Jackpot!

Jackpot!

Harrah's Winning Secrets for Customer Loyalty

Robert L. Shook

John Wiley & Sons, Inc.

Published by John Wiley & Sons, Inc., Hoboken, New Jersey.
Published simultaneously in Canada.

Photographs courtesy of Harrah's Entertainment, Inc.

For general information on our other products and services, please contact our Customer Care Department within the United States at (800) 762-2974, outside the United States at (317) 572-3993 or fax (317) 572-4002.

Wiley also publishes its books in a variety of electronic formats. Some content that appears in print may not be available in electronic books.

For more information about Wiley products, visit our web site at www.wiley.com.

Library of Congress Cataloging-in-Publication Data:

Shook, Robert L., 1938–
    Jackpot! : Harrah's winning secrets for customer loyalty / Robert L. Shook.
          p.   cm.
      ISBN 0-471-26323-0 (alk. paper)
      1. Harrah's Casinos (Memphis, Tenn.)   2. Casinos—United States—Marketing.   3. Customer loyalty—United States.   I. Title.
      HV6711 .S56   2002
      338.7′61795′0973—dc21

                                                    2002013607

Printed in the United States of America.

10   9   8   7   6   5   4   3   2   1

In memory of Sandy Thompson.

Acknowledgments

I AM VERY GRATEFUL TO THE MANAGEMENT OF HARRAH'S Entertainment, Inc. for its cooperation in providing me with access to conduct interviews with many of its employees to research this book. Specifically, I thank Phil Satre, Gary Loveman, and Jan Jones who made this decision. It took both confidence and conviction to permit an independent author to have the free rein I was given. I thank all of the Harrah's people who volunteered to sit through my extensive interviews, some of which lasted several hours, and some whom I interviewed numerous times.

In particular, Gary Thompson worked with me from start to finish on everything from setting up interviews to furnishing research material. I immensely appreciate Gary's support and value his friendship. I also thank Eric Persson, Dawn Christensen, Valerie Trapp, Gina Pinto, and David Strow, also Harrah's employees, for their cooperation.

I had the good fortune to work with some talented professional people at John Wiley & Sons, starting with my editor, Airié Stuart, a woman with immense ability and charm. Emily Conway, Jessica Noyes, Michelle Patterson, and Tess Woods of John Wiley & Sons were wonderfully helpful. Nancy Marcus Land and Brenda Hunter at Publications Development Company of Texas were major contributors to the book production process. All of these people are highly skilled professionals at their crafts.

I thank Debbie Watts, who transcribed the hundreds of hours of recorded interviews I conducted, and Maggie Abel, who assisted me with the preparation of the manuscript. Debbie and Maggie have also worked with me on other books, and they are both talented and reliable. My thanks to Stu Pollak, who helped arrange my itinerary to all the casinos around the country that I visited. Stu, too, is a professional at his work.

I thank Al Zuckerman, president of Writers House. Al is the best agent in the publishing business, and over the 20 years we have worked together, he has become a close friend.

Finally, I acknowledge that information for this book was also drawn from three publications of the University of Nevada Oral History Program (UNOHP). *Every Light Was On* is based on a series of interviews with former Harrah's employees and two of Bill Harrah's wives, while *Playing the Cards That Are Dealt* and *William Fisk Harrah: My Recollections of the Hotel-Casino Industry and as an Auto Collecting Enthusiast* are centered around the oral histories of Mead Dixon and Bill Harrah, respectively. These works are part of the UNOHP's Gaming History Series, which also includes other volumes that would be of interest to researchers in the areas of gaming and business. My gratitude to UNOHP and a special thanks to Mary Larson, the program's assistant director.

Contents

Introduction

MAGINE BEING THE OWNER OF A RETAIL STORE ON YOUR HOME-town's Main Street. Although you have some competition in town, every shop owner is making a good living. Then one day—to your dismay—dozens of retailers come to town, each selling merchandise identical to your store's. Each competitor builds a magnificent storefront and decorates the inside of each store with exquisite furnishings. To build market share, each of these merchants sells below cost and lavishes customers with gifts and prizes.

The competitive environment just depicted is not make-believe; it's an accurate description of Las Vegas' main drag. On Las Vegas Boulevard—the Strip—casino resorts line both sides of the street for a four-mile stretch, each establishment glitzier and more pretentious than the last.

With 15 of the world's 16 biggest hotels, Vegas' lineup of mega-resorts is an amazing sight to behold. Each hotel competes to attract its share of the 36 million-plus visitors that annually pilgrimage to the greatest gambling mecca on the face of the planet. During the past decade, scores of theme casino-hotels have been constructed and renovated. Bellagio, for example, built in 1998 by Steve Wynn for an estimated $1.8 billion, is hailed as the hotel with the largest construction costs in the world. To entice customers through its doors, Bellagio featured a $300 million art collection and a surreal show called "O" that cost a record-breaking $103 million to produce.

Another pricey resort is the Venetian, estimated to have cost $1.2 billion. An all-suite hotel with 3,000 rooms, this theme hotel is Venice in the desert with replicas of the Doges Palace, the Rialto, the Clock Tower, the Bridge of Sighs, and the Campanile. It also features a canal with gondola rides complete with singing gondoliers. To make it even more realistic, white doves are released five times a day. If you feel an urge to stand in the middle of St. Mark's Square, you don't have to travel to Italy—come to Las Vegas.

There's no place on earth like Las Vegas. Where else could you visit a hotel such as the Mirage, equipped with a 70-foot-high volcano that erupts every 15 minutes? Inside the hotel, you walk through a tropical rain forest, get misted by waterfalls, and press your nose against the glass of a 20,000-gallon aquarium stocked with sharks, stingrays, and angelfish. There's also an elaborate habitat housing magnificent white tigers that appear nightly in its famed Siegfried & Roy magic show. Or drop over to the New York-New York Hotel to gaze in wonder at the skyline of the Big Apple. This property features replicas of the Statue of Liberty and a dozen skyscrapers, including the Chrysler Building, a 300-foot-long Brooklyn Bridge, and a Coney Island-style roller coaster that encircles the premise. At the pyramid-shaped Luxor, you walk through a 10-story sphinx entranceway and, once inside, view a replica of King Tut's tomb complete with Egyptian statues that dwarf even those found in the original ancient ruins.

Visitors cross over a moat to enter the Excalibur. You can witness a jousting tournament at this castle-like structure whose drawbridge is guarded by a fire-breathing dragon. Nearby, the "Battle at Buccaneer Bay" is reenacted every 90 minutes each evening in front of the Treasure Island Hotel. The event is staged in a 65-foot-deep lagoon where the pirate ship *Hispaniola* engages the *HMS Britannia* in combat. Twenty dueling actors fight it out in a winner-take-all battle—the defeated vessel does a deep six! And there is MGM's megaresort, the granddaddy of them all, at 5,005 rooms, making it the world's largest hotel. A giant golden lion is crouched at the main entrance to the MGM Grand Hotel—named after the famous movie studio.

The Strip is lined with dozens of casinos, each with its own successful method of luring customers through its doors to sample its products. In the gaming business as in other industries, it can be difficult to differentiate one company's product from its competitor's. Here in Vegas, the products are slot machines and gaming tables.

To compete against other casino-resorts that have invested huge sums of money in elaborately expensive properties, Harrah's Entertainment, Inc., enacted a bold marketing strategy aimed at attracting traffic and enhancing customer loyalty. The company elected to invest heavily in information technology (IT) and management talent. As one Harrah's senior officer said, "With 26 casinos now, and others on the drawing board, it's only a matter of time before a competitor builds a nearby showplace property to entice our customers. We can't continuously build the most expensive property in every market we enter, so we had to take another approach."

In a daring decision to increase market share, Harrah's has invested nearly $100 million in IT so it can accumulate information on its customers—to remember who they are, record their likes and dislikes, and disseminate this data to the appropriate service personnel. All of this is designed to develop customer loyalty. The company has assembled a team of able executives that include a noted Harvard professor, several consumer-marketing MBAs, and a number of gifted strategic thinkers. By putting money into IT and brilliant people rather than bricks and mortar, Harrah's is betting on a marketing strategy that's based on recognizing customers for their loyalty and rewarding them for it.

This is not a book about gaming. It is a business book packed with insightful lessons on how to take market share away from aggressive, strong adversaries. In today's highly competitive marketplace, recruiting and retaining good people and staying ahead of the technology curve are winning strategies for every business. And like Harrah's, attracting customers to enter your front door—whether you're a retailer, a law firm, or an Internet company—is the stuff that builds market share. As in other industries, getting the initial sale is only the beginning. The real test of a successful enterprise is its ability to generate repeat business—which comes from developing solid customer relationships.

Many changes have occurred in the gaming industry during the past 50 years. Despite the fact that Harrah's was founded more than six decades ago, making it the oldest of the established big names in the industry, the company has embraced change more boldly than any other casino operator. *Jackpot* is a story about how a company makes radical changes in a fiercely competitive marketplace—changes that involve investing in people and technology to outsmart and outperform the competition.

You don't have to be in the gaming industry to profit from the many lessons presented in this book. Harrah's business strategies are applicable to every business. As you read this book, note carefully what Harrah's is doing, knowing that these same concepts can be used in your business.

PART I

The Entrepreneurial Spirit

(1937–1978)

In 1937, at age 25, Bill Harrah unwittingly began one of the greatest legends in gaming when he took over a modest card game business in Venice, California, previously owned by his father. The young entrepreneur purchased the illegal "circle game" and operated it out of a storefront for one year. The constant threat of being shut down by local officials drove Harrah to Reno, where he opened a small bingo parlor. Part I recounts Bill Harrah's early struggles to launch the modest enterprise that in time became northern Nevada's most successful gaming company. It closed in 1978. At the time of his death, he had amassed a vast fortune.

1

A RISKY BUSINESS

T'S BEEN MORE THAN TWO DECADES SINCE BILL HARRAH PASSED away in 1978, leaving the unique and remarkably successful company that bore his name. He started his career in the mid-1930s and is recognized as one of the early pioneers in the chronicles of American gaming. In an industry with a shady past, the Harrah name is synonymous with integrity.

Since he opened his first casino in Reno, Nevada, millions of people have passed through the doors of the 26 casinos operated by Harrah's Entertainment, Inc. Relatively few people, however, know much about its founder. As years pass, the number of employees, business associates, and customers who personally knew Bill Harrah becomes fewer. Yet, many of his innovations have become standard operating procedure in gaming casinos across America.

Like pioneers in any field, above all else, Bill Harrah was a risk-taker. As one of the early casino owners, he blazed trails where no one had previously ventured. He is truly one of the great icons in the history of gaming in America.

The history of gambling traces back to primitive man and biblical times. In this country, its roots go back to 1612 when the first lottery in America raised 29,000 pounds for the Virginia Company. George Washington, who deplored the gambling rampant at Valley Forge, nonetheless supported a lottery to help build the city that bears his name. Lotteries helped build General Washington's army and were also responsible for funding several early buildings on the campuses of Harvard, Princeton, and Dartmouth. America's modern gaming era began in the 1940s, a time when Nevada was the only state in the Union where casino gambling was permitted by law. The majority of Americans viewed gambling as sinful. For years, clergymen and politicians preached the evils of gambling to their parishioners and constituents.

The history of gambling in Las Vegas familiar to most Americans revolves around the notorious gangster Bugsy Siegel, who hit town in

1943. The film industry has perpetuated the image of Las Vegas as an underworld haven; blockbuster movies such as *The Godfather, Bugsy,* and *Casino* exhibit this slanted view of its early days.

In the 1940s, Vegas was a small jerkwater town in the desert. However, Vegas held two distinct attractions for Siegel and his Mafia associates: first, legal gambling, and second, a desirable proximity to metropolitan Los Angeles, three hours away by car. Meanwhile, Reno, Nevada, 450 miles to the north, was proudly hailing itself as "the Biggest Little City in the World," and it, too, was in its neophyte stage as a gambling refuge. While Reno had its share of disreputable operators, it also had a handful of commendable small-time casino owners. Although Reno's remoteness was considered a disadvantage at the time, it turned out to be a blessing in disguise, because underworld henchmen stayed put in Vegas. Mafia leaders had no motivation to set up shop in Reno when they were making so much money in Vegas. As the city of Las Vegas quickly became the gambling mecca of the world, Bill Harrah vowed he would never own a casino there. He did not shy away from competition; he simply had no desire to compete head-on against the underworld that had a tight grip on gambling in Las Vegas. Harrah wanted no part of the strong-arm tactics employed by mobster-type casino owners and their business associates.

A Nation of Risk-Takers

Taking risks is the American way. We survived as a nation because our founding fathers were risk-takers. Before the colonization of America, lotteries were conducted in England to determine who would go to the New World. The first to arrive in this country came to America in 1606 and founded the Jamestown colony. By 1609, our nation's first colony had a population of nearly 500 citizens. During the winter of 1610, the colonists were ravished by sickness, starvation, and hostile Indians until the colony's population was reduced to 60. Despite the dangers and hardships, brave men and women colonized our shores and survived. Early settlers encountered enormous risks when they crossed the ocean to a faraway land and ventured into the wilderness. Our forefathers probably embraced gambling because life itself—getting out of the mills and mines, getting through Comanche territory in one piece—was a gamble. Later, during the nineteenth century, Americans pioneered a vast virgin land, building farms and ranches often many miles from their nearest neighbor. Isolated, the settlers became fiercely independent, a characteristic that today epitomizes the American spirit. From its birth, America opened its doors to the world's unwanted. Brave newcomers left their homes and arrived penniless on our shores. They too were risk-takers. This is our American heritage.

In a speech delivered to the Commonwealth Club in San Francisco on November 3, 1989, Philip G. Satre, president and CEO of Harrah's, told his audience:

> Americans have a philosophical drive, an instinct for achievement that includes taking risks. Americans have an inbred tendency, if you will, to gamble. It's been true in our frontier past. I think it is true in our entrepreneurial present. And I think it will be equally instinctive in our high-tech space age future. As long as people strive for the charms of wealth, and try to avoid the pitfalls of poverty, the gamble to win will be a part of our makeup, part of our nature, and part of our future. As luck will have it, gambling will be with us for a long time—you can bet on it.

Business annals are full of resourceful entrepreneurs with humble beginnings who amassed huge fortunes. Irenee du Pont, for example, came to America in 1800 when he was 30 years old. As a boy, he had learned the craft of powder making while apprenticed to famed French chemist Antoine Lavoisier. Not long after his arrival in this country, du Pont bought some gunpowder for a day's hunting. He was shocked by its poor quality. This was his impetus to begin DuPont, today one of the world's largest chemical companies.

The Coca-Cola Company was founded by John S. Pemberton, who was a struggling pharmacist before he concocted his famous formula in 1886. Initially, his caramel-colored syrup was invented to relieve indigestion and exhaustion. He added caffeine because he believed it would serve as a headache remedy. Only after Pemberton failed to market his new product as a medicine did he sell it to Atlanta's largest pharmacy, Jacobs'. Later, when it was mixed with a glass of soda, it became the soft drink that billions of people have since enjoyed. Yet, Coca-Cola was not what could be considered an overnight success. Its first year's sales totaled only $50!

Henry J. Heinz, founder of H.J. Heinz, was another entrepreneur who had a humble start. In 1869, he and his neighbor, L. Clarence Noble, started the famous ketchup company in Sharpsburg, Pennsylvania. They hired two women and a boy, and operated out of Heinz's home. From their kitchen, they peddled their product to grocers, managers of hotel kitchens, and housewives.

In 1920, Walt Disney, an 18-year-old cartoonist, was turned down for a job by the *Kansas City Star,* so he hired on as a graphic artist for a local advertising firm. He started as a $40-a-week illustrator with the Kansas City Film Ad Company, a firm that made 60-second animated cartoon advertisements shown in local movie theaters. In 1923, he left Kansas City for a place where he had heard young filmmakers could find financial backing for their projects: Hollywood. With $40 in his pocket and an unfinished print of *Alice's Adventures* under his arm, Disney boarded a train heading west. Thus began the fabulous career of Walt Disney, one of the legends of the movie industry. Like DuPont, Coca-Cola, and Heinz, the name Disney is known around the world.

Many of America's greatest corporations sprang from humble beginnings. American Express started out as the Pony Express in the 1840s. General Electric dates back to 1878 when Thomas Edison was researching the incandescent lamp. When IBM first began in 1914, it was as a manufacturer of butcher scales.

During the last half of the twentieth century, thousands of companies with modest beginnings became household names in America. In 1954, Roy Kroc was a $12,000-a-year milkshake mixer salesman for Multimixer. Then he came across the McDonald brothers, who operated a drive-in hamburger restaurant in San Bernardino, California. When Kroc saw the crowds of people lined up to buy the one-tenth of a pound hamburgers for 15 cents each, he envisioned opening McDonald's restaurants across the country, each amply supplied with Multimixers. The inventive salesman then convinced Dick and Mac McDonald to give him the exclusive rights to franchise their operation all over the United States. Thus, at the age of 52, when many businesspeople begin thinking about the day they may retire, Kroc embarked on a new career.

Shortly after World War II, Sam Walton, founder of Wal-Mart, got his start with a $25,000 loan from his father-in-law to start his own business. Walton opened a Ben Franklin Store in Newport, Arkansas, and by 1950, had developed it into the most successful location in his region. That year, however, he lost his lease. Forced to sell out, he moved to Bentonville, where he purchased another Ben Franklin store, opening it as Walton's Five & Dime. Throughout the 1950s, Sam Walton continued to add "Walton's Ben Franklin Stores" to his little chain within a chain. This was the beginning of what was to become the world's largest company with revenues in 2001 of $219 billion.

Bill Gates was born in 1955, *after* Kroc and Walton had already started their companies. Still in high school, Gates began programming software with his friend Paul Allen. In December 1974, Allen, four years older than Gates, dropped out of the University of Washington to start a full-time career in computers. Shortly thereafter, Gates left Harvard to join his friend, and, in the summer of 1975, they founded Microsoft. Gates and Allen were not typical entrepreneurs. They had no business plan, no venture capital, and no bankers or Small Business Administration loans. Not yet 21, Gates couldn't even rent a car. But the young duo had everything necessary for entry into the computer industry at the time: a product, programming expertise, and most importantly, a vision of greater possibilities. With this unassuming start, in a relatively short time, Bill Gates became the richest man in the world, and Paul Allen is a close second.

These stories are a tribute to the free enterprise system. There are literally thousands of stories about self-made Americans who started on a shoestring and built empires. The story of Bill Harrah is one of them.

A Humble Beginning

Like so many of our nation's giant dynasty builders, Bill Harrah had a humble beginning. In 1929, at age 18, he went to work for his father, who owned and operated a bingo parlor, the Circle Game, in the sleepy town of Venice, just south of Los Angeles. This hole-in-the-wall operation was housed in a small storefront on a pier built on wood stilts that extended west, standing tall above the Pacific Ocean.

Ironically, it was by pure chance that Harrah's father had acquired the bingo parlor. Before the Great Depression, John Harrah had been a prominent attorney; he even served a term as mayor of Venice. He had amassed a small fortune as an owner of several real estate properties. However, during hard times, tenants couldn't pay their rent, so he was unable to meet his mortgage payments. Consequently, he lost nearly everything, but he did manage to keep a lease that he owned on a storefront on the Venice pier. To keep his head above water, he used this unoccupied space to open the Circle Game. It fit right in with the pier's other tenants; it had several concessions including a hot dog stand, a shooting galley, a pool hall, and a hit-the-milk-bottle game operation. The honky-tonk business was not comparable to a thriving law practice, but it did put food on the table. Like many others during the Great Depression, John Harrah did what he could to survive the hard times.

After completing his freshman year of higher education at California Christian College, Bill Harrah enrolled at UCLA with the ambition of becoming a mechanical engineer. At the end of his first term, he dropped out of college. With millions of unemployed Americans desperate for work, the young college dropout went to work for his father. It was only a temporary summer job, he figured, and both he and his father would find more suitable employment when the Depression ended.

Bingo winners at Circle Game received a carton of cigarettes, which at the time sold for $1.25. Most people played two sets of five cards, which cost 50 cents. Betting 50 cents to win $1.25 was a poor payout, but it didn't matter because the customers had a good time. It was an escape from their hard lives. The Circle Game was bingo with a twist; players sat in a circle on one of 33 stools. In the middle of the table, a roll-down hopper connected to a flashboard. Players bought cards from the dealer, then tried to roll a ball into the hopper in such a way that the flashboard would register a card of a suit and number that would match the cards the players had bought, filling in a four-card sequence. Once out of the hopper, where the ball rolled was random. Still, it was considered a game of skill.

Its being a game of skill was essential because bingo was illegal in the Los Angeles area; however, the law did permit games of skill. There was, of course, some debate on whether skill was actually involved in the Circle Game—and the interpretation varied, depending on the mood of the presiding district attorney.

On slow days when there were only a few customers, John Harrah put house players, otherwise called "shills," in the game to protect the house. Objecting to the use of shills, Bill told his father, "The customers aren't fools. They know when we use shills and it keeps them from playing. Besides, with the extra money we pay for shills, it's bad business."

"If we get rid of the shills and have only two players at a game that pay 25 cents each, we'll be 75 cents in the hole," his father claimed.

The father and son disagreed on many things. For instance, Bill wanted to replace the folding chairs with comfortable stools. He suggested putting drapes over the windows to keep out the glaring sun, and it was he who urged improving the decor. "You have to spend money to make money," he told his father.

An ongoing battle raged between the two Harrahs on how to treat employees. John Harrah would preach to his son, "The help are just like apples or somethin': you need a dozen, you go and buy a dozen." The elder Harrah came from the school that felt employees were like the seasonal walnut pickers who toiled the fields during the Great Depression. He viewed employees as disposable, able to be replaced whenever their services were needed again.

"Help isn't that way. They have to be good, and they have to make a living, and you just can't put 'em out of work," the son argued.

The treatment of help became a sore point. The senior Harrah insisted on laying off workers when business was slow. The junior Harrah wanted to give them steady working hours, regardless of how business was. He believed that turnover and retraining new employees were too expensive. He intuitively thought that by treating people with respect, they'd be more loyal, and that loyal employees treated customers better.

The Circle Game struggled, and in 1932 when its earnings dropped to $100 a week, John Harrah offered to sell the company to his son for $500. The offer was accepted, and the 20-year-old man became the proud sole proprietor of the Circle Game. His first change was the discharging of the shills. This enabled him to lower the price of the bingo cards. In a matter of only a few days, business improved dramatically. Soon afterward, drapes and comfortable stools were purchased. By year's end, the Circle Game was generating between $100 to $200 a week.

By 1934, the Circle Game generated $25,000 in profits, a large sum at the time, for its 24-year-old owner. Later, Harrah purchased two other bingo parlors on the pier—the Plaza and the Vogue.

These were the first of several small-time operations he owned. Some succeeded; others failed. At this stage in his career, Bill Harrah encountered many setbacks. Some of these early reversals were valuable lessons that helped him succeed later in his career. Time, coupled with hard work, slowly taught him the gaming business from the ground up.

One of his biggest hurdles in Venice was the fact that bingo was viewed as a quasi-legal activity. The police would periodically close up his bingo parlors without notice, with little rhyme or reason other than the mood of the governing politicians. Harrah's bingo parlors and the other 20 or so gambling clubs in Southern California would routinely open and close, only to reopen and shut down again.

If there was a pattern, it was political. The Santa Anita racetrack opened on Christmas Day and ran for two or three months. It was no coincidence that when the horses were running, the district attorney would shut down Venice's bingo parlors. Harrah played the cards he was dealt: To remind his customers that he'd be back when Santa Anita closed, he developed a mailing list and sent Christmas presents to his regular customers. This thoughtful treatment of his clientele set a precedent. Throughout Harrah's gaming career, personal touches with customers remained his trademark.

Welcome to Reno

In 1937, the Harrah Venice operation was once more "temporarily" shut down by the local authorities. During that time off, Harrah took a weekend holiday to Reno, Nevada, with friends. After making the rounds at some of the gambling spots in town, Harrah concluded: "What a place! Look at that; they don't close the bars, and they don't close the games, and they [the police] leave you alone." This was in stark contrast to police harassment back home in Venice.

Following a few days on the town with his buddies, Harrah decided to relocate to Reno, a city where he could work in harmony with local law enforcers. During this visit, he spread the word that he was interested in buying a bingo parlor in Reno.

One month later, Harrah received a letter from a bingo parlor owner on Center Street. The fellow was putting his business on the market and willing to accept any reasonable offer. What a lucky break, thought the young entrepreneur. A few days later, Harrah went to Reno and made an offer to buy the business at what he thought was a bargain price. The offer was accepted, and shortly afterward, he shut down his parlors in Venice for the last time. In May 1937, Harrah moved to Reno.

After spending five months setting up shop, on the eve of Halloween in 1937 (coincidentally, the 73rd anniversary of Nevada's admission to the Union), Bill Harrah opened his first bingo parlor in Reno. He paid $200 per month to his landlord, Bob Douglass, a local internal revenue collector. Douglass had some political clout and used it to obtain a gaming license for his new tenant. It was not long before Harrah realized his location was so far off the beaten path, it was doomed to fail. It was two blocks away from where the real action was—on North Virginia Street. That's where the hot gaming establishments such as the Owl, the Bank Club, the Palace, and Harold's operated. Two months later, Harrah rented a vacant building in what he thought was a better location, moved his equipment in, and closed the first parlor. Meanwhile, he continued to pay the rent on his first lease while running an ad in the local newspaper to find a subtenant.

The easy-going Douglass was so impressed that his young renter was attempting to find a subtenant that he refused to accept any more rent for his vacant storefront. Douglass simply tore up the lease! It was a lucky thing because, had the landlord insisted on being paid, Bill Harrah's fledging gaming career might have come to a crashing halt.

The name of Harrah's second Reno bingo parlor was the Plaza Tango. The name came from a deck of bingo cards that said "Plaza" on them, plus the fact that it was on Commercial Row, whose name changed to Plaza Street a few blocks down the street.

Like his Center Street parlor, the Plaza Tango was also a poor location. Next door stood the Wine House, another struggling bingo parlor. Between the two, there was barely enough business for one bingo parlor to remain open. In 1938, the Wine House shut down and Harrah took over its lease. He purchased its equipment for $600.

The winter of 1938 was particularly harsh in Reno, so cold that customers frequently voiced their discomfort. Of course, it was the same all over town—it was cold in every bingo parlor. Harrah's competitors comforted their chilly customers with space heaters strategically placed in various corners of their establishments. Bill Harrah could have done the same for his shivering patrons—a good space heater cost $30 and he could afford to buy a couple. But he went a few steps further, installing an oil-heating furnace in the basement for a staggering $600.

"It was a first-class job. So we bought it. We did need heat, and we wanted the people to be comfortable," he insisted. "They're not goin' to play if they're not comfortable."

Years later, others would attest that going first-class was always a Harrah trademark. When it came to treating customers, Bill Harrah refused to cut corners.

Early in his career, Harrah preached to his employees: "We want our customers to know we appreciate their business, so we will treat them the way we would like to be treated." He continually repeated, "We want our places clean, because that's what we'd like if we were the customer." This straightforward philosophy became deeply embedded in the company culture.

It soon became evident that Bill Harrah knew how to run a bingo parlor. He was doing a great job at the Plaza Tango, but his business continued to struggle. He was only making ends meet. In time, it dawned on him:

> If we got the right location, then there was no reason why we couldn't operate. And there's something I didn't realize, which is very difficult in a new city. Oh, I don't care if you're in the theater business or gas station business or whatever. There's a pattern there, and it looks so great; and you think, "Oh, gee, look at this lot," and you grab it. And all those stations are over here; then you find there's a reason why they're there. The people are used to going there. On the other hand, you can't beat a newcomer.

Sometimes a newcomer can see a lot of things the old-timers can't see. They [the old-timers] are too blind because they're so used to things the way they always were. Just the same, you've got to respect the way a town is laid out. There's a reason for it. And you better really study it before you jump in. Don't just go in and say, "Oh my God, here's a vacant lot! Let me grab it!" If you do, you can sure get fooled.

Bill Harrah discovered early in his career the truth to the real estate aphorism that the three most important qualities that determine the value of a property are location, location, and location. As time passed, Harrah realized that the potential of the Plaza Tango would forever be limited by its poor location, regardless of how well it was managed. All the changes he made to improve the business would not alter its location. That was an irrefutable fact.

Although Harrah longed to buy a bingo parlor on Virginia Street, none was on the market. Then, unexpectedly, along came the opportunity for which Harrah had long waited. A friend who tended bar at the Heart Tango informed Harrah that its owner, Ed Howe, was thinking about retirement. Howe had been in the business for 10 years, working day and night to hold his own against the competition. The word was he was simply tired and wanted out of the business.

Bill wasn't shy about approaching his competitor. He went directly to Howe.

"Would you consider selling this place?"

"I don't know," Howe replied. "I do pretty good here. Let me think about it," was all he said.

Howe apparently saw the offer as a chance to "live the good life" in his trailer down in Arizona because two days later when Harrah stopped by, Howe told him the Heart Tango could be bought for $25,000.

To that, Harrah responded, "I'll have to think about it."

A man is entitled to ask whatever he wants for his business, Harrah thought. After all, it belongs to him. But that doesn't mean I have to pay him all he asks, he reasoned. I'll offer him what I want to pay for it.

The following day, Harrah went back to Howe. "Okay, Ed, I thought about it, and I'm not going to give you $25,000 for this place. I'm gonna give you three. And it's not gonna be cash, it's gonna be a thousand dollars down, a thousand dollars in 30 days, and a thousand dollars in 60 days."

"Let me think about it," Howe said.

"Well, at least he didn't throw me out," Harrah thought. "At least he's thinking about it."

The following afternoon, Howe agreed to sell the Heart Tango at the price and terms Harrah had offered. It was a good lesson for the young entrepreneur: Offer the price that makes sense to you instead of blindly agreeing to the other party's deal.

By the end of the 1930s, there were 17 gaming establishments in Reno. One of the best was the Reno Club, and like the Heart Tango, it, too, was on the main drag. Its owner, Freddie Aoyama, was an Asian who also owned a number of bingo parlors in California with his Japanese silent partners. Harrah would have given his eyeteeth to purchase the thriving casino, but it had never been available. However, when the Japanese bombed Pearl Harbor on December 7, 1941, Aoyama suddenly had a strong incentive to sell. Prejudices against American Japanese literally swelled overnight. So strong was this bigotry that a Japanese entrepreneur could not feel safe operating a business. One week after the bombing of Pearl Harbor, Bill Harrah solicited some partners for financial backing and an offer was made to Aoyama that he couldn't refuse. The deal included ownership of the business, plus a long-term lease with the landlord. Thereafter, the marquis out front read "Harrah's Reno Club."

Once more, Harrah gave the shills the boot, coughed up some customer comforts, and the business rapidly increased. Before long, Harrah's Reno Club was the most successful bingo parlor in Reno.

By now, what attracted customers to Harrah's bingo parlors wasn't just the nicer atmosphere. Harrah casinos had also established a reputation for high integrity. In an industry known for attracting sleazy operators, a reputation as an honest businessman was a highly valued asset. While customers understood that the odds always favor the house, there was comfort in knowing that they could gamble without fear of being dealt from the bottom of the deck.

Early Las Vegas

Today, Las Vegas is synonymous with gambling. Indeed, in the world of gambling, it is Mecca. Although Bill Harrah intentionally stayed far away from the world's gaming Mecca, Las Vegas plays an integral role in his story—as the famed city does in *any* story about casinos.

Around the world, the word *Vegas* conjures up an instant image of flamboyance, excess, and glamour. Few places project such a sensational image by the mere mention of their names—cities like New York, Paris, London, Rome, and Hong Kong. Compared to such a metropolis with a centuries-old history, Las Vegas is an anomaly. As recently as the 1940s, it was a one-horse town with a population under

5,000, yet its spectacular growth and rapid rise to international fame are unmatched throughout the chronicles of modern civilization.

Travel anywhere in the world, and just being from Las Vegas creates immediate interest. "What's it like living there?" people inquire. "You mean people actually live there?" others ask. Youngsters from Las Vegas who attend college in the East invariably get nicknamed "The Vegas Kid" and "Doc Holliday."

In the early 1800s, Spanish-speaking traders routinely visited the gushing springs in the oasis they called *Las Vegas* (English translation: "the meadows"). By 1844, Las Vegas appeared on many Spanish maps. The southwestern desert was still Mexican territory, but the U.S. Army Corps of Topographical Engineers was already at work on a systematic mapping program of its own. By the 1850s, Mormon wagon trains made regular stops at the oasis on their way to California. In 1855, Brigham Young dispatched 30 men to go to Las Vegas to build a fort to protect immigrants from the Indians. Later, the town became a railroad stopover between Los Angeles and Salt Lake City. Ranchers were attracted to the oasis that provided a steady water supply in the otherwise arid desert land. The surrounding mountains contained rich deposits of ore and silver, which, in turn, attracted miners. In an isolated railroad stopover occupied by ranchers and miners, the male population greatly exceeded the female population. Therefore, as in many other towns of the Old West, saloons, gambling joints, and whorehouses became the local source of entertainment. The early town was nothing more than a tent city, a dusty desert depot housing a handful of small trading companies and the railroad office. However, in 1909, Las Vegas became the county seat, giving the site an important government connection. The state legislature named the new county *Clark County* after William Clark, a Montana copper baron and real estate speculator who had also served as a senator.

For most of the nineteenth century, gambling was legal in Nevada. But public opinion can be fickle, and, like alcohol, gambling came to be viewed as a decadent evil. In 1910, under intense pressure from reformers, the state of Nevada banned all forms of gambling. It took the Great Depression to cast gambling in a different light. Twenty-one years later, in 1931, legislation again legalized gambling, making Nevada the only state in the Union to give gambling sanction. It was a desperate effort to boost the economy—and it worked. In time, gaming became Nevada's number one industry. Prostitution—another added attraction—was also legal in Nevada and also prospered.

The federal government played an important role in the growth of Las Vegas. In 1928, Congress passed the Boulder Canyon Act, authorizing spending to construct the world's largest dam on the Colorado River at a site just southeast of Las Vegas. Later named Hoover Dam, millions of dollars were poured into the area while the rest of the nation suffered from the misery brought on it by the Depression. At its peak, the dam supplied jobs to more than 5,100 laborers, almost double the population of Clark County. The dam also became an important source for Las Vegas' water and electricity needs. Equally important, in 1933, Hoover Dam attracted 132,000 visitors and more than 230,000 came to Las Vegas. No wonder the chamber of commerce promoted the city as "the gateway to Hoover Dam."

During the early 1940s, still more millions of dollars in federal government spending poured into the area when the Army Air Corps built the Las Vegas Army Air Corps Gunnery School just eight miles north of downtown Las Vegas. The desert location was chosen because its weather provided excellent year-around flying conditions. In 1949, the Department of Defense changed its name to Nellis Air Force Base. With more than three million acres of ground space and more than five million acres of air space, the base is the largest of its kind in the world.

By the late 1930s, Las Vegas, a city of only 8,000 residents, had a quarter of a million visitors annually. Before long, hotels and small casinos began springing up to accommodate tourists.

One of the earliest visionaries was Thomas Hull, a man who became wealthy building Spanish-style resort hotels in California that featured large pools and recreational facilities in a sprawling, garden setting. In 1941, when he built the El Rancho Vegas in the same style, he threw in a casino. The El Rancho's early success demonstrated the feasibility of combining a casino with a large resort hotel. Moreover, Hull convinced hotel builders everywhere that the spacious tracts bordering the Los Angeles highway were ideal locations to build the mammoth resorts that would eventually make the town famous. One of Hull's early innovations was hiring singers and comedians to entertain his guests. It caught on, and this marked the birth of the legendary Las Vegas lounge act.

Another entrepreneur was R. E. Griffith, a man who made a fortune building and operating theaters during the war. On visiting Las Vegas in the 1940s, Griffith recognized the city's tremendous potential and, with his nephew, built a second casino-resort just south of the city on the Los Angeles highway. They chose a Western motif and designed a huge building with elaborate interior furnishings. Their Last Frontier resort, with a large bar and restaurant, epitomized the grand Western cowboy style of the old Southwest and became an overnight success.

The El Rancho and the Last Frontier were the first casino-resorts, as well as the first theme resorts, in Las Vegas.

A Gangster Called Bugsy

Perhaps the most colorful individual in America's most colorful city was Benjamin Siegel, also known as "Bugsy," a name that no one dared say in his presence. Known for his psychopathic temper, Siegel had a rap sheet that included assault, burglary, bookmaking, bootlegging, extortion, hijacking, murder, mayhem, narcotics, numbers, rape, and white slavery by the time he was 18. Years later, he boasted that he personally killed 12 men.

None of these activities is likely to appear on the resume of a casino owner or employee today, but indeed these were Bugsy Siegel's credentials in the 1940s when gang boss Meyer Lansky dispatched him to Los Angeles on a business trip. Siegel's assignment was to "take care" of some matters with local racketeers who were running what promised to be a potentially lucrative business. Using strong-arm tactics, Siegel's mission was to take control of the "wire" for his boss. The wire was the publication that brought the results of horse races, prizefights, and other sporting events to gamblers in California and throughout the West. Most importantly, it delivered the odds to bookmakers across the country. Siegel did his job well. His recreational activities included visits to Las Vegas, gambling at the El Rancho and the Last Frontier.

Throughout his life, Siegel had been enamored with movies. On arriving in Los Angeles, he renewed his friendship with actor George Raft, one of his closest friends since they were together as kids in the slums of New York. Like Raft, Bugsy had ambitions of being a movie star, but his lack of acting talent prevented him from fulfilling his dream. Raft, one of Hollywood's biggest stars in the 1930s and 1940s, and Siegel formed a mutual admiration society. Known as a tough guy, Raft played leading roles in crime movies. On film, Raft mimicked his good pal, Bugsy, the real-life gangster; he even combed his hair like Siegel's for his gangster parts. In addition to being a dapper dresser, Siegel was handsome—and vain. America's favorite tough guy reputedly slept with a strap on his chin to keep it firm.

On one of his visits to Las Vegas in 1946, Siegel made his usual rounds to the El Rancho and the Last Frontier. He loved everything about them and became determined that he should also own a casino resort, but his would be far more elaborate than anything previously built. After convincing his East Coast Mafia associates—among whom were the notorious Meyer Lansky and Lucky Luciano—to back him with a cool million, Bugsy bought a majority interest in a half-finished Vegas strip hotel being built by Billy Wilkerson Jr., who had put in $600,000 before running out of cash. Wilkerson was the owner of the *Hollywood Reporter* and several upscale Sunset Strip clubs in Los Angeles. Siegel promptly renamed the hotel the Flamingo, and set out to turn it into a playground for the Hollywood elite he was so eager to impress. During the coming months, Siegel got his mob backers to invest more and more cash until $6.5 million had gone into the Flamingo. Rumors had spread that some of the mob's money was going directly into Siegel's pocket.

Years later, Wilkerson's son told the *Las Vegas Sun* that his father had received a late-night visit from Siegel. "Siegel told my dad, 'You're going to turn over your interest to me and if you don't give it to me, I'm going to kill you.'" His father quickly signed over his 48 percent of the unfinished hotel and fled to Paris. Siegel gave this share to his mob cronies to get them off his back.

At the time Siegel made his investment in the Flamingo, the Las Vegas business community was unaware that the source of Siegel's cash—money from the National Distillers—was connected to the money that Murder Incorporated used to go legitimate. National Distillers was one of several Mafia-owned fronts.

Siegel's level of taste finally exceeded his backers' deep pockets. The Flamingo had landscaped lawns and gardens studded with palm trees, an elegant waterfall by its front entrance, plus a variety of distractions for its guests, including a pool, a health club, tennis and golf, stabling for 40 horses, show rooms, and shops. The hotel, low and spacious, had only 105 rooms but reeked of luxury.

As unscheduled Flamingo construction expenses continued to skyrocket, Siegel's mobster partners became wary. Was he cheating them? It didn't help matters that his girlfriend, Virginia Hill, kept shuttling back and forth to Europe, where they suspected she was depositing their money in a secret Swiss bank account. These suspicions put Bugsy in jeopardy. As the story goes, a meeting of the bosses was held in Havana on Christmas Day, 1946, where it was decided that if the Flamingo succeeded, Siegel would be reprieved and have the opportunity to pay back what he owed. If it failed, Bugsy was a marked man.

The Flamingo's grand opening on the day after Christmas made national headlines. Siegel chartered flights, filled them with Hollywood celebrities, and flew everyone into Las Vegas to watch comedian Jimmy Durante open the resort's theater. The casino dealers wore tuxedos, and male patrons were required to wear suits and ties; women wore gloves. The Hollywood crowd partied for three days and then flew home, leaving the casino empty. Local gamblers and tourists were too intimidated to gamble there, and rumors spread that Siegel was pilfering what little profits there were.

Business was so bad that the high-priced entertainers lined up by Bugsy appeared before tiny crowds, sometimes in front of audiences consisting of only a handful of people. The losses were enormous; two weeks after the Flamingo opened, it closed. Two months later, it reopened and, with some changes, began to show a steady profit. However, by then, Siegel's fate had been sealed. On June 20, 1947, while reading a newspaper in the living room of the Hollywood mansion he had purchased for his girlfriend, Virginia Hill, Bugsy's number was up. Nine shots were fired from an army carbine through his living room's quarter-inch-thick pane of window glass. Five shots went wild, but two shots in the head and two more in the chest killed Bugsy Siegel.

It's said that 20 minutes after Bugsy was murdered in Hollywood, three men appeared at the Flamingo in Las Vegas to inform the casino staff that they were taking over. Gus Greenbaum, a man with a casino management background, was put in charge, and the Flamingo became a highly profitable business.

Siegel's funeral was held two days after he died. Although he had spent the last years of his life making friends with a slew of Hollywood celebrities, only five mourners attended his brief service.

Credit is given to Siegel for being the first to recognize the important role that Hollywood would play in the growth of Las Vegas. The gangster called Bugsy added a touch of glitz and glamour, an important influence that has drawn millions of tourists to this gaming Mecca.

Surprisingly, the presence of gangsters in Las Vegas eventually became somewhat of a tourist attraction. Visitors felt as though they were living vicariously when they came to a casino owned and operated by the underworld. Whenever they spotted somebody walking with a violin case, they suspected it contained a lethal weapon—and this excited them. Presumably, they even felt a sense of security with the mob's presence, because they believed the Mafia had an unwritten law that dictated killing only people who were supposed to be killed. Civilians were never murdered by the Mafia—only other bad guys! Many of the tourists felt overly safe in Las Vegas because it was as if there were two police forces. Organized crime worked overtime to foster these feelings—it didn't want to kill its golden goose!

While Bugsy Siegel was the first big-time mobster to arrive in Las Vegas, his arrival marked the beginning of nearly four decades of control under organized crime. To Mafia chieftains, Vegas was heaven on earth, a place where they could set up shop without breaking the law. Among other advantages, it presented an ideal opportunity to launder money. With millions of cash dollars flowing in on a daily basis, skimming—the practice of pocketing cash before it was accounted for—was a temptation no mobster could resist. As infamous Meyer Lansky once put it, "They've given us a license to steal." Mob-operated casinos also enjoyed another edge: a very effective way to collect bad debts. Strong-arm collection tactics greatly reduced the odds of getting stiffed by a deadbeat customer. The Mafia also had an effective way to eliminate the competition. Tales are told to this day about desert burials of those who dared to defy the mob.

Harrah's First Casino

When liquor licenses were in short supply during World War II, Bill Harrah approached Murray Jacobs, owner of a clothing store adjoining the Reno Club. Jacobs had never been keen on operating the small men's shop that had been passed down to him by his father. So, when Harrah suggested they join forces by converting the front of the property into a liquor store and jointly operating a bar in the back in conjunction with his bingo parlor, Jacobs jumped at the opportunity. Thus, the two men formed a partnership to jointly own the bar.

Because blackouts were common during the war, the new enterprise was appropriately named the Blackout Bar. Bill Harrah had set up many deals with other businesses with little or no money down, and the Blackout Bar was another of the many partnerships that he participated in. These deals ran the gamut. In some cases, a partner owned an interest in a bingo parlor; in other cases, it was a piece of the real estate, or ownership in a slot machine concession. Clothier Murray Jacobs was Harrah's partner in the Blackout Bar.

Had there been other options, Harrah would have preferred being a sole proprietor in his ventures. This way, he could make each important decision on his own without anyone insisting on doing it another way. Simply put, he liked the independence that came with being his own boss and not held accountable to a partner. There was another thing about Harrah that made him want to be a solo act. He was always looking for ways to expand his business. He thought big, and partners tended to slow him down. This was especially true with conservative partners, which is what most business people were when compared to a highly aggressive man like Bill Harrah.

Bill Harrah was one of those guys who "just did it." For instance, in the 1940s, there were many restrictive wartime regulations. When there was a freeze on construction and a wall had to be torn out or a bathroom installed, governmental approval was required. The red tape made it extremely difficult to apply for and have permission granted. This didn't stop Harrah. He simply did it before any official board stopped him. "So the trick was just get it done before they knew about it," Harrah is quoted to have said. He believed that when you go to the government to ask permission, it opens a can of worms. Then when bureaucrats turned you down, you'd be in serious trouble by going against their denial. He didn't want a reluctant partner to get in his way. "He who hesitates loses," Harrah believed. And most people hesitated. No wonder he vowed that the day couldn't come too soon when he would no longer have to bring in a partner.

The Blackout Bar attracted an elite crowd, and here Bill Harrah was able to meet many of the leading citizens in Reno, a majority of whom, at the time, he didn't know. To cater to this upscale clientele, he installed his first blackjack table and first crap table. The bar also had a handful of slot machines, and, in fact, a one-dollar slot machine—which, at the time when penny and nickel slots were popular, was a big deal. This small operation was his first entry into the casino business.

On June 20, 1946, Bill Harrah took a bold step beyond bingo parlors when he opened Harrah's Club, his first casino, and he did it sans partners. He borrowed heavily. How well he knew that it would take only a few unpredictable things to go wrong and the risky venture would go under. Despite the risks, he took the plunge, eyes wide open. Harrah's Club had the right location; it was on Virginia Street, the same place that was formerly the Mint, and before that, the Block N. It had 35 feet of frontage and was 140 feet deep. When it first opened, it had a keno game, a faro bank game, two wheels, six crap tables, three crap games, and 40 slot machines. There was also a horse race booking operation in the back room.

One reason for the name Harrah's Club was its location next door to Harold's Club, the area's most successful casino. Harrah figured that people would remember it better because Harold's was so well known. They might even get it confused with Harold's, and this would work in Harrah's favor. Raymond I. Smith, founder of Harold's, came to Reno in the early 1930s, shortly after gambling became legal again in Nevada. Along with his two sons, Raymond A. and Harold Smith, he eventually built an empire from his initial investment of $600. (In 1962, in a sale and leaseback arrangement, they cashed it in for $16,675,000.) The Smiths ran a reputable business and, like Harrah, were well regarded in the community. They were also great promoters. To advertise their casino, they plastered every available barn wall and roof across the western United States with the slogan, "Harold's Club, Reno or Bust." From the Arctic Circle to Jerome Avenue in the Bronx, there were signs promoting Harold's. The key to all Harold's advertising was twofold: the challenge to go west and the total absence of any mention of gambling. This brought in hordes of people by trains, buses, and automobiles. The Smiths ran all sorts of games, including a roulette wheel featuring a live mouse that ran around on the wheel instead of the usual white ball. The mouse would finally tire and sit on a number.

Harold's didn't quite deliver what its advertising promised. When customers came from afar to Reno, they would soon discover that Harrah's Club, although less known, was better run. Like Harrah's other gaming enterprises, Harrah's Club didn't employ shills. From the beginning, Harrah did everything first class. For example, before its grand opening, the bar was redecorated. Although a considerable amount was spent to have it gold-leaf painted, Harrah wasn't satisfied with its look. When he gave the order to remove the gold leaf, the artist informed him that real gold had been used.

"I don't care what it is, if it don't look good, it don't look good," Harrah replied. With that, the bar was stripped with paint remover and the gold was scrapped. This was the way Bill Harrah did things—it didn't seem to matter that he was in debt to most of the gamblers in town for money he borrowed to get his first casino started.

The same thing happened with the rubber tile, inlaid square flooring installed to complement the casino's fine oak and mahogany hardwood fixtures. He didn't like the floor, so he replaced it with terrazzo and carpet. The results were astounding. If nothing else, the carpet set a tone for the place that was far more refined than had ever been displayed in Reno. *Life* magazine had called Harold's "as garish and as nakedly ugly as an unshaded light bulb hanging from the ceiling of a flophouse dormitory." Nor did it hurt to build in a steam pipe beneath Harrah's pavement so customers would not slip on ice or snow. In fact, it was a stroke of genius, for that first winter was bitter—almost bad enough to threaten stillbirth to the new casino.

Here, too, employees were instructed to treat customers the way they'd want to be treated if their roles were reversed. This decree became the modus operandi for all of Harrah's enterprises.

Two pitfalls demand the attention of every casino owner. First, because it's a cash business, an owner must make sure employees don't rob him blind. For this reason, it had always been a sacred ritual for a casino owner to personally supervise the counting room—the place where the cash is counted on a nightly basis. In short, with thousands and thousands of dollars being transacted, when the counting room isn't well guarded and supervised, cash has a way of "disappearing." Although Bill Harrah was a man who ran a tight ship, he delegated the management of the counting room to Bob Ring, a trusted employee who had worked for him since his early days in Venice. When Ring wasn't available, Harrah's father would pinch hit. As the business grew, however, Harrah hired consultants to set up counting room systems—systems that later served as a model for the gaming industry.

Exorbitant expenses are the other pitfall that wrecks startup casino owners. During the first winter when heavy snowfalls kept customers away from Virginia Street, Harrah's Club was also devoid of activity, yet Harrah was reluctant to lay off employees.

"I went in the club and there wasn't a customer. And here we had all our dealers and all our bartenders working. I thought, 'Brother, at this rate and our $8,000 nut, or whatever it was, it isn't going to take long to go out of business,'" Harrah said.

"Many executives in any line of business are very slow to act; they want to quit spendin' the money but they don't want to hurt anybody, and usually you have to hurt somebody. You have to lay people off," Harrah explained. And eventually, he did.

Laying off employees was a hard thing for him to do, especially at a time in his career when he personally knew all of his employees and so many were his good friends. But business is business, and he realized that if the overhead was not reduced, there'd be no business—and everyone would be out of a job.

Owning a Casino Is Not Risk-Free

The start of a new casino is a risky business. Yet, some people think a gaming casino doesn't gamble. True, the odds are in the house's favor, but just like the customers, the casino plays the same games of roulette, baccarat, and blackjack. Hence, the house can and does lose. Even slot machines can lose! Over a period of time, however, the Law of Large Numbers kicks in and favors the casino.

Suppose you toss a coin in the air. The Law of Large Numbers does not tell you that the average of your throws approaches 50 percent as you increase the number of throws; simple mathematics can tell you that, sparing you the tedious business of tossing the coin over and over. Rather, the law states that increasing the number of throws correspondingly increases the probability that the ratio of heads thrown to total throws varies from 50 percent by less than the same stated amount, no matter how small. The word *vary* is what matters. The search is not for the true mean of 50 percent but for the probability that the error between the observed average and the true average is less than, say, 2 percent. In other words, the higher the number of throws, the greater the probability that the observed average will fall within 2 percent of the true average.

Like all businesses, casinos are profit driven, and it is the Law of Large Numbers that provides the house with its profits. In manufacturing and retailing, profits are generated by markups—the difference between the cost of goods and the price received by customers for those goods. Still, like a company with a built-in gross profit, a casino also has overhead that, when too high, can create a stream of red ink. So, even with odds at the gaming tables favoring the house, there is always the additional risk of an unlucky streak, and even casinos have losing streaks. In this respect, a casino owner takes his chances as does any other entrepreneur. Simply winning at the gaming tables does not ensure that a casino will operate in the black.

In a free enterprise system where competition flourishes, it's only a matter of time before the strong become stronger, and the weak fall by the wayside. In a fiercely competitive marketplace like Las Vegas, there is no such thing as a sure thing. Casinos are no different from other companies with expenses that include rent, salaries, advertising, and utilities. If, for instance, expenses run out of control, or marketing efforts fail to get enough customers into the casino, the end may be near. Names such as the El Rancho, Maxim, and Continental can be found on tombstones in the casino graveyard in the Nevada desert. Older casinos such as the Dunes and the Desert Inn—all prominent showplaces in their day—have been imploded to make room for newer and more lavish casinos.

In recent years, several casinos have been built at prices in the $1 billion to $2 billion range. At 8 percent interest, the annual debt service on $2 billion is $160 million, or nearly $500,000 a day! That's just the interest. With thousands of people on the payroll, coupled with expenses for marketing, advertising, maintenance, utilities (imagine the electric bill for all those glitzy Vegas lights), and so on, owning a casino is anything but a sure bet!

2

THE HOUSE THAT HARRAH BUILT

N THE BEGINNING WHEN HIS CASINO WAS NOT WELL KNOWN, BILL Harrah hatched a plan to capitalize on a similarity in names. Out-of-towners who came to gamble at the famous Harold's Club inadvertently stopped at the nearby Harrah's Club. However, Harrah's competition, Raymond Smith and his two sons—the owners of Harold's—ended up with the last laugh by capitalizing on the Harrah's name. That's because Harrah's soon surpassed Harold's as the most successful and best-known casino in Reno, or for that matter, anywhere outside Las Vegas.

Harrah's success didn't happen overnight. Early on, its growth was hardly noticeable. No one who knew young Bill Harrah could have guessed that someday he'd be one of Nevada's most successful businessmen. During his youth, he was not considered "most likely to succeed."

Early in his career, Bill Harrah didn't look like an empire builder. Consider his record: After one year in college, he dropped out to take a job at his father's bingo parlor. There was a time when he was a heavy drinker, described by some as a borderline alcoholic. He hit the bottle throughout the 1940s, and it was 1952 before he finally dried out for good. Even then, two major distractions—women and cars—kept him from focusing on his business.

When it came to women, Harrah must have been rather optimistic about his relationships because he was married seven times—to six different women. Harrah was obviously a passionate man, and some of that passion spilled over into his pastimes. He was an avid car collector, and by his own admission, this was his first love. Acquaintances have said that Harrah's motivation to succeed in the gaming business was so he could afford his addiction to automobiles, which started in 1947 with his purchase of a 1911 Maxwell. During the next three decades, he assembled the world's largest private automobile collection. Included were 1,350 automobiles and an estimated 150 other vehicles such as aircraft and motorcycles. Had the collection remained intact, its present-day value would exceed $200 million.

To spend time with his beloved automobiles, Harrah developed a hands-off style of management. This meant hiring good people— then standing back and allowing them to get the job done. In an industry where owners scrupulously minded the store to protect against skimming, Bill Harrah was an anomaly. He was a perfectionist who paid close attention to minute details, yet he showed little interest in the day-to-day operations of his casinos while they were quietly amassing a fortune for him.

As events would later prove, Harrah did not fit the casino-owner mold. Because he was not afraid to delegate to trusted employees, he was able to create a large organization that would otherwise not have been built.

Harrah was frail in stature, and uncommonly quiet. His introverted personality was atypical of individuals in the gaming industry. His peers were generally gregarious men, comfortable mingling with their customers. In a business where customer relationships are fundamental, casino owners tend to schmooze with VIP customers and employees, but Bill Harrah almost never initiated conversation. While always courteous, he simply didn't engage in small talk.

As described by one 25-year employee: "Bill Harrah is not at first sight the type you would expect to be high priest [of a gambling establishment]. He looks more like a deacon—tall and thin, gray hair, a narrow face, horn-rimmed glasses, a thin smile, a keen look, a quiet voice . . ."

"Somebody once asked me," said another longtime employee, "'Did you ever see Bill Harrah smile?' and I replied, 'Smile? Hell, I never even heard him speak!'"

Harrah's Golden Rule

He wasn't a churchgoing man, but by his actions, Bill Harrah did indeed borrow a verse from the Bible, Matthew 7:12 (NKJV): *". . . do to others as you would have them do to you . . ."* The Golden Rule sums up his philosophy on customer relations. He believed in treating every customer as he would want to be treated if he were the customer.

Some people regard the Golden Rule merely as a cliché, but Bill Harrah's point of view was that no one has yet to improve on it; it has withstood the test of time.

The Golden Rule is such a simple philosophy, yet, in the pursuit of profits, the best way to treat customers often tends to get overlooked.

Sometimes business owners look for ways to cut corners, thinking that perhaps their customers won't notice. But customers do notice—especially subpar service. Bill Harrah believed that exceptional service is what built his customer loyalty.

Harrah strongly believed that when customers are treated well, the bottom line takes care of itself. This is reaffirmed by Lloyd Dyer, who served as president of Harrah's from 1975 to 1980. Dyer recalls what his boss told him at lunch on the first day of his new job:

> Bill said to me, "I want you to understand this—the bottom line to most corporations is the most important thing. I still own 70 percent of the company, and the bottom line isn't that important to me. I do want shareholders to appreciate and join in our profits, but the three things I want done are: I want the customer treated properly; I want the employees treated properly—if we do that we won't have to worry about unions; and I want the place maintained and clean at all times. If we make money after that, fine." He said, "That's my philosophy." And really what he's saying is that if you do all these things you will make money.

A high priority for Harrah was being completely honest with people. Early on, it was hard to find a gambling house being run honestly, because cheating the customer guaranteed a built-in profit. For example, to end a customer's hot streak, some casinos would routinely instruct a dealer to deal cards from the middle of the deck. A dealer who didn't follow orders could be fired on the spot. However, Harrah was determined to play by the rules—his profits would depend on his business acumen, not stacked decks or rigged roulette wheels. At Harrah's, any dealer who cheated a customer was automatically discharged. In time, his reputation for running an honest casino was well known, and he cherished it. "It's why our customers come back here," he lectured his employees.

In the 1940s and early 1950s, Harrah's Club and his number one competitor, Harold's Club, were two of the few casinos that enjoyed a reputation for being on the up and up. Interestingly, they were the two most successful casinos in northern Nevada.

Harrah went a step further, by becoming the first casino that refused to hire shills—casino employees who played alongside the real customers. If a shill plays by the rules, a shill's participation in a poker game doesn't cheat anyone, but just the same, customers might feel that the shills could hurt their odds. To Bill Harrah, customer perception of other customers mattered a lot. He wanted his customers to feel comfortable in his casino—like guests in his home.

Making customers feel comfortable was his forte. This included everything from installing plush carpeting when other casinos still had bare wood floors, and putting real leather on bar stools and in coffee lounges. Harrah was a perfectionist when it came to details. Some felt his insistence on taking care of details was carried to an extreme. He wouldn't tolerate a dirty ashtray. Every 10 minutes, ashtrays on bar counters and dining room tables were to be emptied. Heaven forbid that a cigarette butt would remain on the floor without an employee picking it up! If a light bulb went out, he insisted on replacing it immediately. There was no excuse for a toilet stall to be out of toilet paper. A chipped glass? Intolerable!

Lloyd Dyer explains:

> Bill Harrah felt that if you take care of the little things, the big things are going to get done, which is a little bit opposite to the way many other people feel. I remember many years ago the shift manager would walk outside the casino to check that every light was on for the billboards and above the sidewalks. It was a big deal if a light bulb was out. Scotch tape was forbidden in public areas at Harrah's—no memos, licenses, or notes could be taped to cash registers or on the wall, the door, or anywhere. It was a bugaboo of Bill Harrah's that paintings on the wall oftentimes are crooked, but if you put two hooks there and you level them and then hang the picture, it's always going to be straight. So anything that went on the wall—and I'm sure this came from Bill—anything on the wall had to hang on two hooks. One was not acceptable.
>
> The physical atmosphere of Harrah's was different than other casinos. Early casinos were dark, not well lit. You would go in and it would take 10 minutes for your eyes to adjust to what was going on in there. I don't know if it was Bill who did this or not, but it was always well lit in our casinos. We always had windows so you could see in or out, and it was a cheerful atmosphere. We hired good people—good consultants—to match paints with wallpaper and carpeting. Of course, it all had to be approved.

Some employees thought his focus on minutia rather extreme and approaching paranoia. However, to others, the boss's insistence on taking care of the details set Harrah's apart from competing casinos. Those employees took pride in working for a man who truly cared about customers. They followed his leadership and made sure his orders were carried out. "The customer comes first" were not idle words at a Harrah's casino. The company founder's Golden Rule for treating each customer as you would want to be treated was deeply engrained in the company's culture.

During his early ventures in Reno, Harrah had one or more partners because he had no choice. He didn't have the money to be completely independent. He objected to partners because it sometimes required a compromise in growth or quality. In time, he began to buy out his partners and start new ventures as a solo act. Harrah had so much belief in his own convictions, he was willing to go into considerable personal debt to build his business independently. He was obsessed with making it as a sole proprietorship—partners just got in his way. At times, he was so highly leveraged, a couple of weeks of a cold streak in the casino could have wiped him out. Despite this, in 1955, he went 50 miles north to Lake Tahoe to open another casino. Again, he was ready to further leverage his business, willing to take on more risks, but no partners!

Attention to Details

Maurice Sheppard joined Harrah's in 1946 as a $50-a-week bookkeeper and retired in 1982 as a vice president for community affairs. Between 1969 and 1975, he was president of Harrah's Club. One of his contributions to the company was "the daily report," a company procedure that started as an informal way to let his boss know about the previous day's take. In the beginning, the daily report was an unsophisticated bookkeeping method to provide a 24-hour profit-and-loss statement. The employees who worked on the floor, including dealers and pit bosses, were paid at the end of each shift—they received their daily wages in cash right out of the cashier's cage.

Sheppard describes the daily report:

> It listed department grosses, interest accrued daily, and pretax operating profit. It revealed immediately whether or not the company was within budget. It compared costs year-to-date to the same period of the year previous. We could count the games. I could guess what the bar was doing because cost of sales was 35 percent. The figure we didn't have was the slot machines. So I took the payout figure and worked it backward—a kind of primitive thing.

Lloyd Dyer, who succeeded Sheppard, says, "[It's] unheard of in any business that you get a daily P/L [profit and loss statement]. You usually get one 15 days after the end of the month, or every three months."

Bill Harrah was a stickler for details, and the daily report became an integral management tool that imposed various disciplines throughout the company. In the beginning, its purpose was to show the actual drop and hold for the previous day. It also had wins and losses by sections of the casino, organized by kind of game. It summed everything up, stating the actual final number for the day. At the end of the month, the daily numbers fell into place with the monthly statements with little variance. Eventually, the daily report was extended to include a "daybook," still another report giving other details to be reviewed by Bill Harrah as well as other top company executives.

The daybook was a report of every 24-hour period of the casino's three shifts. Every morning, it ended up on Bill Harrah's desk in Reno at 10 sharp. A copy of the daybook also appeared on the desk of the general managers of each Harrah's casino. Daily couriers were dispatched between Reno and Lake Tahoe to deliver the daybook.

Holmes Hendricksen, who worked for the company in several managerial positions from the 1950s through the early 1980s, describes the daybook:

> When I was a general manager at Lake Tahoe, I knew by 10 in the morning what happened in Reno the day before, and people in Reno knew what had happened the last 24 hours at Tahoe. This was in great detail. If there was a coffee maker that blew up in the kitchen, we knew about it. If there was a guy that beat us badly in the casino on graveyard, we knew about it. If somebody hit the thousand-dollar jackpot in the slots, we knew about it. If an attendant dented a fender in the parking lot, we knew about it. If the men's restroom on the casino floor got plugged up, and we had to shut it down for three hours, we knew about that.

The daybook used a code for casino losses and wins that had words for the numbers one through ten. Shift managers wrote up their reports in code that disclosed, for example, if somebody had won $10,000 in a blackjack game. "This was one of the ways of making management aware of the exact amounts that were involved all the time," explains Hendricksen. "The maintenance manager would have the same report on his desk, but he wouldn't know the money numbers. It was a confidential code used only by top management."

Then there was the policy manual that has been described as being as thick as the Manhattan telephone book. Every policy that the company adopted had to be submitted to Mead Dixon, Bill Harrah's personal attorney, who also represented the company. It didn't matter whether a policy had any legal significance—Dixon still had to pass on it. "Harrah's had a policy on almost everything," says Dixon. "For example, one policy was that all concrete should be painted. The manual went on to say how it should be painted, the color that should be used for painting concrete when there was no other color coordination involved, and the requirement that it be inspected and kept painted and in good condition."

The manual covered the gamut. It contained instructions on fresh plants and flowers—artificial ones were unacceptable. Real leather was acceptable; vinyl was not. The use of scotch tape to post a sign or bulletin was prohibited. A hung painting or picture must have two nails, not one. Harrah personally reviewed every policy; employees were expected to be familiar with them. These policies covered everything—job descriptions, expense accounts, construction, contracts, interior decorations, advertising, and so on.

What kind of a man insists on daily details of a multimillion-dollar business that includes precise information on a blown-up coffee-maker or a dented fender in the parking lot? Bill Harrah's exactness is perhaps best revealed in the orderliness of his bedroom closet. According to Verna Harrah, who was his wife at the time of his death:

> Every year, when we would go to Europe, he'd get his clothes made for him at Brioni's in Rome. He would be there for seven days, and he would get, maybe, 15 different suits made, and he would have two long-sleeve shirts and two short-sleeve shirts made to match each suit, and he'd have a tie to match the outfit.
>
> But Bill couldn't really put anything together (he was sort of color-blind), so everything was hung together and numbered. There would be Brioni one, and then there would be Brioni two, Brioni three, Brioni four, and then every shirt would be Brioni one, two, three, or four, so you'd know that it went with that suit. And on top of that, every jacket had a card attached that was made up at Harrah's, and it would have date, time, and a person's name on it. It would say, "On December 12, dinner with Sammy Davis," so then he would never wear that suit with Sammy Davis again. Now, this is a very anal person!

It figures that a man who would number his suits would also be very punctual. And that was Bill Harrah. "If you worked for Bill, you were either on time or you were early," explains Holmes Hendricksen. "Ten o'clock wasn't 10:01, it was 10:00. If you came a minute late, he would say, 'If I wanted this meeting to start at 10:01, I would have called it for 10:01.'"

Verna Harrah says:

> I can't imagine that any of Bill's managers were ever late coming to a meeting with him, because everybody was very aware of how important punctuality was to him. To him, it was a matter of respect. He wouldn't be disrespectful to someone else, because he really felt that time was all you had. He felt it is your most valuable asset. If

you wasted somebody's time, that was a crime in his mind, so he would never do it to anyone, and he would never expect anybody to do it to him. If you respect a person, you are not late.

Harrah's insistence on punctuality carried over to the casino's headliners. At his first appearance at Harrah's in Lake Tahoe, Willie Nelson came on stage about 20 minutes late. Although some entertainers run intentionally late to keep their audiences waiting, Nelson was informed that Bill Harrah did not tolerate tardiness. Nelson made sure he was on time after that first show.

One of Bill Harrah's favorite entertainers was Frank Sinatra, who performed for years at both the Lake Tahoe and Reno casinos. People close to Sinatra say that he, like Harrah, was obsessed with punctuality. No wonder they became such good friends over the years.

To illustrate Harrah's love of precision, Holmes Hendricksen recalls the time when he headed advertising and public relations:

One day, Bill came into my office waving a newspaper ad that stated, "A thousand cars are on display at the automobile collection."

"I was just over at the collection," he said to me, "and do you know that we're painting a 1917 Chevrolet? And there's another car that we're doing upholstery on. Neither of those cars are on display."

"That's fine with me," I replied.

"But it's not fine with me. This means we only have 998 cars there. We don't have a thousand. I don't want to lie to my customers. If I tell them a thousand, I want there to be a thousand cars out there."

I knew Bill well enough to know how to react to him in this situation, so I said, "Bill, let me get back to you on this," and he agreed.

The next day we met again and I said, "We can't change our advertising every day when you pull cars in and out of the collection."

"I understand that."

"How would you feel if we used a word such as *approximately* or *about* one thousand cars, so it isn't exactly one thousand?"

"That's fine, Holmes." Then he became very serious and said, "I don't lie to my customers."

The Employees' Image

One of Bill Harrah's favorite places to relax was his summer home in Stanley, Idaho. He loved the scenery, the fly fishing, and, most of all, the people. In fact, he was so fond of Idahoans, he opened a company employment office in Twin Falls.

The good people of Idaho were particularly appealing to him because they were fresh and honest. Having clean-cut employees, especially college students, work in his casinos would help offset the shady image of the gaming industry. He was nobody's fool and was keenly aware that many Americans associated legalized gambling in Nevada with the gangsters who controlled casinos in Las Vegas. Harrah figured that wholesome young people from places such as Idaho and Utah would present a more trustworthy image. All it took to come up with this conclusion was a walk through a competitor's casino. Yes, there were some exceptions, but, for the most part, other casino employees looked like the kind of people you wouldn't trust as far as you could throw them. At the very least, you wouldn't buy a used car from them!

The young men and women hired in Idaho and Utah had no prior experience working in a casino, and that was exactly what Harrah preferred. He'd rather train a person without any bad habits than someone who came with excess baggage.

Harrah's hired a high percentage of college students for summer help. This was the busy season in Reno and especially in Lake Tahoe, which at the time was strictly a summer resort. The college kids were full of enthusiasm and energy, and they worked straight through the season, with rarely a day off. Not only were they bright and eager, their clean-cut looks presented a sense of trust. "This young kid is too innocent to cheat me," customers thought. They were right. In addition, cheating a customer was automatic grounds for immediate dismissal at Harrah's.

There were other grounds for being fired. Russ McLennan, who started in 1959 at age 23 as a change person and a few months later was enrolled in Harrah's dealer school, explains:

> You could get fired out of here quicker for insulting a customer or being rude to a customer than you could for any other thing except stealing money. Customers were that important to Bill. He was probably the first guy where the customer was always right not only in gambling, but also in restaurants, and, later on, hotel rooms.

Today, McLennan is vice president of special casino promotions for Harrah's in Lake Tahoe. He emphasizes that, to this day, his employer always insists that the customer comes first. McLennan points out that for the past 40 years, the company has had a rating system for evaluating how well each employee on the casino floor caters to customers.

It's hard to imagine a casino today without female employees serving in all capacities, but for years, few women held positions as dealers or pit bosses. Bill Harrah decided in the 1950s to hire women as dealers when he observed that Harold's Club employed them. Immediately, the old-time employees objected, claiming that women couldn't deal or keep control of the game. Harrah said:

> But the big thing with women and the reason I did it, was because tourists would look in, but they wouldn't *come* in. I overheard people say that there were no women in there. We did have cocktail waitresses, but they'd look in and see all these men standing at the tables and it was kinda scary. But when they looked in Harold's Club they could see ladies there, so in they'd go. They figured that if women were working in the casino, it was a safe place to visit. As far as I was concerned, that's what convinced me.

Unlike the competition's employees, you could always spot a Harrah's person who worked on the casino floor. Everyone was required to wear a pair of black pressed slacks and a clean white shirt. The keno girls wore black skirts, and it was imperative for their stocking seams to be straight. Bill Harrah also insisted that his people having contact with customers be in good physical condition. Employees who were excessively overweight were told to shed some pounds or risk being let go. (Today, employment laws prevent some of the company's earlier practices.) Harrah's concern about overweight employees carried over into the executive suites. There was a scale in the company's conference room on the fourth floor. When senior managers reported to work each morning, they were required to "weigh in." Then they made a calendar entry, recording how much they weighed each day.

It was always easy to spot a new Harrah's employee on a break from the casino floor because that was the person constantly studying a notebook of the company's training rules and regulations. In addition to dress codes, the notebook outlined details about hairstyle and the use of cosmetics. Men, for example, were not permitted to have beards. Employees who worked handling cash were forbidden to put their hands in their pockets. The no-hands-in-pockets rule, of course, had more to do with security than appearance.

The rules were strict, but there were few complaints. In fact, employees took pride in the company's recruiting and training procedures because to work for Harrah's meant having passed the stringent requirements to get the job. Being employed by Harrah's was viewed in the community as being somebody special. Harrah's employees held their heads high—they were among the elite of casino workers.

Evidently, many college students who came to work for the summer at Harrah's in Reno or Lake Tahoe enjoyed the experience. Several of them joined the company after graduation and made it a lifetime career. Lloyd Dyer, who served as the company's president from 1975 to 1980, worked for the company during the summer of 1957 while in college and continued until his retirement. During a semester break in 1956, student Holmes Hendricksen took a summer job as a busboy. He came back the following summer and worked in the cashier's cage. Hendricksen, too, spent his entire career at Harrah's, rising to the office of vice president. He also served as general manager of the Lake Tahoe casino, and later headed the entertainment department during the heyday of big-time entertainment in the 1960s and 1970s. Russ McLennan came to work during the summer of 1959 as a change person, and he continues to work for the company to this day. These and dozens of other students who worked part time during their college years went on to become lifelong company employees.

A Tale of Two Cities

Bill Harrah has been singled out by Nevada gaming historians for having the highest degree of integrity during an era when underworld figures had infiltrated and corrupted the gambling industry in Las Vegas. With his unblemished record, his most significant contribution to the industry could be that he served as living proof a casino could be operated as a legitimate business enterprise. Certainly, there were other honest operators, but they, like Harrah, were an aberration in a disreputable industry. Despite the illicit activities of mob-owned casinos, which many believe provided an unfair competitive advantage, Bill Harrah demonstrated that a legitimate casino could generate a healthy bottom line.

Harrah brought respectability to gambling, an industry that was otherwise frowned on by people across America—including many of the good citizens of Nevada. Even in Reno, where gambling was legal, casino people were not part of upper-crust society. Perhaps it was guilt by association. Following the Bugsy Siegel murder in 1947, the Mob took over in Las Vegas, and it didn't quietly go away. For two decades following Siegel's death, casinos in Las Vegas were controlled by the underworld. The Mafia stayed out of Reno, but only because it thrived in Vegas. Why would the Mob move to a hick town 500 miles due north when it was already in paradise?

An army of underworld characters invaded Vegas after Bugsy Siegel and his associates staked claims. With Siegel no longer in the picture, Meyer Lansky called an old friend, Morris "Moe" Dalitz. As a young man, Dalitz started his career during Prohibition bootlegging on the Great Lakes, running whiskey from Canada to Detroit, Chicago, and Cleveland. He had been a member of the murderous Purple Gang in Detroit and the infamous Mayfield Road Gang in Cleveland. When Prohibition ended, Dalitz and some of his old gang members opened the Beverly Hills Country Club in Fort Thomas, Kentucky, and the Lookout House in neighboring Newport, Kentucky—two casinos on the other side of the Ohio River facing downtown Cincinnati.

Lansky recruited his old pal to Vegas because Dalitz had the casino skills needed to put the Flamingo back on track. "My partner Frank Costello and I have a problem," Lansky said. "We need somebody with your expertise to run our casino in Vegas."

A few days later, Dalitz visited Vegas and immediately recognized that a huge fortune potentially awaited him. However, it would be two years later before he was ready to move out West. In 1949, after his business affairs in the East were settled, he moved permanently to Vegas. One of his partners in his Kentucky gambling ventures, Morris Kleinman, accompanied him. At a meeting with Lansky and Costello, they were told, "Guys, we got a problem. We agree with you that Vegas can be big. But our problem is that if we send the millions it will take to do it right out there, the IRS will be all over us. We can't let it be known we have that kind of money to invest."

Had the Mob put up the money, the IRS would surely want to know how it had accumulated millions of unreported income. On the other hand, Kleinman and Dalitz could substantiate legitimate incomes from their investments in Kentucky, as well as other lawful enterprises they owned, including a successful dog track in Dayton, Ohio.

Dalitz's first Las Vegas venture was taking over the Desert Inn after Wilbur Clark ran into financial troubles. It was a piece of cake. It wasn't long before Dalitz's career in Vegas prospered. Not only did he participate in mob-operated undertakings, Dalitz prospered making smart investments in legitimate enterprises. In spite of his underworld dealings and high profile—especially with the IRS and FBI after him—Moe Dalitz was never convicted of a single crime. This is remarkable considering that law enforcement officials hounded him from his early adulthood until the day he died. In addition to his holdings in the Desert Inn, he owned a piece of the Stardust Hotel, both of which were financed by the Teamsters Union. It was Dalitz, in fact, along with Paul "Red" Dorfman, a long-time associate in the Chicago crime syndicate, who befriended young Jimmy Hoffa during his early years at the Teamsters Union. The Chicago Mob helped Hoffa rise to the head of the union, and in turn, he loosened the purse strings of the Central States Pension Fund to finance the Desert Inn, and years later several other casinos, including Caesars Palace and Circus Circus. Over the years, Dalitz's business dealings in gaming and real estate development made him a very wealthy man. He truly loved Las Vegas and went on to become one of the city's major philanthropists.

The gates to Las Vegas swung wide open, and in marched legions of former bootleggers, bookies, and carpet joint operators. Aware that vast money was to be made, America's ruling crime families declared Vegas an open city. There was a pact among underworld leaders outlawing violence within the city's borders. They wanted to protect "civilians" and encourage tourism. Everyone was in agreement on one point: Tourists must feel safe in Mecca. There was an unwritten law that gangsters could kill only one another.

Who wasn't safe? Anyone working at a casino who didn't play by the rules. The large casinos employed their own goon squads that served as enforcers. According to Ed Reid and Ovid Demaris, who wrote *The Green Felt Jungle*, cheating dealers were routinely dragged into the counting room, a soundproof room that was ideal for torture:

> One dealer was held by two goons while his closed fists were placed on a table. Another goon wielded a lead-encased baseball bat and brought it down on the dealer's hands, smashing them beyond repair. The dealer was then dragged through the casino, with the blood dripping from his crushed fingers. His hands were bandaged by one of the Mob's doctors, who was instructed not to set the bones. Then he was driven to the edge of town and his shoes were taken from him.

It was a 150-mile walk in the desert to the next town, Barstow.

Because the Mob bosses who controlled many of the casinos in Vegas were in distant places such as New York, Chicago, and Detroit, trusted associates served as couriers to transport suitcases filled with cash to their bosses. One such courier from Chicago was Anthony Spilotro, also known as "Tony the Ant." The Ant stood only 5 feet 5 inches. "Spilotro was a suspect in 25 murders, but was never convicted," Seth Rosenfeld reported in the *San Francisco Examiner*. The Ant allegedly carried out one of the murders by putting a fellow gang member's head in a vise and slowly tightening it. His "most important function was to break legs or kill anybody who got out of line," said Bill Roemer of the Chicago Crime Commission.

Tony the Ant loved his chosen profession, so much that he became too zealous at it. Ignoring the order to "lay off civilians," he brutalized anyone who got in his way. He formed his own organization called the "Hole in the Wall Gang" and went on a crime spree that terrorized the good people of Vegas. Bob Miller, who was then the district attorney and later governor of Nevada, recalls: "Before that time, we'd never seen anybody that was associated with organized crime come out and conduct criminal activity at the street level."

Eventually, the big bosses gave orders to take Tony and his brother Michael on a ride to the country. After a suitcase delivery in Chicago, the two brothers were driven to the country in nearby Indiana. Shortly after, a farmer spreading weed killer over a cornfield discovered the Spilotros' bodies.

Hoodlums with rap sheets long enough to wallpaper a room staked their claims in Vegas. Many were colorful and bigger-than-life. One such man was Benny Binion, a Texan who had served a three-and-a-half-year murder rap in Leavenworth Penitentiary, though he claimed self-defense. In 1946, Binion packed his wife and five kids and his cash into a Cadillac and took a vacation to the Southern Nevada desert. The rest is history—the Binions stayed in Vegas and became one of the best-known families in Nevada. A bootlegger in the 1930s, Binion operated a numbers operation in Dallas before settling in Vegas. His Texas mannerisms never left him. He always wore a white cowboy hat, and he packed a Colt Commander .45, which was later replaced by a small .22 Magnum revolver. He also kept a five-shot, semiautomatic shotgun in his golf bag or his car. As the owner of Binion's Horseshoe, Benny prospered in Las Vegas. Throughout the years, he gained some respectability, and like Dalitz, was regarded by many as a philanthropist and innovative entrepreneur. His innovations included redefining high-limit gambling, free drinks to customers, tournament gambling, and being the first in town to provide limousine service to VIP customers.

In 1948, one year after Bugsy's dream, the Flamingo, was underway, the Thunderbird opened with silent partners Lansky and Costello backing it. In 1952, the Sands opened with "Doc" Stacher fronting for its real owners—again Lansky and Costello. By now, the die was cast. The modus operandi would be to have a business person with a clean record to front for the Mob and then "skim the hell out of it." If there was a return on the investment, all the better, but the tax-free money that really mattered was what was taken off the top before any revenues were officially counted. It was important, however, that the front man had a good reputation and would follow orders. It was a good deal for him too. He was paid handsomely to "act" as if he were in charge.

Front men fronted sometimes even for other front men, making it difficult and sometimes impossible to know who the real owners were. This was the intent—to keep the government in the dark. A typical casino/hotel could have as many as 60 shareholders in a corporation that owned the land and building, with the Mob owning only a small percentage of the deal. The basic corporation would then lease out "concessions" for gambling, restaurants, bars, retail shops, and so on. The gambling equipment might be leased from many different companies. When the basic corporation started making substantial earnings, new additions were built by different investment groups, again adding layers upon existing layers, always to hide the identity of the real owners.

One of the most celebrated examples of hidden ownership in Las Vegas became known one night in a flash of gunpowder in New York. On the evening of May 2, 1957, a gunman fired a round of ammunition from a .38 revolver into the head of Frank Costello, reputed to be the boss of bosses in New York. The shooting happened in the foyer of the gangster's fashionable Central Park West apartment building. The bleeding victim slumped onto a leather-covered bench as a frightened doorman spotted an unknown fat man racing out the door. The gunman jumped into a double-parked Cadillac that immediately raced down the street.

Costello was rushed to nearby Roosevelt Hospital, where doctors were able to mend a head wound behind his right ear. While the medical team was saving the gangster's life, New York detectives searched his suit jacket. In addition to $800 in cash, they found a slip of paper that listed the following handwritten notations:

Gross casino wins as of 4/27/57—$651,284

Casino wins less markers—434,695

Slot wins—62,844

Markers—153,745

Mike—$150 a week, totaling $600

Jake—$100 a week, totaling $400

L.—$30,000

H.—$9,000

That same night at the West 54th Street station, Costello was asked to explain the piece of paper in his pocket. He pleaded the Fifth Amendment and received a 30-day sentence in the workhouse for contempt. Even without Costello's cooperation, local police working in cooperation with Las Vegas police discovered the $651,284 figure matched perfectly the gross casino receipts of the Tropicana Hotel for its first 24 days in business. Costello and his associates were ordered to sell their concealed ownership—thanks to the unidentified fat gunman. The significance of the Costello case was that it provided the first conclusive physical proof that the Mob was in Vegas.

In the 1950s, Tennessee's Senator Estes Kefauver's committee aired its hearings on network television to investigate organized crime, and this brought national attention to the Mob's involvement in Las Vegas. The Mormon Church also applied pressure to clean up the town, despite the fact that many Mormons worked in casinos.

The Mob was well settled in Vegas before the Nevada Gaming Commission and its enforcement and investigative arm, the Gaming Control Board, were formed in 1955. However, it wasn't until 1959 when Governor Grant Sawyer gave the order: "Keep organized crime out of Nevada." Under his guidance, Governor Sawyer replaced the Tax Commission with a State Gaming Commission to oversee the industry. He appointed commissioners with high profiles in law enforcement, including former FBI agents, and created the List of Excluded Persons, the infamous "Black Book."

Eight years later, in 1967, the Nevada Corporate Gaming Act was passed, which allowed publicly traded corporations to acquire gambling licenses without the need to license every individual stockholder.

Howard Hughes Comes to Vegas

One of the most fascinating chapters in the annals of Las Vegas began Thanksgiving weekend in 1966, when Howard Hughes, known to America as a "reclusive billionaire," came to town. He arrived on a train that left Boston and went as far as Ogden, Utah, where his party rented an additional locomotive to transport him and his aides directly to Vegas. The Hughes assemblage pulled into town at four in the morning. The thin, pale, trembling bearded man was then put on a stretcher that was placed in a van and whisked to the Desert Inn. A dolly wheeled him into the hotel through a side door. He rode the service elevator to the top floor and did not set foot outside his penthouse until four years later, the day before Thanksgiving in 1970.

When Hughes came to Vegas, he was a skeleton of the man he was during his prime. At one time, as the owner of Hughes Tool Company and later Trans World Airlines, he was one of the richest and most flamboyant men in the world. He courted the most beautiful women in Hollywood—his romances included actresses Jean Harlow, Rita Hayworth, Bette Davis, and Katherine Hepburn. A dashing pilot, he was the holder of several around-the-world flight records. The handsome 6-foot-4-inch Howard Hughes had it all. Yet, on his arrival in Vegas, the 61-year-old man measured in at 6 feet 1 inch and weighed about 120 pounds. His backbone was bent, and several spinal disks were herniated as a result of a 1947 airplane crash that nearly killed him. Hughes took narcotics to ease his excruciating back pain. He developed a dependency on codeine and gave himself daily injections. Needle marks riddled his arms and thighs. An insomnia sufferer, he rarely slept. He was anemic and allergic to sunlight, had a peptic ulcer, and failing kidneys. A prostate blockage hindered his urination, and because his diet consisted of nothing but chicken chunks from cans of Campbell soup and banana-nut ice cream for dessert, his lack of roughage kept him in a state of perpetual constipation. Hughes never exited his Desert Inn penthouse and rarely wore clothes, but did cover his genitals with a paper tissue napkin. His beard covered his chest and his long gray hair came down past his shoulders. His excessively long fingernails curled.

Hughes suffered from a menagerie of phobias, manias, obsessions, delusions, and an inordinate fear of germs. To insulate himself from germs, he shunned handshakes and opened doorknobs with a Kleenex tissue. His eating utensils were wrapped in Kleenex. He seldom bathed and never brushed his teeth. This is the man who came to Las Vegas to buy its most valuable properties, and although it wasn't his mission, he would ultimately rid the town of the underworld.

In four whirlwind years, Hughes became Nevada's biggest casino owner, acquiring the Desert Inn, the Sands, the Frontier, the Castaways, the Silver Slipper, the Landmark in Las Vegas, and Harold's Club in Reno. He also became the state's largest private employer, the state's largest private property owner, and the state's largest owner of mining claims.

When Hughes first checked into the Desert Inn, owner Moe Dalitz was elated that such a wealthy guest had taken up residence. Dalitz's jubilation was short-lived when he realized Hughes and his party didn't frequent the casino and had settled in to become permanent occupants of the Desert Inn's most luxurious rooms. When Dalitz tried to evict his billionaire guest, Hughes made an offer to buy the casino resort for $13.2 million.

The timing was good, because Dalitz was being pressured by the FBI to find an owner because of his mob connections. Meanwhile, Hughes was in need of a tax write-off. This first buy triggered Hughes' purchase of other Las Vegas properties.

"I have decided this once and for all," Hughes wrote in one of his famous memos. "I want to acquire even more hotels and to build this operation to be the greatest thing in the U.S. This is a business that appeals to me."

During his shopping spree, Hughes also initiated an influx of global investment funds, financing his purchases through defense-related profits and Hollywood money, a trend that became more prominent in Las Vegas during the 1980s. Most importantly, Hughes represented legitimate corporate America, and regardless of his unorthodox style, he introduced big business to the gaming industry. Hughes triggered the beginning of the end of underworld control.

Hughes paid top dollar to buy mob-controlled properties, and he led the way for other wealthy entrepreneurs and publicly owned corporations to buy casino properties. Kirk Kerkorian came to Vegas in 1967 after taking his company, Transamerica Airlines, public. On his arrival, Kerkorian announced his ambitions to build the world's biggest hotel-casino on an 82-acre tract on Paradise Road, one block east of the Strip. Kerkorian's 1,500-plus-room International opened the summer of 1969. Barbra Streisand performed in its packed 1,600-seat theater. Elvis came a month later, breaking every attendance record in a Las Vegas theater. The International was later renamed the Las Vegas Hilton. In the early 1970s, Kerkorian bought MGM studios in Hollywood and came back to Vegas in 1973 to build the MGM Grand (now Bally's).

In the mid-1960s, Jay Sarno, another entrepreneur, came to Vegas and built Caesars Palace and then Circus Circus. The Teamsters financed the two properties. Although the Justice Department accused Sarno of several tax code violations, he was never found guilty of criminal charges.

There is no underworld presence in today's Las Vegas. Some people credit Howard Hughes as the catalyst for cleaning up the town. Unquestionably, he was instrumental, but with or without Hughes, it was due to happen. (Thomas Edison is the inventor of the lightbulb, but had he not invented it, we wouldn't be reading by candle today!) Several factors, including the reclusive billionaire and other legitimate business figures, combined to sweep the Mob out of Vegas. The transition would have occurred eventually, and probably earlier with the passage of the 1967 Nevada Corporate Gaming Act that opened the doors for publicly traded corporations to acquire gambling licenses. National pressure put on the Mob by the IRS, the FBI, and Senators Estes Kefauver and Robert Kennedy was also instrumental. In addition, credit must be given to the state of Nevada, which, by cleaning up its act, cleaned up Las Vegas.

Sex and the City

Opponents have long argued that gambling promotes prostitution. In *The Green Felt Jungle,* a 1963 best-seller that defames Las Vegas, Ed Reid and Ovid Demaris wrote:

> Where there's easy money, there's whores; it's that basic. Taken in its logical sequence it goes like this: where there's gambling there's easy money, where there's easy money there's whores, where there's whores, there's extortion and narcotics, and where there's narcotics there's everything else.

In Nevada, however, brothels did come *before* casinos. And when the Reid/Demaris book was published, drugs in America were not as prevalent as they are today. Furthermore, prostitution and narcotics aren't confined to cities where there are casinos. Hookers flock to convention towns attended by large numbers of men, and their presence has nothing to do with gambling. Cities without gambling have their share of prostitution. If you're a nonbeliever, pick up a telephone directory in cities such as New York, Los Angeles, Miami, Atlanta, or Washington, DC, and check out the yellow pages under "Escort Services." (In the Las Vegas yellow pages, these services are listed under "Entertainers.") Be assured these ads aren't for dating services. Remember, too, that there are casinos on Indian reservations in communities sans hookers. Perhaps a sounder conclusion is that convention towns attract prostitution. Simply put, the girls go where men without their wives go.

Working girls also go where the money is. This means that when a single man is out of town with a pocketful of money, odds increase that he'll spend it on a pretty woman. In an atmosphere like a casino's, where there's plenty of loose money and lots of booze, sex sells. It's as simple as that.

Let's not forget, however, the glamour of Las Vegas where nude and seminude showgirls are permanent fixtures. The town definitely has a sensuality of its own; to most men, the mere mention of Las Vegas conjures up an image of lewdness and carnality. Then, too, Vegas had a reputation for providing free sex for its best customers. During the days of the Mob, a high roller had only to suggest that he wanted female company, and a pit boss or casino host would have a bevy of girls lined up to accommodate him. Chorus girls and cocktail waitresses commonly volunteered their services as a special favor to a casino manager. These girls didn't consider themselves "professionals"—that is, they weren't call girls or streetwalkers. Many were even married and had children. Although they were amateurs, they did accept money that was left on a dresser or a handful of chips given by a "date" at the gaming table.

In the old days, the casino requested that showgirls sit in the lounge between performances to "dress up the room." These were the same performers that customers saw naked on the stage. Casino operators knew this practice was good for business, so it became part of the job. Girls who refused to do special favors for the house were replaced by other girls who made themselves available. It was a matter of supply and demand, and the supply of beautiful women always kept up with the demand.

There were also weekend whores—secretaries, bank tellers, college students—females who drove in for the weekend from Southern California for a good time and extra money. They didn't consider themselves prostitutes, and any suggestion that they were would have been vehemently denied.

The weekend whores were strictly amateurs. An illustration of their lack of professionalism and sophistication is the story about two pretty LA secretaries who were invited to a Desert Inn suite where a group of six Japanese businessmen were partying. Throughout the night, the men took turns in the two bedrooms where the girls entertained them. It was a long, hard night, but the girls were sure they would be well rewarded for their sexual services. In the morning, one of the men give each of them 15 chips and explained in broken English that they could be cashed in at another casino. The chips were marked with the number 100. The two exhausted girls had worked hard, but they felt they had been well compensated for a hard night's work. After all, $1,500 exceeded what they earned in a month as secretaries. Imagine their disappointment when they went to cash in their chips and discovered each chip was redeemable for one dollar!

In today's Las Vegas, sex for sale is available but it's not like the old days. The major casinos don't allow prostitutes to solicit in their properties because it's against the law. For the same reason, casino employees don't provide sex to high rollers. They simply won't do anything to jeopardize their gaming licenses. They have too much to lose. Security guards and plainclothes officers at Harrah's and other major casinos who spot a female soliciting on the casino floor or in a lounge will promptly escort her out the door with instructions not to come back. A photograph is taken so she will be easily recognized if she returns. If a customer, however, is with a prostitute, as long as she's his guest, that's another matter. "What we don't want is people on vacation being solicited," said a Harrah's security guard. "But a guy with a broad—that's his business. Besides, who knows, she may be his wife or girlfriend."

On any given day or night, a single man walking down the Strip will be approached by solicitors who pass out X-rated leaflets advertising the services of women who will make room calls. These explicit brochures tout everything from full-body massage to totally nude dancing in the privacy of a customer's room. They leave little to the imagination: Sex is for sale. In some neighboring counties outside Las Vegas, prostitution is legal. Many out-of-county bordellos provide round-trip limousine services. Is it dangerous to be picked up and driven out of town to a bordello? Does a customer risk being rolled? And if he's a respectable family man, will he report that he's been rolled to the police? These are questions to be addressed before being taken for a ride.

The Entertainers

For years, Las Vegas was synonymous with show business. The greatest entertainers came to town—nowhere else in the world did such a heavy concentration of superstars appear within an area only a couple of square miles. A tourist could spend a month in town and see a different terrific show every night.

Show business enamored Bugsy Siegel, and the hoodlum had the insight to recognize that the glamour of big-time entertainers would serve as a magnet to gamblers. Siegel was right on the money, so as early as the 1940s, Vegas was importing top performers. Reno and Lake Tahoe weren't in the same league, and even as late as the mid-1950s, a local band, singer, or piano player was the usual entertainment.

During the early 1950s, the Fortune Club in Reno was paying $275 a week to its entertainers, and Bill Harrah thought it was money being thrown down the sewer. Gradually, he began to recognize that a piano player could play soft music to entertain wives while their husbands gambled. A couple might even come in specifically to hear a singer with a pretty voice. And with the music, they might stay a while longer than they normally did.

Once Harrah understood that entertainers pulled gamblers into the casino, he came full circle in his thinking, and within a decade became one of the biggest purchasers of entertainment in the United States. As one former employee said, "It shows how flexible the man was!"

On December 19, 1959, Harrah's 1,000-seat South Shore Room in Lake Tahoe opened. Bill Harrah was now ready to commit to big-time entertainment. His opening act featured Red Skelton, one of the nation's most famous and beloved comedians. Dignitaries including Governor Grant Sawyer attended the huge gala opening. Each guest was given a silver cigarette box inscribed with the date of the opening and the name of the headliner, Red Skelton. Three weeks later, singer Patty Paige appeared, again to a full house. The opening of the South Shore Room was coordinated with the 1960 Winter Olympics held that February in Squaw Valley, California, a 45-minute ride from the lake resort.

Mark Curtis, who headed Harrah's publicity and advertising at the time, explains:

> We considered the 1960 Winter Olympics a great opportunity to get Lake Tahoe's name out to the world and to get Harrah's name out at the same time. We lined up all those great stars, international stars like Dietrich, Skelton, Borge, to be there during the Olympics. The place was full every night. It was pretty much comped [complimentary tickets], because all those people who went to the Olympics were worn out and too tired to go to the show, but since it was comped, they found the energy to attend.

As far as Curtis is concerned, the Olympics was a godsend to the company:

> It established Harrah's; it established Tahoe. From then on, everybody knew where it was, and business was great. In other words, it was just like a whole new vacationland had opened up, and suddenly everybody knew about it. It was a real turning point, not only for Harrah's, but possibly also for Lake Tahoe.

If the Winter Olympics put Harrah's and Lake Tahoe on the map in 1960, the company's fabulous entertainment program is what kept bringing them back. Holmes Hendricksen held the position of Harrah's director of entertainment in the 1960s and 1970s. His professionalism has since become legendary throughout the show business industry. According to Hendricksen, entertainment played a crucial role in the company's marketing strategy in the 1960s. He explains:

Back then, it was against the law to advertise gambling, so it meant we had to advertise something else. Mr. Harrah chose to go with entertainment. To us, this was something exciting. It allowed us to throw familiar names and pictures of celebrities at the public. This added a new dimension of glamour and excitement. Remember now, there were all kinds of hooks the competition used to induce customers to come through their doors. Some competitors charged ridiculously low rates for their rooms. Others had excellent food at incredibly cheap prices. Our hook was entertainment. That's what we would annually advertise, and each year, we had a different advertising campaign. We built around the entertainers, making it our big drawing card.

In those days, we were still doing dinner shows, and each act performed twice a night. There was one at 7:30 and another at midnight. There were no dark nights—they performed seven nights a week. Depending upon a show's popularity, engagements ran two or three weeks. While the standard engagement was two weeks, it was more economical to have a performer stay for three weeks. This reduced our advertising and publicity costs. The same savings applied when we'd book the same act at our smaller showroom in Reno after it played in Tahoe. Since the Reno showroom was smaller, the act could play there longer. Like everything else in our business, everything depends on the numbers, so the entertainers received less in Reno because audiences were smaller.

"The 1950s and 1960s were the Golden Age for Casino Entertainment," says Lee Ragonese, who's been with Harrah's since 1965. When Ragonese joined the company, he worked as a sound operator and today is director of entertainment at the Harrah's, in both Reno and Lake Tahoe. He explains:

I worked in the Headliner Room, which has since been renamed *Sammy's Showroom,* in memory of Sammy Davis Jr. The Headliner was built on the property adjacent to Harrah's in Reno, where the famed Golden Hotel had stood since 1902. It filed for bankruptcy around 1960, and a fire in 1962 destroyed it. That's when Bill Harrah bought the land and built the 420-seat showroom. Its main competition was the Golden Nugget's showroom with a 700-seat capacity.

Back then, the biggest entertainers in the world worked in Nevada casinos, because it was the best venue in those days. There weren't the big concerts with the huge engagement fees and shared percentage take of the gross like there is today, so playing at a Nevada showroom was the top of the line for an entertainer. It was as far as they could go in the business. Back then, every city had nightclubs, because people went out to see entertainment. Television killed the nightclubs, and it's what's hurting casino showrooms today. And now, the superstars get hundreds of thousands or even millions of dollars for performing in front of huge crowds at concerts, so it has jacked up their fees to where we can't afford them anymore. That's why the Vegas venue has changed to extravagant shows like Cirque du Soleil and Siegfried & Roy. Productions like these cost millions of dollars in permanent fixtures for special lighting, movable stages and so on, which means they can't go out on tour, and this is why the hot acts play in Vegas for years.

Ragonese asserts it was the entertainment that drove the crowds to Tahoe during the winter months:

Nobody ever wanted to come to Tahoe after Labor Day. This place was an outpost in the middle of nowhere where you'd get 20 feet of snow and the roads weren't cleared. But with star performers, a guy in San Francisco would say to his wife, "Honey, why don't we go to Tahoe and see Frank Sinatra?" What he really wanted to say was, "Let's go to Lake Tahoe and gamble," but he knew that wouldn't appeal to her. You have to remember this was before Tahoe became a big ski resort area in addition to being a great summer resort. When I first came here, some of the guys would work here during the summers and Palm Springs in the winters. Those were the days when it was so quiet here, you could shoot a cannon off in the casino and not hit anybody. Today, business is more even, year round.

Holmes Hendricksen explains that in the days when the entertainers performed twice nightly, there were nights it was hard to fill the seats for the late shows:

We used to have all kinds of deals. For instance, our invitee program would permit a customer who had one of our credit or check cashing cards to invite three people as his guest. So a party of four could attend the second show on Sunday through Thursday for free. We played a lot of acts continuously because, if we didn't, there wouldn't be any business during the off months.

Although there was a time when Bill Harrah balked at paying $275 a week for his casino entertainment, he soon recognized the value in big-time entertainment. And when he did, he didn't blink an eye at the company's annual eight-figure budget for the superstar entertainers. Remember, too, that this was in the late 1950s through the 1970s when a dollar went a lot further than it does today. Harrah's lineup of superstars topped all the major casino resorts. Harrah's featured the top stars in show business—performers such as Louis Armstrong, Jack Benny, Danny Kaye, Mitzi Gaynor, Bob Hope, Ed Sullivan, Nat King

Cole, and Liberace. Then came stars such as George Burns, Bobby Darin, Frank Sinatra, Sammy Davis Jr., Bill Cosby, and John Denver.

Competing with Las Vegas for the world's greatest entertainers wasn't simply a matter of anteing up big bucks and the stars would automatically come. Reno and Lake Tahoe were considered the boondocks; and in the beginning, the big stars simply refused to come. To induce the superstars to come, the company's main attraction was Bill Harrah himself. It wasn't as though he wooed them with his charm, because that wasn't his forte. He was an introvert and didn't feel particularly comfortable around strangers. Instead, he attracted stars by using the same draw that the super casinos today use to attract whales—the world's biggest gamblers with credit lines in the millions. Harrah's reputation for treating its stars well was beyond comparison in the gaming industry, or for that matter, in any industry. He housed them in magnificent villas on the lake that came equipped with maid service and chauffeurs. The company's chefs prepared gourmet meals for them. Liquor cabinets were always kept filled with the finest alcoholic beverages, including expensive wines. When the company had its own fleet of aircraft, that, too, was available to the entertainers. Nobody gave them VIP service like Harrah's, and they loved it. Bill Harrah attended every opening act, and afterward, he personally went to their dressing rooms to congratulate each performer. Once the word spread throughout the world of show business, Harrah's was the place to play if you were anybody in the business.

Holmes Hendricksen explains:

> Bill felt that it was his responsibility as the owner to be there to welcome the artist as his personal guest. He'd tell them how much he appreciated them being there and say, "If there is anything you need, let us know. All you have to do is ask."
>
> Bill was a quiet man, and since I was the only unmarried member of management, he'd ask me to sit with him during the show. So I'd go with him and afterward we'd head for the dressing room to personally congratulate each artist. Counting shows in both Tahoe and Reno, I must have sat through hundreds of shows with Bill.

When Hendricksen attended opening acts with his boss, it wasn't the first time he saw them:

> We never bought an act that we didn't see in person. And when I say "we," I'm referring mainly to me, because my job was to look at every act before buying it. Our policy was to see everything before we'd buy it. It didn't matter how big an entertainer's reputation

was—we still personally saw them. And I emphasize being there because we never viewed film clips—it was before video cassettes were available. This meant being on the road five days a week for long stretches at a time, but it came with the job. I was particularly interested in the type of audience they drew. I was interested in such things as: Did they fit a casino crowd? Did they fit our age group? Is the act's material acceptable?

We had a policy that no act could appear at Harrah's that couldn't be viewed on television. If it wasn't acceptable on TV, we passed on it. This meant no nudity or obscene language. Bill didn't want any of his customers to ever come in and be embarrassed by a show. He didn't think you should take your wife out and have her be offended. He believed this was good business, and that was the kind of place we were.

Although Sonny and Cher were headliners when they were still an act, the famous duo played Harrah's only once. There were two reasons they weren't invited back. First, their act contained too many four-letter words, and, second, Hendrickson said they weren't good houseguests—they weren't nice to the people who waited on them!

Relationships with the Stars

Long before customer relationship marketing became part of the vernacular in corporate America, Bill Harrah had fine-tuned it with the treatment he reserved for entertainers. When it came to rolling out the red carpet to these VIPs, nobody did it better than he.

Bill Harrah wasn't the first to comp high rollers. He simply took it to the next level when it came to special treatment for the performing artists who took center stage at Harrah's. Typical of Bill Harrah, it was an agendum calculated to enhance the bottom line. Convinced that world-class entertainers brought a multitude of customers through the door, he wanted to increase his chances of signing up headliners who might otherwise be lost to the competition. Realizing that he couldn't pay the exorbitant fees being paid in Las Vegas, he gave extravagant perks to his guest performers to lure them to Tahoe.

He treated his performers like guests. The treatment they received was on a level otherwise reserved only for royalty or heads of state. First, it was the only hotel/casino that routinely sent its company airplane to pick up and return its headliners. Harrah, with his fanaticism for automobiles, furnished them with expensive cars ranging from Rolls Royces to Ferraris during their stay at Harrah's.

Each headliner could choose between staying in a "star" suite or in one of the two houses Harrah's maintained for their comfort. The star suites were not available to hotel customers—at any price. Entertainers who wanted to stay in the casino's hotel usually chose the Star Suite on the 16th floor, a two-story penthouse comparable today to a $10 million Fifth Avenue condo in Manhattan. Its living room/library/bar at the end of a corridor was sealed off from the elevators by an ornate steel gate, always manned by a security guard. Upstairs were two bedrooms, and a dining room occupied half the space of the downstairs, while the living room was a two-story affair. This stately penthouse had floor-to-ceiling windows that provided a panoramic northern exposure view of the lake and its surrounding snow-capped mountains. A star choosing to dine *en famille* in the suite could select a current movie to view on a screen that descended from the ceiling. Scenes of the suite were filmed and shown in the 1989 motion picture *Things Change,* starring Don Ameche and Joe Mantegna. In 1990, the penthouse was converted to the Summit Restaurant, one of Nevada's finest dining establishments. The Summit has 16 tables that comfortably seat 80 diners.

Another choice offered to headliners was Harrah's Villa, an elegant country home with 400 feet of frontage on Lake Tahoe. It had an oversized master bedroom plus two magnificent bedrooms at the other end. The villa had a huge living room, a restaurant-sized kitchen, and a dining room big enough to host a sit-down meal for 100 guests.

How luxurious was a headliner's stay at Harrah's? Sammy Davis Jr. said it many times: "It used to be an old saying that when you leave New York, you're camping out. Well, anyplace you play when you leave Harrah's is roughing it."

As excessive as the accommodations were, it was the personal touches these special guests most cherished. Hendricksen explains:

My staff kept records on all sorts of information about our entertainers. We knew what they drank, ate, and smoked. We knew who was on a special diet, for instance, who didn't eat fish, who liked pork chops—everything. We sent lavish gifts on their birthdays and even on their spouses' and children's birthdays. I must have spent half my life going to weddings, bar mitzvahs, graduations, and funerals. If one of our entertainers, for example, were nominated for a special award, we'd place a full-page congratulatory ad in the trades acknowledging the occasion. We attended many charity functions in Los Angeles when a particular artist was involved in a fund-raising event. We'd always buy a table and make sure it was filled with people. We'd fly our people to attend—I lost count of how many of those affairs I attended in LA.

It was part of my job to create special relationships with the performers so when they worked at Harrah's, it wasn't just another job to them. Sure, Bill expected them to work hard and do their best in the showroom every night, but he always reminded me, "There's nothing wrong with taking good care of them and making them extremely comfortable."

The entertainers spent a lot of their time resting, but whatever they wanted to do when they weren't performing, we had it available for them. I spent a lot of time on the golf course with them, taking them sightseeing, and of course, Bill's yacht was also available to entertain them.

Hendricksen recalls when English singer Roger Whitaker appeared at Reno and wanted to play a round of golf. "Roger loved the game, but he didn't bring his golf clubs," Hendricksen says. "I thought he ought to have his own clubs, so we gave him a set. He was so grateful. When I mentioned it to Bill, he was delighted. His exact words were, 'Holmes, that's wonderful.' He loved it when we'd take the initiative to be generous."

The entertainers also received extravagant gifts. Recipients of Rolls Royces, Mercedes, Jeeps, and Jaguars, for example, included Bill Cosby, Sammy Davis Jr., Wayne Newton, Don Rickles, and Glenn Campbell. "Back in the late 1960s, Bobby Darin wanted a jeep," recalls Lee Ragonese, "so Bill Harrah had a jeep built with a Ferrari engine. He called it a 'Jerrari.' Articles about the vehicle appeared in all the road and track magazines."

When it comes to lavish gifts, Hendricksen explains:

You have to put things in perspective. In those days, a Rolls wasn't a $250,000 car like it is today. A Rolls cost $50,000 to $60,000 back then, which was about a week's salary for them.

Our pay policy was very simple. We had a top for each room in Tahoe and Reno. Our top acts were paid the top rates for the room, even though we paid a wide range of salaries, depending upon the strength of the act, which was based on how strong a draw the artist was. Sammy Davis Jr., one of Bill's favorites, had been with us for nearly 20 years when Frank Sinatra signed up with us. I made a deal with Sammy that we'd never pay anybody more than we paid him. Our top salary was $200,000, so when Sinatra appeared, Sinatra was told that was as high as we'd go and he accepted it. The top rate was paid to other top performers such as Willie Nelson and Liza Minelli. I made a promise to Sammy that nobody would ever get more than he does, and we never broke our word, so he was happy.

Hendricksen emphasizes that Sammy Davis Jr. worked at Harrah's for 28 years, appearing hundreds of times, doing more shows than any other artist:

> If an act didn't do good business, we wouldn't bring it back. But we'd take into account the time of year, because every act did well at Tahoe during the summer months, but drawing a crowd in February was another story. We monitored everything that happened with our performers. Did he have a new TV show? Did she have a new album out or a television show appearance? Was his career on the rise or going downhill? We looked at everything.
>
> We also had a policy that, unlike Vegas, we never bid on acts. The casinos down there would get into bidding wars over an act, and whoever paid the most money, got it. In show business there are no secrets, so you could always find out what everybody else is making, how much business they did, and so on. However, our policy was: "This is our price, and if you would like to work for us, we'd love to have you. If not, we wish you well." I'd also add, "And if you work for another casino in our area, you don't work for us." Our policy was the same for everybody. Mr. Harrah believed in making them extremely comfortable and treating them like stars. We had houses and suites and cars and airplanes to make them very comfortable. Oftentimes, when our prices were comparable to Las Vegas, they came here just because of the perks. And sometimes, they'd choose us even though the pay was less, because we took such good care of them.

When it came to publicity and advertising, no other casino promoted its headliners like Harrah's. Hendricksen emphasizes:

> Casinos couldn't advertise gambling, but we could advertise what acts we booked. Our performers loved the fact that we were willing to put large sums into a major ad campaign on their behalf, because it was good for their career. Remember now, it also promoted our casino. One of the best campaigns we ever did was our booking in the 1970s with Frank Sinatra and John Denver. At the time, they were two of the biggest stars in the world, and we had both of them do an act together. At the time, we were paying $100,000 a week and they agreed to split the fee. I happened to have good relationships with Mickey Rudin, who was Sinatra's attorney as well as Jerry Weintraub, who was Denver's manager. Ruden and Weintraub were close friends, and they actually approached me to see if we would be interested.
>
> I went to LA with Mark Curtis, our advertising veep, and we worked out a deal in one meeting. We committed a large amount of money to publicize and advertise it. We had advertising on billboards

all over the world, from LA to Tokyo, and New York to London. The billboards featured Sinatra and Denver sitting on a stool back-to-back, and the wording was, "Back-to-back at Harrah's Tahoe," and the date. Once we began accepting reservations, in a period of 12 hours, there were 600,000 attempted phone calls. The lines were so busy, the circuits were backed up clear to Bakersfield, California, and it interrupted the phone service.

It worked both ways. The superstars also promoted Harrah's. Headliners were routinely appearing on shows such as the "Tonight Show" and the "Ed Sullivan Show," being introduced as "now appearing at Harrah's," "has just closed at Harrah's," and "will be opening at Harrah's." The stars loved the star treatment they received at Harrah's, and they raved about it repeatedly in interviews that appeared in magazines and newspapers. They couldn't say enough good things about how well they were treated during their stay in Lake Tahoe and Reno. Hendricksen says:

> For instance, one reason why we booked Lawrence Welk for about 15 years is because he was hot on television. We were the only casino he would consider working because he liked our policy on having only clean acts. We booked him in the summertime for three weeks, and with his full cast, it was a big production show. Welk appealed to an older crowd, and toward the tail end of his career, when we were having difficulty filling the seats for the late shows, we finally decided not to renew his contract.

Harrah's also worked hard to establish relationships with syndicated columnists such as Earl Wilson and Walter Winchell. Its publicists felt that just a line or two in a column with a wide readership in newspapers across the country was as powerful as a full story about the company in a large newspaper. To implement this strategy, Jackie Cannon, brother of the famous sportswriter Jimmy Cannon, was on the company's payroll as a column planter. In this capacity, he was paid to get write-ups in syndicated columns.

Over the years, many close relationships developed between Bill Harrah and show business people. Harrah, for instance, served as Red Skelton's best man, and Bill Cosby served as Harrah's best man when he married Bobbie Gentry in 1969, a marriage that lasted about one year. Cosby and Harrah were such good friends that the entertainer named his daughter Evan Harrah Cosby. Always a class act, Cosby once bought Harrah a Mercedes Grosser limousine for Christmas. A card on the windshield read, "What do you give a guy who has 1,400 cars? Another car, of course!" Another close friend, Jim Nabors,

SAMMY AND THE BIKERS*

During the late 1960s, Sammy Davis Jr. was a frequent guest at Villa Harrah. One of the many perks during his stay was driving one of his host's Rolls Royces. One Saturday mid-morning, Sammy had the misfortune to have the deluxe car break down just a few miles down the road from Skyland, where the villa is located on the Nevada side of the lake.

Frustrated, the entertainer stood by the side of the road, trying to wave down an oncoming car. A couple of Hell's Angel bikers came zooming by, made a U-turn, and offered him a lift. Sammy promptly jumped on the back of one of their bikes and was driven back to the villa.

"That was very nice of you," Sammy told them. "I'd like to do something for you. Let me get some tickets for you and some of your friends for tonight's show. You'll be my guests."

The bikers accepted the invitation and Sammy said he'd make the arrangements with the entertainment manager, who would take care of them.

Bob Trim, who managed the showroom, received a call from the entertainment manager. "Bob, we're in a lot of trouble. Sammy invited some friends of his to tonight's show and we've got to make room for them."

"How many are there?" Trim asked. "As you know, it's Saturday night, and we expect a big crowd."

"You have to make room for 80 to 90. Sammy wants you to meet them at the back dock just before the show."

When Trim walked out to the parking lot at the back dock to wait for Sammy's guests, he was aghast. The English-born gentleman saw nearly 100 long-haired, unshaven bikers wearing weather-beaten leather jackets ride up on their bikes. At the time, attendance in the Harrah's show had a dress code requiring each man to wear a coat and tie. But these were Sammy's guests, so Trim knew he had to make an exception.

"I had a little chat with them," Trim tells with his crisp British accent. "I told them what we expect in the showroom. They listened, and once inside, they behaved quite well. Sammy told the audience how he met his new friends and explained that they were his guests. He asked them to stand up, and they received a big round of applause."

---

* Bob Trim, interview with author, August 26, 2000.

once hosted a surprise party for Bill Harrah in his Beverly Hills home. His guest list of 100 included show business personalities. Another close friend, John Denver, sang at Harrah's funeral.

The Hotel on the Lake

During a two-year period in 1955 and 1956, Bill Harrah purchased several casinos in Lake Tahoe, mainly on the south shore in Stateline, Nevada. Before he came 50 miles north of Reno to the lake resort, there had been some gaming on the south shore of the lake, but the tourism to the area that began on Memorial Day weekend ended abruptly on Labor Day weekend. It was a three-month season, and with a casino's high overhead, it was difficult to generate a favorable bottom line. Another problem was keeping employees year around when, for nine months, the business moved at a snail's pace. The short season was a result of the treacherous weather that hit the mountains on the way to Tahoe, at times rendering U.S. Highway 50 virtually impassible by automobile.

Bill Harrah is credited with a solution for getting customers to come and making it possible for the area's gaming industry to prosper year around. His solution was simple: Bring people in by bus. In 1957, he began a bus program that cost him a bundle in advertising in San Francisco, Sacramento, Stockton, and 28 other cities, offering round trips on chartered Greyhound buses to Lake Tahoe. In the beginning, the cost of transporting customers on three chartered buses to his casino was about $40,000 a month. But even large chartered buses can't travel over mountainous roads that are buried in deep snow.

To keep the roads open, Harrah used his own private fleet of plows to remove the snow. In time, the company's rented fleet had 20 buses leaving each day from Oakland alone. Eventually, Harrah's became the second largest customer of the Greyhound Bus Company. Only the U.S. Army chartered more buses than Harrah's. Interestingly, there are several busing programs in Atlantic City today that have copied Harrah's innovative marketing plan of the 1950s. Thousands of customers are bused in daily from New York and Philadelphia. Ironically, Harrah's no longer buses customers to its marina district casino, although it does have an active busing program at its Showboat casino on the Boardwalk in Atlantic City.

Once large numbers of customers came to Lake Tahoe during the long, snowy winter months, many of them wanted to stay overnight, perhaps for a few days at a time. Consequently, by the end of the 1950s, Harrah's was making an average of 5,000 room reservations a week for its customers—a free service to the local lodging industry. To better serve his customers, Harrah bought a piece of the local Yellow Cab franchise. Because of his obsession with automobiles, he paid particularly close attention to the condition of each taxi and always made sure to hire the most courteous and clean-cut drivers. Customers were routinely taxied back and forth from nearby motels to Harrah's at no cost—they had only to sign a voucher and the casino picked up the tab. And it was good for business that the cabbies talked up Harrah's to their passengers!

Providing room reservations was an excellent service that customers appreciated—and even more so for those who received a comped room. But to Bill Harrah, something was missing. Something big! He needed a hotel. Harvey's and Sahara already had hotels. This meant that when guests came to Harrah's, they stayed at his competitors'.

However, he didn't want to build a run-of-the-mill hotel on what he considered the most beautiful lake on the continent. His ambition was to own the most luxurious hotel in North America. His hotel would be so special that it would lure high rollers from near and far. Instead of spending only a couple of days on the lake in a rustic but modest mom-and-pop motel, they'd now stay for several days, because his casino/hotel would make Lake Tahoe a destination resort. By the 1960s, Bill Harrah's casinos had made him one of the richest and most successful individuals in Nevada. With his enormous wealth, he embarked to build what would be the crown jewel of his gaming empire.

For two decades before the construction, Bill Harrah had traveled extensively around the world, always staying at the finest hotels. Everywhere he went, he took meticulous notes, constantly jotting down ideas about the amenities and elegant services that would someday be provided in his dream hotel. Harrah said:

> I had a file called the "Hotel File." Everywhere I traveled, any idea I liked, I brought back. Then when we got to planning, we went through all that, and it was all in my notes—details about the elevators, the room service, and so on. There were many things in there that I would have forgotten. I'm a great believer in copying a good idea.
>
> Scherry [the wife he married twice] and I had thought for years that if we ever built a hotel how we'd build it. Every place we ever went, we copied every idea. We'd measure the size of rooms. We'd measure the size of the bed. We'd measure this and that.

Harrah demanded the best and put his money where his mouth was. For example, at a meeting with his planners, he asked how fast it would take for the elevator to go from the first floor to the top floor. "That Hilton in New York—I've stayed there—and that's 60 floors, and I was on the 55th floor, and it took me a minute and 12 seconds to get up there, so that was an average of so many seconds per floor."

When it was explained to Harrah that he could purchase an elevator that took 22 seconds, or another that took 15 seconds but cost an extra $250,000 to $300,000, he didn't hesitate to choose the faster model. For an additional cost, he asked, "Can you make it 12 seconds?" One explanation for buying the faster elevator is that he didn't want to inconvenience his customers. A second is that the delay would mean less time spent in the casino.

On one of his trips abroad, Harrah decided to build a hotel with two bathrooms in every room, equipping each bathroom with its own television set. In the early 1960s, it was a big deal to have one television set in a room. It was a time when a big selling point in the lodging industry was to advertise "Free TV."

When questioned about having a second bathroom, Harrah said, "I want to have two bathrooms so that when a gentleman and his wife are in the room, he can use one bathroom and get ready for dinner, and she can use her bathroom."

He also added that it was a big time-saver and a big frustration-saver:

> It's maybe good marital relations—because anyone that's traveled knows that with one bathroom when you're short of time, it could cause a little disagreement. My wife and I travel now; we can afford it, but we always have two bathrooms. And occasionally we'll even have to rent another suite next door just to get that extra bathroom, and they'll look at us like we're crazy. But we'll take it, and we'll pay for it, because that's how we like to live.

He wanted the same luxury for his customers because his philosophy dictated treating customers as he liked to be treated. Having a second bathroom also meant the husband could spend more time in the casino while his wife was still in the bathroom!

In 1973, two years after construction started, Harrah opened his Lake Tahoe hotel, and no expense had been spared. The cost of each of its 250 rooms had soared to $125,000 a room, making it at the time the most costly hotel of its size ever built. Luxury hotel rooms were being built for $60,000 to $70,000. This compared to $16,000 to $20,000 for the cost of a typical Holiday Inn room. When the hotel started booking guests, it was the only hotel in the world with two bathrooms in every room. Each bathroom also had a telephone and television set. Each room had a stocked bar, a bedstead with built-in controls, and a magnificent view. To assure exceptional room service, a special elevator was installed to carry employees and room service orders only. Any order not delivered in 19 minutes or less was to be reported to a full management committee. Department heads were required to answer customer complaints by letter or telephone.

Concerned about the environment, Harrah wanted the hotel to resemble a clump of earth. Earth tones were very important to him, so the exteriors were done like rivulets of clay. Rather than remove trees, Harrah chose to have fewer parking spaces. Originally, the hotel was to have 35 stories, and had the company applied to the county commissioners for it, it would have been granted. Harrah, however, decided such a tall building would have been offensive to the environment and built an 18-story building instead. The original hotel contained 250 rooms; another 290 rooms were added three years later in 1976. Still, no additional floors were added. The following year, the hotel enjoyed a 92 percent occupancy rate.

Mead Dixon, the company's attorney who was later to serve as CEO, accused Harrah of not knowing how to manage capital resources. "For the same amount of money, we could have built a thousand rooms at Lake Tahoe and have been a more successful company."

Harrah disagreed:

> We knew what we wanted. And we got it. There was no compromise. I'm real proud of that because [it] was a little difficult. We have members on the board and in our management that are Return on Investment [people]. Harrah's can't run on ROI because we'd lose all the qualities that have made us as good as we are. Our service would go down. Our cleanliness would go down. Our everything would go down. One of the most difficult things is to keep up the standard. The hell with ROI. I'm proud of that hotel.

Harrah's on Lake Tahoe received a five-star rating from Mobil, as well as the AAA five-diamond rating. It was one of only seven hotels in the United States with both a five-star and a five-diamond rating.

Guests as a matter of course gave the hotel rave reviews. So did the entertainers. Frank Sinatra was known to be a man who didn't mince words. Whenever he'd get a chance to plug Harrah's in Lake Tahoe, he'd simply say, "It's the best hotel in the world." Coming from one of the all-time great entertainers who played and stayed at the most posh resorts around the globe, his praise was a powerful endorsement.

Going Public

Bill Harrah liked to advise people:

> I'm a big believer in getting the experts in. Be sure you get the good ones, pay them what they want, and let them help you. Remember that somebody's already been there before you and studied the problems. This usually means somebody has come up with a good answer. It's worth paying for it, because you'll save a lot of time, effort, money, and frustration.

But did he follow his own advice? Well, sort of. Lloyd Dyer, a past company president, explains:

> Bill was so against going public that he asked me to hire a consultant. He said, "I want you to hire a consultant to tell me why I shouldn't go public." And I did. I hired a man out of Portland, Oregon, and he wrote a ten- or twelve-page report on why we shouldn't go public—but we still had to go public. Bill needed the money, and the only way we could expand was with public financing.

Before the company's first public offering in 1971, Harrah was having financial pressures. He had borrowed heavily to build a 400-room hotel at Harrah's Reno and was in the process of designing the pricey Lake Tahoe hotel. At the same time, he was going through his second divorce from wife Scherry.

Harrah gave two reasons for taking the company public:

> One, primarily, I needed some money personally because I could only pay myself so big a salary, and I could pay some dividends, but I needed more money than that, because I had several divorces, and divorces are very expensive. And I'd been living high, so I just needed money badly. And then the other thing, the convincer, is for estate purposes.

There was one more compelling reason that he later added to the list:

> Another advantage is people like to own something. You can hold people when you own all the stock yourself by paying them highly. But when you're public, you can give or sell stock to them. Plus you can have a stock option plan. When an employee has a lot of stock options, and the stock is worth a lot of money, he can't have it for five years or maybe six. If he quits tomorrow, it's "Good-bye, here's your salary, give us the stock back." It's his stock—all he's gotta do is hold his job.

In 1971, Harrah's became listed over the counter, becoming the first pure gaming company to be publicly traded. It came out with a

450,000-share offering, which represented 13 percent of the company's holdings, and raised $4 million for its owner after taxes and expenses. The following year, the company became listed on the American Exchange, and in 1974, transferred over to the Big Board, making it the first casino company listed on the New York Stock Exchange.

It was not just the direct proceeds from the public offering that changed the financial base of Harrah's. The perception of Harrah's in the financial community changed. That change came because if the company was traded over the counter, then on the American, and, finally, on the New York Stock Exchange, folks figured it must be as clean and healthy as General Foods.

From an activity that was outlawed even in Nevada, gambling had been dragged by its hair to respectability, and Bill Harrah had done the dragging. The SEC and the great national money exchanges had conferred the respectability—well, at least the diploma—but it was Bill Harrah who had qualified the business to ascend into decent society.

Lloyd Dyer explains how unfamiliar the investment community was with the gaming industry:

> They told us, "We've never been in your place in Las Vegas." They'd heard of Lake Tahoe but they had never heard of Reno [except] as the divorce capital of the world.
>
> Not only that, but those people looked at us like we were carrying machine guns under our coats. We were ashamed of the industry's image in the East. But we were god-damned proud of what we at Harrah's were. We developed a rapport with top investment bankers: the Merrill Lynches, the Paine Webbers, the Dean Witters. We had excellent ratings from the rating companies, [but] that was something we had to do ourselves.
>
> We proved ourselves in that financial community, which was a tough nut to crack.

When all was said and done, Harrah's changed the image of gaming in America, opening the gate for other casino companies to take the same route to raise money. Some say this is Bill Harrah's greatest contribution to the gaming industry.

The Man Who Loved Cars

One of Bill Harrah's fondest childhood memories was when his father taught him to drive at the age of eight. Throughout his life, he talked about that experience. He could barely see over the steering wheel of the 1911 Hudson, but still he drove it. Because he was too small to actually start the car, to get the engine running, he coasted it down a steep hill and let the clutch out. Once on level ground, the eight-year-old boy kept the engine running, because if it stopped, he would have been unable to start it again.

Thus began Bill Harrah's love affair with automobiles, one that lasted for the rest of his life. On his sixteenth birthday, he received his first car, a 1926 Chevrolet roadster his father purchased for him. It meant so much to him that, years later, he bought a duplicate of it for his famous car collection. With his laid-back personality and slowness of speech, he didn't appear to be the type who would love fast cars. But like many car buffs, he liked to test a car to see how fast it could go. In 1942, after a night of carousing with a friend, he smashed his 1942 Packard into a steel bridge. His friend went through the windshield and had to have his face sewed up, and Harrah broke his neck. Fortunately, the accident happened in front of the Reno police station, and the police rushed Harrah and his friend to the hospital. After a nine-week stay in the hospital, he was released and classified as 4-F, keeping him out of the army during World War II.

Harrah never stopped driving over the speed limit, and as a result, accumulated many traffic tickets. To keep the number of traffic violations down, a person on his staff was instructed to call ahead to the local police station when the boss was on the road. "Hi, I'm calling from Harrah's in Reno," the employee would say, "and you can expect my boss, Bill Harrah, to be racing through town within the next few minutes. We'd like to donate $100 [sometimes a higher sum] to your community. Now we'd sure appreciate it if you could just let him drive on through."

Every collection has to start somewhere. It wasn't until 1947 that Harrah bought a 1911 Maxwell, the first car in what was to become his world-famous automobile collection. That was the beginning, and then, as Harrah described it:

> You have two cars. Then four cars. All I can tell you [is] the cars came real fast. I was making money, so I could afford to buy a car here and there.
>
> I bought a Duesenberg, I bought this and that. I lived on South Virginia Street then and I remember I had a backyard [with] at one time eight to ten cars out there. [That] worried me and I had to move them. So I started renting vacant buildings around. And pretty soon there were 20 and then 50. Eventually you take a look and, well, what are you gonna do with 100 cars?

Harrah not only bought cars, he restored them. This meant he needed a shop to repair his prized possessions. Initially, he rented an old icehouse in Sparks, just outside Reno. As the collection grew, he rented or bought different properties to house his expensive hobby. Eventually, it was more than a hobby—it was a business. At its peak, it employed 70 mechanics and craftsmen. After adding office staff, cleaning people, and security guards, Harrah's Automobile Collection had a payroll of an estimated 150 employees. The collection kept growing and growing, and ultimately had 1,363 automobiles, or slightly less than 1,500 vehicles if everything was counted—the entire collection included bicycles, motorcycles, airplanes, boats, trucks, fire engines, and even trains.

The collection was too big to be considered a hobby. While it might have started out as a personal hobby for its owner, it became an asset of the company. Harrah's senior managers looked at it as a drain on the casino's reserves even though the collection was used to attract customers to the casino. Car buffs from around the world came to see it. High rollers were given VIP tours. The collection sometimes took road trips to promote Harrah's. For instance, the collection was shipped to Japan for the 1971 World Classic Car Festival and was displayed in Tokyo, Osaka, and Kyoto to big crowds. It made two trips to Germany. Additionally, individual cars were "loaned" for exhibitions around the world.

When Bill Harrah was questioned by the IRS about writing off certain expenses incurred by the collection as business expenses, he argued, "With so many cars, how many do you think I actually drive?" The IRS gave in.

The IRS ruling wasn't based on his enjoyment of automobiles. Mark Curtis explains:

> I think he loved the casino business, but as far as where he'd rather be any day, I'm sure it was with the cars. He did have a definite passion for Harrah's itself and what he'd done with it and the things it allowed him to do. It allowed him so much, so many different ways to express his perfection.

Bill Harrah's dream was to combine his two passions and ultimately open Auto World. It would be a destination casino resort, and had he lived to build Auto World, it would have been a forerunner to today's themed extravaganzas such as Treasure Island and Mirage. He had already purchased property on land that is now the first exit on the new freeway out of Reno in Verde, a small town six miles due west. At the time, people couldn't imagine why he'd want to build so far away from downtown Reno.

"He planned to build a big theme casino resort that honored the American automobile," explains Lee Ragonese, "and it would feature his entire collection. There would be a golf course, restaurants, shops—the whole nine yards."

At the time of Bill Harrah's death in 1978, the Harrah Automobile Collection was valued at an estimated $65 million. Two years later in 1980, when Harrah's was acquired by Holiday Inns, its management was unaware that the car collection was included in the purchase price.

Once cognizant of this sizable asset, Holiday Inns simply didn't want so much capital sitting in warehouses that was not only costly to maintain, but didn't generate a dime's worth of revenue. This was also during the Jimmy Carter years when money was expensive with interest rates in the 20 percent range. As far as Holiday Inns was concerned, the car collection had no business purpose, so a decision was made to liquidate it.

Of the 1,363 cars owned at the time of Harrah's death, 1,188 were sold at auction; the remaining 175 became part of an automobile museum that, today, is open to the public.

PART II

Mergers, Acquisitions, and Expansions

(1979–1994)

The next phase in the evolution of Harrah's saw mergers, alliances, and expansion that further solidified the company's dominant position in the gaming industry. On Harrah's death on June 30, 1978, his attorney, Mead Dixon, was named executor of the estate, which owned the majority of the company's stock. With control of the company, Dixon was elected chairman of the board. In this capacity, his first assignment was to sell the company to raise cash to settle the estate. Two years later, Harrah's was acquired by Holiday Inns, Inc., owner of 1,600 hotels with holdings in two casinos. As discussed in Part II, gambling has spread outside Las Vegas with the opening of casinos in Atlantic City. We witness the growth of Harrah's under Holiday Inns' umbrella, including the opening of Harrah's properties in Las Vegas as well as on riverboats and Indian reservations. Also

featured are corporate changes at Holiday Inns, including the forma-
tion of Holiday Corporation, a holding company consisting of Holi-
day Inns hotels, Embassy Suites hotels, Hampton Inn hotels, and
Harrah's Casinos. In 1989, the British firm Bass PLC acquired Holi-
day Inns. That same year, a spin-off company, the Promus Com-
panies, became the parent company to Harrah's, along with Embassy
Suites, Hampton Inn, and Homewood Suites. This section ends in
1995 when Promus spins off its hotel business and Harrah's becomes
listed on the New York Stock Exchange for the first time.

3

THE HOLIDAY
INNS INFLUENCE

HEN BILL HARRAH DIED AT AGE 66 ON JUNE 30, 1978, HE WAS A very wealthy man, but his philosophy of spending money to make money had left him deeply in debt. Consequently, there was no cash to pay his estate taxes, which exceeded $35 million. He owed $13 million to a bank in Reno and had no savings; his life insurance was a meager $10,000, and his checking account had a balance of about $80,000. He also had interests in several companies, including a large apartment complex in Florida, but by far his biggest holdings were his six million shares in Harrah's.

Mead Dixon, his personal attorney and estate executor, became the company's chairman of the board and CEO. In this capacity, his main objective—to sell the business—essentially meant finding someone to succeed him as top dog. Until then, Dixon would continue to operate Harrah's, looking for opportunities to grow the company.

Meanwhile, Phil Satre, a 30-year-old attorney, had handled some legal matters for Bill Harrah shortly before his death. The Stanford graduate had attended college on a football scholarship and finished law school at the University of California in Davis in 1975. He then joined the Reno law firm Vargas, Bartlett and Dixon—the same firm where Mead Dixon had been a partner before assuming the number one spot at Harrah's. Satre, now chairman of Harrah's, explains:

> I did a lot of work in the area of gaming regulatory matters, litigation, and corporate matters for the company. Prior to Mr. Harrah's death, I worked on everything from his personal estate and tax planning to his plans to establish a large retail automobile sales organization. I had brief encounters with Mr. Harrah, but he wasn't a man who interacted much with people, particularly with somebody at my level back then. But I was able to spend a lot of time with the management of the company.

About the time Satre was scheduled to become a partner at the law firm, Dixon asked him to join the company. The offer was made shortly after Harrah's funeral, and Satre promptly signed on as vice president and general counsel. To help persuade the young attorney to join, Dixon told him of his plans to expand into the Atlantic City market.

"I jumped at the opportunity," tells Satre. "I was aware of what was happening with gaming in Atlantic City, and I wanted to be involved in taking Harrah's from its roots in Reno and Lake Tahoe to the East Coast."

It's interesting that Dixon chose to open the company's first casino outside Reno or Lake Tahoe in Atlantic City—thousands of miles away on the other side of the continent. Earlier, in 1977, Maurice Sheppard, a past president of Harrah's, had been dispatched to the East Coast to appraise what opportunities awaited the company at the famed seaside resort area. When Sheppard returned, he reported to his boss: "Atlantic City is terrible; it's an awful place; it's not going to succeed." Sheppard's report caused Bill Harrah to lose interest in Atlantic City. Yet, the company's founder had been gone less than a year when Dixon set forth to see America's newest and hottest gambling town firsthand.

Dixon's first impressions were: "Atlantic City was over-age and gray; it was a little hick town; 40,000 unemployed people, the town was closing down, and there weren't many talents there. As far as the infrastructure, the political system and the legal system, it was nothing." Although his opinion of Atlantic City mirrored Sheppard's, Dixon was determined that this was where Harrah's should build its first casino outside northern Nevada. There were precious few choices, as casinos were legal only in Nevada and New Jersey.

In the late 1970s, finding a desirable building site and obtaining a gambling license in Atlantic City, where Harrah's was not a recognizable brand name, appeared formidable. For this reason, Dixon considered a joint venture with another company. Having a partner with deep pockets could help fund the casino in case it became tricky lining up financing in the East.

As the company's point man, Phil Satre was given the assignment to establish a Harrah's casino in Atlantic City. His job was to line up a worthy partner and aggressively secure suitable real estate on which to build. To accomplish this chore, over the next three years he spent half his time on the East Coast traveling back and forth from Reno where his family lived.

When Dixon and Satre arrived in Atlantic City in late 1978, Harrah's was already a Johnny-come-lately. New Jersey voters had approved casino gambling in November 1976. In anticipation that the gambling referendum would pass, a few weeks earlier Resorts International had spent $5.2 million to purchase the Chalfonte-Haddon Hall, then Atlantic City's largest hotel, to convert it into the town's first casino. Resorts International had its grand opening in May 1978. Resorts' monopoly lasted 13 months, until June 1979, when Caesars opened a casino resort. Six months after Caesars, Bally's Park Place opened a massive casino-hotel complex, becoming the third company to enjoy a huge operation in Atlantic City.

In June 1978, Steve Wynn came to town and made a big splash in Atlantic City, just as he would later do in Vegas. Wynn says:

> We perceived back in 1978 that the East Coast experience is basically a gray one. And if Atlantic City was ever gonna be exciting and successful, it was because it offered the people in this part of the world a chance to break their ordinary course of disciplined daily life and get a big dose of color and excitement and distraction. So we said everything in our building is going to be bright and twinkling, maybe too much so.

After paying $8.5 million for the Strand Motel on the lower end of the Boardwalk, Wynn tore it down and replaced it with the $160 million Golden Nugget Atlantic City, a Las Vegas-style casino resort, unmatched in glitz and ornateness anywhere on the East Coast. Wynn's casino opened in December 1980, boasting 506 plush rooms upstairs, and enough brass, marble, and glass to convince all who entered that they were in a magical place. The lobby featured a four-story gilded birdcage with five talking mechanical parrots singing in the voices of Louis Armstrong, Bette Midler, Maurice Chevalier, Mae West, and Don Adams. On the second floor, an automated, light-hearted Buddha named Tung Yin Cheek imparted wisdom to visitors. The high rollers' suites on the 23rd floor featured everything from saunas to "opium dens" and bars outfitted to serve monied guests and a hundred of their closest friends. Called the Constellation Suites and designed by Norwood Oliver, these were lavishly appointed with exotic materials: Italian marble, raw silk, even lacquered goatskin.

The Atlantic City Golden Nugget opening in 1980 was a smashing success. Wynn proved what the experts had predicted when casinos became legal in New Jersey: Markets outside Las Vegas could indeed do a booming business.

Holiday Inns and Hilton were among the first major hotel chains to throw their hats in the ring. The Hilton Hotel Corporation had good reason to expand into Atlantic City. Although the chain owned more than 1,000 hotels, 60 percent of its 1979 profits came from the Flamingo and the Las Vegas Hilton, its two Las Vegas casinos.

With other casino operators off to running head starts, the Dixon-Satre team worked diligently to establish a Harrah's presence in Atlantic City. Their first contact with another company was with Holiday Inns. This was a logical choice because when Harrah had dispatched the skeptical Maurice Sheppard to Atlantic City in 1977, he had met with what was then the world's largest hotel chain. Sheppard had spoken at length with Mike Rose, Holiday Inns' Executive Vice President. Rose, a Harvard Law School graduate, was practicing law in his hometown of Cincinnati, where his firm represented a large Holiday Inns franchisee group. Just as Satre had been recruited to work for Harrah's, Rose accepted an offer to work for Holiday Inns at its corporate headquarters in Memphis.

Rose, who became president of Holiday Inns in 1981 and later chairman and CEO, was in charge of the negotiations when the two companies met to talk about a potential merger. Rose says:

> I had met Bill Harrah and some of his executives back in 1977 to discuss a possible joint venture in either Atlantic City or Las Vegas. We looked at MGM, a company that had never been in the gaming business, and after it opened about this same time, its one casino made more money than we made with all our hotels. So we wanted to get into the gaming business, and we wanted a first-rate partner. Harrah's was the single company we identified that had values closest to ours in terms of the way their casinos were run. And unlike some of the casinos in Vegas that had dubious pasts, Harrah's was clean as a whistle. At the time, Bill Harrah was a little spooked about doing business with Holiday Inns because he perceived our approach to be a different quality than what he wanted to do. Consequently, nothing happened, but when Mead Dixon took over, we were the logical merger partners. That's when he contacted us to sit down and talk again.

By October 1979, it was agreed Holiday Inns would acquire Harrah's; but at the last moment, an unexpected event put the deal on hold. Federal Reserve chief Paul Volker, Alan Greenspan's predecessor, invoked credit restrictions that prohibited a bank from making a loan to a company to acquire another company. "The deal had already been signed, and we already had financing committed," explains Rose. "Consequently, instead of giving Harrah's as much cash as we had originally planned, we gave them more convertible preferred stock."

After 19 months of negotiations, Holiday Inns finally acquired Harrah's on February 29, 1980—coincidentally, during a leap year. Bill Harrah's six million shares, which represented 86 percent of the NYSE company, were priced at $35.50 a share, a sum of $213 million.

It was agreed that the Harrah's name would appear on the casino under construction in Atlantic City's Bay Area. The new casino, Harrah's Marina, was located three miles north of the famed Boardwalk, so it was isolated from the other casinos—with one exception. Across the street, Hilton Hotels was already planning to construct a casino resort.

Getting Trumped

Donald Trump became Manhattan's largest private real estate owner when he made a notable purchase from the bankrupt Penn Central railroad—an option to develop 76 acres along the Hudson River on the Upper West Side. Today, he is also Atlantic City's largest private real estate owner as the holder of three properties in Atlantic City—Trump Plaza, Trump's Taj Mahal, and Trump Marina (originally called Trump Castle).

In 1982, after the merger of Harrah's and Holiday Inns, a decision was made to build a second casino resort in Atlantic City in the heart of the action—on the famed Boardwalk. For this expensive venture, it was agreed the company would seek a partner.

In March of the same year, Trump had been granted a casino license from the New Jersey Casino Control Commission and had announced his plans to build a 37-story casino hotel in Atlantic City. He anticipated 614 rooms and a 60,000-square-foot casino.

An unlikely pair met to discuss a possible joint venture—Holiday Inns' CEO Mike Rose and one of America's most infamous businesspersons, known across America as "The Donald." At this first powwow, the hotel CEO was enamored with Trump, according to Mead Dixon:

> Mike had a meeting with Donald, and when he came back, in substance he said—and this is not even a paraphrase—"I feel more comfortable with Donald Trump than I do with Harrah's, so we're going to make a deal with Trump; we're going to be 50–50 partners. Trump has $25 million in equity in his project, and we're going to take the $50 million that we would have put into the Harrah's project, and put it into the Trump project."

That closed the discussion, ending the opportunity to build a second Harrah's casino on the Boardwalk.

"Donald's project turned out to be nothing but a fiasco, with litigation and hard feelings and an impossible relationship between Trump and Mike Rose," explains Dixon. "Not only was it a clash of egos—if you're trying to deal with Trump, you realize you are on a fast track."

At first, it appeared to be a peach of a deal, especially for Trump. In exchange for a 50 percent share of the income, Harrah's agreed to operate the casino free of charge. Holiday Inns reimbursed Trump for $22 million in costs up to that time, paid another $50 million that included a $20 million management fee, financed a $170 million construction loan, and the company agreed to indemnify Trump against any operating losses for the next five years.

The honeymoon between the two companies was short-lived. No sooner had New Jersey Governor Thomas Kean cut the ribbon for Harrah's at Trump Plaza on May 14, 1984, than war erupted between the two parties.

The deal called for certain bonuses to be paid to Trump if he kept construction costs under budget. Consequently, Trump had a strong incentive to cut corners to earn his bonuses. Mead Dixon said:

> I think if he had to omit the kitchens, he would have done so in order to bring it in under projected costs and get his bonus. Our Harrah's people tried to participate in the design of that project—we tried to talk Donald into putting in an adequate number of elevators, and tried to get an adequate showroom, but we couldn't even get him to provide a service elevator . . . and all the entertainment and so forth was on the sixth floor.
>
> We said—this is illustrious—"Suppose we want to put an automobile on stage or a grand piano; how do we get it there?"
>
> Donald's response in effect was, "Put it on the escalator."
>
> We couldn't even get Trump to punch a hole in the wall so we could lift something up with an outside crane to put it into the showroom, because Donald was going to bring the project in under cost to get his multimillion-dollar bonus.

There were other problems: a kitchen too far from the restaurants, a hotel lobby cramped with huge pillars. The deluxe rooms were, at best, ordinary, and the ordinary rooms even less than ordinary. Rooms that could have had an ocean view did not, and public areas that could have overlooked the seascape did not have a view. Then there was the interior decoration—by Trump's wife Ivana—replete with bulky chrome fixtures, and wall treatments done in blaring reds, ostentatious oranges, yammering yellows, and pounding purples. "It's the most magnificent building in the world," claimed her husband. Holiday Inns' people were appalled.

The property bearing Trump's name was hyped as a luxury building, but it was nothing of the sort. Many observers saw the edifice as a monument to Trump's huge ego.

Trump claimed he brought the building in on time and on budget. If he had, that might have been one of the building's few virtues, but Holiday Inns claimed he ran millions of dollars over budget.

Yet another cause of disagreement was parking. Trump acquired land for parking but then informed Holiday Inns that it cost him $10 million, and that unless the company paid its share, he would charge a steep price for every car that was parked on his land. Holiday Inns had no choice but to ante up. The fight over the parking was the last straw, and litigation followed. In the end, the partnership was terminated. Trump bought out Holiday Inns' interests in the hotel, and changed the name to Trump Plaza.

Putting his name on everything he owned had become a Trump trademark. Other holdings include the famed Trump Towers in Manhattan and the airline known as Trump Shuttle. "All he cared about was generating the highest revenue," Rose says of his former business associate. "We always focused on generating the highest profit. To Trump, business is too much about ego. He has not always been financially successful at many of his businesses, because he appears to run them to satisfy his incredible ego."

In February 1985, Hilton Hotels Corporation was denied a gaming license by a 2–2 vote of the New Jersey Casino Control Commission. The denial was based on the company's association with a Chicago labor attorney who had alleged ties to organized crime. The decision was a shocker to everyone. Hilton was so certain the license would be granted that the company already had under construction a hotel 26 stories high, with 703 rooms and 200,000 square feet of public space that included a 30-foot atrium. The 60,000-square-foot gaming area would house 107 tables and 1,688 slot machines. It would employ 4,000 people, 1,000 of whom were already on the payroll. It came equipped with a nine-story parking garage—enough space to accommodate 3,000 automobiles. The property was only 12 weeks from completion when the license was rejected.

The Hilton property was the only other casino resort in the marina area where Harrah's Marina was located. Steve Wynn expressed a strong interest in buying the property, going as far as to make a hostile bid to take over the entire Hilton chain with an initial offer to buy 27 percent of its stock, 6.8 million shares, for $72 a share, $5 above its market price. Wynn's offer shook up the Atlantic City establishment. Some believed that his offer to gain control of the Hilton chain was a hardball tactic to purchase the marina property at a bargain price because it would force Barron Hilton to sell the property to fend off a takeover. Wynn already owned 14 acres of undeveloped land on the

THE BIRTH OF A MAGAZINE

As a young man, Howard Klein had made and lost a fortune in various business ventures. He had done everything from owning a candy import company to trading commodities on Wall Street. In 1978, while between careers, he happened to walk by the Port Authority Bus Terminal in New York City where he witnessed what he later called an unusual happening.*

"This large crowd had gathered at one of the bays," tells Klein, "and I heard screaming and shrilling. There was a lot of commotion and policemen were blowing their whistles, and people were pushing and shoving. Curious, I shoved my way toward the center of everybody, expecting to see two drunks in a fistfight.

"Instead, I saw two old women, maybe 80 years old, taking swings at each other with their umbrellas and canes. They were fighting over the last vacant bus seat.

" 'What going on?' I asked a bystander.

" 'That's the last bus of the day leaving for Atlantic City.'

"The bus was jam-packed with enthusiastic senior citizens. It reminded me of when my kids boarded a summer camp bus. 'Atlantic City?' I questioned.

"When I learned that the gaming casinos were the big attraction, I came back the next morning to take a bus to Atlantic City so I could see it for myself. Again, I encountered another robust crowd. Fortunately, some extra buses were added at the last minute to accommodate the demand, and I was on my way to the seashore. I had to experience firsthand what could cause so many people to get so excited. Two hours later, the bus pulled up to the entrance of Resorts International, and when I entered the casino, I saw an incredible sight. People were lined up waiting their turns to play slot machines so they could lose their money. At the table games, the cash kept pouring in. One blackjack dealer was struggling to push the shunt to jam dollar bills into the box. The money was literally bulging out. He was frantically trying to get another employee to assist him.

"I'm witnessing an American phenomenon, I thought. I had studied journalism in college, so my first inclination was to write a book about the gambling business. I figured what was going on in Atlantic City was bound to spread across the country, so my

---

* Howard Klein, interview with author, September 20, 2000.

(continued)

The Birth of a Magazine (Continued)

book would have a wide audience. I went to the library to do some research, and the first thing I did was look for some articles in the trade magazines on the gaming industry. There weren't any. I did find enough other published material that provided enough information to write a 16-page book outline that I promptly gave to a literary agent I knew. A few rejection letters and a month later, he called to say we had an offer with an advance of $8,500.

"With a wife and kids, I couldn't afford to write the book," Klein continues. "The hell with a book, I figured. That's when I made up my mind that the real opportunity was to start a trade magazine, knowing that the gaming industry was just in its infancy. I set up a meeting with my friend Irv Babson, who owned BMT Publications, a publisher of three successful trade magazines—one for the tobacco industry, a second for the pipe tobacco industry, and a third for the convenience stores industry.

"'What do you mean, the gambling industry doesn't have a trade magazine?' Irv said in amazement. 'I don't believe that.'

"After doing his homework, Babson said to me, 'You were right, so okay, let's make a deal. You be the publisher, you write the articles, and I'll give you a percentage. My partner Irwin Brightman and I will back the whole thing.'

"So that's how I started *Gaming and Wagering Business Magazine,* which is the biggest in the gaming industry today," Klein tells. "Anyone who's anyone in the business reads it."

By sheer coincidence, Irv Babson assigned Gary Selesner, an eager, young editor, to work on the magazine with Klein. "Irv said it was a shoestring operation," recalls Selesner, "and I was going to edit and write articles on gambling but I wouldn't be paid anything extra for it. Still in my 20s, I was able to interview people like Mead Dixon, Phil Satre, Steve Wynn, and many of the top VIPs in the casino industry. And working with a creative guy like Howard Klein was a great experience.

"Then Mark Curtis, Harrah's vice president of advertising, called me," Selesner continues.* "'We need managers for marketing, advertising, and special events for Harrah's Marina and Harrah's at Trump Plaza. We have two other young guys from outside the industry, and we're looking for some more young, bright guys like you to work for us.' My wife and I were anxious to get out of New York, so I took the job and moved to Atlantic City.

---

* Gary Selesner, interview with author, August 25, 2000.

THE BIRTH OF A MAGAZINE (CONTINUED)

"We decided we should reposition Harrah's at the Marina as, 'The Other Atlantic City.' Being three miles from the action, it was struggling, so we decided to subtly promote the marina by emphasizing the negatives about being on the Boardwalk. We pointed out the crime and the tawdriness, and we offered an alternative. We hired Jerry Stiller and Ann Meara to sing the jingle, 'By the bay, by the bay, by the beautiful bay,' to the tune of 'By the Sea,' and sure enough, the people started coming to Harrah's Marina. The property went from being number seven—at the bottom spot—to the number one spot in profits, and it's never looked back since."

For a short period, Selesner promoted Harrah's Marina as "The Other Atlantic City" and Harrah's at Trump Plaza as "Atlantic City's Centerpiece." "We were playing off the strength of the Trump name," he explains, "the glitz, glamour, and location on the Boardwalk, so we differentiated the two to prevent them from cannibalizing each other."

When Trump bought out Harrah's interest in their joint venture, Selesner passed up a job as advertising manager of the western division of Harrah's and remained with Trump. He stayed there for several years as advertising manager, but through a strange twist of fate, he became president of the company. It was in 1984 when Trump's top three casino executives—Jon Benanau, Mark Etess, and Steve Hyde—were killed in a helicopter accident while traveling from Manhattan to Atlantic City. Trump named the 32-year-old Selesner to serve as executive vice president and recruited John O'Donnell, son of William O'Donnell, founder of Bally Manufacturing, to be his president. O'Donnell was unable to work with The Donald, and quit after six months.

"One day, the company's lawyer, along with the CFO, walked into my office and announced that the CFO was going to be the president. The CFO said, 'But Gary's been here longer, so he ought to be the president.'

"With that, the attorney turned to me and said, 'Okay, Gary, you'll be the acting president.'"

Selesner held the position for about a year. The Trump Taj Mahal had opened, and it cannibalized the other two Trump properties. Then, The Donald sent Selesner back to marketing to report to a new president. Not long afterward, Selesner quit the company.

(continued)

THE BIRTH OF A MAGAZINE (CONTINUED)

Next, Selesner worked for President Casinos, the company that founded the nation's first riverboat casino company; and after that, he became general manager for the Hard Rock Hotel and Casino in Las Vegas. In a letter Selesner wrote to Phil Satre, Selesner mentioned that Harrah's had tried to retain him when he chose to go with the Trump organization. "I mentioned in it that I always regretted not going with Harrah's," Selesner tells.

In 2000, Harrah's promoted the general manager at its Lake Tahoe property to manage its casino in New Orleans. Concurrently, Satre invited Selesner to serve as general manager and vice president of Harrah's Lake Tahoe. Selesner accepted at once.

Meanwhile, the magazine thrived, and its name has been changed to *International Gaming & Wagering Business*. Klein sold his interests in the magazine and became a marketing vice president at Caesars and later a vice president of marketing at Claridge Casino Hotel in Atlantic City until his retirement in 2001.

---

adjoining lot. Speculation was that a Wynn takeover of the Hilton property would make him the most powerful figure in gaming on the East Coast.

Trump, who some say was motivated by his ill feelings toward Holiday Inns, submitted an offer to pay the entire $320 million that Hilton had invested in the property. Others speculate that he did it to keep Wynn from becoming the main kingpin in Atlantic City. Regardless of his motivation, The Donald bought the property, sight unseen, having never stepped inside the building.

"If I'd told my father," Trump later joked, "he would have said I lost my mind."

Slots Are Us

The history of slot machines in the United States goes back more than 150 years to the California Gold Rush in 1849. It wasn't until the 1930s, during the Great Depression, that the popularity of slot machines soared. It's interesting that slot machines became more prevalent during a period of hard times and the prohibition of alcohol. After legalized gaming casinos opened in Nevada, slot machines took a back seat to table games.

During and following World War II, slot machines were strictly for the amusement of the wives and girlfriends of the men who frequented casinos. The penny and nickel one-armed bandits were simply a sideline to provide a frivolous distraction to keep women occupied while their escorts tossed the dice and played blackjack. Slots were for women; "real men" didn't play them.

A whole generation of veterans who came home from World War II had spent countless hours fending off boredom during their military days by shooting craps. They shot craps in the barracks and in the foxholes. It was part of the GI experience. Across America, men shot craps in the back rooms of pool halls, bowling alleys, and barber shops. Truckers shot craps in the back of their trailers. When casinos opened in Nevada, nothing matched the excitement generated at the craps table in a casino. It was the shooters against the house—a group activity. Craps provided a camaraderie reminiscent of those old days with their army buddies. Even today, the cheering and noise level at the craps tables far exceeds that of other forms of casino gaming.

Following World War II, couples got together regularly for their Friday night card games—the men played poker or gin, while their wives played bridge and canasta. Families played penny poker on their kitchen tables. By the time the average American boy entered high school, he knew the odds of drawing to an inside straight, a flush, and a full house. At most country clubs across the country, you could find a poker or gin game in progress any night of the week. Unlike today's generation of boys, the average American male of a few decades ago had acquired some card skills during his youth.

It's no wonder craps and table games were the big draw to bring customers through the doors when casinos first opened. While Bill Harrah welcomed these customers to his casino, he also recognized the value in promoting slot machine play. First, table games were so volatile. Conversely, slot machines were more predictable, because the payout could be predetermined. Furthermore, slot machine customers couldn't develop a skill level that would work against the house. In addition, table gaming was more labor intensive. Unlike dealers and croupiers, slot machines didn't require salaries and fringe benefits. Nor did they call in sick, come in late, or demand to be paid for overtime.

To many gaming executives, a slot machine is remindful of valuable shelf space in a supermarket. Some even go further, explaining that each slot machine is much like a little store that measures 22 square feet in area. Each one-armed bandit sits there, luring passersby to take a chance with their money.

Harrah's has a long history of catering to slot players. This tradition began when Bill Harrah started bringing in busloads of customers from San Francisco and Sacramento to fill his casino in Lake Tahoe. Many of these daytime guests were senior citizens and housewives who enjoyed a good game of bingo. Slot machines, although mechanical, were fundamentally like playing a bingo card. Each was based on the random selection of numbers, mindless to play, and could potentially pay a lofty return on money wagered. Other casinos generally ignored their slot customers, focusing their attention on high rollers. But to Harrah's, slot customers represented a good, steady flow of business. Most importantly, their sheer numbers generated a healthy stream of revenue. Over the years, Harrah's mindfulness to these customers earned the company a reputation for being a "slot joint."

To attract slot customers, Harrah's focused on the quality of its machines and promoted that it had the highest payouts in town. With other casinos virtually ignoring their slot players, Harrah's won their loyalty. Over time, it earned the reputation as the place to go to play slot machines.

When Harrah's opened in Atlantic City, the consensus was that a slot joint wouldn't succeed in the East. Some of the so-called experts said, "People in the West play slot machines, but on the East Coast, they're too sophisticated. New Yorkers and Philadelphians aren't about to spend mindless hours pouring quarters into one-armed bandits." Harrah's proved them wrong. When Harrah's first opened, customers stood three and four people deep to wait for an available slot machine.

Frank Quigley, Vice President-Table Games, Showboat Casino in Atlantic City, was one of the first employees to work for the company on the East Coast. "When I first started dealing at Harrah's at the Marina back in 1980, there were 900 slot machines, 130 table games, and 26 crap tables," he explains. "Those were the three-coin mechanical machines. The demand was so strong that we kept adding more slots. Today, there are 3,500 machines. Meanwhile, the number of table games dropped to 61."

"In the early days, our slots were mechanical," tells Bruce Rowe, Vice President of Slots and Research Development at Harrah's. "Later we moved to electro-mechanical slots, and then to video slots that were mainly video poker games. Today, we have video reel slots, sometimes referred to as Australian-type games. Now we see a lot of theming with the slot machines that reflect our culture and lifestyles. Our "The Price Is Right" and "Hollywood Squares" machines are good examples."

With the latest technology, one big drawing card that has popularized today's slot machines is the "winning the lottery" aspect, with a jackpot winner walking away with tens of millions of dollars. Major casinos in bigger markets such as Las Vegas and Atlantic City offer linked video reel slot machines that enable large numbers of slot players to play for seven- and eight-figure payouts. Like a lottery, the pots are progressive, and keep increasing when there are long droughts between winners. By pooling their resources, all the casinos win, because the opportunity to offer huge sums attracts more customers to play. Each casino wants the winner to be one of its customers so it can advertise: "Harrah's Slot Customer Wins Ten Million Dollars."

"The slots always had big payouts," explains Rowe, "but nothing compared to these life-changing jackpots that create instant wealth. Obviously, the odds are very high, but the chance of becoming a multimillionaire in a matter of seconds is the fantasy of millions of people. These humongous jackpots add a whole new dimension."

A native of south New Jersey, Rowe earned a degree in technical theater at American University in Washington, DC. In October 1980, Rowe received job offers from several casino showrooms, but Harrah's was his first choice because of the company's reputation in the field of entertainment. For the next nine years, Rowe worked in the entertainment side of the business; in 1989, he moved into information technology, accepting a new position with the company in Memphis. In 1998, he took a job in slots management. He says enthusiastically:

> I'm still in the entertainment business. When we were looking for acts, it was all about building relationships with agents, and now I do the same thing with slot manufacturers. When I worked with entertainers who were lounge acts—Jay Leno, Arsenio Hall, and Danny Gans, to name a few—we'd track their performances, and the best ones became opening acts in the main showroom.
>
> The same thing happens with slot machines. We have new products that we test and measure to see how well they do. If they're hits, like the entertainers, they become main attractions.

Never in Their Wildest Dreams . . .

After years of affiliation with Holiday Inns and, later, its spin-off company, Promus, several executives from the hotel side of the business now hold key positions in management at Harrah's. Their hotel backgrounds have contributed to making Harrah's the thriving company it is today.

Many of these ex-Holiday Inns people seemed improbable candidates for key roles in the management of a casino. In retrospect, perhaps only in their wildest dreams did they imagine they would someday work in the gaming industry.

One such unlikely individual is John Boushy. The son of two college professors, Boushy attended North Carolina State University, first as an undergraduate major in mathematics, and later in graduate school as an applied mathematics major. "My worst grade was in computer science," he says. "That's funny, considering I now head Harrah's information technology."

Before joining the company in 1978, he worked at IBM as a systems engineer. He soon transferred into sales, where in his first four months, he made his annual quota. Boushy worked in the hotel competency center out of IBM's Atlanta office, setting up systems for large hotels such as the renowned Peachtree Plaza Hotel. With this background, Boushy was transferred to Atlantic City and assigned to work on openings—he opened Resorts International, Bally's Park Place, the Sands, and Holiday Inn Marina Hotel Casino. Boushy recalls:

> On a sales call at the Holiday Inns in September 1979, I was making a presentation to a data processing manager who kept drilling me with a lot of questions. "How do you set up a casino management system?" he inquired. "How would you open a hotel when you don't have users until 30 days before it's scheduled to open?" "You've opened several other properties, so how would you do this?" "And how about this?" He asked some very interesting and legitimate questions which I'd often hear on a sales call. But what I didn't know at the time was that he was actually interviewing me. A week later, I got a call from a vice president in charge of financing at Holiday Inns Atlantic City. He offered me a job as manager of data processing, and I accepted it. My employee number was 13, and by the time we opened what was Harrah's Marina, there were 2,200 employees.

Boushy spent the next 18 months with the company in Atlantic City:

> It was an interesting project because there were many challenges about opening a 500-room Holiday Inns hotel that happened to have a 45,000- to 47,000-square-foot casino attached to it. Its restaurants and parking were geared around a 500-room hotel, and there was little consideration of the needs of the casino customers in terms of numbers of meals, parking spaces, and so on.

Boushy moved swiftly up the ranks at Harrah's; among his key positions, he headed strategic marketing in the late 1980s, where he focused on cross-market visitation. Here, the emphasis was on getting Harrah's customers to visit other properties. Boushy's efforts in marketing research focused on collecting information on customers that could be used to promote customer loyalty as well as provide incentives to visit other Harrah's casinos. Today, he is senior vice president of operations, products, and services, and chief information officer.

A native of Arkansas and a graduate of the law school of the University of Arkansas, Bill Buffalo knew both Hillary and Bill Clinton during his school days. After practicing law for 12 years with his brother in Little Rock and doing some outside counsel work for Holiday Inns, Buffalo accepted a position as an in-house litigation lawyer. Of the six members who worked on Holiday Inns' litigation team when Bass PLC acquired it, Buffalo was the sole lawyer to go with the Promus Company. Today, Buffalo is a vice president at Harrah's, serving as its associate general counsel. In this capacity, one of his key responsibilities involves working in the area of Indian gaming development:

> My mother is a staunch Baptist, so when I transferred from the hotel side of the business into the gaming side, I asked her how she felt about it.
>
> "I prayed about it," she said, "and it was okay with God and me." After I got the okay from her, I knew I was doing the right thing.

Kathy Callahan, a former internal communications director, had been living in Memphis when she joined Holiday Corporation as an assistant in the communications department in 1985. She relays:

> I was an army brat. I grew up all over, but mainly in Florida. I spent my college junior year abroad, and later I attended graduate school at the University of Virginia. I have a Ph.D. in German literature.
>
> Then I went to work at Holiday Inns on its corporate staff and was editor of its in-house magazine, *Frontline.* Later, I wrote speeches for Mike Rose and Phil Satre. So I went with them at the time of the Holiday Inns split with Promus. That's when Holiday Inns was bought by Bass, and the Promus Company evolved to became the new parent company of Embassy Suites, Hampton Inns, Homewood, and Harrah's. At corporate, we all worked side by side as one big family—there had never been any split or separation. So it was quite dramatic when some of the corporate people remained with Holiday Inns and some of us became Promus employees. One day, those of us who would stay with Promus were working at our desks when personal letters from Phil Satre and individual gift bags were delivered to us. The bags were filled with goodies with little things such as pins and t-shirts with the Promus

logo. It was quite dramatic to be seated at my desk and treated so special. This was in direct contrast to the employees who were designated to remain with Holiday Inns and who received nothing. I felt as though I was one of the lucky ones, and it was quite exhilarating to wind up on this side.

Another Holiday Inns transplant is Charles Atwood, a Tulane University MBA and CPA who joined the hotel chain in September 1979 to work on the Harrah's acquisition. Atwood had six years' experience in real estate development before joining the company. In 1978, he was vice president and controller of Canal Ventures, a real estate developer based in New Orleans. By sheer coincidence, Canal Ventures' headquarters was next door to Jazz Casino Company, then the majority owner of Harrah's Casino in New Orleans. One year after joining Holiday Inns, Atwood was put in charge of investor relations, where he remained throughout the various transitions that occurred until the spin-off of the company's hotel brands that resulted in the creation of Harrah's Entertainment. Today, he holds the title of senior vice president, chief financial officer, and treasurer of the company; his responsibilities include planning and analysis, investor relations, development and project finance.

Transplant J. Carlos Tolosa had just graduated from high school in Chile when he first traveled to the United States in 1969. After taking a 10-week English course at the University of Southern Mississippi, he became a full-time student there majoring in business. During his college days, Tolosa worked part-time for Holiday Inns until his graduation, when he became a full-time employee of the hotel chain. By the time Holiday Inns was sold to Bass PLC in 1990, Tolosa was in charge of managing all properties west of the Mississippi. Tolosa explains:

> I stayed with Bass and became chief operating officer for Embassy Suite Hotels, a position I held for five years. Then I was hired by Harrah's to form the first Indian gaming division, and in this capacity, I built four Indian gaming casinos—in Topeka, Kansas; Cherokee, North Carolina; the Ak-Chin Casino in Arizona; and a fourth in Skagit Valley, Washington.

The fourth one opened in 1995, but by mutual agreement with the tribe, the agreement was terminated.

Today, Tolosa is president of Harrah's Western Division. Like Boushy, Buffalo, Callahan, and Atwood, Tolosa had a solid hotel background. And like the others, he was surprised that his career path eventually took him into the gaming industry.

The combination of the diverse hotel experiences of these leaders has helped to shape today's Harrah's.

A Difference in Corporate Cultures

Harrah's first merger would signify the first shift in its meticulous formula since the company's inception. For 40 years, Harrah's was headed by its founder. An entrepreneur with a strong and idiosyncratic personality, a man obsessed with detail and high quality, Bill Harrah was driven by the desire to serve his customers.

Holiday Inns had a similar beginning. The chain was founded by a determined individual who came up with the idea for his business while on a family vacation to Washington, DC. In the summer of 1951, Kemmons Wilson was appalled to find that lodgings available along the way from his native Tennessee were dirty, cramped, and overpriced. He was disappointed that his family was forced to stay in motels that offered little in the way of amenities and eat in restaurants that served poorly prepared food. During his trip, he recognized the need for more comfortable, standardized, and economical accommodations for travelers across the country. When he returned home to Memphis, he told his wife, Dorothy, he'd had "the most miserable vacation in my life," and he vowed to do something about it.

Wilson said, "The experience was so bad that as soon as I got back to Memphis, I decided to build the right kind of motel, one that would have all the things we missed on that trip." Wilson, a building contractor, borrowed $350,000 from a local bank to build the first Holiday Inn, which opened only 20 months after the family's fateful trip to the nation's capitol.

Bill Harrah and Kemmons Wilson shared many similarities. Neither was afraid to go into debt or take risks to build a business. They were from the same generation, with Harrah born in 1911 and Wilson in 1913. Certainly, by today's standards, neither man had much formal education. Harrah had only one year of college under his belt—and Wilson dropped out of school at the age of 14! Both men built empires, becoming legendary figures in their respective industries. Each was motivated to serve his customer. Although the two men's destinies were entwined, remarkably, they never met. Harrah died in 1978, before Holiday Inns' acquisition of Harrah's; Wilson sold his interests in Holiday Inns in 1980, the same year it acquired Harrah's.

By the time of the Harrah's acquisition, Holiday Inns had matured into the largest lodging company in the world. By then, Wilson was far removed from its day-to-day operations, and a team of professional managers operated the international company. Conversely, at Harrah's, founded more than 15 years earlier than Holiday Inns, Bill Harrah made every major decision until his death. It didn't matter that the company was publicly owned; the stock was thinly traded and the founder ran it as if he were a sole proprietor. At the time of the merger, they were in different growth stages—Harrah's was still in its adolescence, while Holiday Inns had grown to full adulthood.

Hence, when Holiday Inns acquired Harrah's, some clashing of corporate cultures was inevitable. It happens in the best of companies, and, in their respective industries, these were indeed the best of companies. Holiday Inns was a more mature company with more than a thousand hotels spread all over the world. To manage its huge operations required a more structured organization, and because of its sheer size, the company had become bureaucratized.

Originally, the acquisition game plan assumed complementary needs existed that would benefit both companies, but there were sufficient differences in the two businesses that dissention resulted instead. From the beginning, there was resistance from some Holiday Inns board members who out-and-out opposed gambling. To these individuals, it was a moral issue—gambling was sinful. Based in Memphis in the nation's Bible Belt, Holiday Inns' meetings always began with an audible prayer, a not-so-common practice in boardrooms. Two long-time board members opposed the acquisition; consequently, when Harrah's came into the fold, those directors resigned from the board.

Traces of Holiday Inns' attitude of disapproval existed long before it joined forces with Harrah's. Holiday Inns built a hotel on the Strip in Las Vegas in 1974—sans casino! It wasn't until 1980 that the company finally showed some interest in gaming when it bought 40 percent of the casino next door.

One significant difference between the two companies is shown in the way the hotel business prioritizes its daily occupancy. In other words, how hotels use their rooms to maximize profit. For instance, there was an assumption by Holiday Inns at the time of the merger that owning a casino would attract customers who would occupy hotel rooms. Phil Satre explains:

> In the gaming industry, hotel rooms only augment our casino business. After working together, we began to understand that hotel customers and casino customers have separate reasons for occupying a room. Casino customers are in a hotel room primarily because they want to visit the casino. On the other hand, hotel customers are

there for a very different reason—an overnight experience. They're there to sleep and then move on to whatever business they have. The action in a casino hotel is downstairs. The action in a hotel, traditionally, is in the room and outside the hotel.

In the casino business, it's common practice to have a certain number of rooms available for high rollers who decide at the last minute to stay overnight. In the noncasino hotel business, the farther in advance that rooms are sold, the better. Vacant rooms are not held, even to cater to VIP customers. As Dave Kowal, a Harrah's marketing vice president explains:

> *Whom* we put in the room is what's important to us, but this is not true for a hotel. We are not like an airline that keeps some seats available for the business traveler, its most valuable customer, and books three days out at a higher rate. We keep rooms available for our best customers, but it's not about getting a higher rate. In fact, the opposite is true because that's usually the customer who gets his room comped.

In the beginning, the two companies were at opposite ends of the spectrum on construction costs. Holiday Inns' original budget called for building Harrah's Marina at a cost of $55 million. "It quickly rose to $75 million, then to $99 million, and ended up costing $145 million," Mike Rose recalls. "That made a lot of people in Memphis very nervous—particularly me! I knew that the operations could support that kind of investment, but due to a casino's ancillary facilities, those numbers far exceeded anything in the hotel business."

Chuck Atwood explains:

> The casino business has the unique position of being both capital- and labor-intensive. With Harrah's under the control of Holiday Corporation, there was an ongoing battle about how much capital to appropriate to build a casino. Historically, a Holiday Inns unit was built for $8 to $15 million, and with Harrah's, the company was looking at spending more on the order of $200 million on a casino operation. With the internal fighting that resulted, we sometimes underspeced new casinos and didn't put as much into the property as we should have, especially when you consider how strong some of those markets were. Capital was treated as a scarce commodity, and this created tension between Holiday Inns and Harrah's.
>
> Take our first casino in Tunica that we opened in 1993. The first casino constructed in the area was built for $20-some million. It was awful. We made a decision to build ours in a cornfield and we put $40 million into it. It generated $40 million cash flow in its first nine months. That's fantastic. We thought we were heroes, but then three

bigger $80- to $100-million casinos opened, and our market share quickly dipped. We allowed the hotel side of the business to influence us to build inferior properties that weren't competitive. In hindsight, more capital should have appropriated in some of the stronger Midwestern riverboat markets.

Satre explains:

A hotel charges everyone the same price for a room. A customer's wherewithal doesn't influence what he pays. In the gaming business, there's a significant variation in the value of the customer to the business. This value is determined by a customer's frequency of gambling, the number of times he visits a property, and his ability to play at high levels. When we build new casinos, we spend money to attract both the masses of the population as well as the high-end customers. Here's where we encountered the most resistance with Holiday Inns. When we built our first property in Atlantic City in 1980, the rooms were not the same quality as the rooms in Harrah's Reno or Harrah's Lake Tahoe.

Mike Rose stresses that with only two locations before the acquisition, the Harrah's culture vastly differed from Holiday Inns, a company with properties around the world. He points out:

Harrah's was typical of the casino business because prior to Atlantic City and subsequently other markets, casino owners had a single property, although a few of them had, at best, a handful of properties. The management was completely centralized, whereas Holiday Inns was very decentralized. For instance, we didn't have much control over our many franchisees other than having franchise agreements that allowed us to control quality. So, our management style was a very different approach.

Another difference was that casino owners didn't tell its management much about the operating numbers. That's just the way casinos were historically managed. They had layers and layers of management, most of whom didn't really know what the overall business looked like. Managers were strictly responsible for their own areas, and at Harrah's, they focused on delivering a high quality of customer service.

Rose also mentions that back at the time of the merger, the casino industry typically did not hire college-educated employees:

The typical guy who grew up in the business in those days didn't have a strong educational background. I observed that many of Harrah's employees were very good operators, but they weren't much when it came to strategic thinking. A noticeable exception was Phil

Satre. I was very much impressed with his thought process, so I kept giving him more responsibility. Even though he came to Atlantic City as a young lawyer, ultimately, I took him out of the legal area and put him in charge of overseeing the opening of Trump Plaza. Although at the time I wasn't aware I was doing it, I was actually grooming him to someday run Harrah's and, ultimately, to be my successor. It was a little early in his career, so we didn't talk about it in those days. I just kept telling Phil, "You've got to have operating experience if you want to run Harrah's someday." He was very willing and very capable, and, I must add, a fast learner.

Holiday Inns as a Catalyst

Unquestionably, Holiday Inns served as a catalyst in bringing Harrah's to Atlantic City. What a strange twist of fate when New Jersey approved gambling in Atlantic City in 1976, while an adamant Bill Harrah emphatically asserted his determination to stay out of what he called a "gangster-ridden state." The same thinking kept the company out of Las Vegas. Most interestingly is that in 1978, Holiday Inns' board of directors resolved to build and operate a hotel/casino in the seaside resort's marina area—two years before the 1980 acquisition of Harrah's was finalized.

Holiday Inns liked gaming for two reasons. First, it wanted to expand its core hotel business and believed there were certain synergies between the ownership of hotels and casinos. After all, casino customers require lodging. Second, Holiday Inns' management had witnessed just how profitable a well-managed casino could be. Other hotel chains were enjoying considerably higher gaming profits in comparison to their lodging profits. Holiday Inns' 1980 acquisition of Harrah's was only the beginning. In February 1980, Holiday Inns bought 40 percent interest in River Boat Casino, Inc., the owner of the Holiday Casino adjacent to the Holiday Inn hotel on the Strip in Las Vegas. The ink had hardly dried on the Harrah's merger papers when the company found itself entrenched in the two markets its founder had refused to enter.

Today, the property on the Strip is the Harrah's flagship casino in Las Vegas. Before 1980, this same site was occupied by Holiday Inns' 500-room casino-less hotel. Next door stood the Holiday Casino, a privately held company founded and operated by Shelby and Claudine Williams. It is no coincidence that the Williamses named their business Holiday Casino. In 1972, the couple wanted to take advantage of the brand name of their neighbor on the adjacent lot. Knowing that the casino would attract lodgers, the hotel chain willingly consented to the Williamses' choice of names.

Shelby Williams passed away in 1978, and his wife, Claudine, ran the business for the next two years before selling 40 percent interest to Holiday Inns. In 1983, the company bought the remaining 60 percent interest. Claudine stayed on in an advisory capacity for several years. To this day, she is referred to as the honorary chairman of the board of the casino. One of Las Vegas' leading personalities, Claudine is a past county commissioner, a past chairman of the Las Vegas Convention Visitors Authority, and a good friend of the company.

In the beginning, the casino kept its name, even though Harrah's managed it. Later, in the mid-1980s, the names of the casino and hotel were officially changed to Harrah's Casino & Hotel. Several renovations were made, and today both the casino and hotel stand under the same roof. After several additions, the hotel now has 2,560 rooms.

Tom Jenkin, who today is senior vice president and general manager of Harrah's Las Vegas and the Rio, was only 20 when he went to work for the Williamses in 1975. Jenkin began his career in the casino's Galley Restaurant working the graveyard shift as a fry cook.

Would Bill Harrah have entered the Las Vegas and Atlantic City markets? Had Harrah lived, it is probable he would eventually have had a presence in both cities, considering they are the top two gaming markets in the United States now without mob connections. However, it's unlikely that the company would have moved so quickly without Holiday Inns' influence.

By the early 1980s, expansion into new markets was old hat to Holiday Inns. The company has a long record of duplicating itself. In one 16-year period, new units were opening every two and a half days. With this experience, it didn't take a fortuneteller to predict that when Holiday Inns opened its first casino, more casinos would follow.

Chuck Atwood explains:

> Back in late 1977 and early 1978, a study concluded the company was a conglomerate with a large number of unrelated businesses. This led us to focus on what was referred to as the *hospitality business*. This meant getting into the restaurant and casino businesses, which were thought to have certain synergies with the hotel business. Those two businesses could benefit from Holiday Inns and vice versa.

At one time, Holiday Inns was a true conglomerate owning dozens of companies—ranging from Trailways Bus Company and Delta Steamship Lines to Perkins Restaurants and a Cessna dealership in Memphis. As the company began to sell off unrelated businesses, new acquisitions focused on its core business. Casinos seemed like a good fit, in particular because hotels with gaming facilities enjoyed exceptionally high room occupancy rates. Additionally, a good casino was a huge moneymaker.

"With its Reno and Lake Tahoe casinos, Harrah's was the Cadillac of its industry," Atwood says. "Almost simultaneous with the acquisition, Holiday Inns began breaking ground to construct a hotel casino in the marina district in Atlantic City."

In contrast to Holiday Inns' vast experience with its market expansion program, Harrah's was a mere novice. Throughout its founder's career, Bill Harrah's gaming enterprises were located in Reno and Lake Tahoe, never more than a 60-minute drive apart. Setting up shop in faraway Atlantic City presented a challenge. Moreover, although Vegas was only 500 miles directly south of Reno, it was equally challenging to make a concurrent move into this highly competitive marketplace.

Phil Satre says:

> We couldn't have picked a better company than Holiday Inns to influence our early expansion program. First, their professional planning process was light years ahead of ours. Holiday Inns was already beyond its growing-pain years of the 1960s, when it metamorphosed from a one-man show headed by Kemmons Wilson to a professionally managed company run by Roy Weingardner and Mike Rose. Under their guidance, Holiday Inns employed a sophisticated planning process, and it was a new discipline that Harrah's badly needed, even though it was resisted by some. Nonetheless, it influenced us positively to think about the long-term aspects of our business.
>
> Second, Holiday Inns was aggressive about development, which is the route it took to increase the scope of its business. If there's one thing Holiday Inns brought to the table, it was that their people knew how to develop properties. They were experts in analyzing a market to determine whether it's a place to be. Plus, they were very good at knowing how to position the company in a new market. They looked at the world from the eyes of a brand. So when we entered the Atlantic City and Vegas markets, their encouragement and support was invaluable.

Chuck Atwood says:

> Holiday Inns' business model had a corporate office with lots of stores out there. The company managed those stores from afar because it wasn't possible to be there with every one of them. This meant the company had to have some type of systematic management technique that delivered information back to its corporate

headquarters. Only then could its home office people manage a geographically diverse set of businesses. Likewise, when Harrah's decided to expand into many markets, it marked a departure from the way casino companies typically go out and look at their business on a daily basis. In the past, Harrah's managed by observation. But we couldn't do that with properties located in many faraway places. So like Holiday Inns, Harrah's had to develop systems for its casino business that could be managed from afar. The company was fortunate to have Holiday Inns serve as its mentor.

In the early 1980s, Harrah's learned still another invaluable lesson from its parent company—how to secure financing for expansion. At the time of the merger, no bank was willing to take a mortgage on a casino. It wasn't that a gaming company was a poor credit risk—a well-managed casino was a gold mine. The problem was not knowing what to do if the bank had to foreclose on a mortgage. In essence, because banks didn't understand the gaming industry, they wouldn't know how to operate a casino if they had to take it over!

Atwood, a key player in corporate development in 1979 at Holiday Inns, gives an interesting perspective on how the Harrah's acquisition was financed:

> Citibank couldn't see itself owning the casino and trying to sell it to someone else. For this reason, the bank wasn't willing to take a lien on those assets [Harrah's Casino]. This meant Citibank needed to have a secured debt position, so we had to find other assets that they could have liens on. This led us to structure the transaction so the bank could get other assets that could be taken back if it ever had to.

The other assets were Holiday Inns hotels—physical real estate used as collateral to finance the $150 million needed to become the sole owner of Harrah's. Its banker, Citibank, understood what to do with tangible properties in the event the company failed to cover its debt. Atwood says:

> When the financial community saw companies like Holiday Inns and Hilton getting into the gaming business, it was a whole new ballgame. The participation of these well-respected blue-chip companies legitimized the gaming industry.
>
> A competitor once remarked to the banks, "Oh, you're making loans to casino companies. They may look like hotel companies, but they are casino companies in drag." Now, you have to remember that back in the late 1970s and early 1980s, it wasn't that long ago from when the Mafia was in the business. There was also some questionable money from the Teamsters' funding casinos.

About the same time that Holiday Inns was financing its takeover of Harrah's, Steve Wynn was seeking financing for the Golden Nugget in Atlantic City with high-yield debt, courtesy of junk bond king Michael Milken. Thus, when the Golden Nugget opened in Atlantic City in 1980, it represented a major shift in casino financing that would change the face of Las Vegas forever. The Nugget was the smallest resort in New Jersey, but it made a hefty $80 million to $90 million in cash in its first year on its owners' initial investment of a paltry $15 million.

Reinventing Holiday Inns

Under the leadership of Mike Rose, no one could ever accuse Holiday Inns of being a company that resisted change. On the contrary, on becoming president and chief executive officer of the hotel chain in 1981, Rose began a spree of selling off the company's unrelated businesses, including subsidiaries such as a bus company, a steamship company, and its restaurant chain, Perkins Pancakes.

"I wanted us to reinvest our money in the growth of our new hotel and casino businesses," he emphasizes, "Hampton Inn, Embassy Suites, Homewood Suites, and Harrah's. Ultimately, we recognized that our Holiday Inns brand itself couldn't grow at the rate we needed it to grow, so we made the decision to sell it."

As Rose explains, the gaming business started to expand rapidly in the early 1990s and was given a much higher multiple by Wall Street than the hotel industry. This was a result of the over-building of hotels in the 1980s, which brought the industry's multiples down. "This was the first time ever that gaming earnings were selling at higher multiples than hotel earnings," explains Rose. "Consequently, it made more sense for us to invest in casino properties than it did in hotel properties. This doesn't mean we stopped investing on the hotel side altogether, but when it came down to making a choice on spending a $100 million here or a $100 million there, we chose the casino business."

Colin Reed, a former senior officer at Holiday Inns who later served as chief financial officer at Harrah's, was put in charge of selling a package of a half dozen of the company's European hotels. The sale would be based on one condition in particular—that the new owner would operate them as Holiday Inns franchisees. Rose had asked Reed to negotiate such a sale with Bass PLC, the parent company of Crest Hotels, Reed's former employer. It had been 12 years since Reed had worked for Crest. Reed tells the following:

Chuck Atwood, Tom Keltner, the development vice president for Holiday Inns' international division, CFO Steve Bollenbach, and I were the team sent to meet in Dallas with Bryon Langton, CEO of Crest Hotels. We calculated the six hotels were valued at somewhere between $128 million and $145 million—the four of us set out to negotiate a price within that range.

When we first entered the room, Langton warmly greeted me, "It's good to see you again, Colin."

After exchanging pleasantries, Langton cut to the chase. "Let's not beat around the bush," he said. "I have authority to buy those hotels for anywhere from $140 million to $155 million."

The four of us looked at each other in dead silence. I was the first to speak out, "We have authority to sell at the high range."

Within five minutes, we shook hands on a deal at a $152 million purchase price for the six hotels.

When the negotiations ended, we went down to the bar at the Embassy Suites to have a drink. "Bryon, I don't understand something. Why do you want to buy these assets as a franchise product when you own Crest Hotels?" I asked.

"The Holiday Inns brand is more international than ours," he replied.

"Have you ever thought about talking to us about getting the rights to franchise a particular territory?" I suggested. "In other words, instead of owning the hotels and being responsible for putting our name on it, you buy the exclusive rights to the Holiday Inns name in a territory, say for Belgium, France, or whatever."

"I never thought about that," he answered. "Let me give that some thought."

Two weeks later, Langton and some other Crest executives met with us in Memphis. "We are thinking about buying the rights to the Holiday Inns name for the international division," he said.

Based on projecting what we thought the business was worth going forward, we said our asking price was $350 million but it did not include getting ownership of Holidex, our system for booking reservations. Then we suggested to Crest that it purchase 13 Holiday Inns hotels in Florida. "This way you'd get some experience in dealing with domestic hotels that will be beneficial in the event you might someday want to run a hotel chain in the United States." They bought the entire package and paid us about $480 million for it, or about 15 times cash flow—a great deal for our company.

In January 1990, Rose sold Holiday Inns for $2.3 billion. The purchaser was the 200-year-old Bass PLC, parent company of Crest Hotels, the largest brewer in Great Britain, and owner of over 2,000 pubs. The following month, the remaining Holiday Corporation's brands consisting of Harrah's, Embassy Suites, Hampton Inns, and Home-wood Suites, under the name of the Promus Companies Incorporated, was traded on the New York Stock Exchange. The Promus headquarters remained in Memphis. Rose states:

> The timing was great for us because it was just before the riverboat gambling boom. This gave us an edge in dealing with the local communities where riverboats sprout up along the Mississippi. We were able to say to them, "We're not really a Nevada company because we're based in Memphis. We're a lot closer to you so we understand your culture and what you want to do. And we know you don't want to be like a Nevada casino."

Rose explains that by the mid-1990s, the demand in the hotel business was catching up to the supply.

> The opposite, however, was happening in the casino business. The jurisdictions were not opening like they did previously, so there were more casinos being built in places like Las Vegas, Reno, and Atlantic City. With an overcrowded, competitive environment, the casino multiples started heading back to their normal level while the hotel multiples were heading upward.
>
> We anticipated this trend beforehand, and because our hotel business consisting of Embassy Suites, Hampton Inn, and Homewood Suites had become a billion-dollar business, it and Harrah's were certainly both big enough to stand on their own. At this point, we believed the hotel earnings would be penalized by the casino earnings, which was the opposite of what happened in 1990. This strategy was based on how we could produce more wealth for our shareholders over the long-term by separating the two businesses.

In 1995, the Promus Company spun off Harrah's Entertainment, Inc.; and for the first time since 1980, the Harrah's name was again listed on the New York Stock Exchange. Michael Rose continued as chairman and Phil Satre as president and CEO. Three years later, Promus merged with DoubleTree, and in 1999, Hilton Hotels bought the combined company.

4

LEAVING NEVADA

LONG BEFORE MOST AMERICANS DISCOVERED LAS VEGAS, RENO, or Lake Tahoe, their favorite destination resort was Atlantic City. In the mid-1800s, Dr. Jonathan Pitney began selling Philadelphia society on the therapeutic benefits of Atlantic City's invigorating saltwater air. Soon, people from all over came to visit what was hailed as the nation's playground. In 1870, six years after Nevada was granted statehood, Atlantic City's world-famous boardwalk was built. The original boardwalk was only eight feet wide, but was later expanded to 60 feet wide and five miles long. In the early 1900s, millions of tourists made annual visits to this gem of the Garden State.

The famous Garden Pier, which opened in 1913, once housed a ballroom where young Rudolph Valentino gave dance lessons and a theater where Irish tenor John McCormick and the John Philip Sousa Band made regular appearances. The first Miss America, Margaret Gorman of Washington, DC, was crowned on the Garden Pier in 1921.

The Steel Pier, the most famous of the city's several recreational piers, was once acclaimed "The Showplace of the Nation." It featured diving horses that plunged off a wooden tower, motorcycles that buzzed along a high wire, and a "human cannonball," who was fired high above the crowd into a net or tank of water. In its heyday, the Steel Pier boasted top performers such as Charlie Chaplin, Benny Goodman, Jimmy Dorsey, the Three Stooges, Guy Lombardo, Bob Hope, and Frank Sinatra. Atlantic City's lineup of star performers was comparable to the great show business talent that later appeared in Las Vegas.

Over time, Atlantic City's mystique became antiquated and worn. Americans grew tired of visiting freak shows on its once-famous piers, and its carnival pitchmen lost their allure. Everything changed. Even the renowned 171-foot Absecon Lighthouse, constructed in 1857, once the symbol of Atlantic City, had moved. Rather, it appeared to have moved. Because of changes in the coastline, the lighthouse is now surrounded by an urban neighborhood, two blocks from the ocean and two blocks from the inlet.

As the number of tourists coming to Atlantic City declined, it was no longer economical to conduct business as usual. Shrinking maintenance budgets prevented owners from putting on fresh paint; their corroding properties were exposed to the punishing salt air. Failure to remodel and redecorate made Atlantic City look shoddy and unkempt. By the 1970s, the area's economy had suffered to the point that its once-celebrated hotels were vacant and boarded up. Unemployment exceeded 40 percent. Even on its sunniest summer days, the nation's playground had degenerated into a third-rate metropolis.

Poverty, drugs, and decay had turned the once-sparkling ocean resort town into an embarrassment. When midget bellhops and the Miss America Pageant failed to hold the public's interest, city fathers hoped that casino gambling would generate the tax revenues needed to fund massive urban renewal projects.

On June 30, 1978, when Bill Harrah died, one year had passed since it became legal to gamble in New Jersey casinos. Previously, in the November 1976 election, Garden State voters had approved a gambling referendum. This change of law meant Nevada no longer had a monopoly on gaming in the United States—Nevada casinos would now be subject to competition. Many believed Atlantic City had a strong competitive edge, because it was accessible to more than 40 million people on the northeastern seaboard between Norfolk, Virginia, and Hartford, Connecticut. No longer would it be necessary to travel 2,500 miles and enter a third time zone to play blackjack and slot machines; now East Coast residents could do it in their own backyard. Atlantic City looked like a serious threat. Nobody could accurately predict how out-of-state gaming would affect the Silver State's biggest industry.

In 1977, the Nevada legislature passed a law allowing Nevada-based operations to run casinos outside state borders. This Foreign Gaming Law opened the doors for expansion into other states. Thus, if there was any good news about Atlantic City to Nevada casino owners, it was that casinos would no longer be confined to the desert.

Although his gaming activities had been confined to Reno and Lake Tahoe, it was not because Bill Harrah was reluctant to move into other territories. In fact, shortly before he died, he had investigated opening a casino in Australia. "We're working hard on Australia. And we looked at other places. If [legal gaming] goes into Florida, we're interested," he said.

However, he felt bad vibes about opening in Atlantic City: "We're not too interested in New Jersey because it's real unhealthy back there. It's just gangster-ridden. I don't think it'll ever get out of that. Florida, I think, will be okay. And anywhere where we can make some money, why, we're interested."

Nonetheless, the handwriting was on the wall when New Jersey opened its doors to gaming in Atlantic City. Eventually, other states would follow suit. A similar thing happened in 1964 when New Hampshire became the first state to operate a lottery; by the 1980s, politicians throughout the country were selling their constituents on "painless taxation" on the pretext of replacing school levies and other tariffs. Slowly, the stigma of gambling lessened. In time, the same Americans who had viewed gambling as a sin began to enjoy it as a legitimate form of entertainment. It was forecast that casinos would spread across America, just as lotteries had. And they did, on Indian reservations and riverboats, in small towns and big cities, gaming spread.

It was a foregone conclusion that Nevada would lose its monopoly on gaming in America. This left Nevada-based casino operators with two options. One, they could focus on their existing properties and reduce expenditures to survive anticipated diminished revenues. Two, they could embrace the approval of gaming in other states as an opportunity to enter other markets.

Not Just Bricks and Mortar

For years, Holiday Inns built look-alike motels. Founder Kemmons Wilson took great pains to standardize the architecture, decor, furniture, fixtures—everything. Even soap and toilet paper were identical in every bathroom throughout the chain. He followed the formula Howard Johnson employed to build its successful chain of roadside restaurants in the 1950s. Other motel and restaurant chains used the same blueprint—because it worked. This repetitious approach may have spread monotony across America, but it made their brands highly visible and recognizable to all consumers. Identical products meant everything from shower curtains to bed sheets was interchangeable. Every order for hamburgers, french fries, and soft drinks was consistent—coast-to-coast across America. Customers wanted consistency and they got what they came for— there were no surprises.

However, when Harrah's embarked into different marketplaces, there were no cookie-cutter casinos. The original Harrah's Club in

Reno didn't resemble the Harrah's in Lake Tahoe, and the one in Atlantic City was nothing like the Las Vegas casino. In 1988, a still-different Harrah's casino was built—this time in Laughlin, Nevada, a small town on the Colorado River, 100 miles south of Las Vegas. At the time, Laughlin was the fifth largest gaming market in the United States, right behind Vegas, Atlantic City, Reno, and Lake Tahoe. No other casino company had bragging rights to a presence in each of the five major gaming markets, all of which were in Nevada and New Jersey.

Certainly, there is merit in having motels and fast-food restaurants look alike—it builds brand identity. However, casinos can't be compared to motels and fast-food restaurants. For starters, a casino is many times more expensive to build and more costly to maintain. Note that Harrah's presently operates 26 casinos in more U.S. jurisdictions than any company in the gaming industry. In comparison, the big fast-food chains have hundreds and even thousands of units. As Harrah's expands its brand, each casino offers a unique experience to its customer. If casinos were alike, a visit to a new casino would simply duplicate a previous experience. This is very different from lodging at a Holiday Inn where a customer wants the consistency of a clean, comfortable room. No matter the distance traveled, when a tired traveler approaches the Holiday Inn sign on the road, a familiar stay at a home away from home is assured. On the other hand, the gaming customer, who seeks enjoyment and excitement, does not seek this uniformity and warm, homelike feeling. A visit to a casino is an escape from his or her normal routine. The nature of gambling is that you never know what to expect. Therefore, while the Harrah's customer anticipates a high-quality product and service, he embraces the unexpected.

To provide customers with adventure, casinos built theme properties. Their themes run the gamut—a visit to a tropical island, the streets of New York or Paris, or even the canals of Venice. Other themes include trips back in time to pirate days or the medieval days of King Arthur.

Today, a drive down Las Vegas's Strip reveals theme casino resorts lining both sides of the street. These include some of the most expensive hotels in the world. The Mirage, Treasure Island, Excalibur, Venetian, Bellagio, New York-New York, Luxor, and Aladdin are the newest of the theme hotels but by no means are they the first. Theme resort-casinos gained popularity in the early 1950s, starting with the Desert Inn and its Miami-Havana style. Shortly afterward, the Rivera, Dunes, Hacienda, and Stardust opened, with various themes. Then Jay Sarno raised the bar for theme casinos in 1966 when he opened the granddaddy of theme casino resorts with a Roman theme—Caesars Palace.

Sarno told reporters, "There's no apostrophe before the 's' in Caesars, because this is going to be a palace for all the Caesars—all the people. Everybody in the hotel is a Caesar!"

Caesars Palace truly was unlike anything anyone on the Strip had ever seen. Guests were supposed to feel as if they had stepped back into the glorious days of ancient Rome. Unlike other Vegas resorts, Caesars Palace was set back from the highway. Its crescent-shaped, 14-story tower contained 680 luxury suites. The 135-foot-long drive-way was lined with imported Italian cypresses. Eighteen fountains sprayed 350,000 gallons of water per minute into the desert air. Inside was $150,000 worth of marble statuary imported from Florence, along with Brazilian rosewood and gold leaf, white marble panels, and black mosaics. The world's largest ceiling fixture, made of fine German crystal, hangs in the center of the Caesars Forum casino. Its swimming pool is the shape of a Roman shield.

Caesars Palace was a tough act to follow, but Sarno outdid himself when he built Circus Circus, which opened in 1968. "Circus was the word Romans used for 'theater,' and that's how I came up with the name for my new resort: a circus inside a Roman circus—or a Circus Circus," Sarno explained. He did not repeat the Roman theme in his new casino on the northern tip of the Strip, but he kept the double name.

Guests at the new Sarno casino resort entered through a four-story concrete tent that led into the mezzanine. There, guests could enter the gaming area only by sliding down a giant metal slide. There were no stairs. Mimes and clowns performed while guests played at gaming tables. Trapeze artists nonchalantly flew through the air above craps tables. Sideshow barkers lured guests to gaudy midway attractions along the inside walls of the massive tent. A 14-piece brass band blared out circus tunes nonstop.

The place lived up to its name; it was indeed a circus in the truest sense. However, it was a circus geared not for children, but for grownups—grownups wanting to act like children. Customers tossed a ball at a target—success meant a blast of air removed a sheet, revealing the body of a semi-nude woman. The Ooh-La-La Theater featured topless showgirls. One exhibit boasted a nude pre-historic woman sealed in a block of ice. Plans initially called for a high-wire flying elephant act. A monorail system in the ceiling secured a custom-made leather harness built to lift a baby elephant through the air. However, when the contraption broke, Tanya the elephant panicked and made a wild dash through the casino. The feature had to be scratched. Fortunately, as a backup act, Tanya had been trained to pull a slot machine lever with her trunk, and the "World's First Flying Elephant" was replaced by "The World's First Gambling Elephant."

Harrah's elected not to build theme casinos to attract customers. First, the investment requirement was too high. Perhaps having one or a handful of casinos with a theme was feasible, but not for a company with a game plan to move into gaming markets across the country. Harrah's knew that having the newest and biggest casino in any given market was at best a short-term proposition. History repeats itself, and once an elaborate property succeeds, an even more lavish casino will be built—across the street, down the street, or next door. Simply put, the company did not believe it was prudent to build and sustain the most expensive properties in every market it entered. Instead, it was necessary to find another way to attract customers to enter its doors—and once inside, to earn and win their loyalty.

A Great Time, Every Time

Harrah's chose not to compete in the theme-casino market, focusing instead on delivering consistently superior service and entertainment. According to Mike Rose, company CEO from 1983 to 1994, the essence of the business is in the excitement of gaming. "The reality of the gaming experience is about as powerful a form of entertainment all by itself as anything there is in the entertainment spectrum," he explained. "If people will actually [drive an hour or two to] go to a cornfield in Minnesota, and stand in line to get into what was essentially a cement-block building, then maybe there is more to this business than big showrooms, pyramids, and volcanoes." In Rose's opinion, an entire strategy focused around family travels is a waste of shareholders' money. "You can make a huge investment for a very small part of the market."

To fuel the excitement of gaming, Harrah's casinos fostered an atmosphere of energetic fun and festivity, with a personal touch. "For the interaction, enjoyment, and excitement that playing in a casino brings," explains Phil Satre, "these trips are not about getting rich on winnings. They are about friends having fun together in an environment of celebration. They are about leaving the passivity of watching whether it is watching TV, watching sports, or watching birds in a park, and becoming actively engaged in the fast-paced action, colors, and sounds of a casino."

Unlike the competition's approach using theme casinos to attract customers, Harrah's ascertains fun and excitement—not bricks and mortar—are its main attraction. It is true that erupting volcanoes, battling pirate ships, and full-scale canals with gondola rides are major tourist attractions—but it takes even more to build long-term customer loyalty. Novelties don't necessarily generate repeat business.

This philosophy spurred Harrah's to provide a consistent experience between its casinos rather than relying on theme properties. The emphasis was not on its tangible assets, but on intangibles. Former Harrah's marketing executive Craig Hudson, who previously worked for eight years at KFC, explains:

> Each property differs in age and design, but over time, we are moving to where our customers will have a very similar experience, no matter which Harrah's they visit. The quality and selection of our slot machines are becoming more consistent at all of our properties. Likewise, we offer similar experiences at the gaming tables. Yet, we have many local differences, more than you find at other casinos. That's because we feel each market is truly different, and we do cater to those differences.
>
> When you're selling fried chicken meals, your customers want to know they'll be served the same food no matter what KFC restaurant they visit. Why does McDonald's have the same logo everywhere? Why the look-alike children's playgrounds? When a vacationing family drives by an out-of-town McDonald's, they remember the good time they had back home. And like a fast-food chain where the original recipe has to be the same everywhere or your customers will be disappointed, our customers feel comfortable with certain consistencies. But equally important, we offer specific differences among our properties. For instance, the slot machines aren't the same at every casino. Or, in some markets, we have more table games. And not every casino will have a steak house, or even a showroom. We allow for those differences. We've learned our customers come to Harrah's mainly for gaming. For the most part, they're not looking for the resort experience we give them at our Rio and Lake Tahoe properties.
>
> So like KFC and McDonald's, we want them to come back because they enjoyed themselves here. We also want them to know they can visit our other properties and enjoy other wonderful experiences. For instance, if they want to ski, we offer them something different at Lake Tahoe, and if they want to play golf, they go to Rio or to Reno. So even though each Harrah's offers uniform services, we have different packages because our properties aren't identical.

Today, Harrah's operates 26 casinos in 20 U.S. markets, and as Rich Mirman, senior vice president of marketing, attests, no two properties are alike.

This is why we've invested in a corporate infrastructure unlike any of our competitors. We have a corporate team, and our 26 individual property marketers break down into five divisions, each with its own marketing vice president. I primarily work with these divisional vice presidents; however, our corporate team also works directly on specific programs with each individual property. I call it a leverage structure, because the divisional vice presidents work with us at the corporate level to develop programs, and we make sure they're properly implemented.

None of our competition currently offers this kind of support at a corporate level. Traditionally, throughout the gaming industry, casinos have been managed independently. In this respect, we're aware of the importance of catering to the local needs, so each of our properties has a marketing department serving its own area. In addition, each Harrah's property has our corporate marketing team staffed with people to provide support and backup not available at a local level.

How the corporate office works with an individual property is explained by Tom Jenkin, general manager of both Harrah's properties in Las Vegas:

Our direct mail program got only a 3 percent response until Rich Mirman and his group showed us how to be more effective and efficient. After that, the response rate more than doubled. Previously, we were sending one message to large numbers of customers, which meant reducing it to the lowest common denominator. Corporate showed us how to tailor our message. We based it on certain factors, such as where customers live, their gaming behavior, when they visit, and what they have told us. In addition, the home office explained that we were actually wasting money sending mailings to certain people. In some cases, it was a matter of getting more results for less effort. We followed their advice, and now we're either getting a bigger slice of the pie, or, in some cases, reducing the size of the pie without reducing our slice.

Mirman points out that with 26 properties, Harrah's has 26 different marketing teams. "These marketing teams are making 26 different sets of decisions," he states. "We've been able to develop a strategy that gives us the capability to treat customers centrally and follow up by executing it at the individual properties."

Chief financial officer Chuck Atwood points out that Holiday Inns' business plan served as a model for Harrah's.

Holiday Inns had a corporate office and lots of stores out there. Management had to manage those businesses from afar. They could not go out and look at every one of them. So they needed a system to bring information back to corporate headquarters. How else could home office people manage such a geographically diverse set of businesses? The discipline that comes from developing Holiday Inns systems has been passed on to Harrah's, and we also apply the same kinds of scientific methodologies. Like Holiday Inns, our central headquarters is far away from our numerous casinos. Most other casino companies can physically visit their properties on a daily basis, so they can manage by observation, but our properties had to be managed from afar. The communication tool that pulls this all together for us is technology.

Different Customers

Not all customers are alike, and with 26 casinos, Harrah's has many kinds. For starters, they can be categorized by the size of their wallets. At the top of the scale are the whales—gamblers with credit lines in the seven- and eight-figure range. There are an estimated 200 whales in the entire world.

Next, there are high rollers and low rollers. To categorize them, casinos keep score by tracking a customer's play. They look at the size of each wager and frequency of play, along with the element of time. Simply put, the more hours of play, the more the house values a customer. Frequency of play is also gauged by how fast a slot machine player pulls the lever or—with today's high-tech slot machines—pushes the button. The more plays per hour, the more activity. Hence, a slow, methodical player is not as sought after as a rapid, decisive player.

There are still more ways to group casino customers. Timothy Wilmott, chief operating officer, explains, "We did some research a few years ago that profiles casino customers into two categories. There's the recognition-driven customer who wants to be pampered and treated like a high roller, even though he may not be a high roller. And then there's the 'escapist,' a customer who wants to be left alone. The escapist comes to the casino to forget about his troubles. He'll play the slot machines for hours and has a great time doing it."

David Jonas, general manager of the Atlantic City Harrah's, consistently one of the top moneymakers of the company's 26 properties, claims there are two different kinds of markets that determine the main difference in customers:

Industry people talk about the categories of Indian gaming, riverboats, and land-based casinos, but it really boils down to being either *destination resorts or frequency markets.* Atlantic City is a frequency market, and we attract frequency customers. These customers come 40 to 50 times a year and stay four hours to 1.2 days. On the other hand, Las Vegas and Lake Tahoe are destination resorts, whose customers stay four to six days. Consequently, both kinds of customers have totally different spending habits. In Vegas, for example, they spend more money on food and will spend $100 on a show ticket without blinking an eye. In Atlantic City, people don't like to spend $10 to see a show. They expect it to be free. They'll play $150 to $200 in a four-hour period and they're gone. In Vegas, it might take four days to get that same money from a customer. There are few similarities between destination resorts and frequency markets.

Before the casinos, we used to play touch football on Pacific Avenue, but now the street is so crowded, you can't even drive down it. If it weren't for the casinos, the place would be deserted. They come strictly for the casinos. Why else would they come? You can get a better meal in New York or Philadelphia, and you can see a better show in New York or Philadelphia. What you can't do in either one of those towns is go to a gaming casino that's legal. It's that simple, and this is why we strive to provide the best gaming experience to our customers. People come here to enjoy the gaming experience and the amenities that come with it.

Of course, there are variations in customers within a specific market. In Vegas, Harrah's and its sister casino-resort Rio attract different customers. Tom Jenkin describes his Rio customer as: "a high-level player who's slightly younger and one who's looking for a little faster pace. We appeal to a crowd that might stay at a Mandalay Bay or a Hard Rock Hotel-Casino. One of the reasons Harrah's acquired this property is that the company wanted to get into a different segment of the business than the mid-level customer that its Strip property attracted."

Likewise, the Harrah's casino in Atlantic City attracts a more upscale customer than does its Showboat property on the Boardwalk. Frank Quigley, vice president of table games at Showboat in Atlantic City, explains:

We bus in some customers who are driven by value. I call them "Depression babies," because they grew up in the 1930s and are very value-minded. You'll see them on an elevator carrying a cooler, a six-pack of Old Milwaukee, and a box of Cheerios to their rooms. They come with their coupons and they go downstairs with their quarters to play the 25-cent slot machines.

The Harrah's here in Atlantic City isn't on the Boardwalk, and it doesn't bus in customers. Its customers come by car or airplane—we call them "drive-ins"—and once at Harrah's in the Marina area, the casino has a captive market—they stay there for a couple of days or so. They're more upscale and tend to play $1 and up slot machines.

A Highly Regulated Industry

Following Bill Harrah's death on June 30, 1978, his executor, Mead Dixon, assumed the role as the company's chairman of the board. Estate taxes were calculated at something over $35 million, but there was no cash to pay them. This left little choice but to sell the business. Dixon spent the next year negotiating with Holiday Inns on behalf of the heirs.

Following the acquisition, Dixon was succeeded by Mike Rose, who became Holiday Inns' CEO in 1981, and in 1984, he became board chairman. Rose was followed by Phil Satre, the company's immediate past CEO and present chairman. Like Dixon, both Rose and Satre are lawyers. Their legal backgrounds serve as a reminder that gaming is a highly regulated industry.

To operate in a state, casinos must be authorized through voter initiative (local and statewide referenda) or legislative action (statute). A gaming license must then be issued by the state gaming board or commission, the regulatory agency that monitors and audits casino activities. Although some form of gambling is now legal in 47 states—the exceptions being Tennessee, Hawaii, and Utah—there is still opposition. Supporters claim gaming is a form of entertainment that provides employment and good wages for large numbers of people, and generates large tax revenues. The opposition argues that gaming breeds crime, compulsive gambling, and prostitution.

Gaming laws and regulations vary by state and are significantly influenced by the business environment. In short, state gaming authorities decide who is licensed and who isn't. They regulate everything from the hours of operation to what is permissible in the casino. Other regulations such as advertising and limitation on wagers are also established by the state. There are special regulations for riverboat casinos; in some states, a boat can be permanently anchored; in others, it is required to cruise for a specific time. Some states, such as Iowa, had earlier limited bets to $5 and losses to $200 per excursion, as well as limiting square footage devoted to gaming to 30 percent of the building.

The history of regulating gambling in this country doesn't go back so far. According to the Cornell Report, commissioned by a trio of federal executive agencies, "The Development of the Law of Gambling:

1776–1976," states: "Before 1850, the West was a crude region, popu-
lated almost exclusively by men. There were no laws, and no formal
government to restrain antisocial behavior. In fact, the early West was
more a collection of individuals than any sort of coherent society."

These individuals, the report adds in a pixyish way, spent most of
their leisure time entertained by CBS. In this case, the acronym stood
for combined "casino, bordello, and saloon." The report continues,
"Gambling, whoring, and drinking took place openly, and were welcomed in the early boom towns for the fat profit they yielded."

One reason Nevada passed a bill in 1931 to regulate gambling was
to bring out into the open what already was common practice in the
back rooms of saloons throughout the state. During Prohibition, the
existence of speakeasies had fostered a culture of political corruption
throughout the country as bootleggers bribed public officials to protect their illegal businesses. Nevada wanted to avoid that experience
with gambling.

Another impetus for the legalization of casinos was to raise
money. Licensing fees were set up with 75 percent going to the
county and 25 percent to the state. If a casino was located in an incorporated municipality, the county shared fee revenues with cities.
The fees were based on the number of slot machines and table games
in a casino.

The history of slot machines traces back to the famous 1849
Gold Rush that induced a huge migration of adventurers to California in search of instant wealth. Following the great gold rush, California soon became a gambler's paradise, because in no other part
of the world was gambling carried on more openly or on a larger
scale. Far from the restraining Eastern influences of home, family,
and church, the California pioneers soon found themselves wagering on practically everything in sight. Bets were laid on everything
from impromptu horse races to bull and bear fights. By the 1880s,
technology opened the door to coin-operated gaming devices,
which were extremely popular in saloons and cigar stores. By 1890,
the city of San Francisco, known as the cradle of the slot machine,
had 3,117 licensed liquor establishments, or about one liquor license for every 96 inhabitants. These watering holes provided excellent outlets for the distribution of nickel-in-the-slot machines. In
1899, a crusade against slot machines was launched in the Golden
Gate City, prohibiting the money payouts; however, cigar machines
were untouched by this law because they were considered trade
stimulators rather than gambling devices. Interestingly, the city's
police commissioner, Moses Gust, operated one of the area's largest

chains of cigar stores. A straight flush in one of his machines yielded 40 cigars!

Slot machines were outlawed in San Francisco in 1909, in Nevada a year later, and in the rest of California in 1911. Nevertheless, coin-operating gaming, with its universal player appeal and lucrative earning capacity, was difficult to stamp out. Through hard times, slot machine revenue could financially assist a saloon, cigar stand, food market, restaurant, drug store, or even a fraternal organization. Consequently, slot machines enjoyed the unusual distinction of being ignored, legalized in various forms, or completely outlawed, depending on their location.

Slot machine history buffs refer to 1910 as the year that the "Gum Age" was born. This began when Mills Novelty added a device that, for a nickel, dispensed a pack of gum. The beauty of this nongambling machine was that it also had payouts in trade checks good for either replay or merchandise redemption.

The Nevada Gaming Commission is the policy organization for the state's control of casinos and slot machines, and the State Gaming Control Board is the law enforcement agency that polices gaming activities. Until 1950, the policing of gambling in Nevada was pretty much a local affair. However, Nevada's live-and-let-live attitude toward casino owners first came under sharp attack during the celebrated hearings chaired by Senator Estes Kefauver during his traveling road show in 1950 and 1951. The purpose of Kefauver's special committee was to alert Americans to the existence of various crime syndicates that made money from gambling. Kefauver's group highlighted the extent to which gangster associates corrupted the gambling industry by bribing public officials. Kefauver, who had presidential ambitions, made sure his investigative activities received national publicity. When the Kefauver Committee conducted nationally televised hearings in Las Vegas, it subpoenaed many casino operators who had mob ties, some of whom had formerly engaged in bootlegging, tax evasion, and other crimes ranging from extortion to murder.

Under federal prodding, the state of Nevada took measures to brand a certain class of individuals—members of organized crime syndicates and associates who obtained loans from them—as undesirable. Never before had a state government in the United States ever nurtured and regulated an industry on the scale of Nevada's gaming industry, only to be coerced by the federal government to enforce harsh restrictions. The notorious Meyer Lansky, for example, could legally and openly invest in the stock market and place his money in many respectable companies. And he did so, as his tax returns showed.

However, he would never be able to get a gaming license in Nevada, although he did secretly invest in several casino companies.

The Kefauver hearing spurred Nevada to a stricter stance toward casino investors for a very practical reason: After the committee hearings concluded, Kefauver proposed a 10 percent federal gaming tax, which would have seriously hampered, if not altogether killed, the casino industry in its infancy. Nevada Senator Pat McCarran had to use all his considerable clout in Congress to have that bill killed. Nevertheless, the threat of federal intervention in gambling persisted.

The FBI didn't pay much attention to Las Vegas, and, in fact, until 1957, it didn't even have an agent stationed there. Everything changed in the early 1960s when Director J. Edgar Hoover began dispatching dozens of G-men to Vegas to flush out mobsters. At the same time, Attorney General Robert Kennedy investigated Jimmy Hoffa and his handling of the Teamster Union's pension fund.

The Nevada Gaming Commission requires all gaming companies to report their winnings so it can compute the taxes for its casino license. Nevada authorities compiled a list of the earnings of the top 30 places in 1961, and three of the top four were not Las Vegas, but northern Nevada. In first place was Harrah's Club at Lake Tahoe, at about $20 million. Harold's Club in Reno was second with about $13 million in gross winnings, and Harrah's Club in Reno was fourth with about $10 million. By this time, Bill Harrah had established himself as the most successful casino owner in the state.

Bill Harrah ran such a clean shop that some of his self-imposed regulations later became an integral part of the Gaming Control Act. For instance, dealers who worked in Las Vegas often came to Reno or Lake Tahoe, and vice-versa. Concerned that his casinos might hire a dishonest dealer, Harrah believed it was essential that casino employment records be kept on file and made available to prospective employers. To avoid hiring anyone with a dubious background, he thoroughly investigated and even fingerprinted dealers. He opened his files to other casinos that wanted to check out dealers who had worked at one of his casinos. He insisted that they reciprocate when he ran background checks on their dealers. The Gaming Control Board was so impressed, it used his dealer registration program as a model in setting up its own.

Harrah is also credited as the originator of the first "eye in the sky." When he opened his Lake Tahoe casino, he installed hidden cameras above the gaming tables to make sure dealers weren't in cahoots with a player. More importantly, it protected customers from a dealer's sleight-of-hand shenanigans such as dealing from the bottom of the deck or other dishonest practices. Before long, the gaming commission required all casinos to install eye-in-the-sky surveillance systems to police dealers.

With 26 casinos in 20 markets, and with each state having different gaming laws, the company hired George Togliatti in 1999 to serve as director of government and community relations. He makes sure each of the company's casinos complies with all state laws in the jurisdiction where it operates. Togliatti's background made him an ideal candidate for this position. After college, he was a Navy pilot for five years and earned an MBA in accounting. He then spent the next 23 years working as an agent for the FBI. For 17 of those years, he was in charge of the Bureau's white-collar crime program in Nevada.

In a highly regulated industry in which gaming laws vary from state to state, Togliatti keeps track of the requirements in all jurisdictions where the company has casinos. He explains:

> There are different procedures within the casinos that dictate what we can and can't do. Take procedures on money handling, for instance. There are more regulations out there than you can shake a stick at. They're intended to make sure everything is above board, so when we keep that in mind, it's not so difficult to stay on top of everything. Just the same, we always make a decision on the side of caution.
>
> Many of the regulations were modeled after Nevada's and New Jersey's because these states were the first to legalize casinos. So on most major issues, the procedures are fairly standard in all states. Thankfully, our attorneys keep their libraries current.

Just how exacting are gaming hiring practices in some states? Togliatti points out that the state of New Jersey has an 80-page application all key employees must complete. "When I started here in 1999, it was 100 pages," he says. "When I filled it out, I had just retired from the FBI, but they didn't cut me any slack. They went through all my canceled checks for the last five years. Even Gary Loveman, who came from outside the gambling industry, had to complete the New Jersey application. As an ex-Harvard Business School professor, he could not have had a cleaner background. Even so, he was required to go through the same procedure."

Richard Klemp, corporate director of government relations at Harrah's, explains:

> My job is twofold. First, my work is to protect our properties from negative legislation, as well as to advance legislation that we need to enhance our operations in existing jurisdictions. Second, I scrutinize

those states where we would like gaming to become a legalized entity, and I work to help make that happen. So, much of my time is spent lobbying state legislatures.

Harrah's has a very strong compliance program, and we make sure everything is absolutely within the letter and the spirit of the law and the regulations. We have excellent inside and outside legal counsel, and we play strictly by the rules. We take nothing for granted. There's too much at stake to do otherwise.

With eight- and nine-figure investments in casino properties, Harrah's takes no chances in losing its license. In recent years, Missouri, where gaming is highly regulated, threatened to revoke the licenses of major gaming operators such as Station Casinos and Hilton Hotels Corporation, reputable companies the state claimed failed to make sure every *T* was crossed and every *I* was dotted.

Indian Gaming

Under the Indian Reorganization Act of 1934, reservations received enhanced recognition from the federal government, were answerable only to Congress, and were exempt from state interference (and taxes) except in criminal matters—a wedge the tribes used to pry open the gaming floodgates. On December 9, 1986, the *California v. Cabazon Band of Mission Indians et al.* was argued in the Supreme Court on appeal from the United States Court of Appeal from the Ninth District. California and Riverside County sought to stop the Cabazon and Morongo Bands of Mission Indians from conducting high-stakes bingo and card games by arguing that Public Law 280 gave the state of California the right to enforce Penal Code 326.5. This statute does not entirely prohibit the playing of bingo, but allows the game only when operated by a charitable organization that cannot be paid for its services, and all profit must be held in "special accounts and used only for charitable purposes; prizes must not exceed $250 per game." Riverside County also sought to impose statutes regulating bingo and prohibiting draw poker and other card games.

In its landmark 1987 decision, *California v. Cabazon Band of Mission Indians,* the U.S. Supreme Court ruled that if a state allowed any sort of wagering—even, for example, at one-night charity functions—gambling became allowable on reservations, too. To impose some control on the subsequent floodtide, Congress passed the 1988 Indian Gaming Regulatory Act (IGRA), which required would-be gaming tribes to first negotiate a compact with their state in order to offer Las Vegas-style gaming. The states, for their part, were instructed to negotiate in "good faith," and if they did not, the tribes could sue them.

With the passage of the IGRA in 1988, the doors opened for Native Americans to engage in gaming ventures on tribal land as a means to gain self-sufficiency. With the IGRA behind it, a tribe notifies the state that it is going to have gaming on its reservation. If the state claims the reservation is not authorized to have gaming, the tribe in essence replies: "We are a sovereign nation. And because gaming in other forms is legal in the state, we can have gaming on our land."

A state is likely to respond: "If this is going to happen within the confines of our state borders, the state will be involved in terms of setting the scope." Hence, a compact is negotiated between the tribe and the state to outline terms specifying three conditions:

1. The scope of gaming, or what the tribes can do. Issues addressed include: Are slot machines allowed? Is table gaming allowed? Is full-scale gaming allowed?
2. What is the economic impact on the state?
3. What is the state's regulatory role?

In 1990, the first Native American casinos opened in Minnesota and Wisconsin. Minnesota, in particular, has many tribes and is considered a very liberal state with a proactive Indian policy. In a compact negotiated with the state, the tribes were permitted to have slot machines and blackjack games. Today, just outside Minneapolis is Mystic Lake, owned and operated by the Shakopee Mdewakanton Sioux Community. Mystic Lake is a casino resort with a four-star hotel and a golf course that ranks among the top 10 in the nation. Its casino has approximately 4,000 slot machines and about 150 gaming tables.

Today, of the 562 federally recognized tribes, 201 have gambling operations; some tribes have more than one casino, and in total, there are more than 300 casinos on reservations. Terms of the compacts vary from tribe to tribe. For example, some permit slot machines but no table games, or vice-versa. Arizona, for example, limits the size of casinos by allowing no more than 500 slot machines in one location. In the state of Washington, slot machines are not permitted, and only table games are legal.

Gaming on Indian reservations is a $13-billion-a-year industry in 28 states and growing three times faster than non-Indian gaming. As a result, the humble slot machine is being hailed as the Native Americans' new buffalo—a single source capable of fulfilling all of a tribe's needs, including jobs, schools, social services, and infrastructure. According to the National Indian Gaming Association (NIGA), Indian gaming is the first—and only—economic development tool that has ever worked on reservations.

Harrah's has been a long-time supporter of Indian gaming. When the Nevada Resort Association (NRA) opposed gaming on Indian lands, Harrah's announced it was resigning from the association. Only after the NRA changed its position did Harrah's rejoin the group. Harrah's was the first major gaming company to establish a Native American gaming division and the first to join NIGA.

In a speech at an NIGA meeting on April 10, 2000, Phil Satre talked about the company's casino partnerships with the Ak-Chin Community near Phoenix, the Prairie Band Potowatomi Nation north of Topeka, Kansas, and the Eastern Band of Cherokee reservation in Cherokee, North Carolina. Later, he mentioned the company's most ambitious-to-date Native American venture, a $125 million casino resort that opened in mid-2002 just north of San Diego, California. This property, a venture with the Rincon San Luiseno Band of Mission Indians, features a 200-room hotel and a 45,000-square-foot casino with 1,500 slot machines and 32 gaming tables.

Satre asked the NIGA audience:

> Why has Harrah's historically supported Native American gaming? We're a publicly traded company. We exist to make money, to generate financial growth for those who choose to invest in us. As IGRA took effect, and the early Native American casinos in Minnesota, Wisconsin, and elsewhere became a reality, we saw Native American casinos in favorable locations performing quite well, attracting the same types of customers we attracted at our Harrah's properties. And as we looked for geographic distribution of our casino brand, we saw that gaming on Indian lands presented opportunities for our company to access consumer markets that otherwise Harrah's could not have reached.

Harrah's Ak-Chin Casino

When Peter Weien joined Holiday Corporation in 1987, he began working in market planning. At the time, the company was engaged in an expansion program, building hotels around the globe. Consequently, Weien became quite knowledgeable in the area of commercial real estate development. In 1991, he moved to the casino side of the business to work closely with the company's treasurer. With his Holiday experience under his belt, Weien was named corporate director of development. In this capacity, he worked on major Indian gaming transactions exceeding $25 million in the development of new properties, as well as the acquisition of existing properties.

In the early 1990s, when it was clear that gambling would no longer be confined to Nevada and Atlantic City, the development department of Harrah's began to look into different markets offering opportunities for expansion. Two internal task forces were formed, one to explore riverboats and the other to explore Indian reservations. Weien served on an Indian gaming task force. In December 1991, after several months of planning, he made a presentation to the company's chief financial officer, Colin Reed. Impressed with what he heard, Reed presented Weien's findings to the board of directors.

Following the board meeting, Reed summoned Weien to his office. "We're going into Indian gaming," he announced, giving Weien a congratulatory handshake. "The board thinks there are Indian gaming opportunities for our company, and your job is to bring them to us."

A key player who would work closely with Weien on this endeavor was Bill Buffalo, another Holiday Inns transplant. Buffalo was an attorney who had practiced law for 12 years in Little Rock, Arkansas. After doing some outside legal work for the giant hotel chain, he accepted an in-house offer to manage the company's litigation department. When Promus was spun off, Buffalo went with the casino side of the business and has since been promoted to vice president and associate general counsel. In this capacity, he is responsible for the day-to-day operational legal work for all properties, with the exception of the New Orleans Casino. Buffalo also does gaming development legal work.

In his research on Indian gaming, Weien met with Sodak, a Rapid City, South Dakota, company that had exclusive distribution rights for all International Gaming Technology (IGT) products sold to Indian reservations. The management of Harrah's was so impressed with Sodak that the company ultimately bought a 20 percent interest in Sodak for $9 million.

Meanwhile, the Ak-Chin Indian Community, consisting of approximately 600 Tohono O'odham and Pima people, was a struggling reservation located outside the town of Maricopa in the Santa Cruz Valley of Southern Arizona, a half-hour drive south of Phoenix. The community was created in May 1912 by executive order of President Taft, who initially signed for a 47,600-acre reservation. The following year, however, Taft rescinded that order and reduced the community to its current size of slightly less than 22,000 acres. While scenic, the reservation's setting is located in an extremely arid Sonoran Desert climate. Although the landscape and terrain are suitable for growing crops by irrigation, water limitations have imposed severe hardships on the local residents. The reservation's main crop is pima cotton and, at the mercy of the desert weather, the Ak-Chin Community has a history of poverty.

In 1992, the Ak-Chin tribal council's five members met to discuss what appeared to be a bleak future. Unlike other areas in Arizona, its land had no minerals or tourism. Life on the reservation looked bleak unless drastic changes occurred.

Leona Kakar, a council member who has since served as a council chairperson says:

> We were desperate. We racked our brains trying to come up with something that would revive the community, but as in past meetings, there was never an adequate solution. This time, one council member suggested gambling.
>
> My first reaction was that gambling is a vice. I thought that way because I had those stereotyped images of Las Vegas gangsters. It's true that I had never been at a casino, but I'm old, so I admit I'm prone to resist radical change. I wasn't the only one who thought that way. Others did too.

"I felt like Leona did," says Terry Enos, another council member. "But hearing about the success that other tribes were having, I thought about how it could help the community. Then gambling seemed like something worth checking out.

One such casino worth investigating was the nearby Fort McDowell Casino, owned by the Mohave and Apache tribes. It had an advantage of being nearly 30 minutes closer to Phoenix than the Ak-Chin Community. There was also the Gila River casino that travelers would pass en route from Phoenix to the Ak-Chin Community. With two casinos in its area, each with a better location, it appeared as though the Ak-Chin Community had two strikes against it from the start.

The Ak-Chin tribal council, headed by chairperson Delia Carlisle, did its homework. After talking to other tribes that were profiting from their gaming operations, the council concluded there was merit to owning a casino. At its next meeting, projections on gaming revenues were presented to the tribal council. After a lengthy discussion, the two members who originally opposed gambling changed their minds. At that same meeting, the council voted unanimously in favor of a casino.

There was also a consensus that no one on the reservation had even a smidgen of experience in operating a casino. "So we decided to seek gaming professionals to run our casino," Kakar says.

The Ak-Chin tribal council conducted interviews with different companies. On the recommendation of Sodak, the council sent a Request for Proposal (RFP) to Harrah's. A cover letter explained that Ak-Chin was predominantly an agricultural tribe. The letter explained that four other tribes already had casinos in the Phoenix area, and Ak-Chin's reservation was in the most remote location.

Peter Weien, Bill Buffalo, and Tom Carr, all Harrah's executives, flew to Phoenix, rented a car, and drove to the Ak-Chin reservation. On the way, Weien said, "This place is so far off the beaten path. Who in the world is ever going to come here?"

The meeting was held in the tribe's government center. The three Harrah's representatives sat facing the five tribal council members. Bill Strickland, an attorney from Tucson, also attended the meeting. He had previously represented the Ak-Chin Community on water issues and had established a reputation as the dean of water lawyers in the state.

In his opening remarks, Carr thanked the council for considering Harrah's. For the next two hours, the three Harrah's executives talked about the company, emphasizing its long experience in the gaming industry. They emphasized that the remoteness of the reservation was a detriment and explained that the Harrah's brand name would be an important drawing card. There was some talk about the company's financial wherewithal to build the casino, and its available manpower to develop and train its workforce. A visual presentation was also given, featuring several conceptual drawings of casinos.

"Ours will be the fifth casino in the Phoenix area," Strickland commented.

"That's not a problem," Buffalo answered. "A metropolitan area like this can handle it."

"Do you think the Harrah's brand will be beneficial?" asked Strickland.

"We already have a strong customer base in the Phoenix area," responded Weien. "We feel they will patronize a Harrah's in this market, so that's a good start."

Buffalo pointed out that some casinos on Indian reservations had failed. "It's no sure thing," he told the council. "They died because they didn't have professional management."

As the council's representative, Strickland asked many questions. The five tribal council members, however, remained silent. "They never said a word, nor did they show any emotion," Weien says. "I'd hate to play cards with them because they've got damn good poker faces."

When the meeting adjourned, the Harrah's threesome bid farewell. On the way to the Phoenix airport, Buffalo asked his associates, "Well, what do you guys think?"

"I don't think they liked us," someone remarked.

"It was a nice trip, but we're not going anywhere with this thing," Buffalo replied.

At the airport, just minutes before they boarded the plane, Weien's cell phone rang. "We like your company," said the tribe's economic administrator, John Long. "We want you to put together a real proposal and come back so we can talk about it."

After the Ak-Chin Community contracted with Harrah's for the development and management of the Community's casino, the company went through the tedious process of seeking approval by the National Indian Gaming Commission (NIGC). Progress was particularly slow because Harrah's was one of the first casino companies to apply for a management contract with an Indian reservation. The NIGC ran a complete background investigation on the company.

After an extensive period of negotiations, it was agreed that a 72,000-square-foot casino would be constructed at a cost of $26.5 million. The contract with the state of Arizona allowed the casino to have 475 slot machines. The state forbid any live table games that were house-banked, which meant players could play against each other but not the house. A five-year management agreement was signed and could be renewed with the mutual consent of both parties. Harrah's arranged for a $26.5 million loan from Wells Fargo Bank and was named the loan's guarantor. This meant that if the casino went bankrupt, the bank would come to Harrah's to collect.

In February 1994, a groundbreaking ceremony was held under a large white tent in a cornfield; to the Harrah's executives and media people, it seemed like the middle of nowhere. In attendance were tribal members and company dignitaries including Mike Rose, chairman; Colin Reed, CFO; Pete Weien; and Bill Buffalo.

Six months later, Harrah's dispatched a team to the soon-to-open casino to hire and train staff. Janet Beronio, a lawyer who had been employed for 10 years by the company, was appointed general manager. Her husband, Ron Beronio, is director of recruiting at Harrah's. Two months before the casino's grand opening, the Beronios moved to a suburb in Phoenix.

On December 28, 1994, Weien drove a rented car down Interstate 10 to the Ak-Chin reservation. By now, he was well familiar with the road and its scenery, but this time was different. This time he was on his way to the casino's grand opening. He felt like Broadway producer with opening night jitters. He didn't know what to expect.

"Every time I come down this road," Weien thought, "I keep thinking how remote this place is. I sure hope we get a good turnout tonight."

He grimaced to think the casino might flop. "I really like these people," he mused. "We built up their hopes, and I'd hate to disappoint them."

Then, driving down Maricopa Road, about three miles away from the casino, he encountered bumper-to-bumper traffic.

"I can't believe it!" he thought. "That's the most beautiful sight I've ever seen in my life!"

When he met Buffalo, who was directing traffic in the parking lot, Weien said, "Look at the traffic. It must be five miles long."

The traffic jam continued through the following day. Inside the casino, people were standing in lines three deep, waiting their turn to play.

The casino was an overnight success. The tribe felt uncomfortable about having so much debt hanging over its head, so it decided to pay off the loan early. Within 20 months, the entire $26.5 million was paid off. When the five-year contract with Harrah's expired, it was renewed for a second five-year period.

"It's been a long process," Beronio says. "The tribe has a long history of farming, and now it's been thrust into a business environment that was foreign to its members. But they're actively involved in running this place. This is their casino, so the tribal council approves the operating budgets, as well as capital expenditures. Once a month, we have a luncheon with the council where we present business issues ranging from marketing issues to human resources matters."

The Ak-Chin casino has a fine steakhouse, buffet, and deli. The main floor in the casino has a stage where entertainers perform. Occasionally, top performers are brought in, including stars such as Percy Sledge, Bo Diddly, and B. J. Thomas. A 146-room hotel developed by Harrah's for the tribe opened in 2001. And it was financed by the tribe.

The lives of the people in the Ak-Chin Community and the surrounding area have dramatically improved since the casino opened. Jobs are plentiful—anyone wanting work finds employment. Of the casino's 800 employees, more than 50 are tribal members, a number that keeps climbing. Millions of dollars have been put into the reservation's infrastructure. Its service departments—fire, police, and sanitation—have been beefed up and so have its community center, elderly services programs, and educational system.

"We have a 24-hour fire and police department now," says tribal council member Terry Enos. "The department serves not only our community but the surrounding area. It doesn't have to, but we believe in being good neighbors."

"In 2000 alone, 90 new houses were constructed," explains Joseph Smith, also a tribal council member. "These homes are valued at $90,000 each, and every member head of household is entitled to one. We give them the key and they move in. The homeowners are entitled to free maintenance on their homes, except for normal wear and tear. Gas and electricity are also free."

The average age of the community is 22. Many young tribal members who left the reservation have since returned. "A main attraction is the opportunity to own a free house," Joe Smith says.

There is a definite emphasis on youth, evidenced by playgrounds and ball fields that have sprung up. Scholarship programs are available to the tribe's college-bound children.

Leona Kakar, a former schoolteacher, has shown a personal interest in programs designed to develop cultural pride in the younger generation. "The children are our future," she says.

"We have a preschool, but our children from K through 12 attend the public school in Maricopa," she explains. "On Indian Day, several adult tribal members visit the school to talk about our culture. Then we have our museum that has classes for the kids during the summer months, where they learn about our culture and traditions. And there is a learning center where students can go to do their homework."

"A higher than average number of the tribal members are diabetic," Beronio says. "In the past, those with diabetes, especially the elderly, had to be bussed into downtown Phoenix for dialysis treatment. Today, the community has its own dialysis center."

The Ak-Chin casino is a wonderful success story and a great source of pride to both its people and employees. Executives at the Harrah's home office in Las Vegas like to boast about it. "The opening of Ak-Chin couldn't have come at a better time for the financially-strapped tribe," says Carlos Tolosa, president of the company's western division. "I can't tell you an exact amount, but that first check was in excess of $1 million. And that was after they made their mortgage payment on the casino—which they paid off in 20 months."

Tolosa smiles when he adds, "We're business people, so we make our decisions based on return on investment. But there are other things even more meaningful. Working with the Ak-Chin Community and other Native Americans, we're learning different cultures— and it's making us better people. Some of the gains we've realized from these experiences don't show on the bottom line."

Foxwoods: A Native American Success Story

When the subject of gaming on reservations comes up, chances are, so does Foxwoods, the largest and most successful gaming casino in the world. The Mashantucket Pequots own Foxwoods, which is located in Mashantucket, Connecticut.

The story of the Pequots is fascinating, dating back more than 10,000 years, the length of time these native peoples have continuously resided in southeastern Connecticut. In the early 1600s, the Pequots had a population of 8,000 and inhabited a 250-square-mile area. They were among the first Native Americans to engage in commerce with the early Dutch and English traders. Following a series of escalating conflicts, in 1636 war broke out between the Pequots and the colonists. On July 28, 1637, a united force of Connecticut citizens, Massachusetts Bay Colony colonists from Plymouth, and some local Indian tribes attacked the Pequot village near what today is Mystic, Connecticut. The surprise night attack was a massacre. The village was burned to the ground, and hundreds of men, women, and children were killed. The Pequot tribe was virtually eradicated.

The few that survived were enslaved by the colonists and by other tribes. They were forbidden to speak their native tongue or to say the word *Pequot*. Those placed under the rule of the Mohegans eventually became known as the Mashantucket (Western) Pequots, and, in 1651, they were given land at Noank. In 1666, the land at Noank was taken away from the Pequots, and they were moved to their present domain at Mashantucket. The tribe originally had 2,000 to 3,000 acres, but over the years White settlers took away much of their land. As their land area shrank, reservation members drifted away. A 1774 colonial census had listed 151 tribal members at Mashantucket, but by the early 1800s, an estimated 30 to 40 members had left the reservation seeking work. Still others joined the Brotherton Movement, a Christian-Indian group that recruited Native Americans in the East to move to a settlement in upstate New York and later, Wisconsin. By 1856, illegal land sales had reduced the 989-acre reservation to 213 acres. A 1935 state commission reported the tribe's population on the reservation had dwindled to 42.

By the early 1970s, the reservation's population consisted of only two elderly women, and then one, Elizabeth George, passed away in 1974. Before her death, she had urged the young generation to return to the land and reunite the tribe. Her appeal inspired her 25-year-old grandson, Richard "Skip" Hayward, a $15,000-per-year pipe fitter at a submarine plant in nearby Groton, Connecticut. In 1975, Hayward began a relentless crusade to recruit Pequot members to the reservation. Little by little, they came. As their numbers grew, they formed a community and elected Hayward tribal chairman. That same year, he lobbied Congress to grant official recognition to the Pequots. Until then, the Pequots had not been recognized as an official tribe with all the rights and privileges Congress grants to Native Americans. More than sentiment was involved. With federal recognition comes "sovereignty," a $900,000 settlement, plus the right to open a bingo parlor. The total settlement designated $600,000 for land acquisition and $300,000 for economic development. By 1983, the tribe had repurchased 1,392 acres that had been placed in trust.

Meanwhile, more tribal members migrated to Mashantucket, and the reservation began a series of economic programs that included the sale of firewood, maple syrup, and garden vegetables; a swine project; and the opening of a hydroponic greenhouse.

In 1986, the tribe opened a small bingo parlor. Two years later, the IGRA was passed, and Haywood set his sights on greener pastures. In 1992, the first phase of Foxwoods Resort Casino was underway. The tribe quickly learned how difficult it was to obtain financing. No U.S. bank was willing to finance a property on land owned by the federal government and held in trust in perpetuity because, in the event of default, with the tribe's sovereignty, such property cannot be repossessed. A $60 million loan for construction financing was eventually secured from Malaysian billionaire Lim Goh Tong, whose wealthy family had major gambling interests in the Far East. Hayward had no intention of being a mere front for big money. He insisted that the tribe retain complete management control over Foxwoods. Tong and his associates would be lenders, not principals.

Foxwoods brought in professional managers, including Al Luciani, its first CEO, who had formerly run Merv Griffin's Resorts Casino Hotel in Atlantic City and had been an assistant attorney general in New Jersey. His experience in the regulatory aspects of gaming, coupled with his strong management background, made Luciani an excellent candidate for the top job. G. Michael Brown, who also came from a gaming regulatory background in New Jersey, followed Luciani as CEO; later, Bud Seley, who served as Hilton's gaming CEO, came aboard to serve as Foxwoods' chief executive.

When Foxwoods opened in February 1992, its 46,000-square-foot casino was staffed for two shifts. At 2:00 A.M. the next morning, the gaming area was so crowded, the first shift was held over, and the second shift was asked to report in early. Immediately, a massive hiring and training program got underway to staff a third shift. Ever since, the casino has remained open 24 hours a day, 365 days a year.

The original Foxwoods Casino had 170 table games, including roulette, poker, and blackjack—sans slot machines. In January 1993, the compact between the tribe and state was renegotiated to allow the tribe to operate slot machines. In exchange, the tribe agreed to pay 25 percent of its annual slot machine win to the state, with a guaranteed minimum of $100 million. The agreement stated that the tribe's obligation to make such payments would cease if the state legalized the operation of slot machines anywhere else in Connecticut, or if any other entity in the state operated slot machines.

After several expansions, Foxwoods now has a 315,000-square-foot casino with 6,000 slot machines and 350 gaming tables. Its three lodging facilities have 1,416 deluxe rooms and suites. The resort has more than two dozen eateries, including four fine-dining restaurants. Its 1,400-seat Fox Theater has featured world-class entertainers such as Frank Sinatra, Kenny Rogers, Tony Bennett, Celine Dion, Jay Leno, David Copperfield, and the Dixie Chicks. The bingo hall also serves as a room for concerts and boxing events. This multipurpose room can hold 4,000 guests and has hosted performers such as Luciano Pavarotti, Carly Simon, and Rod Stewart. There are 17 stores with retail space totaling 15,000 square feet. The Grand Spa and Salon is a 20,000-square-foot state-of-the-art health and exercise center, and the Foxwoods Golf and Country Club has a 6,203-yard championship course. There are 11,500 employees on its payroll, plus another 1,200 people working for the tribal government. Its annual payroll exceeds $300 million. Because the state's cut is based on slot machine revenues, the Pequots' take is public information; the recorded monthly net profit to the tribe from slot machines is $65 million.

Why is Foxwoods the all-time most successful casino? One reason is that 22 million people live within a 150-mile radius, and, until 2000, it was the only casino in Connecticut. Atlantic City, by comparison, has 28 million people within a 150-mile radius and 12 casinos.

The Foxwoods story extends beyond its success as a casino. Its revenues have vastly improved the lives of the 600 Pequots who live on the reservation. To the tribal members, the casino provides jobs, higher education, health care, and financial security. Today, the tribe has a zero unemployment rate. Educational funds are provided to every tribal member, which includes all tuition and other costs associated with education, plus generous stipends while attending school. Most importantly, such affluence has meant self-sufficiency

and self-respect. The reservation has a community center any affluent suburban neighborhood would envy. Its charming, landscaped
Cape Cod-style homes are not what you would expect to see on an Indian reservation. No longer an impoverished people, the Pequots
have used profits from the casino to build a $193 million tribal mu-
seum on the reservation, which houses the most extensive Native
American research library in the world. The Pequots have also contributed $10 million to the Smithsonian Institution's Native American
museum. Although there has been some opposition in the local community, the casino has been a boon to the economy—providing jobs
for the area's citizens and revenues to its businesses.

PART III

Harvard Comes to Vegas: Harrah's Unique Marketing Strategy

Today, Harrah's credits its ongoing success to a unique management team and sophisticated consumer marketing strategy that delivers service according to specific customer needs. The company has emerged from a proud heritage that traces its roots to Bill Harrah, the man who insisted on excellence in quality and service. It is also an organization that has learned to embrace change. With more than six decades under its belt, Harrah's is one of the early pioneers in the gaming industry, yet it is a company that knows how to survive and prosper in a highly competitive marketplace. It is important to note that the time frame in Part III overlaps with the time frame in Part II. Chapter 5 covers the formulation of the Harrah's marketing strategy that was in its beginning stage following the Holiday Inns' acquisition in 1980 and continues through the present. Lest we forget, a marketing strategy is an ongoing process. Today's Harrah's has a disciplined, scientific style of management, foreign in the field of gaming, but considered main-stream by traditional standards in the investment community. Sub-scribing to a management process appropriate for a business school, financial analysts have scrutinized this aberrant gaming company in awe and with esteem. In short, if Bill Harrah were alive today, he would be immensely proud of the company that bears his name.

5

FORMULATING A MARKETING STRATEGY

HE VAST AND VARIED CUSTOMER FOCUS THAT NOW CHARACTERIZES Harrah's took a great deal of time and effort to develop. In 1980, Harrah's opened in both Atlantic City and Las Vegas, but it would be seven years before the company would open another casino. In 1987, the company acquired Barney's, a small casino next door to its Lake Tahoe property and promptly renamed it *Bill's* after the company's founder. The following year, Harrah's built a casino in Laughlin, Nevada, thus becoming the only company to operate in the five largest gaming markets in the United States (Las Vegas, Atlantic City, Reno, Lake Tahoe, and Laughlin). As gaming spread across the country to Indian reservations and riverboats, Harrah's was on its way to becoming the only truly national casino company in America.

For years, Harrah's confined its marketing efforts to what was the norm in the industry—comping its best customers based on their gambling activity. Comps ran the gamut. High rollers were showered with everything from drinks to hotel suites to first-class air travel. For the most part, evaluating these customers was a judgment call made by VIP hosts, casino managers, and pit bosses. The size of the comp was determined by observing customers' play at the gaming tables. Little, if any, attention was paid to slot machine players and, accordingly, rarely were they comped. Casino employees who were authorized to comp customers did so randomly. This was the marketing strategy used by the major casinos to attract high-stakes customers, but computers were not used and comps were not always equitably given to deserving customers.

Beginning in the 1950s and throughout the 1970s, to attract a continuous flow of the masses that included high rollers and slot players, the biggest drawing card for Harrah's was big-time entertainers who appeared at its Reno and Lake Tahoe casinos. Holmes Hendricksen explains:

In those days, it was against the law to advertise gambling, so we had to advertise something else. Bill Harrah chose to go with entertainment. We advertised superstars such as Sammy Davis Jr., Frank Sinatra, and Bill Cosby, who were appearing at Harrah's, and we played off their glamorous reputations by placing their names and photographs in our ads. This way, the public identified us with our star entertainers. Every year, we'd come out with a new advertising campaign, always promoting Harrah's as the casino with the world's greatest performers.

Casinos offered cheap rooms, meals, and drinks—anything and everything to attract customers. Some offered fine dining. Back then, hotel rooms and food were great bargains. Every casino had a hook. But at Harrah's, everything we did was related to entertainment, and, I may add, *entertaining people.* In this regard, we were the first to acknowledge that gaming is a form of entertainment—at a time when gambling wasn't necessarily thought about in this vein.

Starting with the 1960 Winter Olympics in Squaw Valley, California, Harrah's began promoting special events to attract customers to its two casinos. For instance, during the two-week run of the Olympics, the company distributed $85,000 worth of tickets to the casinos' most worthy customers. The company spent so much money promoting and supporting the Olympics that it ranked third among the largest contributors, behind only the state of Nevada and the state of California, both of which had built elaborate visitors' centers. Other special events included boxing matches, car shows, and golf tournaments. Good customers received invitations to play a round of golf with a Harrah's executive and a performing artist, perhaps Jack Benny or Red Skelton. Just as Bugsy Siegel recognized back in the 1940s that his Hollywood cronies would attract the masses to his Flamingo Casino, Bill Harrah understood that his casinos could draw large crowds by providing world-class entertainment at affordable prices.

The world-famous Harrah's Automobile Collection was another drawing card to entice customers to visit the casino. High rollers were routinely given free tours, and, occasionally, Bill Harrah personally ushered a VIP through his collection. Occasionally, the car collection even went on the road to promote Harrah's. For instance, in 1971, 30 antique cars from the collection were shipped to Japan's World Classic Car Festival (the first and only such festival). The cars were displayed in Tokyo, Osaka, and Kyoto, attracting large crowds. Bill Harrah attended and became an instant celebrity in Japan, holding many press conferences and attracting as many viewers as did the cars. The two-week event was a huge success and is mentioned in congressional records as a gesture of friendship from the United States to Japan. In years to come, millions of Japanese visited the United States, many of whom were familiar with the Harrah name because of the car collection. Millions of car lovers from around the globe first heard of Harrah's through its owner's famed automobile collection. Cars from the collection have been shipped to faraway places such as London, Paris, and Johannesburg, keeping the Harrah's name on people's lips.

The days of superstars who entertained for two- to four-week gigs at Harrah's and other major casinos are long gone. Big names performing twice nightly, seven days a week in casinos are a thing of the past. Today, the most popular entertainers are on tour in highly promoted concerts, earning six- and seven-figure paychecks for one- and two-night stands. Harrah's and other major casinos rarely compete with those sums.

"There aren't many headliner entertainers like the Andy Williams and the Paul Ankas out there today," tells Tom Jenkin at Harrah's Las Vegas. "Music has changed so much and today's is geared more to the teens and the 20-to-35 age group. Nowadays, there's pop, metal music, hip hop, and cool jazz—whatever they're listening to—but it's not the kind of music that appeals to a casino's target audience."

Without the superstars to attract customers, Harrah's had to come up with a new strategy to win market share. In the meantime, the competition began building theme casino resorts with price tags in the hundreds of millions of dollars—with some in excess of $1 billion. With its national distribution strategy that called for entering multiple markets, it wasn't economically prudent for Harrah's to open such extravagantly expensive casino resorts across America.

Developing an expansion program not focused around expensive theme casino resorts ran counter to a major industry trend started in 1989 when Steve Wynn opened his tropical-themed Mirage at a cost exceeding $700 million. Wynn's Mirage led the way—the first megaresort built in Las Vegas. At that price, the Mirage needed to take in $1 million per day just to cover interest payments and operating costs. As it turned out, this was not a problem. Soon, the Mirage was taking in $50 million in monthly revenues. News of the Mirage's success spurred more investors to consider building ultra-expensive, themed casino/resorts. Themed casinos had been around for decades in Las Vegas—but this time around, the enormity of their price tags shocked everyone. Steve Wynn, credited as the man who saved Las Vegas, was hailed as a gaming industry visionary.

Harrah's made a bold decision to buck that trend. It was a gutsy move because theme casinos were being built in Las Vegas in record numbers—and tens of millions of people were coming to Las Vegas in record numbers.

Superstar performers and theme casinos share one common denominator: Both are forms of entertainment. In a speech Phil Satre delivered at the National Press Club in Washington, DC, on December 3, 1993, he told his audience:

> People who come to a casino come for entertainment . . . a form of entertainment with several unique qualities—interaction, excitement, and accessibility. Money . . . and the shot to win more money . . . is "the medium." But clearly, the message is entertainment.
>
> At casinos all across America, you can walk in on any given night and see adults of all ages, all races and both sexes . . . playing slots or blackjack together . . . celebrating together . . . interacting with each other and with casino employees in a comfortable, safe environment. Casino entertainment is a truly exciting, truly social experience.
>
> And there are no physical barriers to access . . . an 82-year-old grandmother can place a $10 bet in blackjack, draw 14, then hit a 7 and scream with the same level of intensity that her 28-year-old granddaughter can.
>
> A friend of mine tells me that the opening of casinos in Atlantic City has added five years to his mother's life. Alone in New Jersey and nearly 80 years old after her husband and lifelong companion died, this lady and her friends travel to Atlantic City once a week for the interaction, enjoyment, and excitement playing in a casino provides them.
>
> These trips are not about getting rich. They are about friends having fun and enjoying time together in an environment of celebration. By all measurements, demand for casino entertainment is far greater than existing supply. More than 70 percent of adult Americans say casino entertainment can be a "fun night out."

Michael St. Pierre is general manager of Harrah's in Joliet, Illinois, consistently one of the most profitable of the company's casinos. He credits the company's marketing success to the way it has uniquely positioned itself. "Harrah's is not about a volcano," he states in reference to the Mirage, "or having the most flashy restaurants in town. We provide a unique gaming-centric experience. And we provide great amenities to surround that gaming experience by having outstanding service in a gaming environment."

Company communications director Gary Thompson talks about supply and demand when he explains:

> This is an industry that has historically been about creating supply—the build-it-and-they-will-come approach to grow market share. The bigger and more glitzy the properties, the more they will come. Our

marketing strategy, however, isn't about supply, it's about generating demand by providing a wonderful gaming experience and superior service.

A Growth Industry

In the late 1980s, Harrah's management became very much aware that the public's attitude toward gambling in America was changing, in part because of the onslaught of state lotteries. The first state lottery was introduced in New Hampshire in 1964, and, ultimately, politicians in 37 states sold their constituents on this "painless taxation" under the auspices of replacing school levies and other tariffs. After state governments got into the business and hyped their lotteries through the media, things changed. Millions of Americans took a different view of what had previously been an illegal activity—after all, if the state was in the business, it must be okay. It was only a matter of time before state-run lotteries, in spite of having the worst odds of any common form of gambling, had become a favorite pastime of the American consumer. Phil Satre explains:

> With the lotteries, there was a changing of attitudes toward casinos in America. Subsequently, the nation's baby boomer generation viewed casinos differently than their parents, and at Harrah's, we perceived this as a growth mechanism for our industry. In my own family, I know that had I walked in and told my grandparents I was going to work for a casino, they would have said, "Our poor grandson has wandered off the reservation." But my parents, who were in their late 50s and early 60s, had been desensitized and realized that casinos had become a legitimate business, and they had no problem with it.

Since the mid-1990s, Americans have had less discretionary time than they had in the past. This trend has benefited the gaming industry because visiting a casino is a way of squeezing in a mini-vacation. Full-service commercial and Indian casinos are now spread across America in 28 states, and within a 45-minute to an hour driving distance for most Americans; therefore, many vacationers consider a one-to two-day getaway an ideal way to relax and unwind. What's more, it's an affordable vacation. Most casino visitors don't lose so badly that it hurts them financially. This is evidenced by the fact that 79 percent said they write off their losses as money spent on recreation.

With a strong economy and overtime pay, Americans have cash to spend frivolously—they feel secure enough to blow some hard-earned money and, at the same time, blow off a little steam. One interesting aspect of this trend is the mind-set of those who choose a casino as a getaway—not only from work but also from their kids. It's strictly self-gratification, a break from their tedious routine. A casino is the ideal venue for escape and seems designed for this purpose. The building typically contains no windows or clocks, helping occupants lose track of time. Its action-packed milieu has been well calculated to prevent a participant from thinking about anything outside its walls. To engage in the fast-paced activity of gambling, you must devote complete attention to it. Games such as craps and blackjack require total concentration. It is no wonder gambling gives us a buzz. Certainly, the pleasurable aspects of gambling keep patrons coming back repeatedly.

In a 2000 survey conducted by America's Research Group based in Charleston, South Carolina, 66 percent said they enjoy visiting a casino as a casual recreation, while 34 percent view it as a serious challenge. To many Americans, having fun and being competitive are closely tied.

Being a Niche Player

Every basic Marketing 101 student knows the importance of knowing who his or her customer is. Companies that don't have a firm grasp on their customer's identity handicap themselves: Fearing they may lose customers, they try to offer something for everyone. The unfortunate consequence is that they end up unable to differentiate themselves from their competition in the marketplace, rendering themselves neither fish nor fowl. When this happens, their market share drops substantially.

Thus it was with Harrah's for a time. As more ultra-expensive theme casinos kept being built, Harrah's found itself in a difficult situation. Not having the most luxurious accommodations for its high-end customers, or for that matter, the lowest rates for the budget-minded customers, Harrah's was neither fish nor fowl. Satre explains:

> At one end of the spectrum, there is the high roller. Here, all major casinos traditionally do a good job at going after this customer. Like our competition, over the years, we've built personal relationships with customers, comping them for their business. At the other end, there's the retail segment—customers driven by discounts. These consumers have a low budget, and they usually don't stay in your hotel. And they typically eat at your least expensive restaurant. These people come in by bus rather than by driving their own car.

We made a conscious decision that we were not going to build products to cater to the very high end, the high rollers. We realized the most luxurious properties being built would get the lion's share of that segment of the business. At the same time, we weren't going to go after the nickel and dime slot player, so in a very rudimentary way, we identified our target customer in the middle—the dollar slot player. Keep in mind that back in the mid-1980s, there were mainly single coin slot machines, but today with the multicoin machines, someone who plays a multicoin nickel, dime, or quarter machine is considered a dollar slot player who we identified as our target customer.

In the company, the target market that Harrah's identified as its niche is referred to as an "avid experience player" or AEP. An AEP typically has an annual budget of $1,000 to $5,000 to payroll his recreational gaming activities. Gary Loveman, CEO, explains:

We did extensive research to determine which group of customers was most profitable to us, and, at the same time, which group of customers might be relatively underserved by competitors. We concluded this would be the AEP who typically gambles $100 to $500 a trip and visits us several times each year. This is the customer that our marketing has targeted, and our rewards program is built around encouraging this individual to respond to our promotions.

Rich Mirman emphasizes the company does not try to compete with billion-dollar casinos like Bellagio.

For the segment of customers that likes Bellagio's pomp and circumstance, we don't go after that business. But there's a larger number of customers that we feel will like the low-key, high quality of service they'll receive at Harrah's. That's our market.

To understand our customer, people should read *The Millionaire Next Door* by Thomas Stanley and William Danko. The book emphasizes that the average millionaire in America is unassuming and you'd never know he or she has a seven-figure net worth. These individuals don't live extravagantly, and a trip to Las Vegas is what they consider "living it up a little." When they're in Vegas, they want to eat at a fine quality Chinese restaurant here like the one they go to back home. When they visit an Italian or French restaurant and read the menu, they want to be able to understand what's on it. And when they go to the tables and slot machines, they like the hospitality when the cocktail waitress comps them a Bailey's on the rocks. They have a budget they've set aside to gamble, and they stay within it. They don't have to spend a lot of money to have a great time—and they do enjoy themselves!

Our customer base is people who are middle-aged, their kids are college-educated and grown, and they've worked hard all their lives. They're now at a time in their lives able to afford gaming with the money they budgeted for their trip to a casino. This is what they like to do with their leisure time. It's a safe adventure for them.

The Distribution Strategy

When Harrah's opened a casino in Laughlin, Nevada, in 1988, according to Phil Satre, it was a turning point for the company. "This was our first entry into a smaller market that clearly wasn't a destination market like Reno, Tahoe, or Vegas." Nor, for that matter, could it draw from a large urban market as Atlantic City did. It was the company's first property that was neither in a destination resort market nor near a large metropolitan market. Laughlin (pop. 8,500) was a remote river town on the Colorado River, 90 miles south of Las Vegas.

Until 1941, Laughlin didn't even appear on the map. The town sprang up when construction began in 1941 on the Davis Dam, downstream on the Colorado from Hoover Dam. When the United States entered World War II, funds quickly dried up and the dam was put on hold. It was finally completed in 1953. As in Las Vegas, only on a smaller scale, the town's founding fathers turned to gaming. Gaming, then and now, is Laughlin's only industry, although tourist businesses including retail shops, restaurants, and boating establishments have since opened and prospered. Laughlin is laid-back and very affordable. The rates for attractive hotel rooms run one-fifth the cost of comparable rooms in Vegas. Ads for the town read: "The 'new' place to get away from the over-crowded Las Vegas Strip." Bill Keena, general manager of Harrah's in Laughlin says, "With the beautiful views of the Colorado River and at the low prices for lodging and food, this resort area has to be America's best kept secret."

Today, there are nine major casinos in Laughlin and more than 10,000 hotel rooms. In 1987, when Harrah's made the decision to set up shop in this sleepy river town, six other casinos had already staked their claims. Phil Satre explains:

> We did our homework and determined there was an opportunity for us in Laughlin. We even identified the site where we wanted to build our casino. But this time, when I presented the project to Mike Rose, obtaining financing was a major obstacle, because Holiday Corporation was in the middle of a recapitalization plan.
>
> "Our balance sheet won't permit borrowing that money," Mike replied. "If you want to build in Laughlin, you'll have to do it with project financing."

This meant the real estate itself would have to support the financing, without the backing of Holiday Corporation's credit or any other part of Harrah's to back it. So my colleagues—Chuck Atwood, Colin Reed, and John Boushy—and I aggressively courted bankers, and, ultimately, we succeeded in building the casino. It was an excellent exercise for us, because we became proficient at developing and financing properties without having to rely on Holiday Inns to sign off for us. The casino opened in 1988, and it's been a big success for the company. It's the leading casino in Laughlin and we've added onto it three times, which includes increasing the number of hotel rooms and the size of the casino. Looking back, it was a challenging period, because I didn't want to sit around just managing the properties we had when I took the job. *I wanted to build.*

In 1989, Holiday Inns was acquired by Bass PLC; and Harrah's, along with the three remaining hotel brands—Embassy Suites, Hampton Inn, and Homewood Suites—was spun off into the newly formed Promus Companies.

The building of the Laughlin casino ignited a distribution strategy that has since been repeated many times. Its success marked an important turning point for the company, because it proved that the Harrah's brand could draw customers to a nondestination casino resort. "Even though the property we built in Laughlin was very high quality, we decided to promote the Harrah's brand as its main drawing card," tells Phil Satre.

The success of Laughlin's casino despite its remoteness demonstrated that a significant number of Harrah's customers were loyal to the brand—and the company could build a distribution system on this valuable asset.

About the time Harrah's opened in Laughlin, riverboat casinos were beginning to spring up, and, following the passage of the 1988 Indian Gaming Regulatory Act by Congress, gaming on Indian reservations was just over the horizon. Most Nevada- and New Jersey-based casino owners felt threatened by the new developments. These owners saw the newcomers as threatening to lure away customers who would otherwise come to their properties. However, Harrah's took a positive tack. Taking a Mohammed-goes-to-the-mountain approach, Harrah's welcomed the opportunity to do business where the customers resided.

"Instead of being worried about what these casino openings would do to Nevada-based casino companies, we looked at it as an opportunity," tells former CFO Colin Reed. "We liked the notion of going to these consumers in their indigenous markets. Of course, at the time, we had no way of knowing the potential benefit it would later have on Nevada, but we said, 'Hell, even if it's negative, it's still going to happen, so we should go with the flow.'"

"If there's one thing that ties in with our hotel experience," Satre adds, "we clearly understood that if there's a good corner across the street from our Hampton Inn property, we should build an Embassy Suites or a Homewood Suites on it before a competitor does. The one thing you don't do is let the other guy beat you to it!"

"We took a close look at what was happening across the country with lotteries, on Indian reservations, and the riverboat gaming phenomenon that was creeping in," explains Reed. "After the first riverboat gaming jurisdiction became legalized in Iowa, Mike Rose said to me, 'I think you need to present a plan to our board that expresses what you think is going to happen and what we should do.'"

In July 1992, before a board of directors' meeting held at Blackberry Farms in the Smoky Mountains, Reed met with Satre, who had been named president and chief operating officer of Promus in April 1991. For several weeks, Reed had been preparing a presentation to give to the board, and he reviewed his thoughts with the new president.

Satre listened intently while Reed, a native of Great Britain, explained what he envisioned for the company's future expansion:

What's happening in the United States with gaming is reminiscent of what I witnessed 20 years earlier in Europe with protectionism pertaining to its trading markets. Actually, in Europe, they designed it to protect the borders of their member countries against countries like the United States. In 1991, with America's financial problems brought on by the Resolution Trust Company and the savings and loan debacle, there were some serious economic issues facing the individual states. Just as we saw state after state get into the lottery business to raise revenues, we were going to see the same states authorize gaming casinos as a defensive measure to protect the outflow of gaming dollars that would otherwise go to bordering states. At the time, this was a hypothesis, but it was probable that it would happen. We need to be the first movers.

Satre concurred and said to Reed: "I would like you to take over development for the company."

When Reed presented the same hypothesis to the Promus board at Blackberry Farms, it was agreed the company would appropriate the necessary capital to immediately move forward. Consequently, Harrah's was the first national casino company to open properties in Louisiana, Missouri, and Illinois. One year later, Reed made a similar presentation on Indian gaming, and in December 1994, the Harrah's Ak-Chin casino opened its doors.

A Brand Strategy

It was the simultaneous development of a distribution strategy and a branding strategy that would propel Harrah's to the forefront of the national gaming scene. While the strong national branding program advanced by the hotel side of the business made a definite impression on the Harrah's management, a casual event occurred about the same time as the building of the Laughlin casino that was another catalyst.

Satre recalls the specifics of the incident:

Back in the late 1980s, we sent mailings to customers who'd won big jackpots or a lot of money at the tables. Each received a winner's certificate with a personal letter. I signed hundreds of certificates and letters at a time, so it wasn't exactly my favorite activity. In the letter, I asked customers to write to me about their experience with Harrah's. An enclosed response card asked them to tell me about themselves. What do you like to play? When is your next trip to Harrah's? Is there a particular employee you like?

Admittedly, this was unsophisticated direct marketing, but responses indicated many of our customers were visiting two or three of our properties, and, in some cases, all five of them. Once while I was going through some responses, John Boushy, who headed our marketing at the time, walked into my office. "John, look at this information I'm getting," I told him. "I can't believe this."

John shared my amazement. When we started to track it, we discovered many of our customers visited multiple properties. This is when we realized our customers' primary focus. They want us to give them a great service experience. They want fun. They want to enjoy themselves. They want our employees to treat them well. Rarely did anyone write that the room wasn't fancy enough.

We learned several things from these responses: First, we had customers who gamble in multiple locations. Our Atlantic City customers come to Las Vegas. Our Reno customers go to Lake Tahoe, and so on. Second, when we manually tracked these findings, we estimated 25 percent of our regular Atlantic City customers make an annual pilgrimage to Las Vegas. This planted a seed that there was an opportunity to create a loyalty marketing program to establish relationships with customers who bridge multiple gaming environments.

At the time, my small corporate staff focused primarily on making capital and senior human resources decisions. We were not a source of operating expertise for our properties, nor did we have a common database. Each property had some limited information pertaining to its own customers. In the early 1990s, we decided to invest heavily to centralize our database. Later, when we began opening riverboat casinos, we committed to a distribution strategy based on this loyalty marketing approach. At the time, it was believed that to succeed in this industry, you had to have huge hotels and showrooms, even in riverboat land and Indian country. But we broke from conventional wisdom's big, highly themed casinos.

Shortly afterward, Satre created a strategic marketing department, and John Boushy was assigned to head it. At the time, Harrah's was serving five markets in two states—Nevada and New Jersey. A main function of Boushy's job was to determine what reward a Harrah's customer could expect for visiting multiple locations. Boushy recalls:

When I first took on this assignment, I met with our research people and asked them to explain what cross-market visitation meant to them.

"Well, that's when one of our customers goes to our casino in Reno and also visits our Lake Tahoe property," someone said.

"Or, one of our Las Vegas customers goes to our Atlantic City casino," another replied.

Once we defined what cross-market visitation was, I started looking at some interesting numbers. I was amazed to discover that 37 percent of our customers that went to our Lake Tahoe property also visited our Reno property on the same trip. Incidentally, Reno and Lake Tahoe are about 60 miles apart, which is about a one-and-a-half hour drive. Next, we studied the numbers of our customers who live in San Francisco that go to Las Vegas. Keep in mind that San Francisco is about a three-hour drive to Lake Tahoe and Reno but more than 10 hours to Vegas. The research showed that Tahoe and Reno customers in the San Francisco area were also our customers in Vegas. Wow, I thought, we have a tremendous branding opportunity. We can offer a consistency of experience that builds brand loyalty. We can recognize and reward people for their business at other properties.

After reviewing this information, I immediately commissioned another research project, only this time, it was on a national level. Lo and behold, this study revealed that of the people that visited casinos, about one out of four visited two different markets in a 12-month period. We also saw that people who visited Atlantic City were also going to Las Vegas once or twice a year. With properties in five markets, we concluded Harrah's could definitely benefit from a cross-market strategy.

The strategy's competitive advantage proved its value following the September 11, 2001 terrorists' attacks. Air traffic plummeted across the nation and millions of tourists traveling to destination markets simply stopped traveling by air. Consequently, Las Vegas got hit hard and casino revenues took a nose dive. Harrah's fared the best of the major gaming companies because its drive-in markets weren't affected. On the contrary, visiting a nearby casino offered an excellent alternative for a weekend escape, and revenues actually rose at many Harrah's properties across the country. By October, even the hotel occupancy at Harrah's in Las Vegas was outperforming other casino-resorts on the Strip, a result attributed to the company's cross-market branding strategy.

In 1988, Phil Satre was reviewing a press release to announce that Harrah's was the only casino company with operations in all five major gaming markets. The announcement was sent to Bob Dowd, a former Harrah's public relations vice president. "Dowd read it," Boushy explains, "and he sat back and scratched his head. 'I understand the value this creates for the shareholders,' he said, 'because it creates diversity. I also see the value to employees because it provides career opportunities. But where's the value to customers?'"

Why Frequent Buyer Programs Work

The answer to Bob Dowd's question was a distribution strategy that would reward loyal customers for their business. For the record, Nevada casinos and, later, New Jersey casinos have traditionally rewarded customers by comping them. The major casinos have long excelled in rewarding their high-level customers. They comp known gamblers, who, in turn, spend more time in their casinos than in the competition's. Casino patrons know they'll get more comps by confining their gaming to one or two establishments rather than spreading it out.

But Bob Dowd's question was not directed at the high rollers, because he already understood what was in it for them. High rollers represent a small number of the people who visit casinos, an estimated 1 to 2 percent of all customers. VIP hosts and casino managers know who they are, and they take good care of them. Dowd wanted to know what value would be received by the other 98 percent of the customers in exchange for their loyalty.

For these customers, Harrah's had a frequent player's program. For instance, in Lake Tahoe, preferred customers were issued a Gold Card, and in Atlantic City, they received a Captain's Card. The programs worked like an airline's frequent flyer program. However, these programs were nothing new. Frequent flyer programs had been around since 1981 when American Airlines introduced its American AAdvantage program. When it first came out, it was compared to Green Stamps, a popular supermarket bonus program dating back to the 1950s. Merchants gave stamps for money spent at their stores. Customers glued the stamps into small paperback books, which could be redeemed at Green Stamps outlets for merchandise. The tiny stamps were cumbersome to collect; they had to be licked or moistened before being glued onto a page, and dozens of books of stamps were needed to redeem even a small item such as a toaster. Little did anyone suspect that the long-term impact of American AAdvantage would be felt around the world. In 2002, 63 percent of all American households participated in a frequent-buyer program. These programs go beyond air travel premiums; today, purchase points can be racked up on everything from flowers to charitable contributions. *Inside-Flyer* magazine reports that no fewer than 3.6 trillion miles are sitting in people's accounts. Nearly half of these miles have come from credit card purchases, mutual fund investments, long-distance calls, and similar transactions.

To the credit of Harrah's, each of its casinos had its own frequent player program by the late 1980s. This, however, was its problem, as brought to light in 1990 when Phil Satre received a letter from a customer that addressed the same question Bob Dowd had asked.

The letter read:

> I am a loyal customer of yours in Lake Tahoe, and I like to come up there. I like to play slots and I have a Harrah's Tahoe customer tracking card. I also like to visit your casinos in Reno, Las Vegas, and Laughlin. But I have a different card for each of your casinos, so it's like starting all over again when I visit one of your casinos for the first time. I'm waiting for the day when I have one Harrah's card that's good anywhere I go.
>
> I am also a United Airlines customer. If I get on a United flight in Reno to fly to Chicago, I receive my United frequent flyer points, and I also get them when I fly from New York to Denver or Los Angeles to Dallas. Do you see my point? All my frequent flyer points are credited to my one United account. Why do all of the Harrah's casinos have separate programs when it's all the same company?

Phil Satre points out that when the company "nationalized" its frequent player card so its customers could be rewarded credits on a single company card, some casino managers didn't like it and complained, "My business and my customers are different because this is a different market."

"When I hear those comments," says Satre, "I take out that letter and read it to them."

Dave Kowal, a company marketing vice president explains, "When we were in the early stages of discussing the need to have a loyalty program, we talked about how you could go to Macy's in one city and go to another Macy's in another city and the same Macy's credit card worked. In our industry, that wasn't the case. From a competitive advantage, to leverage our distribution, we viewed this as an effective way to integrate the customer service experience."

A Seamless Experience

An obvious advantage to promoting branding is name recognition. With consumer products, and so many people pressed for time today, it's a real time-saver to buy a brand you're already familiar with. That's why a husband with a shopping list of ketchup, soup, tissue paper, and cola, will come home with a bottle of Heinz, cans of Campbell Soup, a box of Kleenex, and a pack of Coca-Cola. Busy consumers don't want to take chances buying an unfamiliar brand—and they're too rushed for time to read the labels! We do the same thing when we buy everything from underwear to shirts. This is why we stop at McDonald's and Wendy's when we're on the road rather than at Frank's Hamburgers. Although the locally owned hamburger joint may have the best burgers in town, we're not willing to risk getting food poisoning! We feel the same about where we sleep—that's why we stay at brand name hotels like Holiday Inns instead of Betty's Motel. We don't want to come home with bed bugs!

These examples share a common denominator: Consumers want a seamless experience. They don't want any disappointments that a nonbrand product or service might give them. True, the local establishment might represent an outstanding value—just the same, most of us stick with established name brands because we've been disappointed too many times. It does pay to advertise and promote your brand name.

Casino companies, by the way, are not big advertisers. For one reason, depending on the jurisdiction, there are restrictions on advertising gambling. Dave Kowal, a vice president of marketing, mentions another reason:

> One of the things we believe is that gamblers can find a casino. We don't advertise in New York, for example, to come to Harrah's in Atlantic City. The New Yorkers who want to gamble know where we are. We will advertise on billboards on the road to and in Atlantic City, however, because such a high percentage of them do gamble. So we don't go after people who don't already gamble, but with

those who do, we want to get our share of them. We also do direct mailing to consumers who come through our doors and gamble enough to get one of our cards.

According to David Norton, vice president of direct marketing:

It's a more efficient use of our marketing dollars when we use them to attract people who are gamers. This also fits in with our responsible gaming approach. We're not trying to create new gamers. But we are trying to secure a share of the wallet of gamers. So we work hard to identify people who are gamers and make them aware of Harrah's. Our message is: This is a great place for serious gaming with excellent rewards and friendly dealers. We have an environment that a gaming customer will enjoy.

On occasion, Harrah's advertises its brand names in large metropolitan markets such as the Greater Chicago Area where there are two Harrah's casinos, one in East Chicago (which is in Indiana and actually 30 minutes from the Loop), and another in Joliet, just southwest of Chicago. Here, the company promotes the Harrah's brand name via the local media and promotes both hotels, taking advantage of economy of scale—two-for-the-price-of-one advertising. When Harrah's opened its second riverboat casino in Joliet in 1994, its budget was limited when compared to today's budget, and the cost of advertising in the Chicago area was high. But it was a new ballgame when Harrah's acquired Showboat, Inc., in 1998, with properties located in Atlantic City; Las Vegas (which has since been sold); Sydney, Australia (which also has been sold); and East Chicago. To take advantage of the Harrah's brand, the East Chicago casino had a name change from Showboat to Harrah's. It wasn't until March 1999 when the renaming occurred that a move was made to take advantage of the company's brand name. It was an immediate shot in the arm for the East Chicago property; overnight, it attracted large numbers of Chicagoans who regularly frequented Harrah's in Las Vegas. Michael St. Pierre, general manager of Harrah's in nearby Joliet, says:

Now that we rebranded the Showboat/East Chicago property, we can do partnership promotions with our sister property. We have a combined advertising buying power of two properties with one message. As a result, no other casino in this area can match our advertising power. While the East Chicago casino targets a slightly different geographic segment than we do, there's a lot of cross-over play between our two casinos. In fact, 7 percent of the coupons we redeem through our database bounce-back program are cross-property coupons from East Chicago. At one time, these offers were exclusively for our Joliet property, but now we promote both casinos.

Joe Domenico, who has served as general manager of the East Chicago casino since Harrah's acquired Showboat, concurs that certain synergies benefit both properties:

> There's a 20 percent cross-over between the two markets, and we share in our overall marketing efforts. Chicagoland's population is close to 11 million, so the cost of advertising one casino is very expensive. Did you know that this is the third largest and the fastest growing gaming market in the country? Besides that, it's one of the largest feeder markets to Las Vegas. A tremendous number of gamers in this area are Harrah's customers in Nevada, so we want their business when they visit casinos in Chicago.

When it comes to encouraging customers to visit its casinos in other markets, no company does it better than Harrah's. The Harrah's brand benefits its casinos in destination markets such as Las Vegas, Lake Tahoe, and New Orleans because its customers who have good experiences at local casinos in markets such as Chicago, St. Louis, Kansas City, or Atlantic City choose Harrah's when they go to destination markets. The local Harrah's casinos benefit from the company's brand name because they can award their customers trips to company-owned casinos in destination markets. The local Harrah's casinos also benefit from the company's respected national reputation.

In markets such as Las Vegas or Atlantic City where casinos are bumper-to-bumper and within walking distance of each other, it's not uncommon for customers to try to change their luck by spreading their business among several casinos. "We know this is going to happen," says Frank Quigley, table games vice president at Showboat in Atlantic City, "so the challenge is to make our other property the second stop. If they're going to go somewhere else, they may as well stay with Harrah's and keep it in the family. Our cross-marketing strategy is very focused on providing incentives to accomplish this."

Equally important, like people on a family vacation who stop at a Wendy's or a Holiday Inn because they feel comfortable with the quality of service, casino customers also like to have a seamless experience when they gamble. Is this because consumers are creatures of habit? To some extent, yes. But the reasoning goes beyond that. Rich Mirman explains:

> When one of our customers from East Chicago goes to Joliet or Las Vegas, we know him, and we have complimentaries for him. Even though it may be the customer's first visit to the sister casino, this customer has a relationship with us. Our technology allows us to track all of our customers in our database, so we'll treat him with

the same comps he's used to receiving at his local casino—it's not just based on his play on that particular trip.

In the old days, it was based on personal contact with pit bosses and casino managers. A casino manager on the floor personally knows a customer and what his play is. Today, a customer identifies himself when he registers in the VIP area, at the gaming table, or for that matter, by placing his player's card in the slot machine. Once identified, we can treat him like the loyal customer he is—even though it may be his first time in a particular Harrah's casino. Our proprietary technology makes this possible.

The seamless experience that Harrah's creates from one property to another goes beyond comping known customers. George Dittman, director of marketing information planning, says:

A lot of our customers tell us they gamble to relax and escape from everyday cares and worries. Our high-end slot players, for example, like to visit our lounge where they can get away from the gambling scene. And, of course, it's important to provide them with an environment where they feel comfortable—and it's nonintimidating. This is especially true when they're losing and feeling unlucky. When an employee interacts with them when they're losing—perhaps a warm greeting or a friendly chat—this can make the difference between having them stay at our casino or go somewhere else to try their luck.

It's also important to acknowledge that our customers don't gamble 24 hours a day. Obviously, they need to take breaks from the gambling, so we must provide them with ancillary things to do. Here, we must offer them fine restaurants, entertainment, and shopping—this is especially true in a destination market.

For anyone who has visited several of the 26 Harrah's properties across the country, it's immediately apparent that they're definitely not cookie-cutter casinos like, for example, a McDonald's or a Dunkin' Donuts. In fact, their differences are striking if you compare Rio with Ak-Chin, New Orleans with Laughlin, Lake Tahoe with Shreveport, and so on. Michael Silberling, general manager of Harrah's in Reno, explains how this is beneficial to customers:

This brand, at its best, allows people to sample each different property. If you're a golfer, you could be out at Laughlin on the Colorado River, or in Reno on a gorgeous course nestled in the Sierra Nevada, at Lake Tahoe at Edgewood on the water, or at Rio Secco in Vegas where Tiger Woods' coach Butch Harmon has his famous golf school. Each is a different experience and yet complementary to the others. Then there's the rush and excitement of being on the Strip in Vegas, or stepping back a little in time with a slower pace that you'll experience at Harrah's here in Reno. Remember now, some people don't eat the same flavor of ice cream every trip to the ice cream parlor.

Most interesting is the fact that Harrah's seeks to provide its customers with a seamless experience even though its properties cater to diverse niches. The Rio and Lake Tahoe properties, for example, cater to a higher-end customer. Both of these properties have super deluxe suites that compete with those at Bellagio and the Mirage. At the other end of the spectrum are the Harrah's Cherokee Casino in North Carolina and Harrah's Prairie Band near Topeka, Kansas, that cater mainly to quarter slot machine players.

The company's biggest profit-making property, Harrah's in Atlantic City, has as its niche the high-end slot customer. General manager Dave Jonas explains:

> We promote it as "the better Atlantic City" or "the other Atlantic City." We focus on the serious slot customer. Again, our niche is the AEP as well as the VIP customer. Our high-end customers are serious about their slots just as people take their hobbies such as golf or fishing seriously. These customers will put three $100 coins at a time in slot machines, and some have annual budgets in excess of $500,000 for their slot machine recreation. One of our biggest slot customers is a Fortune 500 company heir, but he's a low profile kind of guy and you would never know it.

Creating Customer Loyalty

Gary Loveman describes casino customers as "promiscuous" because when they visit destination markets, they go from casino to casino. "I'm in the business of fostering customer monogamy," he says half-seriously, "like the Ladies' Temperance Movement."

The company conducted a study of customers who visited Harrah's at least once a year. This research revealed that of every dollar of customer losses, Harrah's got only $0.36—the other $0.64 went to other casinos. Loveman states:

> If we could raise that by just a penny, our annual earnings would jump by more than $1 a share. On the surface, that one cent doesn't sound like a lot, but I can quantify this. An increase from 36 cents to 37 cents on the dollar is a cash flow improvement for Harrah's in the neighborhood of $20 million. By applying the usual multiples that exist in gaming industry asset valuation, you'll get a shareholder wealth creation. Divide it by the number of shares outstanding, and it turns out to be around $1 a share, and it's absolutely

independent of capital. By 2001, Harrah's upped that 36 cents of customer losses to 42 cents.

A former Harvard Business School professor, Loveman insists that the consumer behavior of gaming customers is quite different from that in other industries:

> When I first consulted Harrah's, it clearly didn't make sense to me. When you look at the dry cleaning industry, for instance, people don't go to a different dry cleaner every time their clothes need to be cleaned. Nor do people go to a different auto mechanic every time their car needs repair. The same thing is true with your pharmacist or hairdresser. Women go to the same beauty parlor for 10 years and never consider going someplace else. It's not price that wins the loyalty of these customers. It's more about trust-based relationships. But when we did our research, we found that none of the same dynamics were working in this business.
>
> With this information, I concluded that casinos weren't offering the right loyalty-inducing incentives to their customers. In some cases, this loyalty is based on monetary incentives. We had to provide ways to make it financially beneficial for our customer to come to us. This led us to believe we could also win their loyalty with great service and marketing inducements.

Las Vegas on the Strip is unlike any other gaming market. Nowhere else do visitors spend the same amount of time going in and out of casinos, exercising so many options to see novelties such as white tigers, battling pirate ships, Egyptian pyramids, the canals of Venice, the Eiffel Tower and the Arc de Triomphe of Paris, and street scenes of New York. While there are other destination markets, Las Vegas is truly an anomaly in the gaming industry. There's no place like it on earth. Still, after one or two visits to those casinos, you've seen it, and there's no compelling reason to go back. Gary Loveman explains:

> In other markets, customers aren't interested in visiting other casinos. They'll stop in once to check it out, but that's it because casinos are casinos—slot machines in every casino all have pretty much the same yield, and gaming tables are the same wherever you go. It's not like going to a fine restaurant, or deciding on whether you want to eat Chinese, Italian, or French. Casinos have a standardized product. This is why we concluded that the loyalty factor in the casino business should pretty much work like it does in the dry cleaning business.

Loveman admits that comparing the inordinate casino business to the ho-hum dry cleaning industry is somewhat of a stretch. However, his point is well taken. Customer loyalty is equally important in both industries. Loveman has the numbers to back up his statement. His research reveals that the average couple who comes to Las Vegas for three nights and four days visits seven casinos.

Rich Mirman hails American Airlines as the first company to start a loyalty program:

> They were very good at communicating to their customers that 20,000 miles earns a free ticket. As a result, customers started to consolidate their travel on American. One problem, however, was that many customers who fly American will never accumulate enough miles to earn a free ticket. So, to these customers, the big pie-in-the-sky reward wasn't attainable. And if it's not attainable, it has no value to customers. Eventually, the airline realized it wasn't driving much incremental business associated with the program, with the exception of its top customers. Consequently, it partnered with Citibank, and this created liquidity in the program. Now, it was possible for many more customers to accumulate 20,000 miles by supplementing the travel rewards with those granted due to credit card purchases. Before teaming up with Citibank, only the travelers at the top of the pyramid were rewarded. The Citibank connection made the free trip reward attainable to many more customers. I believe this is exactly what a loyalty program should do.
>
> There are four elements of a successful loyalty card program. First, it must provide something perceived to have value to the customer. Put another way, the customer has to want it. Second, a company must clearly communicate what it takes to earn the valuable rewards it offers. Third, the program must be marketed so it creates aspiration. In the case of American Airlines, its customers can earn a trip to an exotic place that they always dreamed of going but was beyond their budget. Fourth—and this is how a company benefits— it must provide an incentive that makes the customer consolidate his or her purchasing—this is what creates greater market share.

Here's how this works with a gaming customer: Let's say a customer has a budget of $400 to gamble during a visit to Atlantic City. The customer may think about taking his or her money and distributing it equally at four different casinos. This means Harrah's must properly communicate to him or her that by exclusively consolidating play at its casino, he or she has a chance to receive a valuable comp. Knowing this, the customer may reconsider visiting other casinos because he or she knows that by wagering only $100 at four different casinos, it won't be enough for any one casino to comp him or her. As with American Airlines, the Harrah's tier program enables its customers to accumulate value over a period of time. But, if an airline customer flies a limited number of miles on many airlines, he or she won't qualify for a free trip on any airline.

Mirman emphasizes that the success of an effective loyalty program has both long-term and short-term incentives. Looking at the long-term side of the ledger, customers benefit by choosing Harrah's over other casinos because, over time, they build a more valuable relationship with the company than if their business had been divided among several casinos. On the short-term side of the equation, Mirman states:

> Our customers at the gaming tables know that if they average, say, $25 per bet and play for four hours, they will receive a specific comp. With the slot machines, our customers know that if they receive X amount of credits based on their activity broken down by time and the amounts of their wagers, they will be rewarded a steak dinner, show tickets, or whatever they select from the reward menu. So here, we give them a short-term incentive to stay at Harrah's rather than going somewhere else. This facet of our loyalty program makes them think, "If I go across the street to play, I'll miss out on my goal because I won't accumulate as many credits at Harrah's, nor will I from another casino."
>
> Another feature of our loyalty program is that we make it easy for our customers to know how many credits are due them. This information is easily accessible to them throughout our casinos at kiosks and Gold Card centers, or by visiting our Web site. Any customer can go to any Harrah's property and have immediate access to his or her account. None of our competitors have the same capacity.

Filling the Casino during Slow Times

Most businesses have slow times. During the off-season, retailers have their winter and summer sales; airlines offer cheap tickets for weekend travel; restaurants have "early bird" specials. Being in both a highly labor-intensive and capital-intensive business, casino managers work diligently to bring customers through their doors during their slow times.

This is why Bill Harrah started the industry's first busing program in 1957—he was looking for a way to generate traffic to Lake Tahoe during the harsh winter months. To many, the idea of busing people in from northern California seemed far-fetched and economically unsound. But Bill Harrah did his homework and calculated his costs compared to his potential revenues. He figured it was a sound business decision. Although Harrah's was shelling out a hefty monthly sum of

$40,000, it paid off handsomely, and to this day, many casinos still have a busing program. Now, it's no longer a matter of busing in people over otherwise impassible roads through snow-covered mountains; it's more about attracting crowds during the week and during slow seasons. Casinos are generally packed with customers on weekends—this is why, depending on the market and time of year, people are bused on Mondays through Thursdays—the slow days of the week.

At Harrah's Ak-Chin casino, for example, which is a 45-minute ride from Phoenix, chartered buses are routinely sent to senior citizen communities to pick up customers. Another attraction is the daytime entertainment, which is free during the afternoon at the Ak-Chin casino. Performers from the 1960s and 1970s such as Percy Sledge, B. J. Thomas, and Bo Diddly are featured, because the older crowd likes them.

During its early days, Harrah's in Kansas City had as many as 200 buses each month hauling in customers. They came from Wichita, Topeka, and even as far away as Oklahoma City. The casino is just five minutes from downtown Kansas City and, typical of Harrah's casinos in local markets, 80 percent of its business comes from a 50-mile radius of the property. The property also has a 10,000-square-foot convention center used to promote weekday business during slow periods of the year. This facility is also used for winter boxing matches and all of the property's entertainment events.

The company's most extensive bus program was at Harrah's in Atlantic City during the early 1980s. "We were busing in 100,000 people a month," tells Joe Domenico, who was the property's vice president of casino operations before being tapped for the position of general manager at the East Chicago property in 1998. "In the beginning, we were losing $600,000 a month. To make it profitable, a bus program has to move rated customers, that is, customers that we know play enough to bus them in. Once we built up a base of rated customers in Atlantic City, the bus program became profitable."

Domenico points out that today at Harrah's in East Chicago, 20,000 to 25,000 customers are bused a month, about 10 percent of the casino's business. "Seventy percent are from the Chicago area," he explains, "but we bus them from as far away as Michigan and Wisconsin. About 60 to 65 percent of them are rated, which is the highest percentage in any market. As far as I'm concerned, if you don't bus rated players, you shouldn't have a bus program."

Today's busing programs differ from market to market. At Harrah's in Reno, for example, the casino offers a limited busing program that caters to people living in the Bay Area's Asian communities. "Here, the focus is on AEPs," explains Michael Silberling, general manager. "It's a chip buy-in program, which means these bus customers are required to buy a certain amount of casino chips that we call 'dead' chips. The chips can't be taken to the cashier and cashed out. The customer gambles with them, and replaces them with 'cashable' chips."

One of the most effective promotions to draw large crowds during slow weekdays is to have a drawing with a grand prize. Ginny Shanks, vice president of marketing for Harrah's Western Division, explains how this typically works:

> We have Wednesday afternoon drawings at our Ak-Chin casino, where $10,000 in cash is given away. Based on a customer's play activity on the previous Wednesday, he or she receives so many entries for the drawing. Now to be eligible, you must be present the following Wednesday. Since Wednesday is the slowest day of the week and an extra 2,000 customers may come as a result of the drawing, at $5 a person, it's an inexpensive acquisition tool. Of course, each customer's play is counted on that drawing day, and again he or she accumulates entries for the following Wednesday, so it keeps generating what we call "repeat visitation."

The most popular major prizes are automobiles, cash, and vacation trips. "At Lake Tahoe, we'll offer a package to Rio that includes a round of golf at the famous Rio Secco Golf Course," Shanks tells. "Likewise, during the hot summer months in Las Vegas, a trip to the mountains at Lake Tahoe is a popular prize. Of course, packages to our other properties reinforce our cross-branding marketing program."

All Harrah's properties have a Total Rewards Give-Away program. No purchase or play is required for entry, but where legal, additional free entries can be obtained based on gaming activity. A customer who visited a Harrah's property in June, for instance, receives a letter that invites him or her back for a drawing in July or August. Better players receive bonus entries. Like the Ak-Chin Wednesday drawings, a drawing is held on a slow day, perhaps a Sunday afternoon, which is a big checkout day, and this generates incremental visits. Again, the prizes are substantial—for instance, a Porsche—and you must be present to win.

Slow times aren't limited to certain days of the week—business slows during certain times of the year—and in the casino business, different seasons attract different customers. In Las Vegas, spring and autumn are the most popular seasons—and the best weather. Vegas is also packed during the summer—even though the temperatures can average in the low 100s for weeks at a time. But the summer is not the season that attracts high-level customers. It's more for tourists. The high-level customers are more likely to come during the spring and autumn seasons.

In New Orleans, however, where the weather is hot and muggy in the summertime, the hotels drop their rates and the town is packed with tourists—and this is good for the casino. Bill Noble, general manager of Harrah's New Orleans, explains:

> There aren't a lot of conventions in the summer in New Orleans, and we've learned that peak convention periods are not peak casino periods. As a rule, conventioneers are not the best segment of casino guests. There's a lot competing for their time. It's also difficult to get a room in New Orleans during the busy convention periods—and the room rates can be high. A basic casino formula has always been to offer reasonable pricing for hotel rooms and for food and beverages. If you come out of the gate with a high retail price for lodging, it keeps a lot of gamblers away.

Repeat Visitations

"Everything we do in marketing is motivated around either extending the length of play or motivating a second trip," explains Gary Loveman.

Here, Harrah's shares a philosophy with all successful companies. Like all great retailers in every industry, repeat business builds market share. This is true with consumer goods products—from gasoline to toothpaste. The same applies to all service industries—from accountants to stockbrokers. Winning customer loyalty is essential.

Giving customers an incentive to come back is the reason it's mandatory to be present for drawings to win large cash prizes, automobiles, and paid vacations. One program offered new customers who signed up for gold cards reimbursement up to $100 of losses for their first half-hour of slot machine play—but they had to come back within 31 days to collect it. Incentives that may include comps such as free rooms, meals, and shows are routinely mailed to new Total Rewards members—all to prompt them to come back within a certain time. David Norton says:

> Some of our properties have what we call "bounce back" offers. Here, a customer earns cash based on his play during a particular visit. He'll receive a coupon of, say, $10 or $20. On his next visit, these coupons can be cashed in at a kiosk—he doesn't even have to go to the Total Rewards desk. At some properties, instead of receiving cash, his card can be inserted in a machine at the kiosk and a comp coupon for a free lunch or dinner will be printed out. In the past, we

gave a 5 percent cashback at the end of the day. So a customer who bet $500, playing $0.25 and $1 slot machines, would receive $25. But we want our customers to have an incentive to come back, so instead of giving them immediate cash, a coupon is mailed at the end of the month. In some markets, people didn't want to wait that long, so to be competitive, they can come back the next day to get their cash. Note, however, that we don't have to give anything to those who don't come back. By doing this, we increase the 'breakage' by not paying what they've earned. In our business, the breakage is the difference in the value of the total offers (cash, coupons, etc.) made and what's paid out. The name of the game is to get them to come back, so why reward a customer if we're not going to see him again?

With our cross-marketing, we'll mail coupons to our Las Vegas customers to give them an incentive to visit a nearby Harrah's property where they live. For instance, customers in the Midwest might get an offer for a free room at one casino in Chicago or St. Louis. Likewise, a Harrah's customer who visits Las Vegas from New York or Philadelphia might receive an offer to visit our Atlantic City property. Of course, we'll also make offers to Harrah's customers from all our markets to visit our Las Vegas properties.

Dan Nita, a financial vice president, explains:

We're constantly testing our direct mail offers to learn what really drives customers to come back. We might, for instance, send a $50 coupon to a certain group of customers who haven't visited us during the past 12 months, and, consequently, have a 5 or 10 percent response. That might look great, but we'll compare it to another group of customers who received no incentive. In some situations, we discovered that even more customers showed up that didn't receive the offer! So, we're constantly experimenting and fine-tuning our direct marketing, always working on ways to drive traffic into our casinos.

The Core Business

"Keep your eye on the donut, not the hole in the donut." This advice is so elementary, many tend to overlook it, especially in the casino resort industry where there is excessive activity 24 hours a day, 365 days a year. In effect, Harrah's is a multifaceted company that in addition to gaming consists of several businesses all wrapped into one that include:

1. A chain of hotels with more than 14,000 rooms.
2. A food and beverage business with annual revenues of $500 million—placing the company in the number 21 spot of the 1999 list of the largest U.S. food and beverage companies.

3. The leasing of retail shops, the total of which would fill a large shopping mall.

Then there is the entertainment side of the business that includes running nightclubs, the personal care side that includes health clubs and beauty salons, and so on. As mentioned earlier, it is a very capital- and labor-intensive business. Large sums of money are constantly changing hands, necessitating tight security measures. To further complicate matters, it's one of the most highly regulated industries in the United States. Overall, it's a business with many distractions.

With several "businesses within the business," it's important for the company to keep focused on its core business—gaming. At the time of the Holiday Inns merger, it became apparent that hotel executives and casino executives had different agendas—the hotel people wanted to fill up hotel rooms—period; casino people wanted to fill the hotel with known gaming customers. "We make considerably more money on casino customers than we do on hotel customers," Phil Satre asserts. "So, our objective is to maximize the revenue per available room for the casino. Unlike a hotel operator who keeps score according to high occupancies, we strive to put people in the hotel who play in the casino."

Just how right is Satre's assessment? In 1989, Harrah's in Atlantic City had earnings of $89 million—more than all 1,200 Holiday Inns properties combined.

Bruce Rowe, vice president of slot research and development, emphasizes:

> We're in the casino business, not the hotel business. We manage codependent inventories, which means our focus is on filling up the hotel with the right people. If they're not the optimal people, we feel it on the casino floor. In the past, some of our people tried to manage this company under the assumption that our game was average daily room rate. That's not our game. The same applies to our restaurants. Restaurants are not our reason for being. Like the hotel rooms, the restaurants support the core business.
>
> This holds true with the entertainment side of our business. I remember hiring a popular rock band because some people thought it was a good idea. But these entertainers were not for us, because they attracted an audience that was scary to our core customers. Hundreds of unkempt groupies adorned with tattoos and body piercing traipsing through our casino actually drove many of our good customers out the door.

Although competing casinos lease space to tenants that operate food establishments on their properties, Harrah's owns most of its restaurants. The company's two Las Vegas properties, Harrah's on the Strip and Rio, own more than 25 eateries. Why doesn't the company lease more space to restaurateurs? Marty Miles, vice president of food and beverage, explains:

> I don't want someone else to be responsible for my guest's experience. It's simple. Since we have a significantly greater vested interest in the relationship with the customer, I don't want anyone with less vesting to be in a position to affect it. For instance, we have several restaurants that are so booked on weekends, if you're not a platinum or diamond member, you won't be able to eat with us. We book reservations for our best customers. But an independent operator's agenda would be to fill the restaurant on a first-come, first-served basis. After all, what does he care about what goes on in the casino? We'll never make the kind of money selling a steak that we make with our core customer in the casino.

A Different Las Vegas Marketing Strategy

There's a new kid on the Strip. The Venetian has come up with a new marketing strategy. Sheldon Adelson, founder and chairman of Las Vegas Sands, Inc., the parent company of The Venetian, is a well-known entrepreneur in town, and he doesn't have a gaming background. Listed in *The Forbes 400* as one of America's most wealthy individuals, Adelson made his first fortune by creating and developing COMDEX, the tradeshow that's hailed as the premier event for the worldwide computer industry. In 1995, Adelson sold that business to Tokyo-based Softbank for $900 million. Two years later, he began construction on The Venetian, a casino mega-resort with 3,036 luxury suites covering nearly 7 million square feet. The standard size of every suite is 700 square feet, which qualified it as an entry in *The Guinness Book of World Records* for having the largest standard hotel room in the world. All rooms have Italian marble, wrought-iron railings, and plush furnishings costing about $20,000 per room. The property includes the Sands Expo and Convention Center, the only privately financed, developed, and operated convention center in the United States.

With his nongaming background, Adelson is considered a maverick in Las Vegas. (The locals refer to him as a convention guy rather than a casino guy.) What's unique about The Venetian is that its core business is not gaming. While it's true that it has its share of slot machines and gaming tables, it was built to be a comprehensive, multifaceted destination resort for leisure travelers, commercial travelers, conventioneers, and gamers. Adelson's business model calls for his $2 billion-plus property (including planned additions) to be a destination resort that features world-class retail shops, internationally famous restaurants, best-in-class health spa facilities (Canyon Ranch Spa Club), state-of-the-art convention settings, *and* the traditional casino and entertainment accommodations known only in Las Vegas. Therefore, while gaming is a profit center for The Venetian, it's not the core business. The Venetian derives 40 percent of its profits from gaming; the other 60 percent comes from its hotel, resort, and conference operations. This is in contrast to the other Strip properties that make their money in the casino and comp food, beverages, and rooms to their high rollers. Yes, The Venetian comps its best gaming guests, but a much higher percentage of its guests pay the full fare for their rooms, which averages $205 compared to $90 for other Vegas hotels. While $205 is the highest average room rate in Las Vegas, it's a bargain compared to other destination cities such as New York, San Francisco, or Atlanta where comparable luxury suites would be triple the price.

Operating a colossal property of this magnitude in Vegas with a business plan that doesn't focus on gaming is indeed a bold marketing plan. Adelson has bet his chips on his belief that Las Vegas is the world's greatest convention town, and for fabulous facilities, business travelers are willing to pay rack rates for luxury rooms and exceptional dining sans comps.

As owner Adelson puts it, "I do not buy into the Las Vegas dogma that you can only make money in the casino, and in order to do that you have to give away the room, the food, and the beverages. Money is fungible, and you can make money from all the revenue centers."

Bill Weidner, the company president, has this to say about the company's strategy:

> First of all, no matter how many rooms we throw at the marketplace, Las Vegas weekends sell out. We looked at 1987 to 1997, and Las Vegas ran almost 95 percent that entire decade, even though the number of rooms went from under 50,000 to 100,000. Second, our mid-week occupancy can be filled with expo business like Comdex for about 35 to 36 weeks of the year, and the remaining weeks can be filled with meetings business. None of the hotels here that developed meeting space in-house actually reached out to that marketplace.

Since its opening, Adelson's game plan seems to be working well. Visitors who come to Vegas to attend a business conference don't seem to flinch at the prices at The Venetian. Remember too, they have expense accounts and their business travel is deductible. And compared to travel expenses in other cities, The Venetian is an incredible bargain.

Centralizing Management

Traditionally, the casino general manager always ran his own show. The consensus was nobody knew his customers better than the boss who worked every day in the trenches. In the early days of the industry, casino companies had only one unit, so the general manager and the CEO were often the same. The "home office" was usually located in the back of the casino or on the second floor.

Presently, the 26 Harrah's casinos are in 20 different markets throughout the United States. It wasn't until 1999, after nearly two decades of being based in Memphis, Tennessee—birthplace and hometown of Holiday Inns—that the company's headquarters relocated to Las Vegas. At the time of the Holiday Inns acquisition, it didn't seem important *where* the home office was—because Harrah's had plans to roll out a national distribution program, following in the footsteps of its parent company. However, as years went by after breaking its ties with Holiday Inns, Las Vegas seemed more logical than Memphis. Remember, too, that Memphis happens to be in one of only three states where all forms of gaming are banned. "It made more sense for us to be in the center of our universe," explains Phil Satre. "Plus, Las Vegas is a better base to recruit employees."

From a company treasurer's viewpoint, Chuck Atwood concurs. "When we were based in Memphis, analysts and portfolio managers rarely visited us. I might see three or four a year. Here in Las Vegas, I probably see someone from the investment community on an average of once a week. There's good reason for them to come here. If you are interested in buying a casino stock, this is where the companies are."

It's also healthy for corporate management to be closer to the customer—both the company's and the competition's customer. This way they get a better "feel" for the business. Although the previous headquarters was only a 30-minute car ride from the Harrah's casino in the thriving riverboat community of Tunica, Mississippi, Memphis is *not* Las Vegas.

Like Holiday Inns in its management style, the company now manages its 26 casinos from its national headquarters. Although everything is centralized, the casino general manager is still boss of his own show. He may receive his orders from the home office, but he's clearly in charge of his property. In this respect, corporate management plays an advisory role, providing support in areas such as human resources, law, marketing, public relations, and technology services. This arrangement provides a level of professionalism that would be unaffordable by a local property.

The company is managed as a system of casinos rather than as a set of individual casinos. This way, customers can perceive a value from viewing the company as a seamless brand of casinos, rather than seeing each property as an unrelated individual experience. With this structure, the company began Total Rewards, a loyalty program designed to generate customer loyalty by rewarding them for visits to every Harrah's property. Previously, each casino had its own card program. To execute this program, Harrah's concentrated its resources at a corporate level, led by a centralized management team. This strategy was in direct contrast to the rest of the industry, where each property operated as an autonomous unit. This was a revolutionary concept for the casino industry.

Beware of the Doomsayers

In the early years, not only did doubts exist in the industry about the controversial marketing strategy of Harrah's, but also there were doubting Thomases in the company. General managers at Harrah's properties initially balked: "These are *my* customers, and I don't want them going to another Harrah's property." In the old days, a person was a customer of a casino. The managers' message was loud and clear: "Don't mess with my customers." Cross-marketing may have been good for the company, but its general managers saw it as an infringement on their personal fiefdoms.

Former CFO Colin Reed compares resistance by the general managers to what he witnessed when he worked in the European hotel industry during the early 1970s:

> A general manager of a major hotel in, say, London or Paris, was a "god" to his staff. He probably spent 20 to 25 years learning at the feet of another god, so when he became god, he wanted to emulate the way his mentor operated the hotel. Consequently, each general manager had his own style of running *his* hotel, and this meant there were different standards throughout the hotel chain. Well, that's just the way the casino industry has been managed in this country. What's more, a general manager's background dictated how he ran his casino. A finance guy did it one way, a marketing

guy did it another way, and a guy who started in the casino as a dealer and worked his way up had his own modus operandi.

For instance, a general manager out of financing was a margin freak. He just wanted to control the margins of the business. If the guy was from the casino side of the business, he was generally good at building customer relationships. There was no standardization among our general managers. It was hit or miss, so we told them, "We must be a consumer-focused company, one that doesn't have a lot of fluff, so we can operate with the tightest possible margins. Everything we do must be through the eyes of the customer." This focus allowed us to build technology systems with the customer in mind. In contrast, many of our competitors think about things through the product lens—they think about big and glitzy because that's the way they were brought up in the business.

The general managers opposed cross-marketing because they didn't want to share their customers with other Harrah's properties. From their prospective, they worked hard to build their customer base, and they didn't see how having their customers go to another Harrah's property would benefit them. Therefore, while cross-marketing would make more money for the company, they viewed it as something that would take money out of their pockets. Explains John Boushy:

> The most important person in the field that I had to convince to buy into the cross-marketing concept was Steve Greathouse. At the time, he was general manager of Harrah's on the Strip. So much of the cross-marketing depended on having huge numbers of our Vegas customers visit casinos in their local areas—and vice-versa. That's because we used this flagship casino in Vegas as a carrot at our other properties in our marketing promotions. It was terribly frustrating because I knew this property would ultimately be the biggest benefactor from cross-marketing, yet Greathouse was my strongest critic.
>
> One day I said to him, "I'd like to have a one-on-one conversation with you, Steve. There are several topics we should discuss." He agreed to meet with me.
>
> We talked about some minor issues, and then I said, "Steve, I would really like to talk about cross-marketing, and I would appreciate it if you'd let me take you through it. I need about a half-hour of your time. Is that okay with you?" He reluctantly consented to hear me out.
>
> "Steve, I think I have a way to make it possible for you to grow your revenues at anywhere from 5 to 10 percent a year over the next 12 months for the next three years. I think I can do this at a rate that's no worse than your present overall margin and probably better."

"I'm listening," he said.

"Here's what customers are doing, I continued, showing him charts and figures I had compiled. "Here's where they're visiting, and here's how much they're not spending with you. Now here's what happens if they do stay in your hotel. Wouldn't you rather have somebody who's a known gamer stay in your hotel than someone whose gaming is questionable, such as a tourist? Of all the general managers in all our properties, you have the most to gain, and I'm at a loss why you're resisting this."

He just sat back and thought about it for a while. "Nobody has ever explained it to me this way before."

After that, he became a strong supporter. At the next operations committee meeting, I announced that Greathouse was now in favor of cross-marketing, and I could sense the momentum shifting around the room among those present. I have since referred to that meeting as a real defining moment for this company. The clincher was when Phil Satre wrapped up the meeting by announcing he was 100 percent convinced it was the right marketing strategy for our company.

The outright contention was expressed not only by general managers. There were managers in senior-level positions at corporate headquarters who had opposed the new marketing strategy. Phil Satre explains:

Many questioned the changes we were making, and some were quite candid with me about expressing their views. The dissenters expressed: "Harrah's will run better as an operating company without a corporate strategy. The new strategy will require significant resources and entail major operating expenses. The high costs associated with implementation are not warranted."

By 1995 to 1996, the marketing strategy was well underway, and while there was some progress, there were also several setbacks. For instance, we had some problems with our casino in New Orleans, and some of our riverboat casinos were off to a slow start. These properties simply weren't getting the right results from our branding and distribution strategies. And for that matter, neither were we realizing loyalty from our target customers—if we were, it wasn't making much of a dent. Concurrently, we had invested heavily in technology, but we didn't have all the talents it took to use it.

What we needed was a stronger cultural shift between the corporate organization and the operating organization. The operating organization still wanted to remain autonomous. So, if a general manager liked something we were developing at corporate, he would use it, but if he didn't like something, he ignored it. Some of them conceded that our marketing strategy might work for other casinos but not theirs. Consequently, we were getting uneven application. We simply weren't moving rapidly enough to implement the marketing strategies and the loyalty strategies we had built.

One day when Colin Reed was in my office, he said, "The platform is in place, but we must move faster to arrive at our goal." His remarks confirmed my thinking that we needed a combination of changing the culture at the properties and enhancing the capabilities at corporate. This meant bringing in high-level talent from the outside.

I went through a period when I questioned if we were using the right strategy. I asked myself, "Should I be trying to create an umbrella that hooked all these properties together?" I knew we were doing something that had never been done by anyone else but then I had some self-doubts that there may be a reason why other casino companies didn't follow this path—something, perhaps, I was missing. Then I asked myself, "Should I eliminate the $40 to 50 million of overhead that all goes to the bottom line?" All I'd have to do is tell our general managers they can run their own show again and allow them to be autonomous just like our competitors are. Sure, I'll come around to measure their performances, but that would be it from the corporate side. I had many sleepless nights thinking about whether I made a mistake.

In hindsight, I underestimated the challenge to implement the marketing strategy, plus there were a few areas where we failed to do what we thought we could do. Sure, there were moments when my confidence was shaken, because by 1997, I could see that the company had not coalesced culturally, nor for that matter, had it executed to my expectations. To get the level of execution I wanted, I had to get rid of the naysayers—the people who were stuck in the past and refused to move forward. This meant bringing in some new talent.

These were challenging years for Harrah's. In the end, Satre's strong will and determination won the day. He was certain the company was on the right path, and he had little tolerance for rigidity and inflexibility. Consequently, some high-level executives either resigned or were dismissed.

It was Mike Rose, Phil Satre's predecessor, whose words summed it up best. Years ago, he had informally said to a group of executives that included John Boushy: "There are three kinds of people—those who make it happen, those who watch it happen, and those who wonder what the hell happened." Having said this, Rose paused and added, "There's a fourth kind of people. Those are the people who get in the way of things happening."

6

WINNING
WITH PEOPLE

EARS AGO, SHORTLY AFTER THE EMPLOYEE BOARD OF REVIEW WAS formed, Bill Harrah fired his chauffeur. The disgruntled driver took the matter directly to the review board. After hearing his side of the story, the board members voted to reinstate the chauffeur. His dismayed boss abided by the decision.

A stickler for rules and regulations, Bill Harrah tolerated no double standard. Whether it would benefit him or not, he put up with no such behavior from anyone—not even himself. His employees may not have agreed with everything that was "company policy," but the majority of the workforce felt good about the company's rules and regulations. Those who didn't like the rules left on their own accord—or were eventually discharged. It was unmistakably Bill Harrah's company. Like many other successful entrepreneurs, he ran his firm as a benevolent dictatorship.

Harrah was a highly principled businessman who worked hard to build a reputation of integrity for his casino. At a time when Las Vegas was regarded as the underworld's playground, in Reno and Lake Tahoe, Harrah's was regarded as squeaky-clean, a reputation that enabled the company to attract the best people. Those who came aboard took pride in their affiliation with the company.

Edwin Wessel, a longtime pit supervisor at Harrah's in Reno, describes working for the company during the Bill Harrah years: "People were proud of the fact they worked at Harrah's. I can recall when somebody would say, 'Where do you work?' and I said, 'Harrah's!' It was something to be proud of because of the standards for personnel and the impeccable integrity of Harrah's itself. Everybody knew that it was run like a regular business, and there were no shady things going on at Harrah's."

When new people joined the company, they became "Harrahized." If a new employee made a mistake, an old-timer might give the excuse, "Well, she hasn't been Harrahized yet."

In the 1999 publication *Every Light Was On*—a 437-page oral history about Bill Harrah based on interviews of 20 employees and two of his wives—unwavering commentary confirms that the company was governed by specific procedures for just about everything. There were even procedures on how to follow procedures! Rome Andreotti, a longtime employee and one-time president of Harrah's, was one of the company's most obedient soldiers. Because Andreotti strictly adhered to his boss's insistence on detail, from time to time he was criticized for nitpicking. But, like all Harrah's managers who held high positions in the company, Andreotti dutifully and respectfully went by the rulebook—no exceptions.

The company was managed by a simple philosophy: If you don't take care of the little things, you won't take care of the big things. James Caselli, who began his Harrah's career in 1958 in Reno and worked there for 28 years, talks about the company's covenant to detail:

> Little things, like he would only serve the best whiskey. Old Crow, Smirnoff, Cutty-Sark—those were the bar pours. Now, nobody in the world at that time was pouring Old Crow, Cutty-Sark, Smirnoff vodka, and Gilbey's gin as a bar pour. These weren't premium drinks; these were the bar pour! So all of this together adds up to give the customers the feeling that they were walking into *the* best, they were going to be treated to the best, and the accommodations were the best. It just built up, and it also built up with the employees.

The constant accent on excellence wasn't just for show. It was everywhere in the company, at every level. Everything had to be sparkling clean and first-class in the kitchen, backstage, dressing rooms, and employees' lounges. Guests or customers wandering through a building got the same impression behind the scenes as they did out front in the casino.

George Drews served as executive vice president of finance and administration in the 1970s and was the company's first Harvard Business School graduate (class of 1947). He saw the strict attention to details as a source of pride for employees. He believed these disciplines permeated the organization, particularly when it came to extending courtesy and friendliness to customers. For this reason, he stated:

> We were so proud to be there. We always wanted to make it better and better. I think he created that atmosphere. We were so enthusiastic about the company that we didn't need any kind of prodding at all. Never. Absolutely never. We were always just absolutely doing our best.
>
> The other thing is if somebody didn't do their job and wasn't superb, they were gone quickly. However, there was never a fear for people that were good employees. There was never a fear of getting fired; but if you weren't a good employee, you were gone—no ifs, ands, or buts about it.

Although he was a strong disciplinarian, Harrah was soft-spoken and has been described as an introvert. He rarely gave a direct order. Instead, he would ask, "What do you think about this?" or "Don't you think we should do this?"

Harrah was also quick to praise employees. Verna Harrah, his wife at the time of his death, tells, "He made people proud, and he always would say to someone, whether it was the lowest janitor or the highest executive, 'You're doing a great job.' He really appreciated every single person. As far as he was concerned, Harrah's was a family, and that's how he made people feel."

A striving for excellence and a sense of pride are legacies Bill Harrah left behind. These qualities remain deeply instilled in the company's culture. During the days that Bill Harrah headed the company, his insistence on perfection became his trademark. Those who bought into his philosophy were not only proud to be associated with the company, but also fiercely loyal employees—so loyal and dedicated that the environment at Harrah's has been described as cult-like.

In their esteemed book *Built to Last*, authors James C. Collins and Jerry I. Porras emphasize that great companies such as IBM, Wal-Mart, Nordstrom, and Walt Disney Company also have cult-like cultures, a quality that contributed immensely to their success. Collins and Porras tell of one Nordstrom employee who "gushes with the excitement of working with the very best—being part of the elite of the elite—very proud to call herself a Nordstrom employee."

This sense of pride instilled in Nordstrom employees begins early on when each employee receives a five-by-eight-inch card that reads:

Welcome to Nordstrom *

We're glad to have you with our Company.
Our number one goal is to provide *outstanding customer service*.
Set both your personal and professional goals high.
We have great confidence in your ability to achieve them.

Nordstrom Rules:

Rule #1: Use your good judgment in all situations.

There will be no additional rules.

Please feel free to ask your department store manager, store manager, or division general manager any questions at any time.

---

* James C. Collins and Jerry I. Porras, *Built to Last*, New York: HarperCollins Publishers, 1994, page 117.

Thomas J. Watson Jr., IBM's former CEO, described the company his father founded as having a "cult-like atmosphere" during its rise to national prominence in the first half of the twentieth century. Thomas J. Watson Sr. consciously set about to create an organization of dedicated zealots. Watson plastered the wall with slogans: "Time lost is time gone forever," "There is no such thing as standing still," "We sell service," and "A company is known by the men it keeps."

Like IBM and Nordstrom, the Walt Disney Company has made extensive use of indoctrination, tightness of fit, and elitism as key parts of preserving its core ideology. The Disney cult even speaks its own language. Employees are *cast members,* customers are *guests,* a work shift is a *performance,* a job is a *part,* a job description is a *script,* a uniform is a *costume,* the personnel department is *casting,* being on duty is *onstage,* and being off duty is *backstage.* When a Disney employee is asked what the company does, he or she responds, "We make people happy."

Harrah's is in good company with other organizations that have thrived with cult-like cultures. Apparently, the concept of being Harrahized is similar to being "Nordstromized," "IBMized," and "Disneyized."

The Gridiron Lesson

To number 52 senior linebacker Phil Satre, the 1970 Stanford football season seems like a lifetime ago. That's the year the Indians had a 9–3 season, enough to win the Pac-8 and a berth in the Rose Bowl.

In 1970, Richard Nixon was president of the United States and still a well-respected leader. It was a good year for the Stanford football team, but not a particularly good year for America. United States casualties in Vietnam totaled 44,241 dead and 293,529 wounded. Four students in a protest march at Kent State were shot and killed by National Guard troops. Four New York-bound airliners were highjacked in Europe that year, and a 747 was forced to land in Cuba. Whites in South Carolina stormed buses to prevent integration. The Penn Central filed for bankruptcy reorganization. On a less serious side, the first Monday Night Football was aired, marking the first time a football event appeared on prime time television. *Patton, Airport,* and *M*A*S*H* were big movie hits, and the top television shows were *The Flip Wilson Show; Marcus Welby, MD; Hawaii Five-O; Gunsmoke;* and *Bonanza.*

All that was going on in the world seemed far removed from Phil Satre's world on an idyllic college campus in Palo Alto, California. His focus was on football and, perhaps, to a lesser extent, his studies.

As Satre looks back, the lessons he learned on the gridiron were as important as those taught in the classroom. He says:

> Coach John Ralston taught us something about life that has stayed with me throughout my business career. The university had not played in the Rose Bowl since 1952, and in order to reach that goal, the team had to win the Pac-8 championship, which in those days basically meant beating USC. The Trojans had dominated the league since the era of O. J. Simpson and continued to do so through 1969. So more than anything else, Coach Ralston worked on having the team envision that it could beat USC. Starting back in our preseason practices in August 1970, he set a goal to beat USC and had us visualizing what we'd have to do to win. He even brought in some people who coached us on visual imagery. While beating USC was our prime goal, Ralston applied the same imagery exercises to every game that season, because our sights were on a Rose Bowl trip.
>
> Once we won the Pac-8 conference, we had a still bigger challenge—on January 1, 1971, we were facing the Ohio State Buckeyes, the number one team in the nation. The Buckeyes came undefeated to Pasadena, and their seniors included several players destined to be drafted in the NFL's first and second rounds. Ohio State's roster had All-American candidates such as Jack Tatum, John Brockington, Rex Kern, John Hicks, and Jim Stillwagon.

There is no question that the Buckeyes were far superior athletes and a strong favorite to win the game. Los Angeles columnist Jim Murray wrote that the computer that could compute the odds against Stanford hadn't yet been designed. Satre continued:

> Going up against Ohio State presented a whole new challenge. We had to prepare for a foe unlike any team we previously faced. Most of us on the team would have agreed that had we played them four times, in all likelihood, we'd lose four consecutive times, and if we ever won a game against them, it would be something we couldn't repeat. So, we accepted the fact that we were the underdog. To win, we'd have to come up with a strategy that would neutralize the impact of their All-American linebacker Jim Stillwagon and do the same to their All-American fullback John Brockington, because we knew Ohio State would eat up the clock with their ground game. So, our game plan was to strike fast and score. To take Stillwagon out of the game, we had to make our quarterback Jim Plunkett and his receivers more effective.

Stanford stuck to its game plan and forced Ohio State to play catch-up football. In the final quarter, Ohio State was behind 20 to 17 and forced to pass, when Stanford intercepted the pass on the Buckeye 25-yard line. The Indians scored on a Jim Plunkett pass to Randy

Vataha, Satre's roommate, winning the game 27 to 17. The Stanford victory marked one of the biggest upsets in the history of college football. Satre explains:

> That season influenced my business career because it made me realize that a team, or for that matter, any organization, can set a goal and with the right planning process, achieve success. That's what we are doing at Harrah's. We create a vision of the future, and then we think through what we must do to achieve our goals. We also identify what the hurdles will be, and what we must do to overcome them. I'm very grateful to Coach Ralston for providing such a valuable lesson to me.

Employee Loyalty and Customer Loyalty

You can't talk about employee loyalty without talking about customer loyalty. The two can't be separated. Study any successful company, and you'll discover how the two work in tandem. People feel good about themselves when their company provides a fine product and outstanding service. Likewise, customers are likely to be loyal to a company with loyal employees.

Customers can sense how employees feel about their jobs and employer. They recognize when employees are treated well and take pride in their company. That's because this pride comes through in an employee's tone of voice, facial expression, and body language. In the retail business, customers sense it in the way a store clerk greets them. Customers sense whether an employee wants to be at work or not. Customers can tell whether a salesperson's suggestions are genuine and sense whether service will be cheerfully given after the sale. A salesperson's subliminal signals can make customers feel comfortable about their buying decisions.

The previously mentioned cult-like companies produce employees who become eager zealots. Every individual wants to carry his weight and not let down his coworkers. Thus, all employees work in harmony, going forward as a team.

Conversely, people feel shame working for a company that makes a shoddy product or fails to deliver on its promises. Studies have shown that when companies take advantage of their customers, employees take advantage of the company. Companies that cheat their customers are more likely to be cheated by their employees. In severe cases, employees steal from inventory. "Why not?" they rationalize. "I'm just getting my share." Some employees "steal" by coming in late, leaving early, taking office supplies, using their expense accounts on personal business, and so on. They behave improperly because it's part of the company culture.

It's a two-way street. Employee loyalty inspires customer loyalty—and the lack of employee loyalty has a devastating effect on how customers feel about a company. Likewise, customer loyalty inspires employee loyalty. A customer's vibes about a company impact employee morale.

In a 1994 *Harvard Business Review* article titled "The Service-Profit Chain," five members of the Harvard Business School faculty and service management interest group wrote: "Profit and growth are stimulated primarily by customer loyalty. Loyalty is a direct result of customer satisfaction. Satisfaction is largely influenced by the value of services provided to customers. Value is created by satisfied, loyal, and productive employees." This study stated that incremental increases in customer loyalty can be traced to substantial bottom-line results. Low employee turnover was closely linked to high customer satisfaction. Gary Loveman, now chief executive officer and president at Harrah's, was one of the five authors of the 1994 report, and he has helped the findings in this article become gospel at Harrah's. Consequently, the company has a strong awareness of customers' loyalty to its casino employees, such as dealers, pit bosses, and VIP hosts. As a result, in spite of the traditionally high turnover of personnel among these casino employees, Harrah's boasts a lower-than-average turnover, an achievement that produces a quantifiably improved bottom line.

The company's focus on employee satisfaction isn't limited to the casino floor. It extends to all employees, even those not in direct contact with customers. As the study revealed, service employees place a high value on having the ability and authority to achieve results for customers. Internal quality is also characterized by the attitudes that people have toward one another and the way people serve one another inside the organization. While it is doubtful that Bill Harrah had ever heard of the service-profit chain, it has long been a part of the company's culture, and today's Harrah's, with revenues of around $4 billion, enjoys a corporate culture centered around service to customers and fellow employees.

In Pursuit of Quality People

The slogan "You win with people" is not a catch phrase at Harrah's. Much of the company's current success can be attributed to the special talents of people brought in from outside.

Gary Loveman is one such person. Before coming aboard, he was an associate professor at Harvard Business School and had received his training as an MIT economist. Loveman was introduced to the company by Stephen Bradley, also a Harvard faculty member. Loveman's previous consulting assignments were mainly with large consumer-service companies such as Walt Disney, McDonald's, and International Service Systems in Copenhagen. During the mid-1990s, Loveman served as a part-time instructor for Harrah's in-house executive training program called *Excellence in Management*. He conducted the program semiannually for a group of about 30 middle-level managers. His mission was to teach them higher level managerial skills with an emphasis on strategic thinking. He gave them projects to work on with the purpose of having them move to the next level in management. His teachings required participants to implement higher levels of service. Soon, Loveman became a "regular" consultant to the company, helping develop a marketing strategy to build customer loyalty.

"Gary was a dynamic speaker," tells Satre, "and I was hearing a lot of rave reviews from our management teams that interacted with him. Some of our general managers hired him for some small selected consulting assignments for their local properties. In 1997, I invited him to make a presentation on branding to our top 15 branding people."

Over a period of time, Satre began to rely on Loveman's advice for still more projects—in particular, a branding strategy at the time of the Showboat acquisition. Satre understood that while developing marketing strategies is a difficult task, implementation could prove even more arduous. Satre's main interest was implementing an effective plan to simultaneously operate Harrah's and Showboat in Atlantic City as two separate brands. Satre focused on the Showboat people's concern that the merger could cause their property to lose its identity. All the while, Satre was convinced that the future of Harrah's rested on its being a centralized marketing company. He had toyed with this premise for several years, and, in fact, once brought in a VISA executive who had headed the credit card company's marketing division. This executive had strong credentials, having also been employed by Procter and Gamble, a recognized premier consumer product marketing organization. The executive had been employed for two years at Harrah's when it was mutually determined that the gaming industry, a highly nontangible service industry, was not his bailiwick.

Satre explains:

We struggled for the last six months of 1997 without filling this position, and it had become evident we needed somebody from outside the gaming industry to implement our marketing strategy. We had developed our Total Gold program, the forerunner to Total Rewards, and we had our WINet marketing system in place, which is our national customer database. I needed to find somebody strong to fill this position, and I thought about several people within our company, as well as in the gaming industry. I even considered hiring a search firm. Not knowing which way to turn, I decided to make a pilgrimage to a man I greatly admired, Sergio Zyman, Coca-Cola's marketing guru at the time. If anyone could advise me, it would be Sergio.

Coca-Cola had been a longtime Harrah's vendor, and it was this relationship that led Satre to seek Zyman's advice. In December 1997, Satre boarded a company jet and met Zyman at the Coca-Cola hangar in Atlanta. It was a fruitful two-hour meeting. Satre explained his business plan to the soft drink executive and presented a job description of the person he was looking for.

"'Sergio, I'd like you to give me some names or places to look for a really strong marketing person,' I said. Then I went through a job description for the marketing position I needed to fill.

"'You don't need a chief marketing officer,' Sergio replied. 'What you need is a chief operating officer who is a marketer.'"

Satre explains:

His thinking was that the implementation of marketing a business like ours doesn't occur in a marketing department but in operations. At the time, I was wearing four hats—chairman, CEO, president, and chief operating officer. I knew what I wanted but also realized that I had neither the time nor the skills to implement it. What Sergio said made sense. My background as chief operating officer of the company made me realize what he said was the way to control implementation. That's because when you have general managers and division managers reporting directly to you as chief operating officer, you control their capital and their human resources. You also have a big say in how they are compensated and rewarded.

I spent the Christmas holidays taking time off to be with my family, but I did put in a call to Gary Loveman to arrange for him to attend a meeting with the Showboat management team in January with me. "Gary, I want you to work closely with me on the integration of this company and, in particular, on the Showboat brand." Three days before the Showboat meeting, I was in my Memphis office preparing for my Atlantic City trip and thinking about my conversation with Sergio, when suddenly a lightbulb went on. "Gary Loveman is the man to fill the marketing position!"

I immediately called Gary. "We're scheduled to be at Showboat at 9:00. I have to talk to you before the meeting. How about joining me in my suite at Harrah's for a 7:30 breakfast?"

Gary accepted my breakfast invitation, and then I started thinking about what his reaction might be. I knew he was intrigued with our company. That was obvious since the very first day he walked into our casino and began consulting us. I knew he was fascinated with our strategy to pursue the demand side and he liked the fact that it was so different from the supply side strategy of our competitors.

Before meeting with Gary, I was on an airplane with Colin Reed discussing the company's lack of focus on marketing. We talked about not having anyone in our organization who was strong on the marketing side. Colin pointed out how we were slow at making decisions to integrate technology and marketing. "We aren't forcing our businesses to embrace the technology side," Colin stressed. "I've been debating about bringing Gary Loveman in, Colin. What do you think?" "It would be a good thing," he agreed.

At my breakfast meeting with Gary, I wanted to probe to see if he had a visceral connection with our operations, our people, and our customers. I was convinced that this quality was crucial because in order to lead people in this industry, there can never be any doubt about one's commitment to the company's employees, the customers, and the industry. By the end of our breakfast, I felt assured Gary had this visceral connection.

"Gary, I want you to consider this offer," I said. "I would like you to come in as the chief operating officer of this company. In this capacity, the executive vice president of this company and the division operating officers will report to you. The entire marketing function will also report to you. You will be given the responsibility for the service strategy, the marketing strategy, and our operation strategies, and integrating them all under one roof."

I didn't have the slightest clue how he would react to my offer. He was noncommittal, but he did say, "I'd like to discuss it with my wife."

Loveman's version of the meeting is slightly different:

When Phil made me the offer, it struck me completely out of the blue. My first reaction was that my family loved living in New England. This thought prompted me to say, "Phil, I am interested, but my family will not relocate to Memphis. If that's a precondition, you will have to count me out."

To Phil's considerable credit, he replied, "I don't think that's a constraint." I asked him a couple of questions on how he'd make room for me to do what I needed to do, emphasizing that all of what he was offering me was presently under his control. I addressed this issue knowing so many Harvard Business School cases that were written about CEOs who had difficulty letting go enough of the operating business to have a COO function effectively. Phil assured me that I had nothing to worry about, and in retrospect, he has never interceded in a way that has stopped me from doing what I thought was right. Sure, there may have been one or two times when he's slowed me down, and on those occasions it turned out that he was right.

The timing of the offer worked nicely for Loveman:

I was at a point at Harvard where I felt like I had accomplished much of what I set out to do and didn't feel as if I wanted to continue to just do that forever. I had an urge to do something else, but at the same time, I hadn't given a moment's thought about taking a senior position at Harrah's or at any other company. I discussed it with my wife, and she was supportive. I also conferred with some of my colleagues, who, for the most part, thought it was a good move for me. My colleagues and I had often compared our work to that of a priest who gives marriage counseling. Like a priest, you give a lot of advice, but it's not something you personally experienced. So after nine years telling people how they ought to do something that I've never done myself, I had the desire to see if I could actually do it and make it work. Phil's offer was the right challenge, because the company wasn't doing what I thought it should do, so now I had the opportunity to do the job right.

In addition to receiving an opportunity to do the job right, Loveman also received a $1.3 million paycheck. Shortly after joining Harrah's, Loveman received a phone call from Rich Mirman, a former University of Chicago math Ph.D. student working for the Booz Allen & Hamilton management consulting firm in New York. Mirman, in his early 30s, had met Loveman, who was on a retainer with Booz Allen in Boston while on a consulting assignment, and ever since had considered the professor to be his good friend as well as mentor. Mirman tells:

When I overheard two partners in the firm talking in the halls, one said, "Gary Loveman joined Harrah's." Then the other guy said, "It doesn't make sense. Why would he go to work for a casino company when he could go anywhere?"

As soon as I heard that, I had to find out what was going on. I called Gary and left five messages, each time saying, "Gary, you have to call me. I need to talk to you." Later that night, he called me at home and took me through his thinking on why he took the job. When he finished, I said, "If there's any opportunity that comes up where you think I can fit in, I want to be part of it."

Harrah's Bingo Club in downtown Reno, 1953. Harrah got his start in gaming after taking over his father's bingo game near Los Angeles in 1929, but decided to relocate to Reno in 1937 following numerous antigaming crackdowns by California officials. The opening of Harrah's first Reno bingo parlor on October 31, 1937, is considered the birth date of Harrah's Entertainment.

Left: 1970s: Bill Harrah receives an award from the state of Nevada for the recognition of his famous Automobile Collection that featured more than 1,500 cars. His collection was shown all over the world.

Right: Actor Kirk Douglas visits Bill Harrah's automobile collection in the 1970s. Over a span of three decades, Harrah built the world's largest private automobile collection, featuring more than 1,500 vehicles. The collection, which once drew celebrities and VIPs from around the world, was sold off after Harrah's death in 1978. Its value today would have been more than $200 million.

Left: Sammy Davis, Jr. and Bill Harrah, mid-1970s. The legendary Rat Packer performed at Harrah's Lake Tahoe for 28 years, longer than any other performer.

Brochure for a Sonny & Cher show, 1974. Since gambling couldn't be promoted in advertisements at the time, headliners helped entice customers to visit a Harrah's casino.

Below: Bob Hope in the late 1960s entertaining guests at Harrah's.

Above: A 1973 show brochure from Harrah's Lake Tahoe featuring Sammy Davis, Jr. Stars from across the country were drawn by Harrah's impressive treatment of headliners. As Davis once said: "Any place you play when you leave Harrah's is roughing it."

Mid-1970s: "Ole Blue Eyes"—Frank Sinatra—and John Denver in a spectacular duo performance at Harrah's.

Above: October 1975. Frank Sinatra chats with crew members from the Apollo-Soyuz space mission following a performance at Harrah's Lake Tahoe. "It's the best hotel in the world," Sinatra often said of the northern Nevada resort.

Right: February 1982. Sugar Ray Leonard invites you to watch his training sessions at Harrah's.

Harrah's CEO Gary Loveman (left) and Chairman Philip G. Satre, in front of the all-new Harrah's Joliet Casino and Hotel. In 1993, Harrah's became the first major casino company to enter the riverboat gaming market and the first major company to open a casino outside of Nevada and New Jersey.

Chairman Phil Satre, a pioneer of Harrah's innovative consumer marketing techniques, stands proudly under the Harrah's globe.

Harrah's was the first to recognize the value of the slot-playing customer, installing more slot machines than any other casino.

The opening of Harrah's Ak-Chin Casino Resort near Phoenix, Arizona, in 1994 marked the first partnership between an Indian tribe and a major gaming company. Harrah's has since signed management deals to operate tribal casinos in Kansas, North Carolina, and California.

Harrah's—St. Louis, Missouri: All eyes are on the "new shooter coming out" luck of the dice roll, one exciting crap game at Harrah's.

Rio Rita and Harrah's model in front of "Rio" logo.

The glittery marquee of Harrah's on the Strip in Las Vegas.

The Mardi Gras-themed Showboat, one of Harrah's Entertainment's two Atlantic City resorts. Harrah's acquired the Showboat in 1998 as part of a $1.15 billion takeover of Showboat, Inc. The buyout was the start of an aggressive growth period for Harrah's. Over the next four years, Harrah's acquired three additional companies, giving it more properties than any other gaming operator in the world.

"I think there is," he answered. That was the beginning of dozens of 5- and 10-minute telephone conversations we had over the next few months. Two things he told me had piqued my interest. First, Gary said the company had already invested in the infrastructure, that is, the technology, to support what he wanted to do. Second, he insisted that there was a tremendous appetite to really make change. As a consultant, I had done a lot of work that has been well received by the few. So often, once a consultant's recommendations get to the most influential decision-makers, if they're not committed to it, nothing happens. Gary assured me, "I will make sure that what we do gets by the top all the way down. Phil Satre wants a corporate marketing team that drives change."

But what really sold me was when he said, "Rich, you're not going to come in to help build the best company in the casino industry—it's going to be the best marketing company—period!"

"Excellent," I kept repeating.

"We're not competing with other casino companies," he emphasized. "It's going to be the best marketing company in *any* industry!"

Gary invited me to the corporate headquarters in Memphis. "It's just going to be a formality," he said, "but I'd like you to come in and interview some of the guys."

I came in and my last interview was with Phil Satre, who I would meet for the first time. Phil was having a busy day, and in the beginning, he seemed somewhat distant. So there I was, sitting across from a CEO, and I'm telling my vision to him about what the marketing for his company should be, and I'm feeling as though I'm not connecting with him. Having been out of school for all of five and a half years, and I was starting to feel a little uncomfortable, even though I'm a relatively confident person. We had been talking for 15 minutes, and Phil seemed like he was anxious to wrap things up.

"Do you have any other questions?" he asked politely.

"Just one," I said. "I know Gary very well. We've worked together and I know his background. He was a professor, and I was a student. I'm familiar with his work, and I might be his biggest fan. So, I understand the brilliance behind your hiring Gary. But what I'd like to know is why you thought bringing him aboard was the right thing to do."

And boom—with that, Phil's eyes lit up. He explained there was a whole new market for the company to pursue, but it was dependent on assembling a team of world-class people. He elaborated on how the company's corporate scenario had grown fat. And because the company had consulted Gary for several years, Phil believed the company could move forward with Gary as its COO, heading its marketing strategy. We ended up talking for an hour and a half. And boy, did we connect. There I was, this nervous kid trying to connect with the CEO, and I did! It was just magical.

On his last day at Booz Allen, a senior partner called Mirman into his office. "We really like you a lot," the executive said, "and I understand that you and Gary Loveman are tight. I think you're making a good move, but I just want to make sure of one thing. Are you comfortable from a morality standpoint about going into the casino business?"

Mirman looked the executive squarely in the eye and replied, "I've worked with national credit card companies and have seen some sub-prime lending companies disingenuous about tying customers to a 25 or 30 percent interest rate. They do so with full knowledge that 20 percent of these customers will not be able to repay the loan. So I have to tell you, sir, I feel more comfortable about working in casinos, because up front we are completely open about the business we run."

After Mirman, Loveman recruited David Norton, a young executive from American Express. Today, Norton is the company's vice president of direct marketing. Landrum Fisher, who worked with Norton at American Express, was the next marketing person from the outside to come aboard. Then came Amanda Totaro, who had previously worked at MasterCard and Dime Bank in New York City. Like Mirman, none of the others had former senior management responsibilities, nor did they have casino gaming backgrounds.

It took courage on Satre's part to recruit people from the outside. It also took conviction to name a professor as his COO, which signaled the company to expect innovation. Satre believed he was doing the right thing and was willing to risk leading his company into uncharted waters. Rarely do leaders in corporate America dare to make such bold structural changes. When change of this nature happens—and works—it has a big payoff. Satre got his big payoff—one that was well earned.

With its distribution strategy, the company's rapid growth pattern requires constant recruiting. In today's tight job market, Ron Beronio, director of recruiting, serves as the company's "internal headhunter." In this capacity, he is constantly searching for managerial talent, both inside and outside the gaming industry. He focuses on filling director and vice president positions.

Why an internal headhunter? "Search firms charge 20 to 30 percent fees for their services," Beronio explains. "If we can find those people ourselves, the savings are substantial."

Like a professional headhunter, Beronio spends his time on the Internet and is continually placing calls to job candidates working for other casino companies. His searching doesn't stop there; he routinely calls middle and senior managers throughout corporate America. He tells:

> It's a relationship business. A lot of my calls are follow-up calls to see how people are doing, and, over time, they remember me when they think about making a change. Some of my best leads come from these people.
>
> Oftentimes I have to sell them on the gaming industry because they ask, "Tell me the truth. Is the mob still in this business?" Others have to be sold on living in Las Vegas. With them, I talk about the year-long good weather, the outstanding outdoor recreation opportunities, our major airport, and the excellent retirement communities in the area, and so on.

Marilyn Winn, senior vice president of human resources, tells:

> When we bring in people for executive positions, we want them to enjoy their stay, so we'll take them to our best restaurants and, if time permits, we'll invite them to a show. We want them to love our business. In fact, one of the questions I ask is, "Do you play?" People may answer, "Well, not very much," because nobody wants to say, "Yes, I'm a really big player." "What do you play?" I'll continue. "I play the tables," or "I play the slots." I want to make sure the people who join us truly love our business—the love is contagious.
>
> Naturally, I want someone who doesn't have concerns about gambling himself, nor for anybody else who gambles. If there's a moral issue about gambling, this is obviously the wrong place for him to work.

Sometimes, a family member objects. When Marty Miles first joined the company, his father asked him, "How do you feel about deriving your income from exploiting the weaknesses of others?"

"My father is very strict," says Miles. "He's a very religious man, and he doesn't drink and thinks drinking is a weakness. I've been with the company two years now, and my father has come to visit. Now, he's been to a few of our properties and has a better understanding of our company. Today, he understands this is truly entertainment and is not about taking advantage of weaknesses."

Hiring from Within

Marilyn Winn explains:

> We don't often recruit from other casinos because we think we're ahead of the curve in our industry. We don't want to bring somebody in who's back someplace where he or she has to catch up to

where we are. This doesn't mean there aren't some talented people with our competition who are also ahead of the curve. We'll often go outside our industry, but when it comes to filling positions in financing and gaming, we tend to recruit within our industry.

Before joining Harrah's, Winn worked in human resources at Abraham & Strauss Department Store in New York City, where she was in charge of training new employees. Following the birth of her daughter, she and her husband decided to leave the Big Apple and move to Las Vegas. They liked its climate and favorable tax environment, and in the event she chose to work again, its large service industry offered many opportunities.

In 1988, she read a newspaper ad for a training manager position at the Harrah's property on the Strip. She got the job and was soon promoted to cashier manager. Later, Winn became a human resources director and then human resources vice president for southern Nevada. Next, she became a slots director, and in 1997, she became the general manager for Harrah's in Shreveport. Winn was the second woman to serve as a Harrah's general manager. Janet Beronio was the first woman general manager in 1994, when the Ak-Chin casino near Phoenix opened.

"The biggest source of talent for filling a position of director and above comes from within Harrah's," Winn tells. "In the year 2000, for instance, of the 145 placements at these levels, 60 percent were from within. We post all of our jobs internally and any employee can go onto the Internet sites that we have to identify available openings."

One source of recruiting top people comes from the company's internship program. Six to 12 college students are hired each year for summer employment; most are recruited from prestigious law schools and business schools across the country. Top executives, including division presidents, visit campuses such as Arizona State University, Harvard, Dartmouth, UCLA, Northwestern, Cornell, Vanderbilt, and the University of Nevada in Las Vegas (UNLV). In addition, 1,500 applicants apply annually for an internship. Those selected are the cream of the crop. These summer jobs run the gamut: Interns work at different Harrah's properties as well as at the corporate offices in Las Vegas. The interns are well compensated and receive allowances to cover living expenses.

On graduation, two or three interns receive offers to participate in a fast-track management program called the *President's Associates Program.* One member of the program is Anika Howard-Weaver, who interned during the summer of 1998 while attending Arizona State

University where she obtained a dual masters degree—an MBA and a Masters of Science and Information System Management. Howard-Weaver was the first African-American woman to be accepted into the program. As an intern, she worked in the human resources department at the Memphis company headquarters.

"During my internship, I was like a project manager," tells Howard-Weaver. "The company was in the process of creating an online system to assist employees with their benefits. It provided such things as health care and 401(k) information to employees and new hires."

On becoming a President's Associate, Howard-Weaver began her full-time career with the company as the Internet marketing manager, based in Las Vegas. In the newly created spot, she describes her work as an "evolving position." Her responsibilities include developing and managing the company site, www.Harrahs.com.

Eric Persson was one of three interns invited to participate in the President's Associates Program in early 2001. Persson was contacted by the company after completing his second year of law school at Georgetown University in March 2000. He had previously worked as an executive assistant for the president of Coast Resorts in Las Vegas. Still in his mid-20s, Persson caught the company's attention because he was a high-profile student. No, he wasn't a college basketball star. Eric was the focus of media attention when he graduated from UNLV with five degrees that he earned in a four-year period—an amazing feat that had never been achieved in the United States. While it has not been documented, his achievement is believed to be a world's record. While earning degrees in political science, criminal justice, sociology, psychology, and communications, he had a 3.8 grade point average. How did he do it? By taking 152 credit hours in a calendar year. During one semester, he accumulated 47 credits and had a 3.98 grade point average, taking 16 classes, getting 15 As and one A–.

"The two keys to taking so many courses," he explains, "are time management and a lot of dedication. Once I decided what I wanted to do, I had to accept giving up a lot. I was in class from 8:00 in the morning to 9:30 in the evening, plus classes on Saturdays. I'd be home by 10:00, and I'd study until 2:00 in the morning. Then, I'd get up at 6:30 and do it again—every day, over and over."

But why did Persson do it? Here's what he explained:

I had an internship in Washington with Nevada U.S. Senator Bryan in 1996, and at a seminar, the dean of admissions at Georgetown Law School spoke about what it takes to be accepted in its law school. I had my heart set on Georgetown because it's in the nation's capital and I wanted to someday be in Nevada politics. When I looked around at the law school candidates I was up against, I knew I wasn't going to make it. I had two choices: I could lower my sights, or I could do something that would qualify me for Georgetown. That's when I decided to earn five degrees as an undergraduate.

Persson did something else perhaps equally amazing while he was a law student. During his second year at Georgetown Law School, he worked full-time for Harrah's, averaging 40 hours a week of work in Las Vegas! "I arranged my schedule so all my classes were from 8:00 on Monday straight through 7:45, taking courses primarily in corporate, constitutional, and criminal law. I'd fly to Washington on Saturday or Sunday night and be on the redeye flight back to Vegas on Monday night. I was able to buy my tickets in advance and, by flying at midnight, I had reduced fares. I accumulated so many frequent flyer miles, I was usually upgraded to first class, which gave me more frequent flyer miles. Plus, every five to six weeks, I'd accumulate enough miles to earn a free round trip.

During his internship, Persson worked in communications, headed by Jan Jones, senior vice president of public affairs. Jones, a former mayor of Las Vegas (1991 to 1999), twice ran for governor of Nevada as the Democratic Party's candidate. "Having the opportunity to work under Jan Jones, one of Nevada's highest profile women in politics," Persson expresses, "was an added bonus I immensely enjoyed."

As a President's Associate, Persson's first assignment was serving as an assistant to Tom Jenkin, general manager of the Harrah's flagship property on the Strip. Former President's Associates who today hold high-ranking positions include Timothy Wilmott, chief operating officer—a 1987 graduate of the Wharton Business School, University of Pennsylvania; Michael Silberling, general manager of Harrah's in Reno—a 1992 graduate of Anderson Business School, UCLA; and Tom Cook, assistant general manager of Showboat in Atlantic City—a 1995 graduate of Anderson Business School, UCLA.

The President's Associates Program has now been around for more than 20 years. It has been a boon for recruiting and developing bright, young people. "When I joined this company as general counsel in 1980 at age 30," says Phil Satre, "the next youngest executive was 45, with most of the others in their 50s and 60s. Very few had a college education, let alone graduate degrees. While I don't judge a person by his or her degrees, a successful company should have a good mix of people with various backgrounds and experiences. As a result of the program, today we have that much needed bench strength of young people."

There are many case histories of Harrah's employees who started at a low entry level and worked their way to key positions. Vern Jennings, for instance, began his career with Harrah's after graduating from high school in Reno in 1976. He tells:

> I parked cars during the summer and continued while in college for 18 months. Actually, that wasn't my first job with Harrah's—at age 14, I bused tables in the employee cafeteria. During the summer of 1976, I met my wife, who also parked cars and worked part time as a beverage attendant. Then I got a job in personnel as an interviewer while still in college. I liked my job so much I took a leave of absence from school after my sophomore year. When I was 25, I worked for the company in Atlantic City and later returned to Reno. In 1984, I decided to get my degree, so Harrah's arranged for me to go back to school full time and work part time at the Reno casino. I graduated in 1986 with a business management degree. In 1987, I went to Vegas to work in human resources.

Ten years later, when Harrah's opened its St. Louis casino, Jennings was named general manager. Of the five casinos in the market, Harrah's was dead last. By the end of 1998, with Jennings at the helm, Harrah's was the number one casino in the area. Today, Harrah's in St. Louis is the number one tourist attraction in the entire state of Missouri, with seven million visitors passing through its doors annually.

Tom Jenkin also had a humble start in the business. Having just graduated from high school, he went to work at Holiday Casino as a fry cook working the midnight shift. Holiday Casino was the predecessor to the current Harrah's site in Las Vegas. Today, he is the general manager of Harrah's on the Strip—the company's flagship property, a 2,560-room hotel-casino, and the upscale Rio, a 2,550 all-suite hotel-casino. From fry cook to general manager of two of the biggest properties in Vegas—that's quite an upward move.

Brandi Jarva joined the company in 1990, and she, too, started at an entry-level position. This bright, attractive woman was hired as a PBX operator, and now, at age 30, Jarva is director of VIP Services at Harrah's on the Strip. In this position, 18 casino hosts report directly to her.

Others who started at entry-level positions include Joe Domenico, general manager at Harrah's in East Chicago, whose first job was as an accounting clerk in 1980; David Jonas, general manager at Harrah's in Atlantic City, whose first job was as an internal auditor in 1982; Frank Quigley, vice president of table games at Showboat in Atlantic City, whose first job was a craps dealer in 1980; and Ginny Shanks, vice president of marketing for the Western Division, whose first job was clerking in the media department in 1983. These are a handful of the success stories of employees who worked their way up the corporate ladder. There are so many, in fact, that it's common at employee orientations for a senior person to tell how he or she worked his or her way up.

Relationships with Vendors

Everyone knows the importance of winning the loyalty of customers and employees. What's seldom mentioned, however, is loyal vendors. Generally, large companies have thousands of vendors. The list of Harrah's vendors can fill a small town's telephone book. Included are everything from suppliers of janitorial supplies and food products to service companies that repair slot machines, copying machines, and so on. Establishing lasting relationships with this army of vendors is crucial to the company's long-term success.

At Harrah's, each vendor is treated as an important team member. The company's respect for vendors traces back to the royal treatment given to entertainers—who, incidentally, also were vendors. True, they were famous show business personalities who attracted hordes of customers to the casino; therefore, understandably, they deserved the red carpet treatment. But at Harrah's, the VIP treatment doesn't stop there. Everyone deserves and *is* treated with respect; it's part of the Harrah's company culture, and it is extended to all vendors.

With thousands of vendors doing business with the company, it would take volumes to write about each; instead, three diverse and interesting vendors are highlighted here: Clint Holmes, an entertainer; Fairfield Properties, a timeshare company; and Butch Harmon, a world-famous golf instructor.

Clint Holmes receives top billing at Harrah's on the Strip as its headline performer. This gifted singer-dancer's talent is frequently compared to that of Sammy Davis Jr. Holmes' original show, *Takin' It Uptown,* is described as "an infectious combination of contemporary music and forgotten favorites performed by a classic song-and-dance man." Others simply describe the show as a mix of adult contemporary, jazz, a little bit of rock and roll, and some old-time favorites. During his act, Holmes wins the audience by telling interesting stories about his personal life, including one about how his father, an American jazz singer, met his mother, a British opera singer. Before starting his gig at Harrah's, Holmes and his family lived in New Jersey where he was a well-known entertainer in Atlantic City. Three times, he was named "Entertainer of the Year" in Atlantic City. Earlier in his career, he was an opening act for performers such as Joan Rivers, Don Rickles, and Bill Cosby. A poll by the *Las Vegas Review-Journal* voted him "Best Singer" in Las Vegas. Holmes received offers from five Las Vegas casinos to be their top act, but he chose Harrah's because of its reputation among entertainers as "the place that treats you like a star." Holmes describes signing a long-term contract with Harrah's in Las Vegas as an opportunity of a lifetime.

"In my business, there's no place on earth like Las Vegas," he says. "When you play here, you're at the top of your career. My wife and I bought a house here, and it's great coming home to be with my family every night. This sure beats being on the road, living out of a suitcase."

Harrah's is investing heavily in promoting Clint Holmes as its star attraction. But it's the word-of-mouth raves about Holmes that are making him one of the most popular acts in Las Vegas.

Fairfield Properties, a company that sells timeshares, is another Harrah's vendor. A division of Fairfield Communities, a New York Stock Exchange company, Fairfield sells vacation ownership units. Generally, each unit is purchased for a one-week-a-year visit to a Fairfield property such as Orlando, Florida; Durango, Colorado; Williamsburg, Virginia; or Las Vegas, Nevada. Fairfield is a member of Resorts Condominiums International, the world's largest exchange network, with an estimated 3,000 locations. This means Fairfield unit owners have a huge selection of places to visit. A customer who buys a unit in Las Vegas, for example—the average sale is around $12,000—isn't limited to vacationing only in Las Vegas. In fact, every buyer becomes the owner of a deed, and the location of the property is simply a place "to park the deed." That's because the owner might, in fact, vacation at the property that's been deeded to him or her only on rare occasion. And, he or she may choose to never visit it. With the huge choices of vacation spots to visit around the world, a unit owner uses "points" that are exchanged each year, depending on the property, because their prices fluctuate, and the length of the stay varies. Available properties are listed in a company publication and can range from luxurious beach resorts to ski resorts. Even cruise vacations are available.

Fairfield's 450-unit Las Vegas 15-story apartment building will be owned by 22,500 owners (450 units × 50 weeks = 22,500). This calculation is based on deeding each owner a one-week unit.

So, what's the connection between Fairfield and Harrah's? With the thousands of tourists who pass through its casino every day, Harrah's on the Strip is an ideal place for Fairfield to sell timeshare units.

"We both cater to the same customer," explains Wilson Moore, Fairfield's corporate vice president. "Our demographics match perfectly with Harrah's. Typically, it's a married couple with 2.3 children, making between $50,000 and $80,000. They are middle-aged baby boomers who want to travel, but they don't want to wait until they're retired. With so many potential customers going in and out of Harrah's, there's a built-in market here.

To attract Harrah's customers to hear a 90-minute sales presentation, Fairfield offers a choice of two tickets to the Clint Holmes' show or $50 in casino chips. Signage at various places in the casino informs customers of its offer. Unquestionably, some people sit through the sales presentation simply to receive the giveaway.

Explains Steve Thull, Fairfield's vice president of sales in Las Vegas:

> We know some people have no intention of buying a timeshare unit. They only sign up to see the show or get the free tickets. But we also know that once they hear what we have, they'll buy because it's a great deal and fits their needs. Every marketing company has a cost to get warm bodies through their doors, and to Fairfield, the money we spend with this approach makes a lot of sense to us. If we didn't do it this way, we'd be spending money on something else such as direct mail and television commercials. But with the traffic that goes through the Harrah's casino, this has been a real home run for us.

It has been an equally good deal for Harrah's. Initially, Fairfield had a small ticket booth in the casino; time-share prospects who signed up for sales presentations were bused off-premises to Fairfield's sales offices. The Harrah's-Fairfield alliance has proven so successful, however, that Fairfield Properties now leases 14,000 square feet of office and showroom space on the second floor at Harrah's on the Strip, where its sales staff give on-premise sales presentations.

Today, in addition to receiving rent from Fairfield, Harrah's benefits in several ways. First, Fairfield promotes the Harrah's brand to its 300,000 members throughout its worldwide system. Keep in mind that Fairfield and Harrah's customers have similar demographics. Second, there are between 2,000 and 3,000 telemarketers who contact prospects nightly. Every night, these salespeople extend invitations to prospects to visit Las Vegas and stay at Harrah's. Third, on completion, 450 of the Las Vegas timeshare units will have prospects with free shuttle service to and from Harrah's. As Tom Jenkin put it, "This is like having an extra 450 rooms in our hotel."

The Fairfield connection has also been a boon to vendor Clint Holmes. "We purchase a block of tickets for his show," Thull points out, "so typically, 25 to 30 percent of his audience comes from us. With the tickets we purchase, Holmes plays to a full house on a nightly basis. And as somebody once said, 'It's always better to have people lined up waiting to get in than to play to an empty house.'"

Moore says:

> In some of our other locations across the country, we sell travel packages at discounted prices that promote coming to Las Vegas and staying at Harrah's. So, it's a two-way street. Harrah's generates business for us, and we do the same for Harrah's.
>
> We chose Harrah's over any other casino company because, like our company, we both have national distribution and listings on the New York Stock Exchange. We also liked the way Harrah's thinks outside the box. This company is willing to do things that haven't been done before in this business. Here, I commend General Manager Tom Jenkin, who championed the Harrah's-Fairfield relationship and is allowing it to grow.

While many people associate timesharing sales organizations with high-pressure sales, this is not the case with Fairfield at Harrah's. "I'd call us a soft-sell company," explains Thull. "We're very sensitive to the fact that we're at a Harrah's property, and we're dealing with their customers. We can't afford to alienate their customers, because if we do, Harrah's isn't going to want to have us around. We truly bend over backward serving as goodwill ambassadors for the company."

Butch Harmon, acclaimed the world's greatest golf teacher, is also a Harrah's vendor. He is deserving of such accolades because he is the current coach of Tiger Woods, the world's best golfer. Harmon also coaches golf greats such as Davis Love III and Mark Calcavecchia. For years, he coached Greg Norman.

Harmon tells:

> I had received a lot of recognition for being Greg Norman's coach, and he had just won the 1993 British Open. That's when I received a call from Tiger Woods' father. His son was only 17 at the time and was playing in the United States Amateur Championship in Houston at the Champion Golf Course. He had lost either his second or third match. His dad asked if it would be okay to bring him over to meet me on Saturday. The three of us had lunch, and I watched him hit some balls. That Sunday, he hit some more balls, and they must have liked what I said because a few weeks later, his father asked if he could turn his son over to me so I could take him to the next level. He felt that he had taken him as far as he could. Although Tiger wasn't very polished in the way he hit balls, I was impressed with his

raw talent. He hit the ball a tremendous length, had a great imagination, excellent short game, and lots of creativity. Plus, he had a real desire to learn, something he has to this day. That's the beauty of Tiger—he continually wants to learn and get better. I could just tell that, with some direction, this kid was going to be unbelievable.

The Woods family were not wealthy, so I told them I'd be happy to work with him for free. Later, when Tiger turned pro, I'd send them a bill. And that's what I did. Today, I go to about 10 to 12 tournaments a year with him, plus we tape every shot he makes during the tour on television. Just about every day we go over his swings and discuss every competitive round he plays.

When Rio purchased the land for its Rio Secco Golf Club, Harmon called the casino's CEO, Dave Hanlon, and explained his concept about a golf school. Harmon explains:

There are golf schools all over, but I had something different in mind. Rather than a school that runs large numbers of golfers through it, mine would keep down the ratio of students to professionals. There would be eight students and five professionals in a class. I felt Las Vegas was the only place a school like this could make it. That's because, with the large numbers of people who come here to have a good time, and with a casino using the golf school as an amenity, it wouldn't have to show a tremendous profit. But it could pay for itself.

The opportunity to be instructed by a man who was hailed as the world's best golf teacher was also a big drawing card.

"I told Hanlon, 'We'll give them a golf experience that's truly unique.'" Harmon says.

"Hanlon liked the idea and took my proposal to Tony Marnell, Rio's owner. They were still in the process of constructing the course designed by Reece Jones. They gave me an end of the driving range, knocked down some mounds, and said, 'You design this area like you want it.'" Harrah's took over Rio Secco when the company acquired Rio in 1999.

Today, in addition to a team of world-class golfing instructors, the Butch Harmon School of Golf has, as Harmon describes it, "the finest technology and camera equipment money can buy. We've upgraded our computer systems four times because we insist on having state-of-the-art equipment." It also has the best learning system. The current three-day package with Harmon costs $4,600 per student and $2,600 with the other staff professionals. A one-day package with Harmon goes for $2,250. At these rates, Harmon acknowledges it's undoubtedly the most expensive golf school in the United States. The three-day packages include four nights' accommodations at Rio, and the one-day packages include two nights at Rio. Harmon's rate for private one-hour lessons is $500, while his other staff professionals charge $150 per hour.

The golf school, which is not available anywhere else in Las Vegas, is a major attraction that Rio offers high rollers. It is an amenity no other casino can duplicate—in short, one of the best comps in town. Harmon personally teaches 30 to 32 schools a year, all booked solid well in advance. However, when Rio asks that the school include a VIP customer, Harmon says, "They call me, and we take care of him. That's part of our job.

"The Harrah's people have been behind us 100 percent. When my contract ended in 2000, I had no desire to leave, so we renewed it. I get along wonderfully with the Harrah's people. I am proud to work with them."

Clint Holmes, Fairfield Properties, and Butch Harmon are but three of thousands of vendors that do business with Harrah's. Each is considered a valued partner by the company.

Similar to the relationship that exists between Harrah's and its vendors are those with government agencies. Richard Klemp, corporate director of government relations, works full-time assuring that the company maintains excellent relationships with local and state authorities. If anyone at Harrah's knows how to build a partnership with state agencies, it's Jan Jones, who has served as a high-ranking elected official. She believes public perception of a company is vital to its overall success. Jones cites pharmaceutical companies as a prime example.

"They've spent hundreds of millions of dollars positioning their companies as a progressive industry that takes its profits and reinvests in research so they can save your mother," she says. "That's their message. And why do they tell it? They don't want price controls, and they don't want the government coming in regulating or taxing what they do."

When it comes to corporate-government relationships, Jones is an expert. "There's nothing wrong with self-promotion. I think you're making a mistake if your company doesn't promote itself."

Jones believes it's good business in a highly regulated industry to build ongoing relationships with government regulators. "You build them when times are good and you communicate with them. If you see them only when something's gone wrong, you're going to have a problem."

Harrah's has a long history of building bonds with state regulators. In 1959, when Gene Evans was hired as the company's director of community affairs, he advised Bill Harrah:

Bill, they passed a law legalizing gambling. And if they can give it, they can take it away. One of these days, somebody could get up and say, "I want to pass a bill to outlaw gambling." If they do, it's going to require votes right here in Carson City. If you can get people here involved, and if they believe in what you're doing—that you're an honest gambler supporting your community and state—you're protecting your investment.

Dean Hestermann, director of public affairs, emphasizes that Harrah's is a strong proponent of strict regulation:

There is an alignment between the government's position and ours on virtually all of the regulatory issues. We want to make sure that the games are fair. We want to make sure that the operators have integrity beyond reproach. We want to make sure that appropriate measures are taken for pathological gamblers. So, we play the role of the White Hat Cowboy. For example, we oppose video gambling in taverns because we know it spells trouble, and it could come back to haunt the entire gaming industry. For this reason, we are always encouraging the rest of the industry to be accountable to high standards. We can't twist anybody's arm, but we can set high standards and hope our competition realizes the wisdom of them.

The Screening Process

It is a safe assumption that Harrah's will open and/or acquire other properties during the next decade. With its distribution strategy in place, the company is in a continual expansion mode. Harrah's is what an investment banker would typically refer to as a "growth company." To achieve this planned growth, the company must promote employees from within and concurrently recruit people from outside. Marilyn Winn explains:

Our major constraint for our growth is our ability to recruit, develop, and promote talent. Right now, we have 20 jobs at the level of director and above that are open, plus another 30 manager jobs to be filled. We're constantly looking for good people, but where we encounter the most problems is finding qualified personnel to place in our properties located in isolated communities with populations under 100,000. We have properties in places like Vicksburg, Shreveport, and Cherokee, North Carolina—many people aren't interested in relocating to these areas. They don't have the shopping, the arts, the professional sports teams, and some of those other things some people think are important. This is why I tell our employees that the fastest way to get ahead is not to be too particular about where the company may ask you to move. People limit their opportunities for advancement when they're willing to live only in Atlantic City, Chicago, and Las Vegas. As senior vice president of human resources, I like it when someone has worked at various Harrah's properties and has been trained under two division presidents. They get more exposure this way.

When it comes to recruiting casino people, Harrah's has a long history of selecting friendly people with a desire to serve people. This tradition is part of the company culture and is practiced today much like it was when its founder was personally hiring. Tom Jenkin, general manager at Rio, explains:

> People come to a casino to have a good time. At Rio, the same customers might stay at Bellagio or the Mirage, so to compete with the top properties that offer fabulous amenities, we must provide an upbeat, fun, exciting environment. To do that, our employees must be friendly and make customers feel comfortable when they visit us. This is why we focus on hiring people who are outgoing and truly enjoy talking to customers. It's more than a winning personality; it's an attitude they have. If we can get this kind of people, we can always train them to do the technical aspects of the job.

Harrah's has long had the best reputation for training casino employees. Larry Kennedy, an assistant casino shift manager at Harrah's on the Strip, can attest to this:

> In 1972, I applied for a job at Harrah's in Reno and was turned down. They weren't hiring anyone with casino experience. Now that's a twist. They wanted to train people their way. I was devastated because I always felt it was the best-managed casino in the business, as well as the one that treated its employees the best. Every time I walked into Harrah's, I noticed their people were professional, and above all else, they enjoyed their work. Most of all, everyone seemed so proud to work at Harrah's. Later in my career, I worked my way up to a shift manager at the Hornsby in Carson City, and anytime someone would apply for a job with us and had worked for Harrah's, I'd go out of my way to find room for them. That's because they were professional, polite, and so good with customers.

It wasn't until 1989, when the company acquired Barney's in Lake Tahoe, that Kennedy joined Harrah's:

> I heard Harrah's needed people desperately and for the first time was hiring outside help to work at Bill's (renamed from Barney's). I walked away from a manager's job to start over again as a dealer— just so I could finally work for Harrah's. I was lucky because eight months later, Harrah's stopped hiring people from other casinos. I

had to go through a lot of training that included classes on dealing, customer service, and Harrah's procedures. It was like starting all over again. But it was worth it. The company has the best benefits and 401(k) program in the industry. And because the company owns multiple properties, employees can transfer to an opening in other areas. That's how I ended up working in Vegas. I'm always keeping my eyes open to see what jobs are posted.

Every interviewee is asked specific questions during the interview process. Basic questions that apply to casino and restaurant jobs are obvious, such as: "Are you of age to do this job," and "Are you willing to work in areas where people smoke?"

Marilyn Winn says:

We also inquire about an employee's willingness to work on weekends, holidays, and during odd hours because we're open 24 hours a day, 365 days a year. This means our employees have to be willing to work at times when other people have time off. Working in a casino means being here versus being with your family on such holidays as Labor Day weekends, Thanksgiving, and Christmas. Then there's our busiest night of the year—New Year's Eve. Not everyone is willing to work when our people must be here.

Geoff Andres, director of table games of Harrah's in Las Vegas, emphasizes:

Our standard interview questions are, "Do you have any shift preferences or shift requirements?" and "Do you require certain days off?" We do have day, swing, and graveyard shifts. If someone wants a nine-to-five job, this business is not for him.

To work in a casino, you have to have a different philosophy about your job. I consider the two days I have in the middle of the week as my "weekend," and my family and I have adjusted to it. In my mind, it has its advantages, because the golf courses aren't crowded and the show tickets are more available on these weekdays. Sure, it takes some adjusting, but you get used to it. For instance, my family celebrates Thanksgiving a day before or after Thursday, and our Christmas isn't celebrated on the same day that everybody else does.

The casino industry has a high turnover of employees, due, in part, to the hours they work. Then, too, some jobs are harder to do than they appear. For this reason, recruits are taken on the casino floor to observe a Harrah's employee at work. Marilyn Winn says:

For example, a woman applying for a job as a cocktail server might say, "I hear a server makes a lot of money on tips." She'll be told, "But she works hard for it, and we'd like you to see for yourself what she does." On the casino floor, she can see what clothes and shoes she will wear, the tray she will carry, and how heavy it is. She will also see the aisles she will have to maneuver through, how she may have to bend over to pick up the glasses, and so on. We want her to know exactly what she'll be doing because sometimes a job may seem more glamorous and exciting than it actually is. For this reason, it's important for people to know it's really hard work.

While there are standard questions in employment questionnaires, each Harrah's interviewer has his or her own favorites to ask. For instance, one favorite question asked by Marty Miles, vice president of food and beverage, during an interview is: "How would your most recent supervisor describe your personality at work?" Another favorite of Marty's is: "Think of a time when you personally improved the customer's experience. Tell me exactly what you did."

Miles explains:

I ask questions of this nature to interviewees who don't necessarily have experience in our industry. These questions would apply to just about anyone—a shoe salesman, a receptionist, or an insurance adjuster. The answers I'm looking for are ones that illustrate how the job candidate was able to change a bad customer experience into a pleasant experience. We have questionnaire forms that ask questions of this nature, and we can quickly evaluate certain behavioral patterns that determine who is likely to excel in specific positions.

Mike Vitale, a table games supervisor at Harrah's on the Strip, first submitted his application to the company online:

Then I came down and met with the casino manager, who, in turn, sent me to the human resources department. I've worked at several casinos, and this was by far the longest process I ever went through to get a job. Besides giving me a personality test and a math test, interviewers asked me dozens of questions to determine if I was the type of person who was acceptable at Harrah's. Later, a vice president interviewed me and asked how I would handle certain situations such as: "Let's say a dealer came in late from his break—how would you handle it? Would you speak to him or just write it up?" The vice president explained, "I want to hire a supervisor who doesn't hassle people but instead coaches people. You must be willing to help people through their weak moments in the day and strengthen them rather than break them down."

I couldn't understand why they asked some of the questions they did, but once I started the company's training program, everything began to make sense. I began to realize that the company's top priority was customer service. We don't have a brand new building here, but we do give them great service that's very personable.

Michael Silberling looks for hard-working people who will enjoy their work. He tells:

> My father is a geologist who's a professor at Stanford like his father was. There's nothing my father would rather be doing than to wander in the hills looking for fossils. As a young boy, he'd constantly tell me, "Son, do something with your life that you have a real passion for and enjoy doing." Well, ever since I've come to work here, I've been having a good time.
>
> After I received my MBA from UCLA, I had several job interviews but none could match the one I had at Harrah's. I spent the day talking to people at both properties in Lake Tahoe and Reno, and that night after taking me to dinner, they took me to see "Skintight," a cabaret show with topless dancers. Now that's something that doesn't happen with other companies that are recruiting MBA graduates!

FOCUS

After an employee is hired, he or she receives a pamphlet, *FOCUS*, an acronym that spells out what gaming customers want:

F stands for **F**ast and **F**lawless service. I don't want to wait, and I don't want you to mess up.

O is **O**ffers and rewards. Gamers like deals, that little extra something.

C is a **C**hance of winning. I'm not going to play a game that doesn't give me a chance to win.

U is **YOU** know me. I want to be recognized. I want you to call me by name, and I want you to ask how my family is. I want you to take a personal interest in me.

S is a **S**potless environment in which to play.

Marilyn Winn explains:

> All newly hired hourly employees go through our orientation program for two full days of FOCUS training that tells them what our guests want. Every supervisor and manager has a third day of FOCUS training to learn how to apply it as managers. There's a one-day program for employees who don't have any direct customer contact, such as kitchen workers and employees at the company's service center in Memphis. The Memphis employees are mainly involved in internal auditing, tele-services, human resources services, and IT [information technology].

During FOCUS training, employees learn the service cycle. The service cycle is how to say "Hello," so it starts with the greeting. It explains how to build a relationship and how to get customers to come back. It's also about what to do when Harrah's did not meet a guest's expectations and what to do when a guest is angry.

Within a 30- to 60-day period, a verbal examination is given by a FOCUS instructor who tests employee reactions in a variety of scenarios. Each employee who passes receives a FOCUS certificate. Anyone who fails the test is given an opportunity to take the test again, but those who fail a second time are not retained.

"We are very clear about what we expect our employees' service attitude to be," Winn stresses.

Communicating with Employees

About three to four times a year, all Harrah's employees are given a toll-free number to call Phil Satre. On designated days when the company chairman will be fielding calls, an announcement is forwarded to all properties that any interested employee can talk directly to Phil Satre.

Some people call simply to say hi—which Satre welcomes. But the serious calls fall into four categories. Satre explains:

First, I get calls that are suggestions on how to improve the business. These can be a marketing idea or perhaps a new game, and we've received some good thoughts that have been implemented. Second, I hear from employees who complain about their supervision—they come to me to protest about being mistreated. Third, many questions are about compensation and benefits—what they like and dislike. And, fourth, they tell me about what they think is a serious violation of our procedures or policies that they feel I should know. While the calls in this last category are rare, in a large company our size, there could be a rogue manager or supervisor that's doing something wrong and getting away with it.

For instance, one woman at our Laughlin property called to complain that her department manager had made an unwelcome sexual advance. While nothing had happened, it had been occurring and she didn't know what to do. The woman said she enjoyed her job and she feared her manager might fire her if she complained. I called the casino's general manager and asked him to privately investigate by observing this manager. A couple of days later, it was confirmed that what the woman told me was the case, and we fired the manager.

Another time, I was informed that a long-term employee was using his position to engage in the sale of drugs on our premises. Again, we followed up with an investigation and fired the employee. In 1989, because of this incident, we started a mandatory drug testing program for our employees. A lawsuit tried to prevent the program, but we won, and we test all employees for drugs in every state where it is permitted by law.

The Call-Phil program generates a lot of valuable feedback—sometimes from overzealous employees. "My favorite story is the call from the 'kissing bellman,'" Satre laughs:

> A bellman at Harrah's Las Vegas called in to tell me, "I just want to say how much I love my job. In fact, I get so excited when I check in guests and carry their bags to the room that I sometimes give them a kiss on my way out." He was so enthusiastic, but I had to tell him, "You know, that's probably not such a good idea." Afterward, I called the general manager to have a talk with the bellman. The general manager called me to report that everything was under control. "I told him that we loved his enthusiasm and he should never lose it. But from now on, a hearty handshake should be given instead of a kiss." The bellman understood and continues to work for the company.

On a more serious note, Satre says he received several calls from employees suggesting the company adopt a single card program. "I was hearing this from both employees and customers," tells Satre, "and it had a strong impact on the early stages of our Total Rewards program."

Often, Satre uses humor to communicate with employees. At the company's 1998 Key Management Meeting, attended by the company's top managers from across the nation, a motorcyclist rode a Harley bike onto the stage and dismounted at the podium. Who would have guessed that the mysterious rider dressed in a black leather jacket, helmet, and dark sunglasses was the company's CEO! In his opening address, Satre told the audience: "I can't think of a better way of getting this meeting off to a roaring start . . ." He also reminded everyone that Harley Davidson represents a hugely successful brand, and a great brand transformation. It was no coincidence that one of the key topics of the three-day meeting was the Harrah's brand.

Satre enjoys communicating with employees, and he's good at it. One reason for his effectiveness is that he's been there. He started work with the company as a waiter in the summers during his college years:

> When I talk to employees, I sometimes talk about lessons I learned waiting tables. "If your job provides service—whether you're a lawyer or a waiter—you must understand your customers' expectations and desires. Once you know that, you must give them that service in as

efficient, effective, and pleasant a way as you possibly can. Being a waiter can sometimes be a difficult job because there are bound to be some grumpy people who get upset because something went wrong. When that happens, your livelihood depends on the gratuities you'll receive, which represent their satisfaction because you turned an unpleasant experience into a pleasant experience. This means you must set aside your personal mood and cater to their needs. Similarly, many people in our organization—whether they're waitresses or dealers—depend on gratuities to support their livelihood. Those experiences I had waiting tables were wonderful lessons that carried over to my practicing law as well as throughout my business career."

One of Satre's strong leadership strengths is his ability to communicate to people at all levels, all the while coming across as sincere and caring. Satre's communication skills were put to the test in early 1999 when the company decided to move its corporate headquarters from Memphis to Las Vegas. The move was based on a sound business decision. Las Vegas is to the casino industry what Hollywood is to the film industry, what Wall Street is to the financial industry, what Detroit is to the automobile industry. Las Vegas is where the company could have the most interaction with vendors and security analysts, and it's the best place to see new ideas competitors are pursuing. Satre explains:

We were at a disadvantage in Memphis because our people at our headquarters didn't have a visceral relationship with what was happening. We were too removed, and, in the eyes of our people at our casino properties, we appeared to be in an ivory tower. I wanted our people who worked in operations across the country to feel that our corporate headquarters people were on the same page as they and had the same passion for the business. Just the same, I knew such a move for employees and their families would be emotional and stressful to them.

Sensitive to what people's reactions would be, Satre wanted to personally tell the Memphis employees about the company's plans to relocate its headquarters to Las Vegas. This way, he could fend off rumors and field questions. To simultaneously tell all 500-plus employees at the Memphis headquarters, there was only one logical place. That would be the breezeway, a wide-open space in the middle of the building where the company had previously made dramatic announcements. It was the same place Satre had announced the Harrah's/Promus split.

All employees in the building were summoned to assemble in the breezeway. Satre promptly told them about the relocation and why management had made the decision. He also explained that 70 to 80 people would be asked to move in Phase I, and they had two months to decide whether they would relocate. Then he told them that there would be two weekend trips for the Phase I people. The company would fly employees and their spouses, and they would stay at a Residence Inn away from the Strip so they could get a feel of what it was like to be in Las Vegas as a nontourist. On Saturday morning, they would board small tour buses to go to the residential areas of Green Valley and Summerlin. During their visit, they would be shown model homes in several new developments.

The reaction to Satre's announcement was mixed. As he anticipated, some people, for a variety of personal reasons, would choose to leave the company. Satre tells:

> I wanted them to understand why the decision was made, and I gave them all the reasons. I empathized with how they felt and told them that it affected my family, too. My wife was very active in the community, and my two children were young and didn't remember living anywhere else but in Memphis. One woman who was standing close to the front gasped so loud, I worried she was going to faint, and I thought we might have to call an ambulance for her. Some people whom I was very close to and who were very passionate about the company had relationships in Memphis that prevented them from moving. As I expected, it was a shock to so many of them.

Following a question-and-answer session, Satre excused himself and immediately drove to the IT department housed eight miles away, where he would deliver the same message. Eileen Cassini, an IT vice president, who had advance notice of the relocation, met with four small groups that morning and personally told all IT personnel what they would soon hear a second time from the CEO. "I wanted them to hear from me," she tells, "so when Phil talked to them, the initial shock would be over. This way, they could concentrate on his message and be prepared to ask questions."

The Harrah's IT department perhaps best exemplifies the company's caring attitude for its 42,000-plus employees. In the world of technology, Harrah's is a special place to work. For the past three years, Harrah's has been listed as one of the five best places to work in America by *Computerworld*. No other company has ever been listed in the magazine's top five list for two consecutive years.

There are many reasons that companies are good places to work. There's the obvious—compensation, fringe benefits, an environment with plush décor and piped-in music, and so on. Harrah's provides all of these, but so do many companies that never make a list of best places in America to work. If it were only a matter of spending money on employees to win their loyalty, the biggest corporations with the deepest pockets would routinely be named the best companies to work for. Small companies wouldn't have a chance. But smaller companies are frequently at the top of the list because their management has not become so bureaucratic that it cannot communicate openly with its people. People want to be heard—to be respected—to know their opinion has value.

One of the best "intangible fringe benefits" in the company's IT department is that employees are constantly shown how their jobs contribute to the company's overall success. Cassini explains:

> All of our IT employees know their linkage. They know what they do every day and what it means for the company. In some areas, technology people are far removed from customers. People are kept in the dark at a lot of companies; they have little understanding about how their daily work benefits customers. We make sure our people fully recognize how they contribute to customer satisfaction. Or, it may be that their work benefits company employees in another area that's located at another premise, perhaps a thousand miles away. We let them know how they're affecting those employees—and we make sure everyone understands how his or her work contributes to this company's bottom line. This creates a strong sense of purpose and inspires people to take pride in their accomplishments. Then we give them a lot of recognition for their achievements.
>
> When job satisfaction levels are high, turnover is low. There's usually a lot of turnover in technology, but ours in IT is only 5 percent. This is why we've won so many awards. Certainly, there will always be some turnover—people retire, spouses get transferred, and so on. Five percent is incredibly low—and of those who do leave, about 40 percent come back within a year, so our turnover is actually only 3 percent!

It's not just at the company headquarters, old and new, that strong communication skills are demonstrated—these skills are demonstrated throughout the organization. Here's what general managers at some of the company's different properties have to say about it:

"When people are recognized for their contributions," says Michael St. Pierre, general manager in Joliet, "they work harder and perform better. In a service industry, we go to extraordinary lengths to listen to employees and respond to their needs."

At the East Chicago property, general manager Joe Domenico communicates quite clearly to his employees through his actions.

When I came here in 1999 after we acquired Showboat, there was a tremendous difference in company cultures. At Harrah's, the emphasis has always been on customers, and our employees take pride in how we service customers. One of the first things I noticed when I came to work here was the limited parking space in the garage. Employees were parking under roof and, consequently, there weren't enough spaces for customers. And with the cold winters we have in Chicago, especially with our lakefront property, it's a long walk from the outdoor parking lot where I instructed all employees to park. Needless to say, my announcement didn't make me the most popular guy in the casino. But when employees saw the outdoor parking was on a first-come basis, and I didn't have a reserved parking space, this sent a message to them that I wasn't asking them to do something I wouldn't do myself.

I come from a farm background and understand hard work, and I never forget my roots. Yes, I am the leader of this organization, but I'm also an employee just like everyone else.

As a Dartmouth graduate with an MBA from UCLA, Michael Silberling, general manager in Reno, came to Harrah's with a fancy education. But Silberling didn't allow it to get in his way. He had worked summers at Harrah's and had done everything other employees did—from parking cars and carrying luggage to dealing cards. "This enables me to speak their language," he explains, "but even more importantly, I appreciate the workload our people have."

Former Harrah's executive Jay Sevigny had rave reviews about Gary Loveman's communication skills, and any fears that the ex-Harvard Business School professor would talk over anyone's head have long since been put to rest. Sevigny says:

Gary comes to the table with exceptional comparative perspective, so when we sometimes go astray and begin to think we have a unique problem, he's able to put it into perspective. A friend of mine once said, "Great professors make complicated things simple." That's what Gary does. As a division president, I got tremendous value from talking to him for half-hour or so sessions and having him walk me through some of my concerns. He brought such clarity of thought to those issues that I could confidently go forward with executing strategies. Having him aboard was akin to having my own on-call professor available for private conferences. Now that's quite a luxury!

I don't think any other casino company would appreciate having a Gary Loveman aboard. However, he was greatly valued for what he brings to the relationship—and the fact that we did made me proud of the organization.

The Code of Commitment

In January 2001, Harrah's formally introduced its Code of Commitment. The code governs the conduct of the company's workforce of 42,000-plus employees who work at properties spread across the United States. With 26 casinos and a distribution strategy poised for growth, Jan Jones, senior vice president of communications and government relations, believed that the written code would serve as a public pledge to the company's guests and employees, as well as the communities it serves.

Jones felt the code was needed so Harrah's could define its stand on important issues. "It's really about who we already are," she explains, "because the code is based on what we've been doing for years. It also serves as an instrument for us to continue to serve the gaming industry as a leader in self-regulation. In addition to being on the cutting edge in marketing, research, and technology, we have assumed a leadership role in conduct—and we feel obligated to set a standard for our competition to follow."

The following is a summary of the Code of Commitment:

1. *Commitment to Guests:* Promote responsible gaming. This means no Harrah's property will cash welfare or unemployment checks. The company honors all requests of customers who want to be *denied* access to the company's casinos. Obviously, these customers recognize they have a gambling problem. At their request, they cannot cash checks or receive credit at any Harrah's property. Marketing promotions to these individuals is restricted. Toll-free help line numbers for problem gamblers are displayed at each Harrah's property, in its ads, brochures, and signs. Additionally, the company contributes financial support to these hotlines. Furthermore, Harrah's employees are trained to recognize the signs of problem gamblers, and they are empowered to provide them with information about how to receive help. Underage individuals are forbidden to play.

2. *Commitment to Employees:* Treat them with respect and provide opportunities to build satisfying careers. This means paying them top wages and valuable benefits that include health insurance and a retirement plan. The company shares its financial successes by paying cash bonuses. To encourage professional and personal growth, the company provides tuition reimbursement, on-the-job training, career development, and promotions from within. The company listens to its people and continually seeks and responds to employee opinions on matters such as their jobs, the quality of their supervisors, and the quality of the casinos.

3. *Commitment to the Community:* Give back to the community and contribute to making it a vibrant place to live and work. This includes responsible marketing. The company conducts its business with honesty and integrity, consistent with the highest moral, legal, and ethical standards, complying with all applicable laws and regulations. The company shares its financial success with the communities by donating 1 percent of company profits to civic and charitable causes. Employees are encouraged to volunteer in civic and charitable causes. The company adheres to responsible advertising and marketing practices.

The Harrah's organization views casino gaming as a recreation enjoyed by millions of responsible adults. And like other kinds of recreation, people budget their time and the amount of money they want to spend so they may enjoy gaming as a pleasant pastime—not a way of life! Company research reveals that customers overwhelmingly say they have fun at its casinos, whether they win or lose on any particular occasion.

The company's culture has long been dedicated to promoting responsible gaming. Customers play for fun—any other reason for playing is the wrong reason. All company advertising and marketing focus on this premise. The company strongly opposes irresponsible or inappropriate gambling. With this focus, Harrah's has adopted a code for its marketing and advertising which caters strictly to adults who choose to play casino games. The following are some highlights of this code:

★ Advertising and marketing materials are consistent with contemporary local standards of decorum and decency. Religious themes, figures, or symbols are not permitted. Nor do the materials degrade the image, form, or status of women, men, or any ethnic, minority, or other group.

★ Advertising and marketing materials do not depict, encourage, or condone excessive, irresponsible, or illegal gambling. They do not (a) state or imply that casino gambling is an acceptable means of satisfying work or family commitments, or an alternative to work or family commitments; (b) state or imply that casino gambling is necessary for financial, physical, or social success; (c) state or imply that casino gambling solves personal problems; (d) portray individuals who are intoxicated, who are compelled to gamble, who have lost control of their faculties, or who have become separated from reality; or (e) suggest in any way that excessive, irresponsible, or illegal gambling is an amusing or acceptable behavior.

★ All company advertising and marketing are geared to adults above the legal age to gamble in a casino. It does not depict customers under the legal age, nor does it use actors under age 25. It does not use any symbols, language, gesture, cartoon, music, animated character, entertainment figure, or child's toy that appeals to persons below the legal age to gamble in a casino. Casino gambling is not promoted as a rite of passage, or otherwise necessary for the attainment of adulthood.

★ All print advertising includes a message offering a toll-free help line for individuals who might have a gambling problem. The company sponsors public awareness, education, and other campaigns on problem and underage gambling.

★ The company will not promote its brands or casinos at any event where the majority of the audience is reasonably expected to be below the legal age to gamble in a casino.

★ No product, name, logo, trademark, or service mark is used or licensed for use on clothing, toys, game equipment, or other materials that are intended for persons below the legal age to gamble in a casino.

★ Advertising and marketing materials are not placed in any media where more than 30 percent of the audience is reasonably expected to be below the legal age to gamble in a casino. This rules out advertising and marketing in college publications.

★ No new advertising is placed on any outdoor stationary location within 500 feet of an established place of worship or an elementary or secondary school. Agreements on all existing advertising of this nature under contract for its placement will not be renewed.

★ The company's Web site specifically states that it is designated for individuals who are of a legal age to gamble in a casino. It takes appropriate precautions to ensure that visitors to the play-for-fun casino are 21 or older. The Web site includes information about the company's responsible gambling philosophy, practices, and programs.

★ A copy of the company's code is given to every casino employee and outside advertising and marketing agency.

★ A Code of Review Board composed of Harrah's employees meets at least once each year to evaluate Code compliance. It also meets when necessary to consider complaints about Harrah's marketing or advertising materials lodged by an interested party. When appropriate, the Board will declare that unsuitable materials be withdrawn. All complaining parties are notified of the resolution of their complaints.

The Code of Commitment is more stringent than current voluntary American Gaming Association guidelines. Harrah's has set higher standards in hope that the entire gaming industry will follow suit. Satre has made it a top priority; the code is not another slick pamphlet meant to be ignored. At Harrah's, they walk the talk. For example, there's Operation Bet Smart, a Harrah's training program that teaches employees to give directional assistance to problem gamblers. The program is so effective, it serves as the standard for other casinos in the states of Missouri and Illinois, and all casinos in Atlantic City have adopted it. The company began its involvement in the area of compulsive gambling in the mid-1980s. As a result of these years of efforts, at the twelfth annual Gaming Hall of Fame Charity Dinner held October 19, 2000, the American Gaming Association's president and CEO, Frank Fahrenkopf Jr., presented Phil Satre with its first-ever award for responsible gaming.

Harrah's employees are trained about problem gambling. There is also signage in the casinos with the message: "Know when to stop before you start," and "If you or someone you know has a problem with gambling, call 1-800-522-4700." Brochures that provide background information on compulsive gambling are distributed. On them are listed the 20 questions of Gamblers Anonymous. Someone who answers yes to seven or more questions may have a compulsive gambling problem.

David Jonas, general manager at Harrah's in Atlantic City, doesn't pull any punches when it comes to problem gambling:

> We built our fine reputation with the message: "Gamble within your means, and if you don't, we don't want your business." In my opinion, this has worked very well for us. We let them know: "We don't want your business so bad that you are going to be hurt." We've all seen that. There are addictive personalities in all walks of life. It's a tiny piece of this business, and it's not what we want.

Welfare checks and payroll checks are never cashed at a Harrah's property. Anyone under age is forbidden to play in the casino. Any customer who wants to purchase a T-shirt in a child's size as a souvenir won't find one in a Harrah's gift shop. That's because the company won't permit them to be made. No matter how great the demand, there are no products sold at a Harrah's property that promote gambling to anyone underage. The Code of Commitment is not idle words. As Phil Satre describes the Code, "It puts in writing the rules we play by."

Doing Good Is Good Business

Caring for the community is deeply ingrained in the company culture. This is particularly true when it comes to doing it in a way that creates win-win opportunities.

For example, in the 1960s Bill Harrah was one of the staunchest supporters of the "Save Lake Tahoe" environmental movement. The company founder had always felt that overbuilding by developers would ruin the natural beauty of the lake, and it could mean the end to casinos on the lake. Therefore, his management team assumed a lead role in the formation of the Tahoe Regional Planning Agency. In a TRPA meeting on his Thunderbird yacht, which California Governor Ronald Reagan and Nevada Governor Paul Laxalt attended, a bi-state compact was agreed on and signed right on the state line—in the middle of the lake. It also turned out to be a major publicity coup. Soon thereafter, Harrah formed a committee to outlaw use of septic tanks at Lake Tahoe. His efforts led to the founding of Douglas County Sewer Improvement District Number One.

Today, Harrah's Casino and Hotel Resort at Lake Tahoe stands 18 stories tall. Initial plans called for a 36-story structure. The taller building was shelved because Harrah felt it would pose an esthetic compromise and thereby distract from the beauty of the natural surroundings. In the minds of some observers, Bill Harrah's commitment to the community was self-serving because had there not been environmental protection of Lake Tahoe, the area would lose its appeal as a major tourist attraction. Likewise, had Harrah not been one of the early movers and shakers to build Barton Hospital, it would have been more difficult to attract employees to reside in the Lake Tahoe community. The same applies to his leadership role in the construction of a better highway to Lake Tahoe or the times he paid for the snow removal on the state's highway to the lake. Self-serving? Most definitely; nonetheless, the community benefited. Harrah always enjoyed win-win situations.

In hindsight, Bill Harrah was ahead of his times. Consider a 1999 survey taken by America's Research Group (ARG). Its findings revealed that 56 percent of Americans stated they would spend more with a company that was active in its community than one that was not. An almost equal amount—55 percent—rated a company's charity involvement as an important factor when deciding where to buy. The same study disclosed that 78 percent of the interviewees trust a company that is active in the community. And how do employees feel about their companies' community involvement? Eighty-six percent claimed it made them feel more loyal. Eighty-eight percent say it's something they talk about with their family and friends. A whopping 95 percent boasted that their bosses' civic activities made them proud to work for the company. The ARG study found that 81 percent of shareholders of even publicly owned companies favor American companies' altruism.

Becoming an active member of the community is also a good way to be accepted by the local citizenry—especially if you're an outsider and came from Las Vegas. When Vern Jennings was promoted to general manager of Harrah's in St. Louis in 1993, gaming had gained approval in the state of Missouri by a slim margin. Vern and his family moved from Las Vegas, and for a while, the reception was downright hostile. Jennings tells:

> When my daughter announced to her seventh grade class we had come from Vegas and her father worked at a casino, her teacher said to her, "Do you know that prostitution is legal in Las Vegas?" The teacher was not only wrong but was also insinuating, "Something is dirty here, and you ought to be ashamed of yourself." This was very hurtful to our family. But we understood where he was coming from. Here we were in a wholesome, clean Midwestern community where a lot of people thought our business was evil, and so anyone associated with the industry was also evil.
>
> My wife, Dana, and I quickly became aware of this attitude. It was very obvious because people were so standoffish and acted as if they weren't sure they should be hanging around with us. It took a while for them to realize we don't carry guns and don't belong to the mob.

Soon after their move, Dana and Vern began joining civic organizations, and the community slowly began to accept them. Today, they are accepted as prominent, highly respected citizens. Says Jennings:

> One of the first things we did after getting our management team in place, was make it a requirement for every manager to participate in at least two local organizations in a significant way. This means serving on boards and chairing fund-raising committees. We have 72 managers, so today, Harrah's managers are active in more than 100 organizations. These include being active in such groups as Ronald McDonald House, United Negro College Fund, and many school and church organizations. Our community involvement in the St. Louis area today is well received and has definitely had a positive impact.

So the good news is that companies that do good things score high marks with their customers, employees, and shareholders. As the ARG survey reveals, it's good for a company's bottom line, because altruism increases customer loyalty and employee loyalty. This loyalty translates into customers' spending more and coming back more frequently; and with employees, it means lower turnover and high productivity. All of that makes for a healthy bottom line.

With large sums of money shelled out to support civic and charitable causes, well-managed companies want to get the most bang from their buck. This prompts them to support causes that directly benefit their customers. A women's apparel company, for example, might support female-related causes such as a shelter for battered women and breast cancer research. Likewise, a toy manufacturing company might support causes for children. Julie Foley-Murray, a community relations consultant to Harrah's, explains:

> Prior to 2001, Harrah's gave to many causes without a specific theme. Today, however, we have a strategic campaign that focuses on giving to senior citizens. One reason is that no other gaming company has done that. We feel there's a great need to support this segment of the population, particularly with the increasing numbers of aging citizens.

In 2002, the company made a three-year, $1 million commitment to Meals on Wheels Association of America to help feed home-bound senior citizens.

Harrah's targets 1 percent of its operating profits from the casinos for charitable giving. In 2001, Harrah's spent $42 million on charities and public–private partnerships in the communities where its properties are located. Some of it has to do with the extra payments that casinos make because they're casinos. For instance, Harrah's New Orleans pays a $60 million tax on revenues plus $2 million to the New Orleans school board, $1 million to the city's tourism agency, $750,000 to the zoo, and $500,000 for development in downtown New Orleans. Then there's the obligation that casinos pay on top of other local taxes. In East Chicago, each year the Harrah's property shells out $10 million to $12 million that goes directly to the city for infrastructure improvements, business development, and two educational foundations. In Cherokee, North Carolina, for example, the company gave $1 million for scholarships. The Harrah's property in Maryland Heights, Missouri, a St. Louis suburb with a population of 25,000, has an effective tax rate of 30 percent that came to $80 million in taxes in 2001. "A majority of the money goes to the state to fund education," explains Vern Jennings, "with $16 million going to Maryland Heights in 2001—before Harrah's, the city's budget was $8 million!" In Metropolis, Harrah's contributed to the repaving of the city's streets. In Atlantic City, funds were given to a senior prescription program that was part of a development fund requiring casinos to give donations. In 2001, the company and its employees contributed more than $1.4 million to victims of the September 11 terrorist attacks.

Long after the implementation of Bill Harrah's giving-back-to-the-community philosophy, today's Harrah's continues this tradition. The company founder did it in an era when casinos were associated with the underworld, and, as a legitimate businessman, he had to work overtime to present a positive image. Jan Jones concurs that the public's perception of the company is equally important today. "There are people who think the gaming industry is villainous," she states. "I believe that part of that is the industry's fault because companies fail to communicate who they are and how they benefit the community. Today we tell our story, demonstrating the impact we are making across the country."

Harrah's, like other leading American corporations, has made philanthropy part of its marketing and public relations strategy. In this respect, many companies now assign their marketing departments to negotiate directly with nonprofit groups rather than through their philanthropic arms. A focus on branding has led many companies to seek naming rights when making large contributions. For example, children visiting the expanded St. Louis Zoo can pet animals at the Emerson Electric Children's Zoo, watch a show at the Bank America Amphitheater, study bugs at the Monsanto Insectarium, and view hippopotamuses at the Anheuser-Busch Hippo Harbor. Major corporations across America are making large donations in exchange for naming rights. In Philadelphia, there's the Please Touch Museum Presented by McDonald's; in Detroit, the General Motors Center for African American Art; in Los Angeles, the Mattel Children's Hospital at UCLA; and in Providence, Rhode Island, the Hasbro Children's Hospital.

"We are looking into naming opportunities," says Foley-Murray, "as a way to have more return on our charitable investments. We want to spread it out across the country, so you might not see our name on a large building, but you might, for example, in a recreation center in a senior citizens' center."

Harrah's now has the technology in place to break down what the company contributes by congressional districts anywhere in the United States. To Jan Jones, this is a godsend. Armed with this data, she says:

> I can meet with elected officials and give them figures on what we've invested in their district. I can also show them the salaries and employee benefits we pay and what tax revenues we generate. With this information, they can see that we have a constituency in their district that matters to them as well as to the company. And by focusing on building an alliance with senior citizens, these constituents can deliver a powerful message to elected officials: "When you hurt the gaming industry, you hurt us."

In addition to the millions of dollars given to charitable and civic causes, hundreds of thousands of hours are given by Harrah's employees who volunteer in their local communities. To encourage its people to become involved, Harrah's Entertainment Reaching Out (HERO) program gives special recognition to employees who give their time doing charitable and civic work. Employees receive rewards based on the number of hours they participate. Not only do these extracurricular activities benefit the community, but the company benefits, too, because the HERO program develops good leadership and team-building skills. In addition, HERO boosts employee morale, helping employees feel good about their employer and themselves.

A Sense of Pride

Years ago, some thought Bill Harrah's attention to detail bordered on the obsessive. They poked fun at his insistence on details such as the immediate replacement of a burned-out lightbulb, the removal of a fingerprinted water glass, or a dirty ashtray. Yet, deep down, the people who worked at Harrah's were immensely proud of the fact that their boss cared so much about doing everything with perfection. And they were pleased that he cared about serving customers. Bill Harrah set incredibly high standards, which in turn put pressure on his competitors to follow his lead. This made him the industry's leader. And employees like to be associated with a winner because that makes them winners, too.

The same sense of pride that employees had during Bill Harrah's era lives on, deeply engrained in the corporate culture. It's unusual in corporate America for employees to feel the same pride and passion instilled by a company founder who has been dead for nearly a quarter of a century. For it is one thing for a strong personality like Bill Harrah to inspire employees during his lifetime, but quite another for the same sense of pride to be passed on to the next generation of senior management.

Employees at Ford Motor Company had this kind of pride when founder Henry Ford was in charge, and it continued when Henry Ford II ("The Deuce") stepped into his grandfather's shoes as CEO. When the Fords walked through a company plant, it was as if the whole world stopped. They were larger-than-life figures, each in his time the most celebrated business personality in America. In Detroit, when a company factory worker was asked what he did for a living, he'd proudly say, "I work for the Fords." It was as if he worked for a family-owned company—even though it was one of the world's largest corporations. The sense of pride of Ford employees has diminished since the days its founder Henry Ford and his grandson, The Deuce, were in charge. Since Henry Ford II retired in 1982, four non-Ford family CEOs headed the company before William Clay Ford, the founder's great-grandson was tapped for the top position in 2001. The sense of pride that once existed among Ford employees, however, has not been restored.

Remarkably, the sense of pride that Harrah's employees had when its founder ruled the roost remains intact to this day. There is no single reason for it to prevail, but instead, a combination of reasons. For one thing, the company has never compromised its integrity, and it continues to be an industry leader, maintaining the highest standards—even above what is required by law. The company continues to provide an excellent workplace for its employees. It continues to give back to the community. Employees are treated with dignity and respect. What's more, the company continues to provide opportunities for personal growth. All this makes for proud employees.

7

THE IT
COMMITMENT

HEN MIKE ROSE RETIRED IN JANUARY 1997, PHIL SATRE, WHO WAS already president and chief executive officer, assumed the additional title of chairman of the board. This promised a very busy and hectic year for Satre. Already on the drawing board was the March opening of a riverboat casino entertainment complex bordering St. Louis, Missouri, and in May, the consolidation of two Harrah's operations in Tunica County, Mississippi, into a newer and larger casino hotel complex. In June, Harrah's Atlantic City would complete a major expansion and renovation that included a new hotel tower and increased casino space, plus additional restaurants. Then there was a $200 million expansion of Harrah's on the Strip in Las Vegas scheduled for completion in October—the company's most ambitious renovation ever, creating a flagship casino resort accommodating guests in 2,560 rooms, 178 of them deluxe suites. The following month marked the November opening of Harrah's Cherokee Smoky Mountains, a joint venture with the Cherokee Tribe in the Great Smoky Mountains of North Carolina.

In addition to its investment in bricks and mortar, the company was gearing up to launch Total Gold, the industry's first fully integrated national players' rewards and recognition program. The forerunner to Total Rewards, Total Gold would seamlessly connect player activity among all properties in the Harrah's brand. While the renovations and openings represented an investment of hundreds of millions of dollars, several other casino companies had already committed even larger sums to build single properties up and down both sides of the Strip. Hence, Harrah's could not claim the biggest, most attractive, or most creative theme casino resort. On this front, the competition had already outflanked Harrah's. At best, the company could play catch-up with its competition, a purely defensive strategy. Total Gold was indeed an offensive play. Harrah's was committed to invest what would total $100 million in information technology (IT) to support its branding and distribution strategy. This was the most notable move Harrah's made in 1997. The future for Harrah's rested on a successful outcome of its marketing strategy.

Understandably, when Phil Satre stepped up to the plate to lead the company, enormous pressures began to test the seasoned corporate head. As the company celebrated its sixtieth anniversary this same year, Satre embarked on a course leading into uncharted waters. If the journey he had carefully mapped out was erroneous, Harrah's would lose its long-held leadership role in the gaming industry. These were indeed stressful times for Phil Satre.

That April, an unexpected personal catastrophe occurred. Satre's wife, Jennifer, was diagnosed with promyelocyte leukemia. Consequently, she was hospitalized for an extended time and concurrently began chemotherapy treatment for six months. Satre says:

> My wife's illness far overshadowed any part of my business life. With her treatments, I knew that I would have to spend far more time at home with my family and be unable to continue in the role of an ambassador, making the rounds to our properties. This allowed me to crystallize my feelings about what I believed—on both what was important and how much tolerance I would give for not getting things done the way I believed was best for the company. Consequently, I curtailed certain activities, and I examined my organization and its people in a different light.
>
> In June, I attended a seminar on building customer loyalty hosted by Gary Loveman at the Harvard Business School. It was an enlightening two days. The lectures, coupled with the commitment I made during my wife's illness about traveling less, helped me decide how to organize the company to succeed in the future. Ultimately, it meant bringing in someone who had both the passion and the expertise to implement our marketing strategy. I knew we had the right tools, but I questioned whether we had the right people in place. This is when I first thought about hiring a chief operating officer with a marketing bias—a bias toward great service, plus a bias toward using these marketing tools to create greater customer loyalty. In hindsight, this is when the seed was planted that led us to consider Gary Loveman for the position.

By autumn, Jennifer Satre no longer required hospitalization; however, she continued to receive treatment for the next year, followed by periodic examinations. Following a period of remission, she received a clean bill of health from her doctor.

Meanwhile, the price of a common share of Harrah's closed on December 31, 1997, at $18.88, down $1 from the previous year. It had been on a five-year downhill slide closing at $45.75 in 1993, $30.88 in

1994, and $24.25 in 1995. For the five-year period, the market price of its common stock had a compound growth rate of −19.9 percent. Consequently, Harrah's was on the list of casino companies most likely to be acquired.

"The year 1997 was an epiphany for me," says Satre. "Certainly, I would never again want to experience a serious family illness like my wife endured. However, it did give me clarity on how to handle my personal life—especially my relationship with my wife and children—and still focus on my business life."

The IT Challenges

Under direct orders from Phil Satre, John Boushy, senior vice president of brand operations and information technology, had started to build a single nationwide database in the early 1990s. Its objective was to create an operating environment that assured Harrah's customers could use their loyalty card at every property, regardless of where they originally got their card. An ideal game plan was to standardize all of the company's disparate IT systems, but Satre had determined the project was too ambitious at a time when the technology wasn't mature. During this period, the company was preoccupied with adding new properties to its inventory.

"While the company thought it important to collect customer information in its database," explains Rich Mirman, "the problem was we had millions of customers to collect information on, but we had no systematic way of turning it into a marketing decision. So we didn't know what to do with it."

In 1993, Boushy began to conceptualize the functionality and architecture of Winner's Information Network (WINet), and the following year he and his team started to build it. To succeed, they would have to redesign the company's IT infrastructure, a task that seemed unattainable at the time. They had to make Harrah's AS400 transactional systems that supported customer activity in the hotel, casino, and events reservations areas at each property communicate with the Unix-based Patron Database, a national customer database that would contain all of the company's customer information.

IBM and AT&T, hardware vendors of Harrah's, told Boushy he would never be able to combine the two systems because the mainframes were incompatible with the Unix systems. Boushy and his team eventually proved them wrong by using middleware and software developed in-house. The technological trials didn't always seem to be the biggest obstacle.

"There were times during this project when the single greatest challenge we faced was convincing the IT people we could do this," Boushy says.

He came up with some creative ways to try to motivate his team. In mid-1996, technical difficulties, a lack of enterprise-wide standards, and an underestimation of the scope of the project had thrown it off track. To demonstrate his confidence in the team, Boushy committed to letting his then-short hair grow until WINet was up and running. A month later, a software bug decimated the entire database; Boushy and his team had to rebuild it from scratch.

Boushy's hair was a Samson-like shoulder length by the time the Patron Database portion of WINet was running in February 1997.

But the pain was worth it. Once WINet was up, Harrah's could share information across its properties, in real-time, for the first time in its history. If a customer who had just been gambling in Joliet, Illinois, hopped a plane to try his or her luck at the Harrah's casino in Reno, Reno's employees knew exactly what the customer did in Joliet and, therefore, what services to provide.

The company's 42,000-plus slot machines now also connect to the AS400 systems, and call center reps are linked to both the AS400s and the Unix Patron Database. The AS400s communicate with the Patron Database through a Unix gateway. Analysts in the marketing department use Cognos' Impromptu query tool to access the data warehouse, and they use SAS software to do predictive modeling.

During the two-year period of 1994 to 1995, Harrah's invested $17 million in technology. Only its property investments had ever approached or topped this sum. At the time, Satre was president of Promus Companies and reported directly to Mike Rose, chairman of the Holiday Inn Corporation. Boushy tells:

> The two had different views on cross-marketing. Mike believed that gamers were like bowlers. Bowlers might go to other markets where there is bowling, but they wouldn't carry their bowling ball with them because they weren't likely to bowl during their visit. Phil believed that gamers were more like golfers and skiers. There are certain places where golfers and skiers go—even for a different purpose—and if they have an opportunity, they will carry their skis or their golf clubs so they could enjoy themselves with some added recreation.

The two men had philosophical differences, which meant Satre would have to sell his boss on the merits of investing in IT for the company to execute competitive branding and distribution strategies. As Boushy points out, Satre faced a difficult task. At 6 feet 5 inches,

Rose was a dominating figure; his deep and often intimidating voice matched his appearance. "I have to admire Phil's perseverance because he hung in there," says Boushy. "There were times it looked like we were going to scrap the project, but in the end, Rose told Phil and me, 'I disagree with you, but okay, let's see what you can do with it.'"

Boushy's title has recently been changed to senior vice president-operations, products, and services, and chief information officer. Previously, it was senior vice president of brand operations and information technology. Having both titles is unusual in *any* industry because companies rarely delegate technology and marketing responsibilities to the same officer. In this respect, Boushy's titles make a statement that sent the message throughout the organization. The message: *Harrah's is a marketing-driven company and technology is a tool to serve marketing.*

Boushy stresses:

> We're definitely a consumer-marketing company that uses information strategically, and we assume an offensive posture. Concurrently, we continually integrate our activities and our information about our customers in an operating context. So, it's not only in a marketing context that we are using that information. For example, IT allows us to provide services at the front desks, over the telephone, and in the restaurants. In the restaurants, we have separate lines for Platinum and Diamond customers, and, consequently, they get seated more quickly. Likewise, at the Platinum and Diamond levels, the hostess might know a customer's favorite wine.

With a background in marketing, John Boushy is not a run-of-the-mill chief information officer. His philosophy is:

> We don't take an R&D approach, which investigates a lot of different technologies and tries to figure out how to apply them. To me, that's like finding a solution first, then looking for a problem to match it! Instead, we take our technology and apply it to improve our capabilities. For instance, if you want to compare customer behavior before and after, you must be able to look at their behavior before and after. While you must have the technology, you must also have the marketing talent to do something with it.

Why All the Technology?

It's true that casinos have slots and security systems that require an investment in technology. But on the customer side of the equation, casinos have never been particularly technology-driven. Traditionally, it's been a business based on one-on-one relationships between casino employees—dealers, pit bosses, and casino hosts—and their customers. There was a lot of note taking on who was betting how much and how often. There was nothing technological about it whatsoever for years, and it was a very profitable business.

The business changed. In a highly competitive marketplace such as the casino industry, companies either adjust to change or fall by the wayside. During the 1990s, phenomenal change took place in Las Vegas. Anyone driving down the town's famed Strip gaping at the towering thematic casino-resorts open or under construction could testify that the casino industry was moving at a rapidly accelerated pace.

Phil Satre recognized this when he saw the palatial edifices being built by his competitors. He also understood that with his distribution strategy in place, his company could not afford to become engaged in a spending war. If Harrah's elected to erect mammoth properties to compete with other casino companies, it could spend itself to the poorhouse. Therefore, for good reason, back in the early 1990s the decision was made to invest in WINet, the first of its kind in the casino industry. Before WINet, Harrah's assumed its customers were partial to a favorite casino they frequented. Each Harrah's property operated independently and competed with all other casino companies—and even among themselves. Each Harrah's property had its own player card that was valid only in its casino. Not only was the Harrah's card invalid at other company properties, but also none of the company's information systems at these individual sites were integrated with those at other casinos, nor could they even communicate with them.

Harrah's was first exposed to the effective use of technology in the early 1980s, starting with the Holiday Inn merger. At the time, the parent company's Holidex was considered the most advanced reservation system in the hotel industry. Colin Reed, who worked for Holiday Inns before the acquisition, explains:

> We were in the process of building our new brands such as Embassy Suites and Hampton Inns. Each had its own reservation systems, and they were all linked together. The Holiday Corporation understood that linking its properties together with technology gave its customers a seamless experience. The company had a frequent buyer program in place, so loyal customers could be identified. Customers liked it because they could call the central reservations office and say, "I'm a loyal Holiday customer, and I want a room in Lexington, Kentucky." Meanwhile, Harrah's had three Nevada properties in Reno, Tahoe, and Las Vegas, plus one in New Jersey. Each was operated as a separate little kingdom where the general manager was

king. It wasn't until early 1992 when we started to uniform our technology so we'd have the same slot management systems and same accounting systems in all our facilities.

Phil Satre says:

> In the 1980s, we had separate customer recognition and reward programs at every single property. Each property had a separate database for its customers. When we started our rapid expansion program in 1992, we wanted to capitalize on our distribution and the relationships we were creating with our customers. Without a national customer recognition and reward program, we couldn't take advantage of our brand. We also knew we needed a fully integrated database on all our customers so we could market to and create relationships with them. So, unlike the past, we looked at the gaming business in the United States as a seamless whole, rather than separate markets in Las Vegas, in Atlantic City, and so on. We stood back and looked at all our customers across the country from a broader perspective. What we saw gave us confidence that our investment in our IT infrastructure would produce high returns for our shareholders. We viewed it as a strong competitive advantage.

Satre saw another competitive advantage: Technology could be used to strengthen the company's relationship with its slot machine players. Here, the company had a long tradition dating back to Bill Harrah's era. The founder didn't like the volatile nature of the table games and, consequently, felt more comfortable with slot machines. At the time of his death in 1978, slot machines had not yet become fully electronic. Many of the mechanical models had an electrical connection, but Bill Harrah resisted converting to them. It was only a matter of time before slot machines became fully electronic and provided more excitement, thus allowing customers to be more interactive. Today's slot machines have everything from video screens to computer chips for multiple coins to be played. This process is not entirely because of the gaming industry—much credit certainly goes to the computer industry. Satre contends:

> We were always a great slot company, and in the early 1980s, we viewed this segment of our business as a tremendous growth opportunity. That's what influenced our thinking when we went from mechanical to fully electronic slots. At the time, it gave us a jump on our competition, and we've managed to keep our lead. Today, we have more slot machine revenues than any other casino company—even though some of our competitors are larger than we are.

The coming of the new electronic slot machine provided something equally valuable. It could serve as a marketing tool by being a source of information to the company. That's because its electronic mechanism had the capacity to track a customer's play. Satre continues:

> We needed the technology to reach out to our AEP customer who likes to play in multiple markets. This customer represents only 12 percent of the universe of players, but more than 55 percent of the total revenues in the casino business. As I previously mentioned, an AEP customer has an annual gambling budget ranging between $1,000 and $5,000. In actual dollars, U.S. casino gaming totals $36 billion, and 55 percent comes to $20 billion. Casinos have traditionally focused on the high-roller customer. Our investment in technology is based on our overriding business model that catered to these customers, and with our branding, we would leverage this across multiple markets.

Explains George Dittman in reference to the AEP customer:

> In 1995, we determined there was a need to find a target customer to zero in on. We didn't want to compete on bricks and mortar going up against the Mirages, MGMs, and the Bellagios. Our marketing research identified the customer with a $100 a day, $1,000 a year budget. This was the customer that the bigger casinos were allowing to fall through the cracks. They simply weren't set up to service this customer. Instead, they were concentrating on the high-end table game player. Concurrently, the slot player was virtually being ignored. This is when we developed a marketing strategy based on consumer research aimed at what this customer liked and didn't like in a casino experience. Once we knew our target customer, we started to develop programs around this particular group.

In retrospect, there was little choice but to come up with a new marketing strategy. The company had to differentiate itself from its competitors—without matching their spending sprees on the construction of billion-dollar properties. Still, no matter how you slice it, investing $100 million in technology is a huge sum for any company, let alone a casino company. It was a bold decision that turned out to be the *right* decision. It was, after all, as Gary Loveman articulates, "a very large infusion of intellectual capital into a business that has very largely depended on physical and tangible assets."

It's Not the Bricks and Mortar *or* the Technology

On February 4, 2001, the *Las Vegas Review-Journal* featured Tom Gallagher, the newly appointed CEO at Park Place. Gallagher was brought in following the October passing of CEO Arthur Goldberg, a well-respected figure in casino circles. Park Place owns well-known brands such as Caesars, Bally's, Flamingo, and Paris. In a question addressed to the new CEO about how he planned to market Park Place properties and its different brands, the reporter referred to Harrah's technology.

Gallagher replied, "I mean no disrespect to Harrah's, but what they're doing is . . . well, first of all, there's no monopoly on technology. Their technology is technology that all of us are using . . ."

While it's public information that Harrah's has invested in the neighborhood of $100 million in technology—a huge investment that far exceeds its competitors—Harrah's does not claim a monopoly on technology. It is true, however, that the company has developed specific proprietary software that is protected under U.S. patent law. In fact, the company filed two lawsuits in 2001 against competing gaming companies to protect its intellectual properties; one defendant settled and the other suit is pending. However, according to Rich Mirman, it goes beyond the money that's invested. Mirman stresses:

> What we do is not about technology. I wouldn't advise anyone to put a lot of time and money into building something that's supposed to replicate the core of what we do without understanding what it is about that core that generates money. For starters, there has to be a plan that presents changes in customers' behaviors because if there aren't strong incentives, why should customers be expected to change behaviors? We had to learn that lesson in order for our Total Rewards program to work.

Gary Loveman explains:

> In order to do what we do to drive customer loyalty and visitation, we needed an infrastructure with the capacity to collect transactional data, pull it across 26 operating businesses, and make it available in a fashion that is easily analyzed and distributed. This is a necessary condition on which all of our marketing activities can occur. At present, no other hospitality company has this, and it's truly a technological advantage. Some of this is embodied in patent protection. There are certain things we do that we hold patents on, so no other company is allowed to replicate it. Once we've collected the data, our marketing activities take over. The two are very complementary with each other.

As marketing executives Mirman and Loveman point out, technology by itself is not enough. It's how the technology is used. Phil Satre learned this lesson personally back in the early 1980s when he and his family were still residing in Reno and he was traveling back and forth to Holiday Inn's Memphis headquarters. He says:

> For a couple of years, I used to check into a Holiday Inn on such a regular basis, I probably slept there more than in my own bed. Every time I registered at that hotel, I had to go through the exact routine. "Hi, I'm Phil Satre. Here's my home address," and then I'd have to fill out the same card. I would say, "You know, I'm here once a week. When are you going to figure that out, so I don't have to go through this same routine?" It didn't matter that I was on the company's board of directors and I headed its gaming division. I still had to do it. That's because they didn't have the ability to do it.
>
> They had a lot of technology and a lot of information on customers, but they lacked the ability to be out-bound with it. All of their information was in-bound. It didn't matter that this customer wants to get a room here, and this is what he likes—a room with a view, a king-sized bed, and so on. Nor did their system let them know that this customer is likely to visit five or six times a year. From a reservations standpoint, Holidex was a breakthrough product in the 1970s and early 1980s, but it didn't offer much that contributed to building a relationship with the customer.

Before Gary Loveman and his team came aboard, Harrah's did have the technology to collect all of the transactional data, and it was capable of getting it to one place, which was its IT headquarters in Memphis. "The problem was," as Loveman puts it, "nobody knew what to do with it."

Bruce Rowe, vice president of slots and research development, declares:

> It's not about technology, because a lot of companies have great technology but don't have access to the information. It's what you do with the data—or to put it another way, how you turn it into good information. The technology is the conduit through which that information is conveyed. In the early 1990s, we thoughtfully planned a strategy technology architecture that provides aggregate enterprise-wide information, which, in turn, enables us to understand what each of our business units is doing. This makes it possible to know how our customers are spending time and money with us in each of our properties. By having a uniform system for all properties, we are able to benefit from the power of large numbers. In contrast, many of our competitors can be described as portfolio managers, meaning they run their companies independently of one another, so they cannot combine and utilize the power of the math.
>
> In my area, this allows us to look at our slot machines as a point-of-sale device. It's a place where we communicate with customers,

and it's where they spend a lot of their time and money. With standardization, when a customer uses a card, we are able to collect very accurate point-of-sale information about each and every customer transaction. The slot machines tell a lot about the customer, but how this information is used upstream is where we really create our value.

When Gary Loveman joined the company in 1998, the company had the right technology and transactional data, but this by itself wasn't enough. He points out:

> We knew who came into our casinos, and we knew when and what they did. But we didn't know the potential value of a customer based on the little we knew from having seen him. We observed that a large number of our customers visited us only once in a 12-month period. If we compared these customers to those who visited twice or more, the gap in profitability was enormous. So the challenge was, "How do we convert a single-time visitor to a multiple-time visitor in any given year?" That was a marketing problem. Another way to put that question is: "Why is a person that we want only visiting once and not choosing to visit again, when in all likelihood, he is visiting a competitor in the marketplace for a subsequent trip?" This thinking is what led us to the notion of modeling what a customer ought to do rather than just what he does. This was the basic insight that prompted us to think about marketing as a potential profitability versus an observed profitability. We then took our data and did retrospective analyses to see if we could predict behaviors of customers based on what we observed about them.

Says Boushy:

> When I went down to Memphis in 1992, one of the first things we had to agree on was that we weren't going to have different systems in each of our casinos. To do otherwise, we would never have been able to meet our speed to the market. We also knew that aggregating had a significant long-term value. American Express originally thought it was in the transaction-processing business. Eventually, they realized they were in the information business. Well, from day one, we started this knowing we were in the information business.

Where Are the Customers' Yachts?

There's a story about a man who visits his stockbroker in Fort Lauderdale. "I want you to look out the window," the stockbroker tells his client. "Do you see all those beautiful yachts at that dock?"

The customer glances outside and nods his head. The stockbroker continues, "See that big one in the first row. That's our president's yacht. The one right next to it belongs to our top salesman. The big one on the other side is our chairman's yacht. And mine is beside his," he says with obvious pride.

"Yes," the man says, "but where are the customers' yachts?"

This story is reminiscent of the question Bob Dowd asked in 1988 when Harrah's began focusing on generating more business at its five properties through its cross-marketing efforts. Dowd said that he understood the value created for the shareholders and employees, but he questioned, "Where's the value to customers?"

To answer Dowd's question, Rich Mirman explains, "It's true that we collect information about our customers for marketing purposes. But from a customer's perspective, it's in their best interests to show us as much information as they can, and at the same time, for them to consolidate their play. This is true for all casinos, or for that matter, any loyalty program. The more credit they get for consolidating their play with us, the more they play. That's the fact of the program."

George Dittman says:

> In the past, we were no different from the rest of the industry. We were ignoring mid-level customers and focusing our attention on high-level customers at the table games. But once our technology was in place to identify customers with annual $1,000 budgets, we could pay special attention to them. Our research revealed that the customer that we designated as an AEP was not being serviced. This is who we now cater to—this is our bread-and-butter customer.
>
> Now that we have defined our niche in the marketplace, we can conduct research on these customers to find out what they like in a casino, what they go for, what facilities they want, and so on. For instance, we learned that these customers want a gaming facility where employees recognize them. They complained about feeling lost in large casinos such as MGM or Caesars. Knowing this, we can establish a relationship with AEP customers, the same customers that, in other casinos, would have to gamble at a $3,000-a-day level before anyone gives them any attention.

An important piece of information revealed about customers at the AEP level was that, primarily, they come to the casino for the gambling. They're there to escape their everyday, humdrum life. Gambling is exciting. Other things are secondary—the shows, the restaurants, the shops, the hotel rooms, and so on. While those attractions do reward casino play, the customers' main interest is gambling. It's their favorite form of recreation. So, what should the casino do to satisfy them? *No hassles.* They don't like to wait for anything, so be sure to give them their drinks on time, give them fast and friendly change service, speed up their check-in time at the hotel, get them seated quickly in the restaurants, and bring them their cars without delay.

One of the biggest changes in the gaming industry is the huge crowds that come to casinos today. The numbers have increased tenfold since the 1970s and 1980s. Tom Jenkin says:

> It's more mass marketing today. Years ago, all of us knew 20 or 30 customers that we had good relationships with. We knew their wife, kids, and even their dog's name. We talked to them on the phone, sent birthday cards, and when they came in, they'd ask for us and we'd join them for a drink or perhaps lunch or dinner. We had a relationship with those customers, but we never knew the vast majority of all the other people who came through our doors. Sure, we did our best to provide a good experience to those people—but we didn't get to know them. Our technology has since allowed us to deliver a high level of service and establish relationships with different segments of customers. None of our competitors are able to match us when it comes to making the appropriate offers and incentives to mid- and lower-level players.

Under the old business model that was used in the casino industry for years, customer relationships were limited to individual employees who worked with a small number of key customers. However, with the growth and increase in number of Harrah's properties, that business model no longer worked. The old method had still another flaw—customer loyalty was to an individual employee as opposed to the company. Today, the customer receives value from the company that is delivered by employees. Dave Kowal explains:

> At the VIP level, everybody does a good job treating customers well. But with our technology, when I'm dealing with you as our customer, I can look at you and know who you are beyond my four walls. If you visit me in Chicago, I know who you are, and I'll know who you are when you visit me in Atlantic City. A competitive advantage that we enjoy is even when you spend only $30 or so every couple of weeks, we can still track your play and reward you. You can be a first-time visitor at Las Vegas or Lake Tahoe—or any of our 26 casinos. When you stick your card in the machine, you are instantly recognized and any value in terms of comp value or cash value in your account can instantly be transported and available to you. As I said, all casinos do it well at the VIP level. But we've been able to take it down to a lower level. This is accomplished by our technology—if we had to depend on manpower, below a certain level it wouldn't be cost-effective.

From a customer's viewpoint, it's a good feeling to walk into a casino for the first time and be treated like an old friend. While the AEP may not be a high roller, he or she is a valued customer, and it's probable that the customer will appreciate receiving a comp in a far-away casino that knows who he or she is and makes him or her feel important. The company's objective is for the customer to receive the same level of service and relationship that would have been delivered by a host who was in charge of the account. The existing available information on each customer makes this possible. It also allows Harrah's to customize its relationship with large numbers of people. For instance, a customer might require a refrigerator in his or her room because of a medical condition; another may prefer a specific brand of wine. Information technology offers an endless list of ways to tailor-make each guest's experience.

As Rich Mirman points out:

> There is consistency on how a customer is treated at every touch-point. This is true at the property, at the call center, through the mailbox, at the kiosk, and at the Total Rewards center. At every touchpoint, there is the exact set of information about this customer that includes every single interaction at any Harrah's property he has ever visited.
>
> While this is an exceptional tool from a marketing perspective, from a customer perspective, it's all about rewards.

The Value of a Customer

Formulas that assign value to a customer are nothing new. A car dealer, for example, determines that a 30-year-old customer who buys a $30,000 car will potentially buy 20 more cars during his or her lifetime. With inflation factored in, the dealer determines he has a $1 million customer. You can do the same thing with any customer—the total fees someone will pay for cable television if the customer renews the service for the rest of his or her life; the total number of golf balls a golfer will consume; the number of soft drinks, razor blades, and cosmetics products will be purchased; and so on. Every business can place a value on a customer by projecting repeat sales based on the assumption the customer will remain loyal for the rest of his or her life.

This simple math *assumes* the maximum long-term value of a single customer. It brings to mind the story of an engineer, a chemist, and a marketing vice president who are shipwrecked on a desert island.

Their sole source of food is a crate of canned beans, but they must first figure out a way to open the cans.

The engineer suggests that they build a catapult and fling the cans against a large rock to smash them open. The chemist vetoes the suggestion, and instead recommends starting a fire, so the cans will burst open. "No, no," exclaims the marketing vice president. "Assume that we have a can opener."

As in this story, many marketing people place a value on their customers based on assumptions, but, in truth, they are playing a guessing game. Assuming that you have a loyal customer for life after the initial sale is wishful thinking. It's preposterous to deny that customers can be wooed by a competitor, or to try to predict whether they will want your product in the future. Yet, if a value can be placed on a first-time customer, Harrah's has figured out a way to do it. Gary Loveman says:

> Compared to other products in the consumer businesses, one defining factor about Harrah's is that we know what every customer is worth. Think about that. That's a transforming event in marketing. The airlines don't know. The banks don't know. Even the grocery store never bothers to calculate it. They can't tell you about their customers with the precision we do. You'd think the banks, catalog retailers, and supermarkets would excel in this area, but they don't.

Harrah's tracks a customer's play at the table games much the same way its competitors do. A pit boss tracks how much they buy in for and how much they buy out for. Average bets are also tracked. Based on this, casinos have a fairly accurate gauge to size up a customer. However, Harrah's excels at knowing its customers in the slot machine area. Bear in mind that, in the past, slot machine customers were overlooked—casinos knew little about them and cared little about them. This is not the case today at Harrah's. With two-thirds of its revenues coming from its slot machines, Harrah's is paying very close attention to these customers. Considering the large number of slots customers, with its technology in place, Harrah's knows a great deal about these players. Rich Mirman emphasizes:

> We tap into a wealth of information about our slot customers. Remember now, we have all the demographic information that customers give us when they sign up for a Total Rewards card. We have their name, address, phone number, e-mail address, age, birth date, and so on. We also know which of our properties they frequent. Next, there's the information we find out about them at the slot machines. We know their actual wins and losses, the duration of play,

the frequency of their play, the denomination of their play, and how many coins they put in the machine. And most importantly, we know the velocity of their play. Velocity is the rate that they put coins in the machines—naturally, the faster the better. When players slowly push the button, it indicates they're not frequent players—the slowness of play means hesitation and unfamiliarity with the game. On the other hand, serious gamblers will rapidly hit the button to make their bets. They know what they're doing—they're there to play. They enjoy the thrill—it's a lightning-quick, passionate thing. And it's a strong signal that this is a good player! After one hour, we can look at this and get a sense of the player we want to be our customer—and we also know that we should start comping this individual.

We even know how many different machines they play. We track their play on every machine—and at every Harrah's property. Then we aggregate it all up. And we have the ability to look at it by property or aggregate. And we know whether they predominantly play slots or predominantly play table games. This is all we need to know. With this information, we can determine the value of our customers.

When we have our first contact with a customer—and this is true with every industry—we get only a small share of his total budget. Let's say a Las Vegas player is staying at the Mirage or Caesars, and he comes across the street to check out Harrah's. Consequently, the time spent on his gaming here is only a small piece of his wallet. In this respect, it's like an investor who places an order with a stockbroker for the first time—it's a single transaction—he doesn't transfer his entire portfolio when he tests the waters. The same thing applies when someone flies an airline that's not his regular carrier, purchases a new kind of golf balls, or eats at a different pizza parlor.

At Harrah's, we call these customers "first trippers," and when I started here in '98, they were 70 percent of our database. These customers took the time to sign up for a Total Gold card and played; yet, a high percentage of them never came back. Now why is that? The reason is that they were staying somewhere else, so after coming to our casino and playing for a while, they went back to their hotel. Consequently, they played 10 hours there, and perhaps one hour at Harrah's. Because the other casino got the lion's share of their business, it might have comped them with a free room, two steak dinners, and perhaps show tickets for their next visit. For their one hour of play at Harrah's, we sent them a two-for-one offer for a buffet dinner. Instead of figuring, "Well, the buffet offer from Harrah's was generous because I only played there for a short time," they think, "Who are those guys? I'm never going back to Harrah's again. I'm only going back to the Mirage (Flamingo, Treasure Island, etc.) where they took great care of me."

That's how we used to treat first-trippers, and, sure enough, we rarely were able to dislodge customers from the host casino that had their loyalty. However, casino customers are, by nature, promiscuous. They want to check out a lot of different places. They like seeing what's going on at different casinos, and they visit other places for a change of luck. But they are loyal to the one casino that treats them well.

For obvious reasons, we didn't have much chance of winning over new customers with our two-for-one buffet offer. It paled in comparison to what the other casino comped them. After analyzing our low batting average with the first-trippers, we decided to use a different strategy. We took a long, hard look at the information we had on them, and it was the same that we had on our loyal customers. That's because in addition to the information we knew about them because they filled out the Total Gold application, we had all the data about their slot play even though they played for only an hour or so. We knew the size of their bets, the rapidity of their bets, their wins, their losses, and so on. We had all the information that we needed to predict what they would have played staying with us for two or three days. This meant we *could* determine what the upside would be if they played more with us—just as we could with customers who do stay with us. So, by making offers to them that match or exceed where they stay—even though we received only an hour's worth of their play—first-trippers could be converted into loyal customers. And imagine their reaction when, after they spend an hour in our casino, we offer them generous comps inviting them to be our guests when they next come to town. "Wow, this is amazing," they exclaim. "Harrah's is willing to give me a free room and steak dinner the next time I'm there. I was there for only one hour—what a fantastic casino!"

With this approach, we started to dislodge customers from the casinos that had their loyalty. This is where our direct mail and tele-marketing campaign kick in.

A Pavlovian Approach to Marketing

Mirman reveals:

Our objective is to build a relationship with those first-trippers. Once they've signed up for a Total Rewards card and played for a brief time in one of our properties, we consider it the beginning of a relationship. Admittedly, it's not a strong relationship, but it is a relationship. These customers are placed in our New Business Program.

We built a marketing strategy that buckets customers, putting first-trippers in one of three groups. The first group of people play in the $500 a day and above range, the second group, in the $100 to $500 a day range, and a third group play less than $100 a day but visit with high frequency. In some of our Midwest properties, for instance, it's not uncommon for this last group of customers to come 50 times or more a year. The program uses different criteria and fluctuates depending on the market where the property is located. In one market, for instance, a first-tripper could be defined as a customer we have known for less than six months, and has visited perhaps two or three times. In another market, the customer has visited us maybe only once during the last 12 months. A destination resort area like Las Vegas or Lake Tahoe would have a longer time frame between visits than a market like St. Louis or Kansas City, both defined as high-frequency markets (also referred to as day-trip markets). Our first objective with first-trippers is to get them over the hump of that first trip. We want them back in our casino. So, we offer them excellent comps that they view as disproportionately generous for the short time they spent at our property compared to where they normally play.

Once they come out of the New Business Program, our "Pavlovian" marketing takes over. Here we have a mathematical model that tells us what appeals to specific gamblers based on data tracking their previous behavior at our properties. Our computer is programmed to spit out behavior modification reports that target customers for specific offers. With one customer, a cash offer will trigger a response, and another customer is motivated by the offer of a free room. If a customer doesn't respond to an offer, the customer is automatically moved into the retention program. Here, offers are made that, hopefully, trigger another visit, and if that succeeds, the customer is transferred into the original cycle.

We classify each customer, regardless of whether it's his first visit or his hundredth. We use two categories: frequency and budget. Frequency is determined by several factors. For instance, customers who live close to the casino are much more apt to frequently visit it than those who live farther away. Likewise, an older customer is more apt to frequently visit a casino than a younger customer. The other dimension is budget, and that is determined by the denomination the customer bets and his play velocity.

If a customer's frequency is lower than we think it should be, say, someone comes twice a year, and we think he could be a once-a-month customer, we'll start making attractive offers, but we might tighten up the expiration. For example, a 30-day expiration period gives the offer a sense of urgency; he might come sooner than he had otherwise planned to visit. Likewise, a customer might want to take advantage of our offer and stay with us rather than where he had originally planned to stay.

Note we don't collect some data that might seem to be important. Remember now, they've put down their birth date and address when they signed up for their Total Rewards card, but we don't have any income or credit information (unless they specifically sign up for credit). That's because everything we do is based mainly on behavioral, not demographic, information. We know there are high-income people who spend small amounts of their leisure time gambling and low-income people who spend a majority of their leisure time gambling.

Once we know the potential value of a customer and what offers motivate him to visit us, we rely on our Pavlovian marketing approach to be the carrot to get him to visit our casino. Our objective is to change a customer's behavior. This is quite different from what our competition does—their marketing efforts are geared to reward but not necessarily change the customer's behavior.

Mirman points out that the company is constantly relying on "test control." Mailings are continually being sent to customers in test groups to determine which offers are more effective. Either/or offers are also made, such as a free room or $50 in cash. These offers are limited to specific periods—and if not used, they expire. Here, too, the objective is to inspire the customer to make a decision. Some offers must be redeemed within a week or two. Others are tightened up and although they are good for a long time, they are packaged so a customer may receive 10 offers, each redeemable on a specific week over a 10-week period. This way, a customer can look at his calendar and determine, "I'm going to Atlantic City anyway, so I should take advantage of this offer from Harrah's."

The Harrah's model sets budgets and calendars for gamblers, calculating their "predicted lifetime value." When a gambler's value is less than predicted—say he skips a monthly visit—Harrah's "intervenes" with a letter or phone call offering a free meal, a show ticket, or a cash voucher. Telemarketers are trained to get customers to talk about their casino experiences, and then to listen for particular phrases such as *hotel room,* or *steak dinner,* to come up with the most alluring offer.

Gary Loveman thinks that too much attention is given to the physical attributes of the gaming business. An outsider who joined Harrah's in 1998, he took an entirely different approach. While casino companies have traditionally relied on the addition of supply to increase growth, the ex-Harvard Business School professor had what many gaming experts considered a sophomoric premise. He proposed that growth could occur by stimulating demand. Gary Thompson, communications director, says:

Our competitors use a "pull" strategy. They rely primarily on bricks and mortar to pull customers into their properties. Their approach is: "We built this expensive casino resort, come see it." Ours is a "push" strategy that uses database marketing to push people to markets. We do this by giving them offers tailored for them. With our marketing analysis, we anticipate their needs and desires.

With the data Harrah's keeps on its customers, it can quickly respond when patterns change. CFO Chuck Atwood explains:

We may notice a certain customer who visits our casino every third Thursday, and then we notice she missed a couple of turns. One of our telemarketers will call, "We haven't seen you for a while, and we wanted to know if everything is okay. Is there something we might have done? What can we do to make it up to you?" Not only does this enable us to correct an unpleasant experience, it opens dialogue to let the customer know we care about her.

With more than 25 million gamblers in its database, Harrah's is able to track individual customer play—a remarkable competitive advantage that has been achieved through IT and marketing people working side by side. At present, no other casino company has the combination of technology and marketing expertise to duplicate it. Doubting Thomases have questioned the method as too impersonal, but others acknowledge accuracy is increased by reliance on the law of large numbers. Here, Harrah's enjoys a competitive advantage because its distribution is geographically spread out in 20 markets and its 26 properties are linked to a common database.

The Harrah's marketing team is convinced that the information gleaned from its technology is superior to researching customers via typical surveys. For example, an airline surveying travelers may ask, "How many flights on all airlines do you fly in a 12-month period?" A customer might be less than truthful on a questionnaire and answer 100, thinking he or she will receive better treatment by being viewed as a big-time flyer. Likewise, a casino customer may overstate how many times he or she gambles with the belief that an inflated number will entitle him or her to more comps.

Predicting Customer Behavior

With many Harrah's slot machines set to pay out at 95 percent-plus, it may seem a huge gamble to offer future comps to people who walk in off the street for an hour's worth of play. Not so. It's simply a cost of doing business.

Every business incurs an acquisition cost to land new customers. For instance, selling costs include anything from sales commissions to travel expenses. Even when no salespeople are involved, acquisition costs can range from mailing catalogs to primetime advertising. Consider the extravagant billion-dollar casinos built to lure people to come through their doors—the huge investment and overhead associated with these properties are also costs to acquire new customers.

So while the comps that Harrah's dishes out to first-trippers to entice them to become second-trippers may seem extravagant, in retrospect, they are not so far-fetched after all.

Remember that Harrah's doesn't have a big budget for advertising to the public. As Ginny Shanks, a marketing vice president, explains:

> Our occupancy in our hotels is over 90 percent, and we know that people who stay elsewhere will leave their hotel. They primarily visit other properties for three reasons: dining, entertainment, and, to some extent, as a result of a promotion. So, when we do advertise, our messages focus on the above. For the benefit of tourists, our advertising appears at the airport, and on taxicab tops, billboards, and tourist publications in hotel rooms. We don't do much television or radio advertising because those media don't reach tourists. As a company, we rely on our customer database as our number one source. Why? Because when you think about the price of getting somebody you know to come back, versus getting somebody that doesn't know you at all to come in, it's far more economical to go after the people with whom you already have a relationship.

Rich Mirman puts it another way. "It's hard to economically determine where to fish for customers who have a high propensity to want to gamble. What's more, of those who do, you have to find customers that would enjoy gambling at Harrah's."

Lavish comps for first-trippers are revolutionary in the casino industry and don't guarantee profit. To make it work, a sizable investment in IT was required, plus abundant resources for research and development. As Rich Mirman emphasized earlier, it would be foolhardy for a competitor to think it can duplicate the success of Harrah's simply by investing large sums of money in IT. Explains vice president Dan Nita:

> We refer to what we do here as *decision science*. In the past, we took a different view of a customer who came in for a half hour and put in three coins at a time every time he pulled the handle on a slot machine. Previously, we'd take a look at that customer and think of him being worth $15 to us. And we'd treat him accordingly, perhaps sending him a coupon good for a half-price meal at one of our less

expensive restaurants. Now, with the data we have on this same customer, instead of looking at him as a $15 player, we may evaluate him as a $300 player. And that's how we'll treat him.

Gary Loveman illustrates how this works:

Let's say we have a 60-year-old woman who lives in a comfortable suburb of Memphis. She visits our Tunica property on a Friday night, briefly plays a dollar slot machine, and goes home. Based on traditional casino methods, she'd have a low theoretical worth, perhaps a few dollars. Consequently, she wouldn't be a likely prospect to pursue, and little effort would be made to get her to come back. And in all likelihood, she wouldn't respond to it. Our present system draws a distinction between the observed worth of a customer and what we predict their worth is. The fact that this player is 60 years old, female, plays slots, and lives in an affluent Memphis suburb that is near Tunica now suggests to us that she's a good customer, but we just haven't seen it yet. Today, instead of ignoring her, we market to her in a way that's intended to test the proposition that she's been improperly categorized. So, with the little information we know about her, we are going to make a prediction based on what we know about people like her—that she's probably a terrific customer, even though our exposure to her is not yet inspiring. And if we predict she's a great customer, we are going to give her a very rich offer. In this particular incident, we'll give her a marketing offer that has a short redemption window to see if she responds quickly. It won't include a hotel room offer because she lives nearby. And since we know she's slot-centric, she'll receive a cash offer to play the slot machines. We'll measure how fast she responds and how much she plays. If the woman responds the way we think she will, that verifies the prediction that then puts her into a new category for the next marketing wave. What we did with this woman, we have the capacity to do across a 25-million person database and have it executed in 26 locations by modestly trained people.

David Norton, marketing vice president, asserts:

We have a lot of transaction data on our customers. We know how often they come, what they like to play, if they stay at our hotel, and so on. Since we know past behavior, we can also understand what our customers' potential is, and we can determine what their future value is likely to be. We know who's likely to be a long-term customer and who's not. We take a look at their observed behavior, and our group of analysts builds models to show their predicted behavior. We look to see if there's a gap between how many times a person comes here and the share of his wallet we receive now, versus what our models say is possible. Using this segmentation strategy, we bucket people into groups and see who comes perhaps twice a year but should come as many as 20 times a year. Within the traffic our casinos generate, we isolate these groups of customers and send them customized messages. A letter might say, "Thanks a lot for your loyalty but we'd really like to see you more often." To incent them to come, we'll shorten up their redemption window. This is Pavlovian marketing because we give them carrots such as a $20 food offer or a $20 coin offer to come. In the past, everybody would get the same redemption offer, say 60 or 90 days in one of our frequency markets in the Midwest. Now, we look at these groups, and with one of them we'll determine, "These people over here come twice a year, but we can change their behavior. So maybe we'll give them $30 if they come within 15 days, but we will still give them $20 if they come within 60 days."

With our direct mail strategy, we split people into five core segments. Because we emphasize a customer's life cycle, first, they're put in our new business group. These are people we've known less than one year, and we split them into segments one and two—low frequency and high frequency. Remember these are new customers, so we have limited data on them, such as their age and addresses. We don't have more detailed information, such as their occupation or income, but then we really don't want it. Then there's a loyalty group, people we've known for more than one year. These are segments three and four—low frequency observed, and high frequency predicted. And then there's the fifth segment—our high-frequency people. All of our show campaigns (mail campaigns) place customers into these five core segments.

In the past, 80 to 85 percent of the company's revenue was generated from its high-frequency segment, or about 10 percent of its customers. Today, 20 percent of the customers generate 80 to 85 percent of the revenues. Norton adds:

We were doing what everyone else did, and we focused our marketing energy and dollars on the group of customers who were already coming to our casino. For instance, in North Kansas City, if customers were coming 30 times a year, we were trying to entice them to come still more. But it wasn't realistic, and incrementally we weren't generating more trips from them. Now our marketing focuses on first-trippers that, for some reason, prefer going to one of our competitors. Our objective is to make attractive offers that will influence their behavior so they'll come to us more often.

At first, it was a challenge to persuade our general managers to change their thinking. "These are my core customers," they'd say, "and I don't want to do anything to lose them." In other words, the general managers were concerned that a focus on first-trippers would mean less attention given to their best customers. But those core customers came because they liked our product, had a favorite dealer, and so on. Today, with our tiered program, at the Platinum and Diamond level, they get quicker check-in service, valet parking, and a lot of other services that aren't necessarily monetary incentives. So, we kept our core customers and successfully increased our customer base.

The Right Offer

Gary Loveman attests:

> The trick here is to get the right level of marketing offer and solicitation attached to the right level of customer profitability. If you go after a broad band of customers with an undifferentiated marketing approach, then the majority of the time you fail to offer the appropriate value to the right group of people. To be cost-effective, we've focused on getting highly customized offers into the hands of carefully selected groups of people to generate visitation.

When Harrah's wants to drum up business to fill its 1,300 rooms in Lake Tahoe during November and December, it goes to its huge database of customers—the best place to find the right level of customer. According to General Manager Gary Selesner in Lake Tahoe, the average hotel guest's daily game play is $700. This means Selesner has a large number of high-level players from which to draw. "We'll send offers to fly them into Reno and pick them up by bus or limousine. My constant goal is to put the best-worth customer into the room."

Likewise, when Michael Silberling, general manager at Harrah's in Reno, wants to drum up business by flying in a chartered jet filled with high-worth gamblers, he, too, solicits people from the Harrah's database. He explains:

> If I want to bring in a plane of high-level customers from Shreveport, Chicago, or Houston on a charter program, I invite them to come on out on such-and-such a date. And to incite them, I'll give them a compelling reason about something special that's going on at the time. It could be a golf tournament, or perhaps a major entertainer such as Ray Charles will be appearing in our showroom. To fill a chartered jet or a commitment that's been made for a block of seats on a commercial airline, other casinos must place ads in the newspapers. Our database is a tremendous competitive advantage.

To determine which offer is most cost-effective, the company will examine two groups of "observationally equivalent" customers. The two groups share the same age bracket, live in the same area, and have the same history with the company. One group may receive $50 cash for the next visit, and the other will receive $25 cash, plus a free room and a free buffet. Then the company observes which group responded more favorably and how much play each group had. When the profitability of each group is determined, the company will recalibrate based on their response.

Other tests are made with offers for special events such as a concert, golf tournament, or boxing match. Customers who have been dormant for a time and are not responsive to mailings are turned over to telemarketers. Again, offers are made to trigger reactivation. And still more tests are run to see what generates favorable responses.

When the telemarketers call, they ask specific questions about why the customer hasn't returned. Depending on the customer's reply, the caller can refer to several different menus that list appropriate responses. Each response has different offers. An estimated 75 percent of the customers will consent to receiving a mailed package with a specific offer; afterward, a direct mail piece is immediately dispatched. Of these recipients, 20 to 25 percent come back to the casino.

When offers are made to a group of customers, they receive unlike offers. "One group may get an offer for $10 cash," Dan Nita says, "while another receives $5 cash. We might send food coupons to a third group, and so on. We experiment to see what offers generate the best response rates so we can determine what really drives those customers to come back."

The objective of test marketing is to see what gets the most bang for the buck. For example, Harrah's in Atlantic City sent a $50-cash offer to a group of customers who hadn't visited the casino during the past year. The offer attracted a 10 percent response rate. "After seeing those numbers, everybody was patting themselves on the back," says Nita. "Then someone suggested, 'Well, maybe just sending a letter reminding customers that we haven't seen them would also work. Let's do this with 20 percent and see what happens.' Surprisingly, we discovered we'd sometimes get more customers to show up without making an offer."

Test marketing is a good tool to access procedures so they can be improved, revised, or eliminated. For instance, in the early stages of the Total Gold program, customers were awarded bonus points for their play. A customer would receive 50 bonus points after earning 100 bonus points during a particular time frame. The objective was to incent more play. After surveying customers, it was discovered that few understood how the bonus points worked, and because the extra

50 points had a value of only $1.50, it didn't get anyone to play more. Spread throughout all Harrah's properties, the bonus points had an aggregate cost of nearly $14 million in expenses, yet each individual customer perceived it to have practically no value. Tests run on small groups suggested the bonus points program could be terminated—and no one would care. After the program terminated, not a single complaint letter was received.

For years, the company awarded cash payments to customers for their daily slot machines play, just as its competitors did. This meant that when customers put their cards in the machines and earned cash awards, they could cash in the same day. Test marketing revealed that customers weren't motivated to play more for these cash awards. Mirman explains:

> The cash was not the real motivator to get them to play. They have a budget, they have time, they have luck, they have enjoyment—all those things were what motivated them. So, the same-day cash was not a differentiator. They could walk out, go to another casino, and earn the same rate of cash there or with us. This meant that same-day cash payments were not a good investment for us. This prompted us to stop investing in a trip we were already getting, so we discontinued same-day redemptions. It was replaced by delivering cash offers through the mailbox. This way, the investment goes toward purchasing the next trip. And if they don't come back, it doesn't cost us anything.

Rich Mirman points out special offers made to some groups to change customer behavior. This occurs, for instance, when a model has predicted that a group of frequent players, identified as low-worth customers, has the potential to be high-worth customers. This group is categorized as "upside potential customers," and an objective is set to capture a larger share of their gambling budget when they return to play at Harrah's. He explains:

> Remember now, we already get them to come to our casino. So, what we might do is give them $10 for just showing up. But we'll give them $50 if they play for two hours. Why two hours? This gets them over the hurdle to tag them as a high-worth customer. What's intriguing is, they are already coming to the market and playing for that number of hours, but they had been making us their second or third stop. Now, we're changing the offer to give them a reason to switch the priority of casinos they visit. Hence, we're changing behaviors.
>
> We did another test and found out 50 percent of the customers couldn't care less how we distribute the cash to them. Twenty-five percent actually preferred mailbox delivery, and the remaining 25

percent preferred to receive it the same day. Then, we found if we slightly upped the reinvestment in cash, those people who preferred it the same day were neutralized. They were equally happy to receive a bit more in the mailbox than they would otherwise receive the same day. From our standpoint, by not giving cash that same day, the slightly higher cost we incurred generated a better return on our money.

When these customers respond to our offer and play at our casino, another offer is sent a few weeks afterward to get them to come again, and then we repeat this with a follow-up offer still another time. As I said, it's a Pavlovian marketing approach. Over time, we are capturing a significant amount, or even better, of the total share of their gaming wallet in terms of both trips and budget.

A customer recently e-mailed Phil Satre about an article that appeared in the *Wall Street Journal* May 4, 2000. "While it was an impressive article," the customer wrote, "I was offended by its reference to your company's Pavlovian approach that would characterize me as a salivating dog."

The customer ended his message by stating, "By the way, my wife and I will be out at your kennel in Las Vegas and looking for bones on the 21st and 22nd. Then my wife would like to visit your kennels in Reno and Lake Tahoe." Satre responded with a personal letter, which he signed, "Phil Satre, DVM." Satre grins:

> I knew where this guy was coming from. I'm an avid fly-fisherman, and when I get an offer for equipment or a fishing trip, I want the offer made to me. I don't want to read a lot of literature about bass fishing in Michigan's Upper Peninsula or buying an offshore boat— that's wasting my time. And don't offer me a cheap trip because I buy $5,000 fly-fishing trips to places like Alaska and Canada. I'm not interested in reading a lot of junk mail that goes to a general audience. I want them to know where I fish, what I like, and what my budget is. Similarly, we attempt to customize our offers to groups of customers that properly match their interests.

Other IT Applications

IT primarily serves Harrah's as a marketing tool, and as such, provides the company with a decisive competitive advantage. But its applications aren't exclusively limited to finding marketing solutions. IT contributes to many other areas throughout the company. One such area is surveillance. Gone are the one-way mirrors where casino security people keep a watchful eye on potential cheaters at the gaming tables. Instead, hundreds of closed circuit television monitors are strategically located throughout the casino. This technology is not unique to Harrah's—all the casinos use it.

Yet, Harrah's uses many technologies not duplicated by its competitors. For example, in addition to obtaining information on customers, IT conducts employee opinion surveys. John Boushy, chief information officer, tells:

> Periodically, we survey our employees for their feedback. We ask questions such as: "Do you have the tools to do your job?" "Do you have the training to do your job?" "Is it clear what the company expects of you?" "Is it clear that customer satisfaction is important to the company?" In 2000, for the first time, we had the technology to conduct surveys over the Internet. We had PCs set up at various points at all our properties, and within a four-day period, employees spent 10 to 15 minutes completing the survey. Using this paperless survey, we cut eight weeks off our turnaround time in getting back to our workforce. Then we told them: "This is what you told us, and here's what we're going to work on." This had a substantial effect on morale, and we intend to do this on a regular basis in the future.

A recent pilot program that's generating a great deal of interest is known as the company's *Career Development Plan*. At present, the program enables IT employees to chart their careers with Harrah's. Explains Eileen Cassini, an IT vice president:

> What an employee formerly did on paper can now be done on a computer screen. Someone can plot his career by typing in, "Here's where I am today, and here's where I want my career to take me." Our technology responds by telling this individual what skills he needs to develop in order to realize his goal. It also lists the employee's strengths and weaknesses. The employee can then hyperlink to suggestions and assessments, or if he chooses, he can sit down with his supervisor for a personal conference. Employees can also log onto a page that provides recommendations on how to build his skill sets in order to move up to the next level or into another role that he desires. Online training is also available. Today, IT employees have all the tools they need to plot their careers, and this, we think, is very empowering. As I said, this is presently available only to IT personnel, but once we get the kinks out, we'll roll it out so all company employees can access it.

Boushy says:

> An employee can say, "This is where I want to be in three years," and the program responds by listing the series of skills and experiences generally required to fill the position. Based on that, a self-assessment capability, along with an integrated component from

the employee's supervisor, offers an evaluation of where the individual is, and what is necessary for him to move forward.

Another project that is currently being used almost exclusively by IT employees is its Manager's Meeting, an informal "live" Internet conference that participants can join. Boushy explains:

> About once a month, I communicate to all IT employees to see who is interested in joining me in a casual conversation. I make a few announcements, and then I turn it into a Q&A session. I get asked everything, and about 50 percent isn't even related to technology. They want to know things ranging from "How's the company doing in New Orleans?" to "What's the status on our rising health care costs?" I think it's great that they express their interest in challenges that the company faces that are outside their area. It tells me they care about the company.

It's no surprise that a technology-savvy company like Harrah's has found many internal and external ways to use the Internet. Anika Howard-Weaver explains:

> Customers can log onto our Web site to check their Total Rewards account, and if they're interested in receiving e-mail offers and correspondence from us, we will communicate with them on a regular basis. They can visit our Web site for information ranging from show times to room availability. Here, they can log on our Guest Book that contains everything from our latest deals to amenities available at our different properties. The Internet is also an excellent source for customer information so we can present customized marketing offers. Above all else, the Internet is an incredible cost-saving tool that can convey messages to large numbers of people in a matter of microseconds.

In the late summer of 2000, Harrah's formed an alliance with iWin.com, a Web site where users vie for prizes and sweepstakes. These users play free, but they can win prizes. As one of the 20 most visited Internet sites, iWin.com is an ideal partner for Harrah's. In August 2000, there were 13 million registered users of iWin and its sister site, Uproar.com. Rich Mirman says:

> The demographics are an excellent match. Their users tend to be a little older—middle America-type people who have time to spend on the Internet and a propensity to enjoy gaming. This is a large source of potential customers, and in exchange for a chance to win prizes, we get their e-mail addresses. Iwin users can click onto a Harrah's prize section and play games that entitle winners to trips to our properties. Since gambling on the Internet is illegal, the site

makes its money strictly on advertising revenues. MGM has its own site offering games and prizes, but we're happy to partner up with a company that has expertise in an area we don't have.

With the millions of people who walk through the Harrah's casinos but don't sign up for a Total Rewards card, or those who don't use their cards, making offers to these customers is an expensive proposition. Typically, less than 1 percent respond to offers. Mirman says:

> The economics of going after this business, however, changes when the Internet becomes the communication vehicle used to pursue this large group of people. If we have their e-mail addresses, and we have distressed inventory at certain properties, we can contact these people very inexpensively by e-mail, whereas previously it was too costly. [In the lodging industry, *distressed inventory* means rooms that are vacant; as the night for renting them approaches, the more distressed they become.] It's like an airline with vacant seats: An unsold seat on a flight generates zero revenues. If, however, we can offer a room in Lake Tahoe, say for $50 a night—at the last minute via the Internet in a targeted way—we're better off than having it not sold.

According to Dave Norton, IT makes it possible for the company to have a yield management program that keeps current and accurate records of available rooms at all Harrah's properties:

> We're now able to project booking patterns for each level of our different types of customers, always with a preference to fill our rooms with the highest level guests—starting with VIPs, followed by AEPs, and, last, customers who pay the full retail price. Always mindful of the room rate, we might charge a retail customer $200 for a room but sell it for $50 to an AEP. But because the gaming revenue is such a high component, it's the most important equation in determining our maximum profitability. So, while we don't want the room to remain vacant, our objective is to never be in a position where we displace VIPs and AEPs. IT makes this yield management possible in a very automated way, whereas in the past, it was somewhat of a guessing game.

8

ALL CUSTOMERS ARE NOT CREATED EQUAL

HROUGHOUT CORPORATE AMERICA, YOU HEAR LIP SERVICE ABOUT how companies treat their customers. For example, we've all heard the boast: "We treat all customers the same—big or small." Equality is a fine ideal for a democracy, but in the business world, does anyone treat all customers the same, without regard to revenue?

It isn't practical to treat all of your customers alike, nor is it good business. It is prudent to treat your small customer courteously as you do a big customer, because mighty oaks from tiny acorns grow. But do you really think a large food supplier extends the same level of service to a mom and pop grocery that it gives to a giant national supermarket chain? Every customer is deserving of respect, but considering the huge volume and profit margins generated by a large account, prioritizing pays off. Certainly, you shouldn't ignore small customers to care for your big accounts, but there are different levels of service that should be reserved for your biggest customers. For instance, a large ticket item may have a higher level of service built into its sticker price—a luxury car versus an economy car, a grand resort hotel versus a budget motel, a four-star restaurant versus a neighborhood family style eatery, and so on.

In certain industries, it isn't possible to promise equality to all customers, regardless of size, and this is definitely true in the casino business. Depending on the level of play, customers receive a wide range of comps. Unquestionably, no other industry is so obvious about the pecking order of its perks. This is apparent from the moment you register for a hotel room at a Las Vegas casino. On your first visit to a casino during a busy day, be prepared to stand in a long line that snakes around the lobby several times. Waiting in line gives you plenty of time to notice that not all guests have to wait to check in. At Harrah's, rated players and Total Rewards members with Diamond cards register in a hassle-free, deluxe VIP lounge. In addition, depending on their rating, there may be no room charge on their bill. The very best customers are comped an exquisite suite, including meals.

After their express reservation experience, hungry Diamond and Platinum cardholders again avoid long lines in the restaurants. At Rio's famed seafood buffet, for instance, cardholders stand in an express lane that short-circuits what could otherwise be a two-hour wait on a busy night. On weekends, some of the finer Harrah's restaurants take dinner reservations only for the casino's best customers. This is the way it is at all fine dining spots in casinos in Las Vegas. At Bellagio's premier restaurants, dinner reservations before nine are given only to its registered hotel guests and rated players.

Anywhere else, customers would be enraged to see VIPs ushered to the front of the line and whisked off to a waiting table. But in the world of gaming, this is how the game is played. It's a fact of life that a customer's gambling activity determines how he or she is treated. Casinos don't care whether you win or lose—only that you play the game. The more time and money you put into your game, the more royally you are treated. Casino patrons accept this favoritism as standard procedure.

The practice of comping goes back to the 1940s in Nevada and has prevailed throughout the industry ever since. No matter what a person's net worth, if he or she is not a player, he or she isn't comped. Harrah's doesn't know how much money a customer has—that only becomes a consideration if an individual requests a line of credit. Otherwise, the company makes no attempt to find out, because it doesn't matter.

Michael Silberling, general manager at Harrah's in Reno, explains:

> I look at the way customers are treated in this business, and I think it's the greatest equalizer with a total lack of prejudice, more so than anywhere I've ever been. It doesn't matter if you're male or female, young or old, white or black. If you come in prepared to wager, then you're going to be treated accordingly, based on the amount of money you put at risk. And we don't care if you win or lose. It's refreshing to be in a business that has such a lack of prejudice.
>
> Now this doesn't imply that we'd ever treat someone poorly. We take great pride in giving excellent service to all customers. However, if you're gambling in an area of the casino where you're betting black chips (worth $100) or above, your drink comes faster, and if your jackpot is paid, you wait in a shorter line.

Phil Satre recalls his days at Holiday Inn, where all customers were treated alike:

When a customer pays X amount of dollars for a room, it doesn't matter who you are. If you stay in a Holiday Inn room, the company receives the same rate from you as it does from any other customer for that room. That's because the profitability on all customers is equal. In the gaming business, however, there is a considerable variation in the value of the customer. Certain customers can be extremely valuable to the business due to their frequency of gambling and visitation, plus their ability to play at high levels.

In most service industries, there's a 20/80 principle at work: 20 percent of a company's customers generate roughly 80 percent of its revenues. Gary Thompson explains:

> Our research reveals that about 11 to 12 percent of gaming industry customers represent more than 50 percent of its total revenues. These people have a passion for gaming, and it's their favorite pastime. And, for the record, they're not putting hundreds of thousands of dollars on the table. They spend between $3,000 and $5,000 a year. Gaming puts some excitement in their lives. At Harrah's, we're trying to make sure we capture our share of these customers. We do it by offering uniformity in the way we service them.

Comping

When it comes to gaming tables and slot machines, there's not a whole lot of difference from one casino to another. In a free-enterprise system where there are marginal differences in product, the struggle for market share becomes highly competitive. This prompted the trend to build theme casinos. Driven by competitive forces, casino owners engaged in a race to outbuild and outspend each other. Soon, bigger and more expensive casino resorts were constructed, and when the dust settled, Las Vegas was home to 15 of the world's 16 largest hotels. Bellagio and the Venetian may be the two most expensive hotels ever built.

Elaborately expensive properties are considered today's main drawing card to attract customers. In the past, present, and, no doubt, the future, other enticements include big-time entertainment, fine dining, and special events. The list of special events runs the gamut, including boxing matches, golf tournaments, concerts, poker tournaments, and slot machine tournaments. Their purpose is to attract customers to spend their time and money in the casinos. If it were possible to fill the casinos to maximum capacity without these attractions, none of these enhancements would exist. Under such a scenario, there would be only gaming tables and slot machines; additional trimmings would be unnecessary overhead.

Comps are by no means a recent innovation. Comping is as old as the casino business itself. The practice began when casinos started to provide free alcoholic beverages to preferred clientele. Complimentary meals were a natural for casinos. After all, customers had to eat, and casino owners didn't want anyone leaving the premises. Likewise, free lodging kept guests from straying elsewhere, which meant they could spend more time at the tables. When executed by astute businesspeople, the costs of comps are built into a casino's business model. Conceptually, this requires casino management to calculate comps as routine expenses to acquire and retain customers. Properly done, it's no different from building in other expenses such as advertising and payroll. In addition, most businesses allocate a budget for entertaining customers and clients. Casino companies just take it to another level!

Since the early days of Las Vegas, steady bread-and-butter casino customers have earned comps—most commonly free drinks, meals, and show tickets. The more expensive comps—a room, air travel, or the companionship of a beautiful woman—were reserved for high rollers. The VIP treatment served to motivate aspiring players: By increasing their play, they, too, could acquire high-roller status.

In the early 1960s, many casino resorts began flying in players from across the country on junkets. A company employee or an independent junket agent arranged these trips by inviting known players from a particular metropolitan area to spend a few days in Las Vegas at a host casino. The concept was reminiscent of Bill Harrah's busing people to Lake Tahoe during the winter season. Based again on the theory of bringing the mountain to Mohammed, junkets were packaged to woo known players. Depending on a player's credit line, junkets included free transportation, lodging, meals, and whatever else might be available to a high roller. The heyday of junkets was before the advent of computers; consequently, they were arranged on a hit-or-miss basis. Now and then, an overzealous junket agent would extend a free package to a low roller whose gambling activity did not merit the comps. The concept of junkets is basically sound; if executed properly, a junket with an airplane filled with high rollers is money well spent.

Harrah's has a long history in comping customers. A popular comp was free tickets to see Bill Harrah's famed automobile collection, one of Reno's major tourist attractions. A tour personally guided by Bill Harrah was a rarely given comp, reserved for major high rollers. Another drawing card has been entertainment. For many years, Harrah's was the showplace of the casino industry's biggest entertainers. Front-row seats were awarded to the most deserving customers. There was always an obvious hierarchy in the showrooms. While you couldn't detect the biggest gamblers by their appearances, you could easily spot them by which tables they occupied in the restaurants and showrooms. Introductions to the superstars were reserved for high rollers. In addition, at the celebrity golf tournaments, high rollers often played in foursomes with an invited celebrity.

Superstar entertainers received the comps normally reserved for the casino's high rollers. Harrah's, in fact, was even more generous with its top stars, housing them in its Lake Tahoe hotel penthouse, as well as in leased lakefront homes. They were given the use of Rolls Royces during their stay, and the company jets would whisk them in and out of town; indeed, they received the red carpet treatment. These amenities enabled Harrah's to compete with the Las Vegas casinos by attracting the superstars to Reno and Lake Tahoe. Some entertainers also liked to gamble, so the comps they received served a dual purpose. Nat King Cole, for instance, was one of the biggest stars in the late 1950s and early 1960s to appear at Harrah's. In those days, he was paid $17,500 a week, the company's highest salary at the time. Cole loved the action in the casino and couldn't stay out of it between performances. It was not unusual for him to ask for his entire salary the first week, even though he had another week to go, and still get advances on his next engagement. Sometimes, it was the entertainer's spouse who was the heavy gambler. Singer Teresa Brewer's husband, Bill Monaghan, would draw an advance against her $30,000 weekly salary paid by Harrah's; occasionally, he lost her entire salary at the tables before her opening act.

Many entertainers, known for their big egos, insist on receiving the star treatment. Those who draw large crowds into the casino get it—and at Harrah's, they got it in spades. Feeding egos is an important factor in comping customers, for receiving the red carpet treatment at a casino is indeed an ego trip. Casino owners understand this well and diligently work at satisfying the biggest of egos. They start by making sure their employees greet rated players by name. Desk clerks in the VIP lounges review daily guest lists so they can recognize and welcome high-level players on arrival. Everyone on the floor—casino hosts, pit bosses, dealers, and cocktail waitresses— works overtime to make sure he or she is current on names of guests to acknowledge. Restaurant managers conduct daily meetings during which they review names of main players they will serve during the evening. All headwaiters and each maitre d' are tipped off in advance so they can personally welcome VIPs. This treatment is no different from the treatment received when a good customer walks into a restaurant in his or her hometown and is greeted by the maitre d' or owner. Likewise, customers relish being greeted by a store manager or an owner of a small haberdashery or boutique shop. Although a seemingly small gesture, a simple verbal acknowledgment massages customers' egos and keeps them coming back.

Of course, customers in particular enjoy perks that are reserved only for a chosen few. Therefore, in addition to having a floor manager walk across a crowded aisle to extend a warm hello in the casino, a perk such as a guest's favorite cognac goes far to stroke an ego, particularly with the right presentation. "Mr. Smith," a casino host may say, "I remember you like Godiva chocolates, so I wanted you to enjoy these during your visit." Royal treatment makes customers feel important and sends an immediate message to everyone in the vicinity: "This is Mr. Big, our valued customer."

Depending on a customer's rating, "customized comps" can range from a special brand of wines to a bouquet of flowers delivered to a guest's room. The bigger the player, the more he or she is showered with comps—and the more attention to detail. Customers are aware of what comps they are entitled to receive, and those with big egos aren't shy about asking for what they think is due them. Ray Gambardella, a former director of table game hosts at Rio, says:

> One customer loved to be comped a box of Royal Jamaica cigars. As soon as he walked into the casino, he'd ask his host for a box. "You have to play first," the host told him. This customer would bicker with the host for a few minutes and then settle down to play. An hour or so later, he'd ask, "Can I have my cigars now?" "Not yet," the host answered. A little later, the customer asked again, "Have I earned my cigars yet?" "Okay," the host finally said, "I'll get them for you now."

Considering the large sums of money involved, to many, the casino industry's practice of comping customers seems like a sloppy way to do business. After all, even in relatively small casinos, millions of dollars are spent on comps. If comps are indiscriminately dished out without a system to control who gets what, a casino company could gravely imperil its bottom line. In the early days when the mob controlled the business and skimming was prevalent, comping may have been a way to artificially expense unreported profits. Comping is also a carryover from those days when casinos were not operated by astute businesspeople. Nevertheless, comping remains a common practice in the casino industry—and when properly controlled, it is an effective way to retain customer loyalty. With the Harrah's technology in place, customers' play is tightly tracked; therefore, comps are not dished out in a slipshod fashion.

There was some initial resistance to scientifically designated comping. Long-time Harrah's employees may have been accustomed to comping a customer based only on their hunches. Old-timers in the business who thought they knew their customers intimately didn't appreciate techies invading their turf, telling them how much customers were entitled to receive based on computer printouts. These employees resented having their judgment questioned by home office personnel from afar. It took time for employees to embrace the new systems, to accept change after years of doing business another way.

Today, Harrah's casino employees have adapted to and accepted the new methods of tracking customers' play. They now spend considerably less time taking notes to track bets. Casino technology is designed to relieve them of some of their former chores. The new system keeps accurate records on customers and, consequently, allows casino employees to follow concise guidelines on comping. There is no foolproof system to assure that every player at the gaming tables is comped exactly as he or she should be, but certainly today, there is less chance for error at the slot machines because computers keep accurate score. Recently, there have been several published articles and books that offer instruction on how players can earn more comps than they deserve—to try to beat the system. One tip that has been passed on to thousands of gamblers is to place more chips on the table when a floor supervisor is watching and to cut back on bets when he or she isn't. By doing this, a player tries to appear to be a bigger player than he or she actually is.

To people unfamiliar with the casino industry, comping seems to be a way to buy a customer's business by showering him or her with gifts. Regardless of what outsiders may think, customers like it, and the casinos view it as an accepted business practice. At Harrah's, it's a major expense to the company, with comps running about 7.5 percent of annual revenues—in 2002, an estimated $300 million. Because that's a huge expense, comps are monitored and judiciously rewarded to "deserving" customers.

Swimming with the Whales

It was a Saturday night and the Harrah's casino in Lake Tahoe was packed. Thousands of people were playing the slots; impatient customers stood behind playing customers and waited for them to vacate their seats at the table games.

It was a good night for celebrity watching. In the high-limit area, Charlie Sheen, Emilio Estevez, and a few of their friends were playing baccarat, and hundreds of passersby tried to catch a glimpse of the show business celebrities. Meanwhile, beyond the gawkers, at the next table an unassuming man from Hong Kong was hardly noticed. The horde of people passing never gave him a second look. Yet, high-ranking managers of the casino were carefully watching every card of baccarat as it came out of the shoe. The Asian bet huge sums of money on each hand, sums that dwarfed all others in the casino. On this particular night, the casino's entire profits or losses were dependent on whether this one individual won or lost, making the play of all the other customers in the casino seem inconsequential. A single man would determine how the casino did that night.

The man from Hong Kong was a whale—a designation given only to the world's biggest gamblers. They are so identified because a whale is the biggest fish in the ocean. Actually, a whale is not a fish but a mammal, but the analogy is a picturesque way to describe these big-time gamblers. There are an estimated 200 whales in the entire world, and their gambling credit lines run into the seven and eight figures. Eighty percent of whales are from Asian countries where gambling is often publicly taboo but privately acceptable. On a given stay at a casino, a whale could win or lose $10 million to $15 million. At this rate, one or two whales' winnings can dramatically modify a casino company's quarterly earnings. In 2000, Rio's losses to whales made a big dent in Harrah's reported earnings for two consecutive quarters.

When Harrah's acquired Rio in January 1999, it did so with the intention of owning one of the premier resort casinos in Las Vegas. In effect, Harrah's wanted a property that could compete favorably with Bellagio, the Mirage, Caesars, and other ultra-deluxe casino resorts. While Harrah's on the Strip was a popular and profitable casino, it was not in the same league as newly built billion-dollar properties that had become the "in" places to stay. There was no question that the magnificent newer properties had more appeal to high-level gamblers. This is particularly true when it comes to catering to the whims of whales. After all, anyone who can afford to gamble for such high stakes is indeed a very wealthy person with an eight-figure-plus net worth. Such people live a very rich lifestyle— and when they travel, they go first-class all the way. They can have the best that money can buy, and that's what they want and demand from a casino. Accordingly, when whales come to Vegas, they expect red-carpet treatment comparable to that normally reserved for royalty and heads of state.

Just how wealthy some whales are is illustrated by a story told by Russ McLennan, vice president of player development:

> A while back, some potential high rollers from Hong Kong visited us in Lake Tahoe. Their party, which included their children, totaled 18 people. After staying a few days, they asked us for transportation back to Reno. At the time, we had two Rolls Royce limos and a Cadillac limo. When the Rolls pulled up to the front of the hotel, I said to one of them, "This is your limo. Have you ever been driven in a Rolls before?" "Yes," he answered, "I own three of them." Not long afterward, I went with two of our vice presidents to Hong Kong, and this customer sent three Rolls Royces to the airport to pick us up— one for each of us.

When it comes to rolling out the red carpet, nobody does it better than Las Vegas. Why else would the super rich travel from Hong Kong, Taiwan, and Tokyo to a remote place in the Nevada desert to place their bets? After all, casinos are everywhere, including across the United States. In Vegas, whales are treated literally like kings. They usually arrive on their private jet planes. Or, if they prefer, a casino will dispatch its own jet to fly them in—Harrah's will send its own G-4 aircraft. On arrival, they are chauffeur-driven in a stretch limousine to one of the world's largest and most spectacular hotels, and their suites—*suite* is hardly the word to describe the accommodations— range in size from a few thousand square feet to as much as 45,000 square feet. The suites have Italian marble floors; exquisite decorations and fine art; huge, elegant bathrooms with Jacuzzis, steam and sauna baths; exercise rooms; massage rooms; private beauty-shop facilities; restaurant-quality kitchens; enormous bedrooms with walk-in closets; deluxe living rooms and dining areas; and entertainment centers. The suites are so large that the size of one suite prompted one Japanese guest to complain that he was unable to locate his wife in it.

At Rio, its Palazzo suites are housed in a tower attached to a remote end of the main hotel. Ground-level villas have their own swimming pools. Each villa has its own entrance and security guard. The Palazzo suites opened in autumn 1998. The eight suites cost $53 million, a huge investment that the Rio's original owners believed was necessary to attract whales, in particular, Asian high rollers.

Each Palazzo suite comes equipped with its own concierge, and the guest has a casino host on call 24 hours a day via a beeper system or a cell phone. Each suite also has a staff of housekeepers, a full-time chauffeur, and chefs from Rio's finer restaurants available to prepare gourmet meals in the suite's kitchen. The Palazzo suites also has a butler's quarters that provides 24-hour service, which assures each guest of an available butler during the entire stay. Few hotels in the world offer such luxury accommodations. Anything a whale requests, if it's possible, is given, gratis. For instance, if a whale's wardrobe is missing something, it will be delivered—a dozen expensive imported shirts, a dozen silk ties, even a different Italian suit or sports jacket for every night of the week. Whales have hosted cocktail parties and dinner parties in their Palazzo suites—serving gourmet food, wine, and liquor, all on the house. The finest wines are at a whale's beck and call. According to Marty Miles—and as Harrah's vice president of food and beverages, he should know—in one month last year, the cost of room service for the eight Palazzo suites was $160,000, averaging $20,000 per suite.

Gambardella tells:

> A whale or his wife may want to go on a shopping spree, and we'll pick up the tab. Recently, one customer said to me, "I've lost a lot of money this past trip, and it's my wife's birthday. Can you buy something for her?" "Sure," I said, "Let's go shopping." "Just pick out something nice for her," he answered. We bought her a $50,000 diamond necklace, and I kept it in my office. When they were in the restaurant that night, the general manager and I went to their table, wished her a happy birthday and handed it to the gentleman. "I believe this is yours," I said. His wife was in a wheelchair, and she nearly fell out of it when she saw it. "Would you put it on for me?" she asked, so I did. He pulled me aside and whispered, "It's beautiful. It cost me about $800,000 for this necklace." I smiled and said, "I know."

Not too long ago, *Hustler* magazine founder and owner Larry Flynt and his girlfriend stayed at the Palazzo suites. A Rio chauffeur dropped the girlfriend off at Fashion Mall and came back to the hotel. Twenty minutes later, when she looked for the limousine, it wasn't there. Imagine the commotion when she called the casino and said she was stranded at the mall—the girlfriend of one of the biggest customers in the business! Meanwhile, she paged the driver and waited 20 minutes until he arrived. To placate her for the inconvenience, the casino gave her $40,000 to go on a shopping spree! It's rumored that during a two-month period, Flynt lost $10 million at Rio, so, understandably, the casino allocated a budget to make sure he and his guest never left on a sour note.

A few years ago, Microsoft's Bill Gates came to Las Vegas to attend the Comdex Convention (Consumer Electronics Convention). His offer to pay $20,000 to $25,000 a night for a five-day stay in a Palazzo suite was turned down. Why? Bill Gates is not a rated player and plays $3 to $6 hold 'em poker. "Those rooms were available only to very high-level players who had credit lines of $2 million to $3 million," explains Gary Thompson. "We believed in those days that we couldn't afford to tie up a room for $100,000 and take the risk of losing a whale because we couldn't accommodate him. Our thinking has since changed. Today, we'd be delighted to have Bill Gates as one of our guests."

"It doesn't matter how much money you have," says Dan Nita, "but how much you gamble. Comps are only given to gamblers based on their play activity."

In October 1999, Vice President Al Gore was in Las Vegas to attend a fundraiser. His entourage, which included Secret Service personnel, stayed at Harrah's. Brandi Jarva, the casino's VIP host director, says:

> When we first received the call to accommodate them, the casino didn't want to do it. But when Phil Satre, who personally knows Al Gore, said, "It's important to me," we agreed to do it. They occupied three floors of the hotel, and because they weren't rated customers, we charged them the full rate. That's right, because they displaced potential casino customers during a busy time of the year, we didn't make an exception and give them a special price. It was strictly a business decision. Meanwhile, Gore never went into the casino, nor did any of the Secret Service agents.

The Palazzo suites can all be turned into connecting rooms, so it's possible a single whale could occupy the entire area. By opening corridors, the Palazzo suites area could be converted into one gigantic, multilevel 45,000-square-foot suite with 18 bedrooms! Normally, when divided into separate units, the smallest unit is a two-bedroom, and the others are three and four bedrooms, averaging about 5,000 square feet each. Cary Rehm, Rio's former general manager, says:

> The most rooms I've ever seen connected together were 10 bedrooms. It was a large Asian group. Generally, due to the long distance they travel, our Asian customers come in larger groups and stay for longer periods. There is usually just one key player, but there may be several other gamers in the group. A whale's entourage will include family members and friends.

Tom Jenkin emphasizes that whales generally have a staff of their own servants, so when they come to Las Vegas, Rio's mission was to accommodate all of them with the same level of lifestyle:

> They travel in a class of service unknown to most people across the world. They are extremely discriminating, and we render a level of personalized service comparable to their expectations. For example, with one guest, we have a four-page list of amenities to prepare for

his visit. Even though he comes by himself, we give him a six-bedroom suite because he likes that environment. Each bathroom is specifically arranged to appeal to him. Our attention to detail is extraordinary. We even know his favorite brand of razor blades and how many he requires. Having a staff that can provide the absolute finest quality of service is a competitive edge Palazzo Suites enjoys. Our staff people understand to the nth detail how to serve these most discriminating guests.

Fishing for whales is like hunting big game—it's a high-stakes venture. At $100,000 a bet, there's an exchange of big, big bucks. Although the odds favor the house, a gambler on a hot streak can walk away with a bundle. One advantage of the house is that it has deeper pockets than players. This means that if a customer wins 25 hands in a row, the house can afford to pay him or her. When it goes the other direction and the customer loses 25 hands in a row, he or she is out of money, so the house wins. However, when the customer has deeper pockets than the house—and most whales do—this equation works in reverse. Moreover, there are whales with more net worth and liquidity than even the world's largest casino companies. The casino business is also based on the law of large numbers. With thousands of players in a casino, the risk is spread over a large number of transactions. With a single whale, anything can happen on a given night.

During Dave Hanlon's tenure—Rio's CEO for two years in the mid-1990s—the decision to cater to whales was made. Going in, Hanlon knew the risks were high, but so were the rewards. Another motivation for going whale hunting is that it's unquestionably the most glamorous end of the gaming business. Having the world's biggest high rollers patronize your establishment is a casino owner's dream come true—but it can also be his or her worst nightmare. Hanlon tells:

> During our first six months with high stakes tables limits set at $150,000 a wager, it was exciting, and right off the bat, we got lucky. I mean, we were killing everybody. Some of our people who had never been in the high-roller business were saying, "We should have done this a long time ago." But then our luck changed and for the next six months, we got killed. Every night that we had a whale in the casino, I made sure to be there, and believe me, when you're down a couple of million in a matter of a half hour or so, it makes you sick in your stomach. When we were behind, I'd be calculating our losses in my head and, at the same time, I'd be thinking how long it would take for the casino to make it up. In this end of the business, you're either a big hero or a big idiot. Back then, the Rio

wasn't owned by Harrah's, and as a single casino, it only took one whale to seriously hurt us. There were times when things got so bad, I worried, "Will we be able to borrow enough money to pay these guys off?" When it gets like that, it's not business, it's real gambling. Today, with 26 Harrah's properties, the company is in a better position to weather the storm.

Unlike Captain Ahab, the Rio has stopped hunting whales. The company has made changes to reduce its erstwhile vast exposure to high-risk play. These changes occurred after June 2001 when high rollers won enough to dent the company's second quarter earnings by 10 percent, or four cents a share. The company cut its maximum acceptable wagers enough to effectively put Rio out of the high-roller table game business. "The slot machines were subsidizing high rollers," explains Gary Loveman, "and we became the reverse Robin Hood of the casino world. Taking from the poor and giving to the rich is a stupid way to run a business."

With 200 whales spread around the world, competition for their business is fierce among some casino operators. Comps have long been the main attraction to win their business, but, in recent years, another incentive has been offered. Before they head for the tables, some whales negotiate with casinos to have their losses discounted by as much as 18 percent. This means that a high roller who wins $10 million takes home $10 million. But if he or she loses $10 million, he may pay only $8.2 million. The favorite games for these customers are blackjack and baccarat. The house edge at baccarat is one of the thinnest in a casino, averaging 1.3 percent—as little as half that of games such as roulette and some slots. In baccarat, it takes at least 15 million hands for a casino to have a 95 percent certainty of winning that 1.3 percent.

One crucial risk that a casino takes is the high credit limits it extends to whales. In states where gaming is legal, gambling debts are collectible; however, even after running careful credit checks, wealthy people have financial setbacks and, as the expression goes, you can't get blood out of a turnip. For instance, in the late 1990s, 95 percent of high-level players were from the Far East; when its economy became severely depressed, many billionaires with large illiquid real estate holdings were unable to pay their gambling debts. This, coupled with currency restriction problems, caused a few whales to tell casinos, "I don't have any buildings to sell so I can pay you, so you'll have to sit and wait."

In addition, it is difficult to collect from a player who is from a foreign country. As Dave Hanlon points out:

When a casino has a customer from Bangkok or Taiwan, it's basically giving him an unsecured line of credit. The main thing the casino has going in its favor is that a gambler will pay off his gambling debt because he wants another line of credit to go gambling.

Let's say a whale has a line of credit of $2 million and his losses total $2 million. Even if he doesn't intend to pay, he's not going to tell us. Instead, he'll say that he'll pay later. He might go to the Mirage where they also know him, and hit them for another million or two, and then Mandalay Bay and so on. By the time he leaves Vegas, $10 million worth of credit could have been extended to him. The risk is that he could get himself so buried in debt that he can never get out. He might have been good for $2 million, but if he loses $10 million, he might not pay anybody. There's not a lot of cooperation between casinos in a situation like this. A friend at another casino might say, "Oh, he's a slow pay, but he'll pay you when he comes back next year." In this respect, there is some informal intelligence in this town. But just because he doesn't pay here doesn't mean he can't get credit down the street. Historically, bad debts in this industry are less than what MasterCharge and VISA experience. Just the same, when a whale isn't able to cover his gambling debts, the casino takes a huge hit.

Refusing to extend more credit to a demanding customer who's over his or her limit is a delicate situation, as Tom Jenkin explains:

How we work with each whale depends upon who the person is. Our policy is not to allow our customers to lose more money than they're comfortable losing. We try to take the person away from the tables, sit down with him, and, if we can, suggest that we should talk about it the next day. Usually, the next day, players will thank us for stopping them and say, "That's enough, I don't want to lose any more. I'll see you the next time I'm in town."

When a customer with a high credit line loses it and asks for more credit, we use due diligence to ensure that the customer is not overextending himself. And if we do give him the money, we'll say, "Good luck. This is as far as we'll extend your credit." We feel we have an obligation to the property as well as the customer.

Tales of Whales

Depending on a whale's line of credit, a certain sum of money is allotted during his or her visit. As long as a customer is under this budgeted amount, he or she may ask for anything; and as long as it's legal, the request will be granted. One whale was given a $100,000 diamond watch; another asked for—and received—an around-the-world, expense-paid, two-week trip. Harrah's in Lake Tahoe rented a lake-front house for one whale, a billionaire Internet company owner from Silicon Valley. The casino also bought four snowmobiles for him—not just for his visit—the four snowmobiles were delivered to his residence. Every high roller has a theoretical value to the casino, and a formula determines the amount of comps he or she can receive. As long as whatever the player requests is under this amount, the casino will comp him or her. Within these set perimeters, a whale could ask for a Mercedes Benz, and the casino would buy it.

Frank Quigley, vice president of table games at Showboat in Atlantic City, says:

> Last week a customer lost $200,000. He stayed in a beautiful suite, and we picked up his tab on everything, including a first-class ticket back to Charlotte. We also knocked 10 percent off his losses. A few days later, he called and said, "If you guys want me to come back, I want you to book me on a Mediterranean cruise." We gave it to him and it cost us 10 grand.

One of the most famous and colorful whales is Kerry Packer, who reputedly is Australia's wealthiest man, with an estimated net worth of $4.6 billion. A regular visitor to Las Vegas, the media mogul is legendary in gaming circles. Packer is a gentleman who is highly respected by casino people, is considered a folk hero by the masses, and is known for his generous tips. There's a story about the time he accidentally bumped into a cocktail waitress, knocking over her beverage tray. Packer apologized and asked for her name and address. A few days later, her bank notified her that her $50,000 house mortgage balance was zero. Packer had paid off the mortgage.

A front-page story during the summer of 2000 in *The Australian,* his homeland's national newspaper, detailed Packer's Las Vegas losses during a recent trip—an estimated $34 million in his native currency, the equivalent of U.S. $20 million. Consequently, Labor Party member Mark Latham criticized Packer's love of gambling and said, "Notions of public morality and justice are under threat when it is possible for one person to accumulate such extraordinary wealth and then use it in such an extraordinary way," according to the *Australian Financial Review.* Packer denied that his losses in Las Vegas were $20 million; he also stated that his losses were less than his donations to a Sydney children's hospital.

Packer has been known to play five hands of blackjack simultaneously, betting $200,000 a card—a fast way to drop or make a million dollars. People have asked what motivates such a wealthy man to gamble so heavily. He reportedly answered, "I do it so when I walk through the door at a casino, I can see the fear in the executives' eyes."

"I know Kerry Packer," says Dave Hanlon, "and he's a very pleasant man, a totally nice guy. He's played at Rio, and once after he lost $3 million, he simply wrote a check. There was no bull about, 'What's my comps?' or 'What's my discount?' It was strictly, 'How much do I owe? Three million? Thank you very much.'"

When a whale is on a hot streak, a casino's losses can accumulate quite rapidly. "We were beaten for $3 million in three hours," says Jay Sevigny, "and I once saw one player bet $150,000 a hand at the baccarat table and win $1 million in six minutes."

Like other gamblers, those that wager the highest stakes are a superstitious lot—and so are the casino owners. Just how much is revealed in a story told by Gary Selesner, vice president/assistant general manager at the Rio. Selesner recalls that in the 1980s, while he was working at Trump Plaza in Atlantic City, Japanese billionaire Akio Kashiwagi came to the casino. At the time, Kashiwagi was reputed to be the biggest casino gambler in the world. Selesner, who at the time was president of Trump Plaza, tells:

> Kashiwagi regularly bet $200,000 on each hand of baccarat, and Trump was anxious to get into that high-end business. Kashiwagi had won $6 million from Trump Plaza during a previous two-day visit to Atlantic City earlier in the year, and we were anxious to have a chance at beating him. After some courting, he accepted our invitation to return and arrived with $6 million in cash. We gave him a credit line for another $6 million.
>
> Once he started playing, we kept going back and forth with him. First, he'd be up, then it was our turn, and so on. Every hour or so, Trump would call to get a report on how we were doing. At one time when he called, Kashiwagi had us for $8 million.
>
> "You've got to beat this guy," Trump instructed me.
>
> "Donald, we're trying to do that, but you know that's not the way it works. He can beat us."
>
> "No, you've got to beat this guy."
>
> "He beat us last time, and he can beat us again," I repeated.
>
> I was aware of Trump's financial problems, so I knew a lot was at stake for the casino. My boss, Ed Tracy, who was in charge of all of Trump's Atlantic City operations, also felt the heat. Out of the blue, he asked me, "Gary, do you have any good luck charms?"
>
> "Yes, I do happen to have one," I answered. "When I was on a player development trip in the Far East, I picked up one of those rubber two-headed dragons for two bucks while in Bangkok."
>
> "Great!" Tracy said. "Now let's send a limo to get it."

I don't believe in such nonsense, but just the same, I had a limo sent to my house. When the driver returned, we placed my lucky dragon on the podium across from the baccarat table facing Kashiwagi. Sure, it was part levity to relieve some stress, but when you're down $8 million, there's no telling what you'll do. But damn if that two-headed dragon didn't change our luck. We ended up beating Kashiwagi for $10 million. He lost his $6 million in cash plus another $4 million he was playing on credit.

The deal was that Kashiwagi could play for $12 million. But at $10 million, Trump told my boss, "We've got the money, and I want to stop the game."

"It's not fair," I protested. "We brought the guy all the way over here from Tokyo, and we made a deal with him. We have to let him play through to his $12 million."

Trump insisted that it was his casino and the game was over. Kashiwagi angrily picked up his $2 million in chips and went next door to Caesar's where he called a press conference, calling Trump a cheapskate. It was all over the *New York Post*.

Did the two-headed dragon actually bring good luck to Trump? Or bad luck to Kashiwagi? Meanwhile, Kashiwagi, who had been described as a gaming warrior, tried to negotiate a 20 percent reduction in what he owed the casino, which, at the time, was the standard discount given to whales. Trump insisted he wanted it all. Several months later, Kashiwagi was murdered by the Japanese Yakuza. As it turned out, he died and Trump got stuck for the $2 million—obviously bad luck for both parties!

Howard Klein, a former marketing vice president at Caesars in Atlantic City, tells a hilarious story about Sir Tang, a whale from Hong Kong and a frequent visitor at Caesars in the mid-1980s:

He was a legitimate "Sir," actually knighted by the British government and a multibillionaire. Back then, Caesars was the pioneer gaming company in international marketing to high rollers. At the time, I worked in domestic and international marketing at Caesars, when I received a call from the company's Los Angeles offices. "Sir Tang and his entourage are en route to Atlantic City. Make sure you're set up for them," I was told.

Sir Tang had a credit line of $5 million, and Asian protocol required that a high-ranking company official greet him at the airport upon the landing of his private jet. Just before I headed to the airport, I alerted all of our people to get everything ready for Sir Tang and his entourage of eight. Several of our marketing people came with me, including a Chinese executive who would serve as an interpreter. Each of Tang's party was a wealthy businessperson, and each had a significant line of credit. Imagine our surprise when each of them stepped out of the plane and were so casually dressed, wearing $4.99 short-sleeved shirts and sandals. Tang, however, was quite different. He was dressed in a black mandarin robe. With his shaven head, he looked like a character right out of a 1930 black and white movie about pirates on the China coast. Tang didn't speak a word of English.

When we got back to Caesars Palace, the interpreter told me, "It is a matter of protocol among wealthy Chinese that the top people escort the top visiting people to their suites." Since the company president wasn't in town, as the vice president of marketing, I would be the executive to take Tang and his party to their suites. On our way to his suite, Tang didn't utter a word. He simply smiled and nodded his head. When I opened the door to his suite, he glanced around the room, and suddenly his eyes widened, and he started talking very rapidly, spitting out his words to my interpreter. Tang stood at the entrance, refusing to enter.

"What's going on?" I asked.

The two bellhops with Tang's luggage stood in the hallway. Like me, they, too, were stunned. Meanwhile, Tang and his associates were conversing in Chinese, and from the way they were shaking their heads and frowning, I knew something had upset them. But what? It was an exquisite suite. What could possibly be wrong?

"The room has the wrong feng shui," a Tang aide said.

I didn't know it at the time, so the aide quickly explained that according to Chinese lore, it's important what direction various objects face in a house, and this would be Tang's house during his visit with us. Staying in the room would bring bad luck. There were two deluxe penthouse suites in the hotel, so I called downstairs to have Tang moved to the other one. Another big player from New York and his girlfriend occupied it—and they weren't going anywhere. If we attempted to move this customer, we'd lose him.

The aide explained our dilemma to Tang and his associates, and, fortunately, the Chinese are resourceful people. After huddling with them for five minutes, he turned to the two bellhops and me and said, "We've got some work to do," and the four of us followed him into the suite. Tang and his group stood in the hallway, while we moved nearly every piece of furniture to face another direction. We moved beds, dressers, and even took a dark sheet from a bed in an unoccupied room so we could cover a large mirror in the suite's hallway. About half an hour later, one of Tang's associates entered the suite. He stood by the windows, looking out to test the sun and the direction of the wind. Through the aide, he instructed us to move a few more items in the room, and finally brought Tang in. Although the suite looked like a hurricane had gone through it, Tang looked around approvingly. Suddenly, he stopped in his tracks and pointed to a statue of a lion on a coffee table. The lion's mouth was wide open, and, symbolically, it represented the casino and meant Tang would be eaten alive.

I picked up the statue, and placing it under my arm, I bowed to Tang. He nodded to me and made a slight motion signaling to bring in his luggage. That night, he won slightly more than $1 million at the baccarat tables. Later that same evening, through the aide, I informed Tang that the other suite would be available for his occupancy the next day and for the remainder of his stay. I explained that it had correct feng shui and since his suite was in such disarray, he would be more comfortable there. I thought he'd be pleased, but he said that he was staying exactly where he was. He was up in the casino and he wasn't about to change his luck. I suppose its feng shui did bring him good luck, because he won $2.5 million on that particular trip. Upon his return in six months, he insisted on the same suite, and again, we rearranged everything in the same disheveled way we did the first time. This time, Sir Tang wasn't so lucky. We beat him for the $2.5 million, plus some.

Rated Players

It doesn't take long for Harrah's employees to identify a customer whose gaming activity is deserving of recognition as a rated player. A rated player is someone who spends enough money and time at the gaming tables and slot machines to be "courted." And how does a casino court a customer? With comps. Comps are based on what the casino stands to make on a gamer who plays for a given time and who places bets at a certain denomination. Comps are not determined on a customer's losses. The house is willing to take its chances, knowing that with enough volume, odds are it will make a profit—not on any particular player—but on a large number of players.

Sometimes, a new customer requests to be rated so he or she can receive comps. If the casino doesn't know this person, a casino manager might say, "Okay, instead of charging you the rack (retail) rate for your room, we'll give you the casino rate. [The rack rate may be $300 while the casino rate is $100.] Depending on your gaming activity, we may deduct the cost of your room plus other items you charge to it." Other items could include meals, bar charges, show tickets, and so on. During the customer's stay, designated casino employees track his or her play—always based on the amount of time spent at the tables and the denomination of bets. If a customer asks, "What's it going to take to comp me?" a casino manager may respond, "If you average $100 per hand at blackjack and you play for four hours, there will be no charge for your room. And if you play six hours and your average bet is $200, we'll also comp your meals and other room charges. And if you play eight hours, averaging this amount, we'll reimburse you for your airfare, plus on your next visit, we'll put you in one of our deluxe suites." Although not cast in stone, each casino has its own criteria for comping rated players.

At Harrah's, slot machine players are rated by computers. Rating players this way is relatively easy. A customer inserts his or her Total Rewards card into the slot machine and credits are earned based on time, denomination of bets, and velocity—the number of bets made during a given period. This doesn't require a pit boss or casino manager to jot down little notes on a customer. The computer records everything very efficiently.

Total Rewards players who are at the Diamond and Platinum levels register in the Harrah's VIP reception area. A player's tier level does not qualify him or her for comps. Comps are based on play activity. If a customer doesn't come to a Harrah's casino for a long time, comps are based on his or her play during a particular visit. Like the Total Rewards program, with IT in place, comps are determined on a customer's play activity at all 26 Harrah's casinos. Just the same, there are certain entitlements for Diamond and Platinum players. In addition to bypassing the main check-in counter, there are express lines at restaurants, preferred treatment for making reservations at the top-of-the-line restaurants, special toll-free numbers for reservations, and at some properties, special parking privileges—free valet service, and so on. Diamond players have visiting rights to Diamond lounges that provide alcoholic beverages, hors d'oeuvres, and snacks scrumptious enough to make a delicious lunch. The interiors of the lounges are comparable to an airline members' club. All food and drinks are on the house. Throughout the year, Diamond and Platinum players receive a variety of offers from Harrah's, including coupons for discounted and/or free rooms, meals, shows, and special events.

Diamond and Platinum members are not automatically rated players. The qualification for a Diamond card is $5,000 of theoretical loss per year, while a Platinum card is based on only $1,500 per year. Because a high percentage of Harrah's revenues are generated from customers at the Platinum and above level, the company works overtime to please these special customers. Perks represent only a small investment to the company, compared to the considerable customer loyalty they generate. For instance, there is practically no cost for

providing conveniences such as line-cutting privileges, special parking, quick room registration, and so on.

In the VIP reception area, a VIP representative welcomes guests
to Harrah's and doubles as a concierge. Diamond members have a
designated VIP host to arrange everything from making dinner reservations to sightseeing tours. Platinum members are not assigned a
VIP representative. Brandi Jarva, director of VIP services of Harrah's
on the Strip explains: "Like the Diamond lounges, having a VIP host
is for Diamonds and up. It's not a privilege that Platinums receive.
It's what I call an aspirational thing."

Every rated player has a casino host, a sort of combination
concierge and goodwill ambassador, who discusses comps with a rated
player. In the case of the high roller who asked for a box of cigars and
was told he had to play more to earn it, the casino host held out that
carrot. Likewise, the casino host might comp a customer for show
tickets at another casino or arrange a golf game at the Rio Secco Golf
Club. Because comping is not cut-and-dried, at checkout time, it's
common for a guest to sit down with his or her casino host and review
the hotel invoice. Often, there's room for negotiation. "Why was I
charged for Friday night's dinner?" a customer may ask. "Next time, I
want a suite instead of a room," insists another.

Harrah's Las Vegas has 39 casino hosts; this includes 22 executive
hosts, 6 player development hosts, 6 Asian hosts, and 5 casino hosts.
In addition to greeting guests and working with rated players, casino
hosts contact inactive players—customers who haven't visited the
casino for an extended period. Pit managers rate new customers who
are betting heavily at the gaming table and then tip off a casino host.
In response, the host introduces himself or herself and invites the
player to be the casino's guest for dinner and the show. A host might
invite a high-level player on a tour of Harrah's suites. In short, an
alert casino does whatever it takes to attract a high roller to stay at
Harrah's.

It's not just casino hosts who cater to rated players. All employees do. And all casino employees are trained to keep a lookout for a
rated player. Michael Silberling explains:

> Our long-time employees will absolutely know our top 100 cus-
> tomers. These customers will be recognized on sight when they
> check in here in Reno, eat at our steakhouse, and play at our high-
> stake tables. If a player we don't know comes in and plays at a high
> level, our listening posts will definitely identify him, and within 15 to
> 20 minutes, our people who are supposed to know will be informed.

Good casino hosts are aggressively on the prowl to bring in new high-roller customers. They're constantly attending dinner events and other functions to meet people. For example, it's an annual tradition for a Harrah's host to go to the Kentucky Derby to drum up business. Hosts also travel to different markets to meet potential customers, usually at affairs set up by a junket representative. On occasion, Harrah's hosts a party for as many as 500 people that includes dinner at a fine restaurant such as a Ruth's Chris Steak House or Morton's Steak House. The party will have some form of entertainment, plus raffles for expense-paid vacations to a Harrah's gaming resort.

Casino hosts jump through hoops to satisfy their best-rated players. Winning their loyalty can be a fiercely competitive undertaking. What will a casino do to woo high rollers? Steve Wynn developed Shadow Creek Golf Course. This verdant mirage sits on 320 acres north of downtown Las Vegas, carved into the desert like an emerald river. Its total cost was in excess of $48 million. The land was purchased for just under $3 million, a pittance compared to the cost of the more than 20,000 mature pine trees. Wynn imported not only the pines, but also the fallen pine needles to make the course appear mature. The fairways are wide. The greens are large. The wildlife—including wallabies and pygmy deer—and waterfalls are numerous.

Golfing is limited to a handful of players per day, ferried to the course by limousines. With 70 employees at Shadow Creek, including nearly 50 gardeners and maintenance workers, players barely outnumber the staff. On an average day, as few as four foursomes tee off.

For years there were no green fees. There was no tipping or bribing the starter caddy, or the waiter who was happy to serve caviar on the course. Players had to carry a minimum $100,000 credit line. When the city of Las Vegas insisted that Shadow Creek be open to the public, Wynn reluctantly agreed, and, accordingly, set the daily green fees at $1,000. Any golfer who shells out the outrageously high fee is a probable high roller that the course's owner would welcome as a customer.

While no other casino has anything comparable to Shadow Creek, Harrah's has its Rio Secco Golf Course—and the Butch Harmon Golf School. Having Tiger Woods' coach as an instructor is a special comp an ardent golfer would die for. All guests who stay at Rio have access to its golf course; likewise, all guests at Harrah's on the Strip are welcome to play the Secco course. This privilege is not extended to guests who stay at any other Las Vegas hotel; however, rated players from other casinos certainly would be welcome.

While visitors in Las Vegas associate gaming casinos with giant-sized hotels, a majority of casinos in frequency markets are actually stand-alone operations. For example, during its first seven years in business, Harrah's Ak-Chin casino did not have a hotel. General manager Janet Beronio explains:

> Our customers are mainly from Phoenix and Tucson, which are only 45 minutes from here. They come here to gamble, and afterward they go home to sleep in their own bed. Nonetheless, this didn't stop us from building a beautiful 146-room hotel. Why would we build a hotel for our customers who live so near? For the most part, the hotel is an amenity much like our steakhouse. Comping rated customers with a hotel room is a nice way to show our appreciation for their business.

For the same reason, Harrah's built a 293-room hotel adjacent to its East Chicago casino. General manager Joe Domenico claims:

> We have the finest property in Chicagoland, including the downtown hotels. Our seven super suites are comparable to our Lake Tahoe property. Now, instead of catering only to locals, we're a destination casino. We can also use the hotel to reward our premium customers. And our statistics tell us that if our customers get the extended stay, they will spend more of their gaming budget with us versus our competitors.

Similarly, at Harrah's in Joliet, the vast majority of customers are within driving distance, residing in the greater Metropolitan Chicago area. Still, this property has a beautiful 200-room hotel with four deluxe suites and several more second-tier suites. Michael St. Pierre, general manager, explains:

> We use the hotel rooms as a carrot so we can comp our rated players who don't feel like driving home after a fun night in our casino. It's also an amenity that we can offer Harrah's customers in other markets to attract them to visit us for a few days.
>
> For rated customers living nearby who prefer going home, we send a limousine to their house, pick them up, treat them to dinner, and when they're through playing in the casino, we take them back home.

While every customer receives excellent service, as Michael Silberling says, "Our people do go that extra mile for a rated player. For instance, when a high roller puts in a call for room service on a busy day, it's likely that his order will get preferential treatment and arrive at his suite before one that was called in earlier."

Marty Miles points out that a rated player's order in the restaurant also receives special treatment. "If a high roller orders a veal chop dinner, and the kitchen receives the order after someone else ordered the same meal, and there's only one veal chop left, be assured the high roller gets it."

Rio still has a high-limit salon, a private gaming area that caters to high rollers who don't qualify as whales. Tom Jenkin explains:

> We like to keep these players in this area because its high level of service caters to the most discriminating customers. It's a matter of being able to control the environment. As an example of the service we give here, we have a designated employee who cleans the restroom after every use. Other employees are constantly making sure the room is spotlessly clean.

The Personal Touch

With 25 million customers in the Harrah's database, it's impossible to know every customer personally. However, with high rollers, it's a different story. "With a rated player, you can be assured that a casino host knows this customer very well," says David Norton. "At this level, nobody has to wear a name tag. Getting to know these customers is a critical part of our business."

While the generous comps that were described earlier in this chapter border on overindulgence or what could be described as conspicuous consumption, perhaps it is the personal relationships formed with customers that truly build customer loyalty in the gaming business. This is not to suggest that the luxuries bestowed on high rollers could be entirely replaced by endearing casino hosts. A customer is not likely to forsake a stay at a Palazzo suite for a standard Harrah's room because he or she is enamored with his or her casino host. However, the personal relationship a customer has with a Harrah's employee can be the tiebreaker that wins his or her business from Bellagio or the Mirage. In this respect, the gaming business is like all other businesses—customer loyalty is built on one-on-one relationships. The world's best IT doesn't replace the personal touch. In an era of high tech, there is always a place for high touch.

Over the years, casino hosts develop close relationships with their customers. These friendships often extend beyond the business. Hosts join their customers for dinner, rounds of golf, and an occasional round of drinks. And it goes beyond the walls of the casino. They attend customers' family weddings, bar mitzvahs, and funerals.

It doesn't have to be something extravagant to win a customer's loyalty. Brandi Jarva understands this quite well:

> One of my good friends is a woman from California who used to come here with her husband; he recently passed away, and she's been coming here about once every two weeks. I know she's a big Tom Jones fan, so on her birthday, I hired an impersonator to sing to her in the high-limit slot area. This guy was the spitting image of Tom Jones, and he did a half-hour performance just for her. His singing drew a crowd of people and everybody had a really good time. Most importantly, the woman loved it.

This was a customer who Jarva befriended over a period of time; and, at little expense to the casino, she did something far more meaningful than a comp for a dinner or show.

Undoubtedly, the woman will never forget it. Oftentimes, it's the personal touch that is so much appreciated. Jay Sevigny tells a favorite story that illustrates how the personal touch wins customer loyalty:

> A gentleman wanted something done for his wife, who for some unknown reason was upset with him. So he said to one of the Palazzo Suites butlers, "Can you do something special to make my wife happy?" The butler said he'd take care of it. He then went out and purchased dozens of vases of fresh flowers and arranged them around the bath in the suite's master bedroom. When the customer's wife came back to the suite and saw the flowers, she was so overwhelmed, it took her breath away. She thought her husband was so romantic and thoughtful, she couldn't stop thanking him. Later, the customer told the butler that what he did was "absolutely perfect."

Sometimes, it's just a friendly employee who adds a nice personal touch with a sense of humor. Geoff Andres, a former blackjack dealer at Harrah's in Reno, tells a cute story:

> I'm not much of a celebrity gawker, but when Clint Eastwood sat down at the table, it was exciting. He was in Reno to shoot *Pink Cadillac,* a movie he starred in with Bernadette Peters. Not only was he a cool guy, I was impressed about how down to earth he was.
> While Clint might have been cool, he wasn't too adept at blackjack, and he was by no means a high roller. He had a stack of $10 chips in front of him, and he'd carefully study each hand as if he was betting the ranch on it. Each time, he'd stare at his cards with his piercing eyes. Then, he'd look into mine and finally, he'd give me a slight hand motion for a hit or a pass. This went on for about an hour. Then I dealt him a four and a seven and I was showing a jack.

When it was his turn to bet, he kept looking at his cards and glancing at my face card. Clint seemed somewhat nervous. Finally, he asked, "What should I do? Should I double down?"

I couldn't resist using a line from one of his *Dirty Harry* movies. "I don't know, Clint," I said in a whisper, "Are you feeling lucky?" He gave me a strange look and then burst out laughing. With that, the other players at the table just howled.

When it comes to a personal touch, Jerome Robinson, maitre d' gourmet at the Steak House at Harrah's in Atlantic City, knows how to do it with a touch of humor:

A very distinguished gentleman was dining alone when I came to his table to greet him. Although I tried to start a conversation with him, he hardly spoke a word. The waiter received the same cold treatment when the man ordered his dinner.

Although the man was very formal, I noticed he removed his shoes. This is the only sign I noticed that he was trying to unwind. That's when a lightbulb lit up over my head. I had the waiter create a diversion and when the customer turned his head, I lifted his shoes from beneath the table. Then I sent a busboy to a nearby shoe store. "Buy the most gaudy women's high heels in the store. Get the ones with the fuzzy fur."

Upon his return, we created another diversion, and I placed the newly purchased pair under the table. About 45 minutes later, the customer paid for his check and was getting ready to leave. He felt with his feet for his shoes but couldn't find them. Then he reached under the table and picked up the high heels. The poor guy was dumbfounded, but still he showed no emotion. His eyes wandered around the room as if he was trying to find a logical explanation.

That's when I walked to his table and placed a large covered silver tray on the table. "Sir," I said, "this is our specialty of the house. Please enjoy it with our compliments."

"Er, thank you," he mumbled politely.

At the precise moment that I lifted the lid, the waiter took a photograph of him to capture his expression when he saw his shoes on the tray. Instantly, a huge grin appeared on his face. "This is absolutely the funniest thing that's ever happened to me," he roared.

This customer has visited Harrah's many times since that night, and he always has me come to his table when he's with friends. "This is Jerome," he tells them. "He's the one I was talking about. Tell them again, Jerome, so they can hear it from you."

Bill Keena, Harrah's general manager in Laughlin, came up with an original idea that went over big with many of his rated players, and, again, it was something that didn't cost the casino an arm and a leg. Keena explains:

> I give naming rights for some of our suites to our best customers. Based on their annual play, I name a suite after them for the following year. They're so proud of it that they invite some of their friends to come to Laughlin to show them "their" suite. They also realize that if their gaming activity drops, the plaque with their name on it won't appear on the suite.

A master at developing strong relationships with customers is Russ McLennan, a long-time company employee since the days of Bill Harrah. Today, in the role of vice president of player development, McLennan has one of the most unusual, as well as most enjoyable, jobs in the casino business, or for that matter, any business. An avid sportsman, for the past 20 years McLennan has been entertaining high-level players by taking them on hunting and fishing expeditions to Guaymas, Mexico, and Kenai, Alaska. The Mexican trip is mainly dove hunting and fly-fishing. McLennan has a favorite lodge for his guests, about 500 miles south of the border on the inland side of the Gulf of Mexico. The Alaskan trip is a four-day combination of salmon fishing and halibut fishing. McLennan says:

> The Kenai River is the most famous king salmon fishing in the world, and we have a ball. We started doing this back in the early 1960s when we took our customers to Bill Harrah's lodge in Idaho on the Salmon River. Back then, we'd fish and also hunt elk. Now, it's mostly fishing and dove hunting.
>
> Generally, a group of 10 to 12 customers goes with me. When we first started these trips, we'd invite $10,000 to $20,000 customers, but since our costs have gone up, we raised the ante. My next trip is composed of $50,000 to $250,000 players. Some of the guys go with me on a regular basis, so we've become close friends. And they've also become good buddies with each other. Since Harrah's picks up the tab, we fly them to Lake Tahoe or Vegas for a couple of days before the trip, and afterward we return to the casino and have their wives join up with them for a couple days. Phil Satre is a fly-fish enthusiast, so every now and then, he will join me with a group of customers. Phil is such a regular guy, he fits in well and is a lot of fun to be with.

In addition to the hunting and fishing trips, Harrah's customers are frequently invited on golf trips. McLennan, a great outdoorsman, also hosts golf trips to places such as Palm Springs, Cyprus Point, Spanish Bay, and Pebble Beach, but he confesses that his golf game is not much to brag about. It all sounds like fun—and it is—but it's also business.

Business executives often travel to faraway places to drum up business—and top gaming executives do it, too. On a recent trip to the Far East, for example, Phil Satre visited Taiwan, Hong Kong, and Singapore. He explains:

> We have some important customers in the Pacific Rim, and the trip was a way to demonstrate that the company cares about them. In the Asian culture, a trip to where they live, combined with entertaining them in their locale, shows respect.
>
> When Harrah's was the sponsor of the Miss Chinatown United States, which attracts contestants from across the U.S., I served as Grand Marshal of the San Francisco Chinatown Parade in celebration of the Chinese New Year. Along with San Francisco's Mayor Willie Brown, I had the honor to crown the winner. Some of our biggest customers are members of the San Francisco Asian community, so our participation in their celebration is a small token of our appreciation for their patronage.

Over the years, the Satres have celebrated New Year's Eve at different Harrah's properties including Reno, Lake Tahoe, Las Vegas, and Atlantic City. "Again, I like to spend time with our customers. They're really fun people my wife and I enjoy."

One of the company's most popular customer mixers is its Brand VIP Event, an annual three-day weekend that serves as another way for Harrah's to thank its best customers for their business. Each year, the company's 26 casino managers invite VIP customers across the country; the event is hosted by a different Harrah's property each year, and has recently been held in Atlantic City, Lake Tahoe, and Shreveport. The strength of a property's marketplace determines how many guests are eligible to be invited by each general manager. In 2000, for instance, Harrah's in East Chicago invited 12 customers and their significant others, Harrah's in Atlantic City invited 30 customers, and so on. Generally the company's CEO hosts the event, which includes activities such as golfing, boating, and, of course, gaming. There's always a Friday evening cocktail party hosted by Phil Satre and a Saturday night dinner with a major entertainer, who is flown in for a single performance. Jay Leno was the performer in 2000.

Entertaining high-roller players is an important part of the business, and Harrah's executives at every level get involved. Inviting customers to the Super Bowl is an annual happening—as well as Super Bowl and New Year's Eve parties at all of the company's casinos. Not surprisingly, casinos look for reasons to party. And what better way to personally get to know customers!

Service Is Not a Department

In a 2002 survey conducted by America's Research Group, 16 percent of Americans claim they have ever had a problem with a piece of furniture they've purchased. This means 84 percent of all furniture buyers have never in their lives had to call a retail store with a problem. This remarkable statistic attests to a meaningful phenomenon that carries over to enterprises in every field. Any businessperson who thinks servicing customers is centered on the company's service department is likely to wind up with many dissatisfied customers. That's because a large majority of customers never have a single contact with the service department.

There isn't a service department per se at Harrah's; every employee is a walking, talking service center. Serving customers is included in every employee's job description. As previously mentioned, the company is a strong advocate of the "Service Profit Chain" dictum described in a 1994 *Harvard Business Review* article penned by Gary Loveman et al. Today, as chief executive officer of Harrah's, Loveman underscores the importance of satisfied employees as a first step to achieving customer satisfaction.

Marilyn Winn, senior vice president of human resources, claims:

> Our management philosophy is truly an inverted pyramid. We believe that the people who serve our guests should be served by supervisors, and supervisors should be served by managers. All of us at the corporate office are focused on how the company can serve our customers and our employees who serve our customers. The idea behind the Service Profit Chain philosophy is that profit comes from loyal customers, and loyal customers come from loyal employees. To earn an employee's loyalty—which we don't take for granted just because someone is employed here—we focus on making sure that Harrah's is a good place to work. We pay people well, give them excellent benefits, and treat them fairly. We also recognize good performance and reward them for it. Sometimes, it's the small things that go a long way. For instance, an employee might ask to leave early on a particular day to attend her daughter's school play. Or, a supervisor might ask for an employee's opinion and then listen intently to what he's told.

There is an adage, "No matter how much training you give an old gray mare, it ain't ever going to win the Kentucky Derby." This is applicable in every service business when hiring employees—a company must handpick the right people, best suited to serve others. Winn explains:

> We look for people who enjoy serving people. There are people who receive pleasure by pleasing others, and we try to seek them out. For instance, a Harrah's cashier will serve as many as ten times more customers than a Home Depot cashier. It takes a special person to do this. Remember now, there will be casino customers who are in a grumpy mood during the course of a day—they've lost money, they've been drinking, they couldn't find their favorite parking space, and so on. On such occasions, the employee may have to dig down deep to ensure that every customer interaction is a pleasant one. This requires good eye contact, a warm smile, a pleasant personality, and, of course, being professional. Not everyone can behave this way under stressful conditions. To make this happen, we put in a lot of interviewing hours to make sure we hire the right person.

Harrah's has a management talent scouts program to recruit high quality service people. Winn goes on to say:

> When our managers come across somebody in their community who gives them outstanding service—an employee at the dry cleaners, a restaurant, or, perhaps, a convenience store, they'll hand them a specially printed card. By showing the card when they come to the casino's employment area, the person will be given preferential treatment. She won't have to wait in line and will immediately be granted an interview. The card reads, "I spotted your quality service and if you are ever interested in working for Harrah's Entertainment, please come and see us. We would love to talk to you." Our managers are constantly looking for the best people in their communities to recruit.
>
> We also have a long-standing employee bonus program. If an employee recruits somebody who comes to work for us and remains on the payroll for a specific period of time, the employee who recruited her receives a bonus, depending on the property and the position, that ranges from $300 to $2,500.

While there are different tiers of Harrah's casino customers in regard to who gets what comp, every customer who walks in the door receives a high level of service. Tom Jenkin explains:

> Every customer is important to us, high roller or not. We're continually asking ourselves, "How can I make our customers' stay better?" The bottom line is that serving them is what we do for a living. Our employees know that the quality of service they give is going to

show up in their wallets. Naturally, the people whose earnings directly depend on tips are directly and immediately compensated for the quality of service they extend. But even employees working in positions in which they don't receive gratuities are indoctrinated to understand that their future is impacted by satisfying customers who come back.

How does this work? In fine restaurants at Harrah's, servers know everything on the menu, and at preshift meals, they test food so they can properly make recommendations to customers. "I just loved tonight's tuna," a server may say. "And the veal is absolutely scrumptious." They are also given tickets to the casino's shows so they can make personal recommendations. If a customer inquires about Clint Holmes, the star attraction at Harrah's in Las Vegas, a server can enthusiastically respond, "He's sensational. I've seen his show three times, and I can't wait to see it again."

"Before we open for dinner," explains Marty Miles, "we have 15-minute meetings with our staff. We discuss what happened the night before, how many customers we'll serve tonight, who will be serving what customers, and so on. 'Susie, you'll be serving these reservations, and here's yours, Jon.' This way, our servers can greet customers by name when they're seated."

All employees on the casino floor accommodate guests. It takes just a stroll through the casino to observe this firsthand. For instance, if you need directions—and it's easy to get lost in a casino—just ask a Harrah's employee for assistance. You'll be pleasantly pointed in the right direction, and if you ask somebody on a break, chances are you'll be escorted to your destination. You don't have to be a high roller to receive this treatment. On a crowded day, the casino employees can't tell a high roller from a low roller with a poor sense of direction. *Everyone does it for you just because you're you!*

If a customer is dissatisfied, the Harrah's satisfaction guarantee kicks in and ensures that whatever is broken will be fixed or it's on the house. Restaurant servers and housekeepers are trained to spot customer dissatisfaction and report the problem; what it takes to satisfy the customer is decided at the supervisor's discretion. Or, for example, a seemingly small thing, such as having slow valet parking service, delays a customer. Depending on the property, the casino may appease a customer with a buffet pass good for two, or something equivalent. In cases like these, even a nongambler is comped!

If a slot machine malfunctions, Harrah's refunds the bet to the customer. Once, a customer was sitting in front of a slot machine that he had been playing. Another customer reached over his shoulder, deposited $1, and pushed the play button. The machine hit a $5,000 jackpot. Both men claimed the jackpot! The two customers were ushered to a nearby office, where each told his story to the casino's general manager. "It belongs to me," said the one man, "I had been playing that machine for an hour." The other man shouted, "He wasn't playing it when I put in my dollar. And since it was my dollar, it is my jackpot."

The general manager called the surveillance technicians and asked for a review of the tape. On reviewing the video, a decision was made to give $5,000 to each customer. The jackpot could have been split 50–50, but that may not have satisfied either customer. Incidentally, neither customer was a high roller—but they were customers!

Britt Beemer, CEO of America's Research Group, says, "A satisfied customer will tell six people, but a dissatisfied customer will tell 41 people. That's a ratio of nearly seven to one. This means every time you have one unhappy customer, a business needs to have seven very happy customers to offset the badmouthing it will get from a single disgruntled customer."

New Orleans—What's Wrong with This Picture?

It has been anything but easy for Harrah's in the Big Easy. When Harrah's became a 44 percent minority partner in the casino owner, JCC Holding Company—a public corporation that is the parent of Jazz Casino Company, LLC—it had high hopes for a successful venture in New Orleans. Plans called for a subsidiary of the company to be engaged as a casino management company; the casino would operate under the Harrah's brand when it opened in October 1999. On completion, the company's investment would be $350 million.

As the only land-based casino in New Orleans, one of America's most popular destinations, the 100,000-square-foot property was destined to be a flourishing enterprise. It couldn't have had a better location, on Canal Street along the Mississippi River in downtown New Orleans, and adjacent to the French Quarter, the Aquarium of the Americas, and the convention center. Across the street is the Riverwalk, an upscale shopping mall, and only a short walk away is another mall with a Saks Fifth Avenue as its anchor store. Because there were three gambling riverboats in the immediate vicinity, being the only land-based casino was considered a competitive advantage because gambling on Louisiana riverboats was restricted to certain cruising hours on the Mississippi. This meant riverboat gamblers could not come and go as they pleased—an inconvenience that kept them in the floating casino until it docked. In a land-based casino, customers are free to come and go at any time. Most people don't want to be stuck on a riverboat for a couple of hours after exceeding the budget they set for the day.

With millions of tourists visiting New Orleans, a city with one million residents, potential casino revenues seemed enormous. On completion of the casino, its 2,500 slot machines and 106 gaming tables would generate enormous proceeds. In exchange for exclusive rights to the only land-based casino in the Big Easy, the state of Louisiana demanded a heavy toll. The casino would be required to make a minimum payment of $100 million to the state each year regardless of performance—about $275,000 a day! Foxwoods, the Native American-owned casino in Mashantucket, Connecticut, had a similar compact with the state when it agreed to cough up $100 million each year for its right to be in business. As it turned out, it was money well spent. Foxwoods has since become the most successful casino in the world. With Foxwoods' tremendous success as a model, operating one of the world's premier casinos built in New Orleans might be worth the high tariff. To its owners, the potential return on investment in pursuit of this market was a risk worth taking.

Before the casino was built, Harrah's had to make other concessions. After the restaurants in the French Quarter banded together in protest, the local authorities decided that the casino would not be permitted to have fine dining establishments. Why? The restaurateurs feared unfair competition from the casino lowballing the food or comping meals altogether. In a tourist city known worldwide for its fine dining, the combined forces of the city's main attraction were a powerful foe. Local politicians did not want to upset the apple cart. For similar reasons, the city's hotels claimed that they, too, would be unable to compete. Even local shopkeepers feared retail stores in the casino would cut into their revenues. After considerable debate, it was agreed that the casino would be void of fine restaurants and lodging facilities, and limited to a single small retail shop selling sundries and gaming-related paraphernalia. Permission was granted for a 250-seat buffet-style dining area. However, with visitors estimated as high as 16,000 per weekday and 60,000 per weekend day, it was hardly enough to handle the traffic. Imagine a town of 16,000 with only one restaurant, or worse, a small city of 60,000. It's equally difficult to imagine a world-class casino without these amenities.

Lest anyone forget, it has been a long tradition in the gaming industry to comp customers to win their loyalty. This is true today even with a casino that has the only game in town. (Forget for the moment that there were gambling riverboats—a subject to be addressed shortly.) Gamblers have long been accustomed to receiving comps from casinos. What's more, they *expect* comps, and when they don't receive them, they are more than mildly disappointed. A casino without comps would be like an airline's first-class section without food and beverages. Therefore, even without fine restaurants and luxurious hotel rooms, Harrah's had no choice but to comp its customers. However, to do so meant sending them away from the casino, which defeats the purpose of comping. A basic rule in casino marketing is to use comps to attract customers to the casino—not to send them off elsewhere. Everyone knows that the more time customers spend on the premises, the more likely they are to play. Hence, operating one of the most elegant casinos in the world sans fine dining and lodging severely handicapped Harrah's. Consider, too, that comping meals and hotel rooms owned by third parties is still another expense because when casinos comp amenities consumed on their own properties, they don't pay a retail price. On top of this, there was the $100 million annual state fee, equivalent to a 41 percent tax rate on gross revenues for the casino's first 12 months of operation!

When the casino opened in October 1999, it soon became apparent that the company wasn't playing on a level field. While the company paid top dollar for exclusive rights to operate the area's one and only land-based casino, it wasn't so exclusive after all. The three riverboats on the Mississippi rarely left dockside, so they, too, were land-based. Not only did the riverboats reduce their expenses by not sailing up and down the river, being land-based, but also they attracted larger crowds—that, in turn, reduced traffic at the Harrah's property. Clearly, the state's unwillingness to enforce the sailing of the riverboats was in violation of its agreement with Harrah's and its partners. What happened, in fact, was that the riverboat management made weather-based decisions not to sail and did it to an extreme. A slight chance of rain, for example, would be reason to dockside the riverboats for an entire day. Harrah's employees "tested the waters" by making personal inquiries about riverboat sailings. "Well, the weatherman said there's a five percent chance of rain today, so we won't be leaving the dock today, but our casino will be open," a riverboat employee would report, with a wink. "Do you see that little cloud up there? Well, it could rain today, so we don't want to take any chances. There will be no sailing today. But you're welcome to come aboard and enjoy our casino." In effect, these were not riverboats; they were land-based casinos.

In hindsight, New Orleans itself wasn't the incredible market that Harrah's management had projected. Although the metropolitan area has a population exceeding one million, an estimated 28 percent of its residents live below the poverty line; hence, the casino has a lower than anticipated frequency of customers. The presence of a billion-dollar-plus casino industry in nearby Biloxi and Gulfport was an unknown factor when the Harrah's New Orleans project was on the drawing board. These markets have drawn customers who would otherwise gamble in New Orleans. In addition, tourists who come to New Orleans are not necessarily gaming customers. Although Harrah's has used the New Orleans property for cross-marketing purposes, sending high-level customers to its casino where they are comped at nearby hotels and restaurants is not the way Bill Harrah would operate a casino.

Meanwhile, Harrah's expressed its dissatisfaction with restrictions imposed on it by state and local politicians. The company warned that if this dissatisfaction was not resolved, it would close the casino. With 2,500-plus jobs at stake and a payroll of nearly $100 million on the line, the state listened carefully.

In March 2001, the Louisiana Legislature approved key elements in a reorganization plan for JCC Holding Company, owner of Harrah's New Orleans Casino. In essence, the $100 million annual tax was reduced to $50 million for the year ending March 31, 2002, and $60 million for each of the next three years. Permission was granted for the casino to have restaurants and a hotel. In 2002, Harrah's Entertainment decided to buy the 51 percent of JCC Holding Company that it didn't own. The Louisiana Legislature also granted permission to gambling riverboats to have gambling while dockside, and, accordingly, they will be taxed at a higher rate.

Superstitious People

One trait gaming people have in common is a superstitious nature. Surprisingly, this includes both sides of the table—players and casino employees.

Depending on the game, some skill is required to win in a casino. But, as gamblers often say, "I'd rather be lucky than good." Never downplay Lady Luck in a game of chance. Bear in mind that slot machines operate by random selection. For that matter, so do the roll of the dice and the spin of a roulette wheel. And while knowing when to "hit" in a game of blackjack necessitates understanding certain probabilities, it's luck that determines the card actually dealt.

Accordingly, at any given time, a lucky unskilled player could have better fortune than an unlucky skilled player. Of course, luck is an elusive force. Hot streaks and cold streaks come and go. What causes them, however, is unpredictable. Still, this does not stop gamblers from trying to influence their luck. When it comes to enhancing one's luck, anything goes. The most common are lucky charms. Casinos are full of people carrying odd little objects, including the old standard rabbit's foot or four-leaf clover. Other players come equipped with statues, dolls, polished stones, jade jewels, rings, bracelets, necklaces, old coins, and so on. To many, it's a culture thing. For example, Asian women wear mother-of-pearl bracelets and other forms of jewelry, sometimes with religious significance. Other folks wear lucky T-shirts, hats, and ties.

Every dealer tells stories of customers who have specific ways to stack their checks (chips). Their piles vary, sometimes arranged in triangles, according to colors, or perhaps with a dollar bill on top. When they're on a cold streak, they like to change things. They demand to have the deck and dice changed. They switch seats, change tables, or request new dealers. They also go to another casino for a change of luck. Gamblers have lucky ways to snap their fingers, particular ways to cut cards, and bizarre body gyrations to toss the dice. Men touch body parts—theirs, their wives', and their girlfriends'. Breasts and buttocks are favorites. One croupier tells about a customer who put his hands inside his pants, removed a piercing jewel from his genitals, and placed it on the table for good luck. The man never even winced. But the croupier surely did.

Many people look for omens to determine their luck before coming to the casino. A flight number containing a "7" or an "11" is considered a good sign. So is an upgrade to first class, a completed crossword puzzle, or an on-time flight. Conversely, bumpy and delayed flights are bad omens. Drivers who have all green lights on their way to a casino interpret it to mean good luck. A major traffic jam means, "Don't press your luck today." And heaven forbid a fender-bending car accident!

One Harrah's customer spent three consecutive days and nights at the roulette tables, refusing to change his clothes. To make matters worse, it happened to be a particularly hot August. He wore the same shirt and pair of shorts, never once leaving the casino. He sweated profusely, using a box of moist wipes that he periodically placed under his armpits to "bathe" himself. People in his proximity who got a whiff of him fanned their faces for relief. Was he embarrassed? Who knows? But it didn't stop him because his sweaty clothes were bringing him good luck!

A customer at Harrah's in Atlantic City had a superstition that takes the cake. He had a Shar-pei that loved chewing on Gucci loafers. So, guess what he fed his prized pet before heading to the casino? Once when he stayed a particularly long time at the tables and was having an unlucky streak, he requested his casino host to purchase ten pairs of Gucci loafers and have them delivered to his residence. The request was granted and a limousine driver was dispatched to the customer's house. His butler promptly placed the loafers in front of the small Chinese dog. Then he called his employer. "Yes, boss, he's chewing on them as we speak."

"That's what I wanted to hear," the man said. Moments later, he tried his luck again at the tables. If you're thinking about trying this to change your luck, don't bother. Over time, this customer lost a few million dollars at Harrah's, as well as a lot of Gucci loafers.

Some gamblers resort to prayer to change their luck. A well-known televangelist used to play blackjack regularly at the Desert Inn. A heavy bettor, the man of cloth and his wife would hold hands and pray for the right card before they'd take a hit. Once they lost $150,000 that turned out to be the church's money. Mike Vitale, today a table games supervisor at Harrah's on the Strip, says, "They actually thought God would give them good luck to play with money that belonged to their parishioners."

It's not only the customers who have superstitions. So do casino owners. In the old days, it was taboo for a dealer to wear white shoes in the pit. Dealers who were cold got the boot. Dealers also changed the way they shuffled cards to change their luck. And, of course, casino managers would routinely replace cold dealers with new dealers.

There's always a lot of excitement in the casino when somebody is on a lucky streak and a crowd accumulates to cheer for it to continue. It's even better when a craps player is on a hot roll and everybody at the table is sharing in his or her luck. Not long ago, a crowd of bystanders gathered around a 22-year-old man who was playing the end seat at a full blackjack table. An elderly Asian man stood behind him, observing the young man's lucky streak. It was truly remarkable. The dealer had a picture card showing and the young man hit on a 16 and drew a 5. The young man doubled down with two 10s and drew two aces.

On winning seven consecutive hands, the young man placed his usual $10 wager on the table. This time, the Asian politely asked him, "Do you mind if I give you some money to bet for me?"

"No problem," he replied, glancing at the dealer for approval.

"Fine with me," the dealer said.

"I want to bet $10,000," said the Asian.

The dealer got the attention of his boss, who, in turn, nodded to accept the wager. With that, the Asian reached into his pocket and placed his money next to the young man's chip. The cards were dealt around the table. A small smile appeared on the young man's face when his first card was a jack. The Asian's facial expression never wavered. When his second card was a king, and the dealer had an 8 showing, a small grin appeared on the young man's face. The Asian remained stoic.

Each of the other players played their cards. Finally, after the woman seated next to him drew to a 13 and busted, the young man turned to the Asian and said, "Give me $1,000, or I'm going to hit another card."

"You can't do that! You have 20," the Asian said.

Again, the young man repeated, "Give me $1,000, or I'll . . ."

"Okay," the Asian answered, reaching into his pocket for his checks.

On putting $1,000 of checks in his pocket, the young man stood up from the table, picked up his winnings and said to the dealer, "I'll stay."

His next words were, "I'm out of here," making a quick exit from the table, leaving his $10 wager behind.

Bill Keena tells:

A few years ago, a well-known NASCAR racecar driver, was in the casino late one night after having raced here in Laughlin. His luck was really bad at the blackjack table, but sitting next to him, a man with a stupid-looking fishing hat was beating the house again and again. The driver finally asked the man if he could use his hat. "No way," the man said, "it's good luck for me." "Would you consider selling it to me?" "Yeah, for $100." "It can't be worth more than a couple of bucks." "Yeah, but I still want $100."

The driver handed the man a hundred dollar bill and, like magic, his luck changed. He started to win hand after hand, and the other guy couldn't steal a card. Finally, the guy says, "I'd like to buy back the hat." "I want $500 for it," the driver answered. "But you only gave me $100 for it." "That's right, but it's $500 now."

9

THERE'S NO BUSINESS LIKE THE GAMING BUSINESS

ICH MIRMAN STATES, "IF THE HARRAH'S MANAGEMENT TEAM WERE transposed, and we applied our same business model, I feel we could successfully run a large number of consumer products companies in America."

Mirman's statement elucidates why Harrah's Entertainment, Inc., is the gaming industry darling of Wall Street. Analysts are attracted to the company whose track record reads like a business school case history. Its management team comprises many individuals with professional careers from outside the gaming industry. They come from everywhere—academia, the financial services industry, consulting firms, marketing, ad agencies, and so on. As Gary Loveman says, "These people never had anything to do with the gaming industry; they developed skills in other fields which they are now applying at Harrah's."

In short, investment bankers understand Harrah's. For many years, dating back to the Bugsy Siegel era, Wall Street steered clear of casino companies. Outside Nevada, gambling was an illegal activity, and even in Las Vegas where it was legal, it was a Mafia-controlled business.

In this respect, Bill Harrah was an anomaly—he was a businessman of high integrity who happened to own a gambling casino. In his eyes, Harrah's was a form of entertainment; a casino was a place where customers came to escape for several hours to have some fun.

To others, a gambling house was a den of iniquity. Never mind that millions of Americans privately participated in gambling—placed bets, played poker, shot craps—in public, they disdained gambling. For years, gambling was viewed as a vice in America. Clergymen preached that it was immoral. Government officials strictly enforced laws banning gambling, and offenders were incarcerated. Even though gambling was legal in Nevada, upper-crust society ostracized casino people.

Interestingly, in many states where casinos are banned, other forms of gambling such as horse racing and lotteries are permitted. The most widespread form of gambling—the state-owned lottery—has paybacks considerably lower than casinos. And for years, churches have been permitted to operate bingo games. With this in mind, legislators and clergymen have selectively given their approval to some forms of gambling. Could it be that their approval is more readily given when they have the advantage of being the house?

Today, even distracters acknowledge gaming as a major segment of America's expanding entertainment industry. In an industry that was illegal for nearly a century, with a notable exception (gambling is legal in the state of Nevada, although it was banned between 1910 and 1931), its current popularity is convincing proof that gaming has become America's favorite pastime. Forget about baseball! Today, legal gaming revenues exceed the combined amount Americans spend on movie tickets, recorded music, theme parks, spectator sports, and video games.

In the annals of American business, no other U.S. industry has been banned for so long. Categorically, gaming has an unusual past. Those who scorn gambling claim it corrupts people, while supporters contend corruption prevails only when corrupt people are permitted to operate casinos. Here, gaming may be a victim of guilt by association: People who haven't kept up with the times, or who have been watching too many Hollywood films, still conjure up an image of gangster-controlled casinos. The Mafia and the unions long ago relinquished control of casinos, and corporate America has permanently moved in. Likewise, state legislators have scored high marks in keeping undesirables out of the business.

There are the antagonists who claim gambling is addictive and, therefore, harmful to society. Studies, however, document that gambling disorders—estimated to be 1 percent of the adult population—are minimal in comparison to the abuse of alcohol or tobacco, both of which are substances. Gaming is not a substance; it is a form of entertainment.

Still other critics oppose gaming because the house always has an "edge." But, isn't every for-profit organization supposed to have an edge? In retailing, for example, goods are marked up 40 to 50 percent above the cost of merchandise, which is, in effect, the retailer's edge so he or she can make a profit. In retailing circles, it's known as the "markup" or "margin." Similarly, a casino is entitled to a built-in profit, or margin, and that's why the odds slightly favor the house. However, the house is never guaranteed to win. Many customers come to a casino, have a wonderful time, and go home winners. "That's something you can't do when you go on a vacation to Disney," says company CFO Chuck Atwood. "If you have a budget for $1,000 at

Disney or another vacation destination, you will always walk away with less money. But, in this business, you can walk away with a lot more than you came with."

Unlike other businesses, casinos know they will incur losses. Even with the odds favoring the house, there is no guarantee a casino will turn a profit. It is a highly capital-intensive business. In addition, in many markets, casinos are open 24 hours a day, 365 days a year; hence, three shifts are required. This makes it a highly labor-intensive business, too. Moreover, in a dog-eat-dog marketplace, casinos that aren't efficiently managed fall by the wayside. Therefore, contrary to what some people think, owning a casino is not like owning a money machine. The graveyard is filled with casinos that have gone under. As Atwood notes, "In the early 1990s, a Wall Street analyst studied the financial statements [which are public record] of Las Vegas casinos and reported that there were ten casinos making nearly all of the profits. The other casinos were just eking by."

Comping is a direct result of the fierce competition between casinos. Where else do businesspeople extend themselves to satisfy every whim of their customers? It is true that, on occasion, a restaurateur or bartender serves a drink on the house; a businessman might treat a client to a round of golf at his or her country club; a manufacturer might invite a valued customer to the Super Bowl. Promotion and creating goodwill are commonplace in today's business world. However, when it comes to comping, casino companies are in a league of their own. The cost of comping is no nickel and dime thing for casinos. In the year ending 2002, Harrah's comped an estimated $300 million to customers, or about 7.5 percent of the company's gross revenues—a huge chunk right off the top. You can call it marketing—but $300 million worth of customer freebies happens only in the casino business!

Certainly, comps are a powerful inducement luring customers to a casino. It is particularly true at the high-roller level where private jets, limousines, and suites several times larger than the average American house invite customer loyalty. But, the thrills of a gaming casino are guaranteed to mesmerize anyone with a sense of adventure who enjoys having fun. Undoubtedly, it's the rapturous ambience that drives people to gamble, because everyone knows the odds favor the house. Why else would grown men bet thousands of dollars on a hand of baccarat, a game less challenging than a child's card game of fish!

Managing a casino is no simple task. There are so many services to provide customers. Gary Loveman explains:

> In addition to the casino games, we park their cars; feed them; put them to bed at night; entertain them in showrooms; sell merchandise

to them in retail shops; offer them bus, limousine, and air transportation; and, in some cases, we lend them money. This is a very rich collection of service activities, all being generated millions of times every day, under one roof. It's a complicated job to get all of these things done well. With the exception of a theme park like Disney or a cruise liner, no other service company must execute so many different kinds of service delivery to one customer. Airlines, for example, fly you from one place to another, and hotels put you to bed at night, but they don't feed you as much and provide all the other things we do.

A casino is a happening. No other place has such incredible nonstop excitement. This is especially true in Las Vegas, the world's gambling mecca, where something is always going on, 24 hours a day, 365 days a year. No other business in the world provides this constant, nonstop entertainment. This is what people come for—and even when they lose money, they don't go home disappointed.

Nor do they always go home single. In 2001, 243,198 people tied the knot while visiting the world's gambling capital. Thousands more renew their wedding vows. That's averaging a wedding just about every three minutes, around the clock, 24 hours a day, 365 days a year. The most popular date is Valentine's Day, a day when 2,130 lovebirds got hitched in 2001. The second favorite choice is New Year's Eve. Since the Clark County courthouse started keeping a tally in 1909, more than three million people have been married in Vegas.

Why Las Vegas? It's hard to imagine that the jangling slot machines and bright neon lights inspire wedding bells. There are, however, several romantic spots in town. One such place is the fountain outside the Bellagio hotel with its more than 1,000 spouts of water that are choreographed to music and light. The display features more than 1,000 feet of fountains with water spouting skyward to heights of 240 feet. Others are swept off their feet at the Eiffel Tower replica at Paris Las Vegas or on a gondola, cruising down The Venetian's Grand Canal. And, typical of Vegas, there are theme weddings. Favorite themes are beach party, western, Harley, Victorian, Egyptian, gangster, and an Elvis wedding package! You can even get married in a taxi at a drive-up window!

Even Odds

Gary Loveman takes exception to critics who argue that casino companies operate unfairly because the gambler's odds are in the house's favor. He asserts:

I believe that argument is sheer nonsense. It's simply the way we price our product.

We could reprice casino gaming by setting an admission price just like you pay to see a show or a sports event. All we'd have to do is calculate what the average customer loses—we already have that information. Then, we'd factor in our overhead. Once we did this, we could have our slot machines set so we paid out exactly the amount of money that they take in. We'd do the same on all of our table games. We'd change the dealer's rules so the house advantage was zero. Our roulette wheels wouldn't have zero and double zeros, so we would even their odds, and so on throughout the casino.

After we did all of the above, we'd then charge a flat rate of say, $40. We could either charge customers for drinks, or give them for free, again figuring out what it would cost—much like we do with our buffets. This way, every customer who came in the casino would pay a flat $40—win or lose—so immediately upon walking through the door, every customer would be down $40. Concurrently, he or she would be playing against the house at even odds. But, this isn't how we do it. Instead of charging a flat fee, customers come in for free. But, they do play at a slight disadvantage on average—and on the average, they lose about $40.

We could keep doing what we do now or the way I just explained, and how we get our money really wouldn't matter to the casino. Frankly, I really wouldn't care. But customers wouldn't want it this way. Customers prefer not having to pay an admissions fee—they want to take their chances with the cards on the table. They'd rather not pay to walk through our doors, cognizant of the fact that the house has a slight advantage.

When you stop to think about it, it would be like a movie theater giving away free popcorn and candy at the concession stand and building it into the price of a ticket.

Charging a flat fee to every customer would undoubtedly be a more efficient way to operate a casino, and it would also appease critics who call the house's built-in edge unfair. However, the customers enjoy the challenge of trying to beat the house, and when their play warrants it, they love being comped. Much would have to change if the house had even odds—many things that customers wouldn't like.

Change Is Constant

"These are the same questions you asked on last year's exam," a student said to his professor—Albert Einstein.

"It is true that all of the questions are the same," replied Einstein. "But this year, all of the answers are different."

Had the course been casino management, the same reply could be given. The casino industry, constantly experiencing change, seems to reinvent itself every few years. There has been so much change during the past decade that the 1980s already seem like ancient history. Anyone who hasn't visited Las Vegas since the early 1990s would hardly recognize it. During the past decade, when several of the world's largest, most expensive hotel casino properties sprang up, arriving in town on a night flight that passes over the Strip was a dazzling sight. No wonder that when shuttle astronauts did a light study of the earth, Las Vegas was deemed the brightest city on the planet.

Inside the casinos, changes are less obvious, but equally impressive. Today's slot machines are as different from their predecessors as today's most cutting-edge laptop is from yesterday's manual typewriter. Technology has brought rapid change to the casino industry, enhancing everything from security measures taken to guard against cheaters, to storing customer information. Technology has made slot machines much more exciting; their popularity is soaring. And thanks to technology and some very smart marketing people, there is also the information that Harrah's collects from customers' slot play. This valuable marketing tool could not have possibly been imagined several years ago. This data enables the company to recognize its best slot customers and award them for their loyalty. Consequently, many formerly "invisible" customers are courted and comped in a manner formerly reserved only for high-level gaming table players.

Today, the Harrah's database holds 25 million customers, a number that keeps growing. As more Americans go online, Harrah's will communicate with its customers more quickly and at greatly reduced costs. This makes it possible to extend last-minute offers on available rooms, show tickets, airfares, and a host of other products and services.

Presently, gambling on the Internet is an illegal activity. If Americans are someday able to gamble online, how will it be regulated? Harrah's public affairs director Dean Hestermann says:

> There is probably a right way and a wrong way to go about regulating Internet gambling. One of today's concerns is the issue of restricting access to anyone under the legal age to gamble. To date, this isn't something technology has solved. At Harrah's, we're certainly not opposed to Internet gambling, per se, nor are we in favor of it, per se. It's like casino gaming—there's a right way and a wrong way to go about doing it. Another hurdle is the issue of determining what happens if someone in State A gambles on an Internet site in State B, when that form of gambling is not legal in State A. How do

you determine where someone is physically located when he or she is gambling? This is a big technical and legal issue that has to be answered.

There are antagonists who criticize the use of technology for the purpose of gathering information on consumers, claiming it is intrusive and smacks of "Big Brother." Jan Jones answers:

I look at it as being smart marketers. It's about giving the best possible service to your customers by accessing information about their specific needs. If you check into one of our properties, and I say, "Good afternoon, Mr. Smith, and welcome back. We have your suite ready on the sixth floor. We've preordered your breakfast—an omelet, bagels, and orange juice—just as you prefer. Since we know you like playing baccarat, we have a special seat for you in VIP. I've also made reservations for you at 8:30 at the Range with the best bottle of our Beaujolais, which we know is your favorite brand." Do you think that's being intrusive? Or, do you think it's being smart? I think it's being smart.

It's also being smart for Harrah's, with its 26 casinos, to use its technological and marketing skills to enhance its brand name. Gary Loveman emphasizes that this is similar to the development of a brand in industries that are more traditional:

There's an emotional attachment between a purchaser and a provider that exists with great brands in the automotive, cosmetics, garment, and pharmaceutical industries. We want the same sort of thing to exist with all of our brands in our business. Each year, we give back in excess of $300 million to our customers in what is referred to as reinvestment, or, in this industry, comps or givebacks. This process is rife with a lack of sophistication. It's done in a careless and costly fashion. Our objective is to improve it, and by doing so, we can make considerably more money.

Harrah's has been in the gaming business for more than 60 years. No other major casino companies can match this longevity. The company has survived and continues to prosper because it adapts to change. In this respect, Harrah's is a rarity in business chronicles. Most commonly, it is the fledging start-up venture that dares to be innovative and risk-taking. Older, more staid companies often take a conservative route. The company's founder, Bill Harrah, was indeed a risk-taker, and his management style permeates the corporate culture. An early pioneer, he introduced many innovations to the industry. For example, as we've discussed, he was the first to bus customers to Lake Tahoe, a marketing program still practiced by many casinos across the United States. Perhaps it's a small touch, but even the box lunches served on the Harrah's buses were a first.

Although Bill Harrah didn't invent comps, he was the first to do it in the most grandiose style through the star treatment he gave to the Harrah's entertainers. His star suites were predecessors to luxury suites reserved for today's high-level players. Harrah catered to the stars, spending millions in advertising dollars to promote them—in an era when it was illegal to otherwise advertise a gambling casino. He was one of the early sponsors of golf tournaments—the forefather of today's major sporting events, including boxing championships.

When Harrah's opened its hotel in Lake Tahoe in 1973, its cost of $100,000 per room made it the most expensive hotel ever built. Since then, the world's most costly hotels have been built in Las Vegas, but it was Bill Harrah who proved to the casino industry that if you build the most elegant and exorbitant property, the people will come. A quiet man, he didn't shy away from seeking out ideas, and when needed, copying them from others. "We don't always have to do everything right," he told employees. "Other people do things better than we do. And if they do, let's find out what they're doing and let's copy it."

One of the accomplishments Bill Harrah was most proud of was founding the first casino to be listed on the New York Stock Exchange. The listing was in 1973, two years after Harrah's first traded on the over-the-counter exchange. Being the first NYSE casino established Harrah's as an industry leader, a highly professional, stable, business-like company. In 1973, this was very different from the image of Nevada casinos.

A Look into the Future

According to Tim Wilmott, chief operating officer, Las Vegas is an anomaly of U.S. casino marketplaces:

> A typical customer goes to Vegas once a year and stays three or four days. Most customers who go to casinos in markets such as Atlantic City, Chicagoland, riverboats, and Indian reservations visit about once a month and stay about four hours. It's just another night out on the town. Casinos are another entertainment option competing for their discretionary entertainment dollars.

Wilmott describes an accurate portrayal of today's marketplace in which most Americans live within 45 minutes to an hour driving time of a casino. As a result, people are taking weekend vacations at casinos to add a little excitement to their lives. With less discretionary time to spend, they see casinos as a way to squeeze in a quickie vacation. Casinos offer a way to get away for a few hours, or a day or two, and blow off a little steam.

In a research study conducted in 2000, America's Research Group revealed that 68 percent of gamblers stick to their budgets; they have the discipline to walk away after losing a predetermined amount of money. Seventeen percent don't, and they exceed their budgets; 12 percent said they walk sometimes, but not always. Only 8 percent said that they have lost sleep because of gambling losses.

In spite of these numbers, many people think gamblers typically play for much higher stakes than they actually do. Gary Loveman says:

> I was on a flight and sat beside a U.S. Congressman who serves a district that has gaming, and yet he had so many false notions about the industry. During our conversation, I asked him what he thought the average win per visit for the casino was, and he said, "It probably exceeds $200." He was shocked when I replied, "In your state, it's about $27." I was in Shreveport last week, and it's $63. That's less than an expensive dinner.

Concerned legislators keep a watchful eye on the perceived social consequences that transpire from irresponsible gambling. While certainly these watchdogs have good intentions, overzealous regulations fail to serve anyone's best interests—the casino companies or their constituents. Undoubtedly, regulatory authorities must govern gambling.

However, according to Gary Loveman, there comes a time when enough is enough. Something is wrong with the system when "moving a slot machine ten feet from one spot to another requires regulatory intervention," says Loveman. He compares this regulation to overseeing HMOs and other health care providers:

> [They] can make a thousand life or death decisions about the allocations of scarce resources without the slightest degree of regulatory intervention. That strikes me as peculiar.
>
> When we built a hotel tower as an addition to our Atlantic City Harrah's, it created a lot of jobs in the area. The construction of that tower had to pass a New Jersey regulatory body that reviews the construction of only two types of buildings—casinos and nuclear power plants. Now I have a difficult time understanding the common characteristics of these two industries. And why should a casino hotel structure that doesn't even have a casino in it, but simply hotel rooms that serve a casino, be subjected to this level of regulatory scrutiny! This kind of regulation isn't beneficial to problem gamers,

our customers, shareholders, employees—nobody. Certainly, having sensible regulation directed at the right set of problems is efficacious. At present, however, it's costly to us as well as to our customers. In the future, I hope legislators will see the wisdom and will no longer burden our industry with meaningless regulation.

Michael St. Pierre believes many regulatory requirements that sprang from good intentions are frivolous:

For example, in Missouri, there's a $2 admission charge for every passenger who comes aboard. The state also has a loss limit law, which means a passenger can buy in only up to $500 in any two-hour gaming session. Furthermore, passengers come aboard for a two-hour simulated excursion because the boats remain dockside. Until last year, customers could come aboard only during the first 45 minutes, but this requirement has been eliminated.

Dean Hestermann explains:

There was a lot of social engineering kinds of experiments like Missouri's loss limits and riverboat cruising requirements. Intuitively, these regulations had some appeal in terms of mitigating the alleged social consequences, but with years of actual gaming experience, it's hopeful legislators will realize restrictions of this nature are costly to casinos and inconvenient to customers. By making our business less profitable, the state penalizes itself by reducing tax revenues.

While the future may see an easing of some cumbersome rules and regulations, it will be increasingly more difficult for Johnny-come-lately casinos to enter existing marketplaces. Most of the markets have matured over the past several years, and like any industry—from shopping centers to movie theaters—there is a saturation point to the number of casinos that the United States can support. It's likely that established casinos won't expand into new markets; instead, they will reinvest in their existing properties.

At present, there are still parts of the United States that are underserved by casino gaming—areas such as the New England states, Ohio, Pennsylvania, Maryland, and Florida. "I think the benefits to these states will be so apparent and the negatives so inconsequential," Hestermann says, "we will witness more states legalizing gaming. This will also mean some of the companies already in existing markets will do their best to protect their interests by keeping their competitors out. So I don't anticipate much unanimity among casinos."

In the near future, Harrah's will continue to improve its existing properties, adding rooms, restaurants, players clubs, and convention and ballroom facilities. Phil Satre says:

We will continue to look at acquisition opportunities. By adding new properties to our portfolio, we increase our access to more customers. It's also a way to have proximity to large numbers of people living in certain markets. The Cherokee Indian casino in North Carolina and newly opened Rincon casino in Southern California are good examples of how this works.

Aside from the bricks and mortar, I foresee many ways we can communicate to our customers on the Internet. There are so many new ideas on the drawing board that as far as I'm concerned, we're just scratching the surface. The additional services we'll be able to provide our customers are mind-boggling.

Using the past and present to foretell the future, Harrah's will continue to challenge conventional wisdom and be a trendsetter in the gaming industry. With its dynamic management team and $100 million IT infrastructure in place, the company is set to move forward, dedicated to its commitment to give "the best value experience" to its customers. The company is in an enviable position. None of the competition has such in-depth information about its customers, nor does anyone have the talent to implement the information. In short, Harrah's is in a position to predict trends and make fact-based decisions—a powerful competitive advantage to move forward.

To stay ahead of the curve, Harrah's must continue to embrace change because what it does today, its competition will copy and do tomorrow. This is the nature of the free enterprise system. Rudyard Kipling could have had Harrah's in mind when he wrote his nineteenth-century poem, "The Mary Gloster," that read: "They copied all they could follow, but they couldn't copy my mind,/And I left 'em sweating and stealing, a year and a half behind." The company that Harrah's is today will not be able to compete with the company Harrah's will be tomorrow.

Notes

Chapter 1

Page 4 "In this country, its roots go back to 1612 when the first lottery . . ." C. Britt Beemer and Robert L. Shook, *It Takes a Prophet to Make a Profit,* New York: Simon & Schuster, 2001, p. 220.

Page 6 "Not long after his arrival in this country . . ." Clinton Woods, *Ideas That Became Big Business,* Baltimore, MD: Founders, Book 25, p. 382.

Page 6 "They hired two women and a boy . . ." Eleanor Foa Dienstag, *In Good Company,* New York: Warner Books, 1994, p. 24.

Page 7 "He started as a $40-a-week illustrator with the Kansas City Film Ad Company . . ." Daniel Gross and the Editors of *Forbes* magazine, *Forbes: Greatest Business Stories of All Time,* New York: John Wiley & Sons, 1996, p. 126.

Page 7 "Thus, at the age of 52, when many businesspeople begin thinking . . ." Carrie Shook & Robert L. Shook, *Franchising, The Business Strategy That Changed the World,* Englewood Cliffs, NJ: Prentice-Hall, 1993, p. 143.

Page 7 "Walton opened a Ben Franklin Store in Newport, Arkansas . . ." Daniel Gross and the Editors of *Forbes* magazine, *Forbes: Greatest Business Stories of All Time,* New York: John Wiley & Sons, 1996, p. 270.

Page 8 "Gates and Allen were not typical entrepreneurs . . ." Daniel Gross and the Editors of *Forbes* magazine, *Forbes: Greatest Business Stories of All Time,* New York: John Wiley & Sons, 1996, p. 340.

Page 9 "The Circle Game was bingo with a twist . . ." Leon Mandel, *William Fisk Harrah: The Life and Times of a Gambling Magnate,* New York: Doubleday, 1981, p. 31.

Page 10 "To remind his customers that he'd be back when Santa Anita closed . . ." Leon Mandel, *William Fisk Harrah: The Life and Times of a Gambling Magnate,* New York: Doubleday, 1981, p. 33.

Page 11 "Look at that; they don't close the bars . . ." Leon Mandel, *William Fisk Harrah: The Life and Times of a Gambling Magnate,* New York: Doubleday, 1981, p. 34.

Page 12 "It was a first-class job. So we bought it . . ." Leon Mandel, *William Fisk Harrah: The Life and Times of a Gambling Magnate,* New York: Doubleday, 1981, p. 53.

Page 15 "By 1844, Las Vegas appeared on many Spanish maps. . . ." Barbara Land and Myrick Land, *A Short History of Las Vegas,* Reno, NV: University of Nevada Press, 1999, p. 12.

Page 15   "The early town was nothing more than a tent city . . ." Barbara Land and Myrick Land, *A Short History of Las Vegas,* Reno, NV: University of Nevada Press, 1999, p. 3.

Page 16   "With more than three million acres of ground space . . ." M. Gottdiener, Claudia C. Collins, and David R. Dickens, *Las Vegas: The Social Production of an All-American City,* Malden, MA: Blackwell Publishers, 1999, p. 14.

Page 16   "One of the earliest visionaries . . ." M. Gottdiener, Claudia C. Collins, and David R. Dickens, *Las Vegas: The Social Production of an All-American City,* Malden, MA: Blackwell Publishers, 1999, p. 17.

Page 16   "They chose a Western motif and designed a huge building . . ." M. Gottdiener, Claudia C. Collins, and David R. Dickens, *Las Vegas: The Social Production of an All-American City,* Malden, MA: Blackwell Publishers, 1999, p. 18.

Page 17   "Known for his psychopathic temper, Siegel . . ." Barbara Land and Myrick Land, *A Short History of Las Vegas,* Reno, NV: University of Nevada Press, 1999, p. 93.

Page 18   "Siegel promptly renamed the hotel the Flamingo . . ." Pete Earley, *Super Casino,* New York: Bantam Books, 2000, p. 45.

Page 18   "The Flamingo had landscaped lawns and gardens . . ." Barbara Land and Myrick Land, *A Short History of Las Vegas,* Reno, NV: University of Nevada Press, 1999, p. 97.

Page 18   "The Flamingo's grand opening on the day after Christmas . . ." Pete Earley, *Super Casino,* New York: Bantam Books, 2000, p. 45.

Page 21   "So the trick was just get it done . . ." Leon Mandel, *William Fisk Harrah: The Life and Times of a Gambling Magnate,* New York: Doubleday, 1981, p. 77.

Page 22   "In 1962, in a sale and leaseback arrangement . . ." Wallace Turner, *Gambler's Money,* Boston: Houghton Mifflin, 1965, p. 42.

Page 22   "The key to all Harold's advertising was twofold . . ." Leon Mandel, *William Fisk Harrah: The Life and Times of a Gambling Magnate,* New York: Doubleday, 1981, p. 83.

Page 22   "I don't care what it is, if it don't look good, it don't look good . . ." Leon Mandel, *William Fisk Harrah: The Life and Times of a Gambling Magnate,* New York: Doubleday, 1981, p. 75.

Page 22   "If nothing else, the carpet set a tone . . ." Leon Mandel, *William Fisk Harrah: The Life and Times of a Gambling Magnate,* New York: Doubleday, 1981, p. 80.

Page 23   "Suppose you toss a coin in the air . . ." Peter L. Bernstein, *Against The Gods, The Remarkable Story of Risk,* New York: John Wiley & Sons, 1996, p. 122.

Chapter 2

Page 27   "Bill Harrah is not at first sight the type . . ." Leon Mandel, *William Fisk Harrah: The Life and Times of a Gambling Magnate,* New York: Doubleday, 1981, p. 94.

Page 30 "It listed department grosses . . ." Leon Mandel, *William Fisk Harrah: The Life and Times of a Gambling Magnate,* New York: Doubleday, 1981, p. 104.

Page 30 "[It's] unheard of in any business . . ." Leon Mandel, *William Fisk Harrah: The Life and Times of a Gambling Magnate,* New York: Doubleday, 1981, p. 104.

Page 32 "If you worked for Bill . . ." Interview with Holmes Hendricksen on September 21, 2000.

Page 37 "Guys, we got a problem . . ." William F. Roemer, Jr., *War of the Godfathers,* New York: Donald I. Fine, 1990, p. 56.

Page 38 "One dealer was held by two goons . . ." Ed Reid and Ovid Demaris, *The Green Felt Jungle,* New York: Trident Press, 1963, p. 52.

Page 38 "Spilotro was a suspect in 25 murders . . ." Barbara Land and Myrick Land, *A Short History of Las Vegas,* Reno, NV: University of Nevada Press, 1999, p. 105.

Page 40 "Gross casino wins as of 4/27/57 . . ." Ed Reid and Ovid Demaris, *The Green Felt Jungle,* New York: Trident Press, 1963, p. 82.

Page 41 "Under his guidance, Governor Sawyer replaced the Tax Commission . . ." M. Gottdiener, Claudia C. Collins, and David R. Dickens, *Las Vegas: The Social Production of an All-American City,* Malden, MA: Blackwell Publishers, 1999, p. 27.

Page 42 "His backbone was bent . . ." Jack Sheehan, *The Players: The Men Who Made Las Vegas,* Reno, NV: University of Nevada Press, 1997, p. 133.

Page 42 "Hughes suffered from a menagerie of phobias, manias . . ." Jack Sheehan, *The Players: The Men Who Made Las Vegas,* Reno, NV: University of Nevada Press, 1997, p. 134.

Page 42 "In four whirlwind years, Hughes became Nevada's biggest casino owner . . ." M. Gottdiener, Claudia C. Collins, and David R. Dickens, *Las Vegas: The Social Production of an All-American City,* Malden, MA: Blackwell Publishers, 1999, p. 132.

Page 43 "I have decided this once and for all . . ." M. Gottdiener, Claudia C. Collins, and David R. Dickens, *Las Vegas: The Social Production of an All-American City,* Malden, MA: Blackwell Publishers, 1999, p. 132.

Page 43 "Hughes also initiated an influx of global investment funds . . ." M. Gottdiener, Claudia C. Collins, and David R. Dickens, *Las Vegas: The Social Production of an All-American City,* Malden, MA: Blackwell Publishers, 1999, p. 23.

Page 43 "Barbra Streisand performed in its packed . . ." Pete Earley, *Super Casino,* New York: Bantam Books, 2000, p. 65.

Page 44 "Where there's easy money, there's whores . . ." Ed Reid and Ovid Demaris, *The Green Felt Jungle,* New York: Trident Press, 1963, p. 111.

Page 48 "Back then, it was against the law . . ." Interview with Holmes Hendricksen on September 21, 2000.

Page 48 "The 1950s and 1960s was the Golden Age . . ." Interview with Lee Regonese on September 21, 2000.

Page 50 "Bill was a quiet man . . ." Interview with Holman Hendricksen on September 21, 2000.

Page 51 "First, it was the only hotel/casino . . ." Leon Mandel, *William Fisk Harrah: The Life and Times of a Gambling Magnate,* New York: Doubleday, 1981, p. 128.

Page 52 "Scenes of the suite were filmed and shown in the 1989 motion picture . . ." Interview with Greg McGlown on August 26, 2000.

Page 52 "It used to be an old saying . . ." Leon Mandel, *William Fisk Harrah: The Life and Times of a Gambling Magnate,* New York: Doubleday, 1981, p. 130.

Page 52 "My staff kept records on all sorts of information . . ." Interview with Holmes Hendricksen on September 21, 2000.

Page 53 "Back in the late 1960s, Bobby Darin wanted a jeep . . ." Interview with Lee Ragonese on September 21, 2000.

Page 58 "Scherry [the wife he married twice] and I had thought for years . . ." Leon Mandel, *William Fisk Harrah: The Life and Times of a Gambling Magnate,* New York: Doubleday, 1981, p. 161.

Page 60 "For the same amount of money . . ." Leon Mandel, *William Fisk Harrah: The Life and Times of a Gambling Magnate,* New York: Doubleday, 1981, p. 169.

Page 60 "We knew what we wanted . . ." Leon Mandel, *William Fisk Harrah: The Life and Times of a Gambling Magnate,* New York: Doubleday, 1981, p. 169.

Page 62 "It was not just the direct proceeds from the public offering . . ." Leon Mandel, *William Fisk Harrah: The Life and Times of a Gambling Magnate,* New York: Doubleday, 1981, p. 180.

Page 62 "We've never been in your place in Las Vegas . . ." Leon Mandel, *William Fisk Harrah: The Life and Times of a Gambling Magnate,* New York: Doubleday, 1981, p. 181.

Page 63 "To keep the number of traffic violations down . . ." Interview with Michael Silberling on September 24, 2000.

Page 63 "You have two cars . . ." Leon Mandel, *William Fisk Harrah: The Life and Times of a Gambling Magnate,* New York: Doubleday, 1981, p. 181.

Page 65 "He planned to build a big theme casino resort . . ." Interview with Lee Ragonese on September 21, 2000.

Chapter 3

Page 70 "He owed $13 million to a bank in Reno . . ." Leon Mandel, *William Fisk Harrah: The Life and Times of a Gambling Magnate,* New York: Doubleday, 1981, p. 208.

Page 70 "I did a lot of work in the area of gaming regulatory matters . . ." Interview with Phil Satre on June 15, 2000.

Page 72 "We perceived back in 1978 . . ." John L. Smith, *Running Scared: The Life and Treacherous Times of Las Vegas Casino King Steve Wynn,* New York: Barricade Books, 1995, p. 112.

Page 72 "Wynn's casino opened in December 1980 . . ." John L. Smith, *Running Scared: The Life and Treacherous Times of Las Vegas Casino King Steve Wynn,* New York: Barricade Books, 1995, p. 112.

Page 73   "I had met Bill Harrah and some of his executives . . ." Interview with Michael Rose on December 18, 2000.

Page 74   "Donald Trump became Manhattan's largest private real estate owner . . ." John R. O'Donnell, *Trumped!*, New York: Simon & Schuster, 1991, p. 24.

Page 75   "In exchange for a 50 percent share of the income . . ." John R. O'Donnell, *Trumped!*, New York: Simon & Schuster, 1991, p. 25.

Page 76   "All he cared about was generating the highest revenue . . ." Interview with Michael Rose on December 18, 2000.

Page 80   "If I'd told my father . . ." John R. O'Donnell, *Trumped!*, New York: Simon & Schuster, 1991, p. 28.

Page 82   "When I first started dealing at Harrah's . . ." Interview with Frank Quigley on September 9, 2000.

Page 82   "In the early days, our slots were mechanical . . ." Interview with Bruce Rowe on June 14, 2000.

Page 83   "The slots always had big payouts . . ." Interview with Bruce Rowe on June 14, 2000.

Page 83   "I'm still in the entertainment business . . ." Interview with Bruce Rowe on June 14, 2000.

Page 84   "The son of two college professors . . ." Interview with John Boushy on May 16, 2000.

Page 85   "A native of Arkansas and a graduate . . ." Interview with Bill Buffalo on May 15, 2000.

Page 85   "Kathy Callahan, a former internal communications director . . ." Interview with Kathy Callahan on June 15, 2000.

Page 86   "Another Holiday Inns transplant is Charles Atwood, a Tulane University . . ." Interview with Charles Atwood on April 20, 2000.

Page 86   "Transplant J. Carlos Tolosa had just graduated high school . . ." Interview with J. Carlos Tolosa on June 14, 2000.

Page 87   "In the summer of 1951, Kemmons Wilson was appalled . . ." Carrie Shook and Robert L. Shook, *Franchising: The Business Strategy That Changed the World*, Englewood Cliffs, NJ: Prentice Hall, 1993, p. 93.

Page 88   "After working together, we began to understand . . ." Interview with Phil Satre on July 18, 2000.

Page 89   "*Whom* we put in the room is what's important to us . . ." Interview with Dave Kowal on June 15, 2000.

Page 89   "It quickly rose to $75 million . . ." Interview with Mike Rose on December 18, 2000.

Page 89   "The casino business has the unique position . . ." Interview with Charles Atwood on April 20, 2000.

Page 90   "A hotel charges everyone the same price . . ." Interview with Phil Satre on June 15, 2000.

Page 90   "Harrah's was typical of the casino business . . ." Interview with Michael Rose on December 18, 2000.

Page 91   "You've got to have operating experience . . ." Interview with Michael Rose on December 18, 2000.

Page 92   "Back in late 1977 and early 1978 . . ." Interview with Charles Atwood on August 23, 2000.

Page 93   "We couldn't have picked a better company than Holiday Inns . . ." Interview with Phil Satre on June 15, 2000.

Page 93   "Holiday Inns' business model had a corporate office . . ." Interview with Charles Atwood on August 23, 2000.

Page 94   "Citibank couldn't see itself owning the casino . . ." Interview with Charles Atwood on April 20, 2000.

Page 95   "Thus, when the Golden Nugget opened in Atlantic City in 1980 . . ." M. Gottdiener, Claudia C. Collins, and David R. Dickens, *Las Vegas: The Special Production of an All-American City,* Malden, MA: Blackwell Publishers, 1999, p. 33.

Page 95   "I wanted us to reinvest our money . . ." Interview with Michael Rose on December 18, 2000.

Page 95   "Colin Reed, a former senior officer at Holiday Inns . . ." Interview with Colin Reed on August 2, 2000.

Page 97   "The timing was great for us . . ." Interview with Michael Rose on December 18, 2000.

Chapter 4

Page 100 "The famous Garden Pier, which opened in 1913 . . ." Tom Feeney, "Atlantic City, N.J., Had Plenty of Glamour before the Casinos," *Knight-Ridder/Tribune News,* PITEM002468C, September 1, 2000.

Page 101 "Poverty, drugs, and decay had turned the once-sparkling ocean resort town . . ." John L. Smith, *Running Scared,* New York: Barricade Books, 1995, p. 109.

Page 104 "Circus was the word that Romans used for 'theater' . . ." Pete Earley, *Super Casino,* New York: Bantam Books, 2000, p. 60.

Page 105 "The reality of the gaming experience is about as powerful a form of entertainment . . ." Stephen P. Bradley, *The Promus Companies,* Boston: Harvard Business School Publishing, 1995, p. 11.

Page 105 "For the interaction, enjoyment, and excitement . . ." Stephen P. Bradley, *The Promus Companies,* Boston: Harvard Business School Publishing, 1995, p.12.

Page 106 "Each property differs in age and design . . ." Interview with Craig Hudson on May 16, 2000.

Page 107 "This is why we've invested in a corporate infrastructure . . ." Interview with Rich Mirman on September 9, 2000.

Page 107 "Our direct mail program got only a 3 percent response . . ." Interview with Tom Jenkin on May 15, 2000.

Page 107 "These marketing teams are making 26 different sets of decisions . . ." Interview with Rich Mirman on September 7, 2000.

Page 107 "Holiday Inns had a corporate office and lots of stores out there . . ." Interview with Charles Atwood on August 23, 2000.

Page 108 "We did some research a few years ago . . ." Interview with Timothy Wilmott, President of Harrah's Eastern Division, on October 6, 2000.

Page 108 "Industry people talk about the categories of Indian gaming . . ." Interview with David Jonas, September 19, 2000.

Page 109 "Tom Jenkin describes his Rio customer as . . ." Interview with Tom Jenkin on July 18, 2000.

Page 109 "We bus in some customers who are driven by value . . ." Interview with Frank Quigley on September 9, 2000.

Page 110 "Estate taxes were calculated at something over $35 million . . ." Leon Mandel, *William Fisk Harrah: The Life and Times of a Gambling Magnate,* New York: Doubleday, 1981, p. 208.

Page 110 "Some states, such as Iowa . . ." Stephen P. Bradley, *The Promus Companies,* Boston: Harvard Business School Publishing, 1995, pp. 6 &12.

Page 111 "One reason Nevada passed a bill in 1931 to regulate gambling . . ." Jack Sheehan, *The Players: The Men Who Made Las Vegas,* Reno, NV: University of Nevada Press, 1997, p. 2.

Page 111 "Following that great gold rush, California soon became a gambler's paradise . . ." Marshall Fey, *Slot Machines: A Pictorial History of the First 100 Years,* Reno, NV: Liberty Bell Books, 1997, p. 101.

Page 112 "Slot machines were outlawed in San Francisco in 1909 . . ." Marshall Fey, *Slot Machines: A Pictorial History of the First 100 Years,* Reno, NV: Liberty Bell Books, 1997, p. 13.

Page 112 "The purpose of Kefauver's special committee . . ." Jack Sheehan, *The Players: The Men Who Made Las Vegas,* Reno, NV: University of Nevada Press, 1997, p. 4.

Page 112 "Under federal prodding . . ." Jack Sheehan, *The Players: The Men Who Made Las Vegas,* Reno, NV: University of Nevada Press, 1997, p. 6.

Page 113 "Everything changed in the early 1960s when Director J. Edgar Hoover . . ." Pete Earley, *Super Casino,* New York: Bantam Books, 2000, p. 62.

Page 113 "Nevada authorities compiled a list of the earnings of the top 30 places in 1961 . . ." Wallace Turner, *Gamblers' Money,* Boston: Houghton Mifflin, 1965, p. 3.

Page 114 "There are different procedures within the casinos . . ." Interview with George Togliatti on August 28, 2000.

Page 114 "My job is twofold . . ." Interview with Richard Klemp on January 23, 2001.

Page 115 "Under the Indian Reorganization Act of 1934 . . ." Jerry Useem, "The Big Gamble," *Fortune,* October 2, 2000, p. 240.

Page 115 "In its landmark 1987 decision . . ." Dyan Machan, "The Last Article You Will Ever Have to Read on Executive Pay? No Way!" *Forbes,* May 20, 1996, p. 1.

Page 116 "Gaming on Indian reservations is a $13-billion-a-year industry . . ." "The Big Gamble," *Fortune,* October 2, 2000, p. 224.

Page 118 "We're going into Indian gaming . . ." Interview with Peter Weien on April 21, 2000.

Page 119 "We were desperate . . ." Interview with Leona Kakar on June 13, 2000.

Page 119 "I felt like Leona did . . ." Interview with Terry Enos on June 13, 2000.

Page 119 "So we decided to seek gaming professionals . . ." Interview with Leona Kakar on June 13, 2000.

Page 120 "This place is so far off the beaten path . . ." Interview with Peter Weien on April 21, 2000.

Page 121 "It was a nice trip . . ." Interview with Bill Buffalo on May 15, 2000.

Page 122 "Every time I come down this road . . ." Interview with Peter Weien on April 21, 2000.

Page 122 "I really like these people . . ." Interview with Bill Buffalo on May 15, 2000.

Page 122 "It's been a long process . . ." Interview with Janet Beronio on June 13, 2000.

Page 122 "We have a 24-hour fire and police department now . . ." Interview with Terry Enos on June 13, 2000.

Page 123 "In 2000 alone . . ." Interview with Joseph Smith on June 13, 2000.

Page 123 "The children are our future . . ." Interview with Leona Kakar on June 13, 2000.

Page 123 "A higher than average . . ." Interview with Janet Beronio on June 13, 2000.

Page 125 "More than sentiment was involved . . ." Dyan Machan, "The Last Article You Will Ever Have to Read on Executive Pay? No Way!" *Forbes,* May 20, 1996, p. 17.

Chapter 5

Page 133 "In those days, it was against the law . . ." Interview with Holmes Hendricksen on September 21, 2000.

Page 134 "There aren't many headliner entertainers . . ." Interview with Tom Jenkin on May 15, 2000.

Page 135 "Harrah's is not about a volcano . . ." Interview with Michael St. Pierre on November 6, 2000.

Page 135 "This is an industry that has historically . . ." Interview with Gary Thompson on February 13, 2001.

Page 136 The first state lottery was introduced . . ." C. Britt Beemer and Robert L. Shook, *It Takes a Prophet to Make a Profit,* New York: Simon & Schuster, 2001, p. 225.

Page 136 "With the lotteries, there was a changing of attitudes . . ." Interview with Phil Satre on May 17, 2000.

Page 137 "At one end of the spectrum . . ." Interview with Phil Satre on May 17, 2000.

Page 138 "We did extensive research to determine which group . . ." Interview with Gary Loveman on September 28, 2000.

Page 138 "For the segment of customers that likes Bellagio's . . ." Interview with Rich Mirman on May 16, 2000.

Page 139 "With the beautiful views of the Colorado Rive . . ." Interview with Bill Keena on January 20, 2000.

Page 139 "We did our homework and determined there was an opportunity . . ." Interview with Phil Satre on June 15, 2000.

Page 140 "Instead of being worried about what these casino openings . . ." Interview with Colin Reed on June 15, 2000.

Page 141 "If there's one thing that ties in with our hotel experience . . ." Interview with Phil Satre on June 15, 2000.

Page 141 "What's happening in the United States with gaming . . ." Interview with Colin Reed on August 2, 2000.

Page 142 "Back in the late 1980s . . ." Interview with Phil Satre on July 18, 2000.

Page 143 "When I first took on this assignment . . ." Interview with John Boushy on May 16, 2000.

Page 145 "Merchants gave stamps for money spent at their stores . . ." Interview with C. Britt Beemer on September 18, 2002.

Page 145 "The letter read: 'I am a loyal customer' . . ." Interview with Phil Satre on July 8, 2000.

Page 146 "When we were in the early stages of discussing . . ." Interview with Dave Kowal on June 15, 2000.

Page 146 "One of the things we believe . . ." Interview with Dave Kowal on June 15, 2000.

Page 147 "It's a more efficient use of our marketing dollars . . ." Interview with David Norton on August 23, 2000.

Page 147 "Now that we rebranded the Showboat/East Chicago property . . ." Interview with Michael St. Pierre on November 6, 2000.

Page 148 "There's a 20 percent cross-over between the two markets . . ." Interview with Joe Domenico on November 6, 2000.

Page 148 "We know this is going to happen . . ." Interview with Frank Quigley on September 9, 2000.

Page 148 "When one of our customers from East Chicago . . ." Interview with Rich Mirman on May 16, 2000.

Page 149 "A lot of our customers tell us they gamble to relax and escape . . ." Interview with George Dittman on July 18, 2000.

Page 149 "This brand, at its best, allows people to sample . . ." Interview with Michael Silberling on September 24, 2000.

Page 150 "We promote it as 'the better Atlantic City' . . ." Interview with Dave Jonas on September 19, 2000.

Page 150 "I'm in the business of fostering customer monogamy . . ." Christina Binkley, "A Casino Chain Finds a Lucrative Niche: The Small Spenders," *Wall Street Journal,* May 4, 2000, p. A1.

Page 151 "When I first consulted Harrah's, it clearly didn't make sense to me . . ." Interview with Gary Loveman on July 18, 2000.

Page 152 "They were very good at communicating to their customers that 20,000 miles . . ." Interview with Rich Mirman on May 16, 2000.

Page 154 "We were busing in 100,000 people a month . . ." Interview with Joe Domenico on November 6, 2000.

Page 154 "Here, the focus is on AEPs . . ." Interview with Michael Silberling on September 24, 2000.

Page 155 "We have Wednesday afternoon drawings at our Ak-Chin casino . . ." Interview with Ginny Shanks on August 22, 2000.

Page 156 "There aren't a lot of conventions in the summer in New Orleans . . ." Interview with Bill Noble on April 22, 2002.

Page 156 "Everything we do in marketing . . ." Interview with Gary Loveman on July 18, 2000.

Page 157 "With our cross-marketing, we'll mail coupons . . ." Interview with David Norton on April 21, 2000.

Page 157 "We're constantly testing our direct mail offers . . ." Interview with Dan Nita on April 20, 2000.

Page 158 "We make considerably more money on casino customers . . ." Interview with Phil Satre on May 17, 2000.

Page 158 "We're in the casino business, not the hotel business . . ." Interview with Bruce Rowe on June 14, 2000.

Page 159 "I don't want someone else to be responsible . . ." Interview with Marty Miles on June 15, 2000.

Page 160 "I do not buy into the Las Vegas dogma . . ." Gabriel Erem, "Sheldon & Dr. Miriam Adelson, an American Success Story," *Lifestyles Magazine,* Spring 2001, p. 6.

Page 160 "First of all, no matter how many rooms . . ." Rex Buntain, "Hard Target, Who's Out to Get the Venetian, and Why?" *Casino Executive,* February 1998.

Page 161 "It made more sense for us to be in the center of our universe . . ." Interview with Phil Satre on June 15, 2000.

Page 161 "When we were based in Memphis . . ." Interview with Charles Atwood on August 23, 2000.

Page 162 "A general manager of a major hotel in, say, London or Paris . . ." Interview with Colin Reed on August 4, 2000.

Page 163 "The most important person in the field . . ." Interview with John Boushy on May 16, 2000.

Page 164 "Many questioned the changes we were making . . ." Interview with Phil Satre on August 24, 2000.

Page 165 "There are three kinds of people . . ." Interview with John Boushy on May 16, 2000.

Chapter 6

Page 171 "Watson plastered the wall with slogans . . ." James C. Collins and Jerry I. Porras, *Built to Last,* New York: HarperCollins, 1994, p. 124.

Page 171 "Like IBM and Nordstrom, the Walt Disney Company . . ." James C. Collins and Jerry I. Porras, *Built to Last,* New York: HarperCollins, 1994, p. 127.

Page 172 "Coach John Ralston taught us something about life . . ." Interview with Phil Satre on August 24, 2000.

Page 174 "Profit and growth are stimulated . . ." James L. Heskett, Thomas O. Jones, Gary W. Loveman, W. Earl Sasser, Jr., and Leonard A. Schlesinger, *Harvard Business Review,* March/April, 1994, p. 164.

Page 174 "Internal quality is also characterized . . ." James L. Heskett, Thomas O. Jones, Gary W. Loveman, W. Earl Sasser, Jr., and Leonard A. Schlesinger, *Harvard Business Review*, March/April, 1994, p. 168.

Page 175 "Gary was a dynamic speaker . . ." Interview with Phil Satre on June 15, 2000.

Page 177 "When Phil made me the offer . . ." Interview with Gary Loveman on July 18, 2000.

Page 178 "When I overheard . . ." Interview with Rich Mirman on April 21, 2000.

Page 180 "We really like you a lot . . ." Interview with Rich Mirman on April 21, 2000.

Page 180 "Search firms charge 20 to 30 percent fees . . ." Interview with Ron Beronio on July 19, 2000.

Page 181 "When we bring in people for executive positions . . ." Interview with Marilyn Winn on January 22, 2001.

Page 181 "How do you feel about deriving your income . . ." Interview with Marty Miles on June 15, 2000.

Page 181 "We don't often recruit from other casinos . . ." Interview with Marilyn Winn on January 22, 2001.

Page 183 "During my internship, I was like a project manager . . ." Interview with Anika Howard on February 2, 2001.

Page 183 "The two keys to taking so many courses . . ." Interview with Eric Persson on January 23, 2001.

Page 184 "When I joined the company . . ." Interview with Phil Satre on August 24, 2000.

Page 185 "I parked cars during the summer . . ." Interview with Vern Jennings on February 9, 2002.

Page 187 "In my business, there's no place on earth like Las Vegas . . ." Interview with Clinton Holmes on August 22, 2000.

Page 188 "We both cater to the same customer . . ." Interview with Wilson Moore on August 22, 2000.

Page 188 "We know some people have no intention . . ." Interview with Steve Thull on August 22, 2000.

Page 188 "This is like having an extra 450 rooms in our hotel . . ." Interview with Tom Jenkin on May 15, 2000.

Page 189 "We chose Harrah's over any . . ." Interview with William Moore on August 22, 2000.

Page 189 "I had received a lot of recognition . . ." Interview with Butch Harmon on January 20, 2001.

Page 190 "There are golf schools all over . . ." Interview with Butch Harmon on January 20, 2001.

Page 191 "They've spent hundreds of millions of dollars positioning their companies . . ." Interview with Jan Jones on May 16, 2000.

Page 192 "There is an alignment between the government's . . ." Interview with Dean Hestermann on February 13, 2001.

Page 192 "Our major constraint for our growth . . ." Interview with Marilyn Winn on January 22, 2001.

Page 193 "At Rio, the same customers . . ." Interview with Tom Jekin on May 15, 2000.

Page 193 "In 1972 I applied for a job at Harrah's in Reno . . ." Interview with Larry Kennedy on August 29, 2000.

Page 194 "We also inquire about an employee's willingness to work . . ." Interview with Marilyn Winn on July 18, 2000.

Page 194 "Our standard Interview questions are . . ." Interview with Geoff Andres on August 23, 2000.

Page 194 "A woman applying for a job as a cocktail server . . ." Interview with Marilyn Winn on May 3, 2000.

Page 195 "How would your most recent supervisor . . ." Interview with Marty Miles on July 18, 2000.

Page 195 "Then I came down and met with the casino manager . . ." Interview with Mike Vitale on August 29, 2000.

Page 196 "My father is a geologist who's a professor at Stanford . . ." Interview with Michael Silberling on August 24, 2000.

Page 196 "All newly hired hourly employees go through our orientation program . . ." Interview with Marilyn Winn on January 22, 2001.

Page 197 "First, I get . . ." Interview with Phil Satre on February 14, 2001.

Page 198 "When I talk to employees . . ." Interview with Phil Satre on August 24, 2000.

Page 199 "We were too removed, and, in the eyes of our people . . ." Interview with Phil Satre on August 24, 2000.

Page 200 "I wanted them to hear from me . . ." Interview with Eileen Cassini on February 13, 2001.

Page 201 "All of our IT employees know their linkage . . ." Interview with Eileen Cassini on February 13, 2001.

Page 201 "When people are recognized for their contributions . . ." Interview with Michael St. Pierre on November 6, 2000.

Page 202 "When I came here in 1999 after we acquired Showboat . . ." Interview with Joe Domenico on November 6, 2000.

Page 202 "This enables me to speak their language . . ." Interview with Michael Silberling on August 24, 2000.

Page 202 "Gary comes to the table with fabulous comparative perspective . . ." Interview with Jay Sevigny on June 15, 2000.

Page 203 "It's really about who we already are . . ." Interview with Jan Jones on January 23, 2001.

Page 206 "It puts in writing the rules we play by . . ." Meredith Hartstern, "Harrah's Entertainment Honored for Responsible Gaming Leadership," *Harrah's People,* Fall, 2000, p. 19.

Page 207 "Its findings revealed that 56 percent of Americans stated that they would spend more . . ." C. Britt Beemer and Robert L. Shook, *It Takes a Prophet to Make a Profit,* New York: Simon & Schuster, 2001, p. 63.

Page 208 "My wife, Dana, and I . . ." Interview with Vern Jennings on February 9, 2002.

Page 209 "Prior to 2001, Harrah's gave to many causes without a specific theme . . ." Interview with Julie Foley-Murray on January 23, 2001.

Page 210 "There are people who think the gaming industry is villainous . . ." Interview with Jan Jones on May 16, 2000.

Page 210 "For example, children visiting the expanded St. Louis Zoo . . ." Julie Edelson Halpert, "Dr. Pepper Hospital? Perhaps, for a Price," *New York Times,* February 18, 2001, p. BU1.

Page 210 "We are looking into naming opportunities . . ." Interview with Julie Foley-Murray on January 23, 2001.

Page 210 "I can meet with elected officials and give them figures . . ." Interview with Jan Jones on January 23, 2001.

Chapter 7

Page 215 "My wife's illness far overshadowed any part . . ." Interview with Phil Satre on August 24, 2000.

Page 216 "The year 1997 was an epiphany for me . . ." Interview with Phil Satre on February 14, 2001.

Page 216 "While the company thought it important to collect . . ." Interview with Rich Mirman on May 16, 2000.

Page 216 "They had to make Harrah's AS400 transactional systems . . ." Meridith Levinson, "Jackpot," *CIO,* February 1, 2001, p. 84.

Page 217 "The two had some different views on cross-marketing . . ." Interview with John Boushy on May 16, 2000.

Page 218 "We're definitely a consumer-marketing . . ." Interview with John Boushy on May 16, 2000.

Page 218 "We don't take an R&D approach . . ." Interview with John Boushy on May 16, 2000.

Page 219 "We were in the process of building our new brands . . ." Interview with Colin Reed on August 4, 2000.

Page 220 "We were always a great slot company . . ." Interview with Phil Satre on July 18, 2000.

Page 221 "In 1995, we determined there was a need to find a target customer . . ." Interview with George Dittman on July 18, 2000.

Page 221 "A very large infusion of intellectual capital . . ." Gary Loveman, "Where Gambling Will Take Us in the 21st Century," speech at the 11th International Conference on Gambling and Risk-Taking, Las Vegas, NV, June 12, 2000.

Page 222 "I mean no disrespect to Harrah's . . ." Jeff Simpson, "Nevadan at Work: Tom Gallagher; President and Chief Executive Officer, Park Place Entertainment," *Las Vegas Review-Journal,* February 4, 2001.

Page 222 "What we do is not about technology . . ." Interview with Rich Mirman on February 5, 2001.

Page 222 "In order to do what we do to drive customer loyalty . . ." Interview with Gary Loveman on February 15, 2001.

Page 223 "For a couple of years, I used to check into a Holiday Inn . . ." Interview with Phil Satre on July 18, 2000.

Page 223 "It's not about technology . . ." Interview with Bruce Rowe on January 22, 2001.

Page 224 "We knew who came into our casinos . . ." Interview with Gary Loveman on July 18, 2000.

Page 224 "When I went down to Memphis in 1992 . . ." Interview with John Boushy on January 22, 2001.

Page 225 "It's true that we collect information about our customers . . ." Interview with Rich Mirman on February 5, 2001.

Page 225 "In the past, we were like our competitors . . ." Interview with George Dittman on July 18, 2000.

Page 226 "It's more mass marketing today . . ." Interview with Tom Jenkin on May 15, 2000.

Page 226 "At the VIP level . . ." Interview with Dave Kowal on June 15, 2000.

Page 227 "There is a consistency on how a customer is treated . . ." Interview with Rich Mirman on May 16, 2000.

Page 228 "Compared to other products . . ." Interview with Gary Loveman on July 18, 2000.

Page 228 "We tap into a wealth of information about our slot customers . . ." Interview with Rich Mirman on May 19, 2000.

Page 232 "Once we know the potential . . ." Interview with Rich Mirman on May 19, 2000.

Page 232 "The Harrah's model sets budgets and calendars for gamblers . . ." Christina Binkley, "A Casino Chain Finds A Lucrative Niche: The Small Spenders," *Wall Street Journal,* May 4, 2000, p. A1.

Page 233 "Our competitors use a 'pull' strategy . . ." Interview with Gary Thompson on April 23, 2002.

Page 233 "We may notice a certain customer . . ." Interview with Charles Atwood on April 20, 2000.

Page 234 "Our occupancy in our hotels is over 90 percent . . ." Interview with Ginny Shanks on August 22, 2000.

Page 234 "It's hard to economically determine where to fish for customers . . ." Interview with Rich Mirman on February 5, 2001.

Page 234 "We refer to what we do here as *decision science* . . ." Interview with Dan Nita on April 20, 2000.

Page 235 "Let's say we have a 60-year-old woman . . ." Interview with Gary Loveman on July 18, 2000.

Page 235 "We have a lot of transaction data on our customers . . ." Interview with David Norton on August 23, 2000.

Page 237 "We'll send offers and fly them into Reno . . ." Interview with Gary Selesner on August 25, 2000.

Page 237 "If I want to bring in a plane of high-level customers from Shreveport . . ." Interview with Michael Silberling on September 24, 2000.

Page 237 "The trick here is to get the right level of marketing offer . . ." Interview with Gary Loveman on September 28, 2000.

Page 238 "One group may get an offer for $10 cash . . ." Interview with Dan Nita on April 20, 2000.

Page 239 "The cash was not the real motivator to get them to play . . ." Interview with Rich Mirman on May 16, 2000.

Page 240 "I knew where this guy was coming from . . ." Interview with Phil Satre on May 17, 2000.

Page 241 "Periodically, we survey our employees for their feedback . . ." Interview with John Boushy on February 12, 2001.

Page 241 "What an employee formerly did on paper . . ." Interview with Eileen Cassini on February 13, 2001.

Page 241 "An employee can say . . ." Interview with John Boushy on February 12, 2001.

Page 242 "About once a month . . ." Interview with John Boushy on February 12, 2001.

Page 242 "Customers, can log unto . . ." Interview with Anita Howard-Weaver on February 2, 2001.

Page 243 "The economics of going after this business . . ." Interview with Rich Mirman on April 21, 2000.

Page 243 "We're now able to project booking patterns . . ." Interview with David Norton on August 23, 2000.

Chapter 8

Page 247 "I look at the way customers are treated in this business . . ." Interview with Michael Silberling on September 24, 2000.

Page 248 "When a customer pays X amount of dollars for a room . . ." Interview with Phil Satre on June 15, 2000.

Page 248 "Our research reveals that about 11 to 12 percent of the gaming industry . . ." Interview with Gary Thompson on April 23, 2002.

Page 251 "One customer loves to be comped a box of Royal Jamaica cigars . . ." Interview with Ray Gambardella on August 23, 2000.

Page 254 "A while back, some potentially high rollers from Hong Kong . . ." Interview with Russ McLennan on January 21, 2001.

Page 255 "A whale or his wife may want to go on a shopping spree . . ." Interview with Ray Gambardella on July 18, 2000.

Page 255 "Those rooms were available . . ." Interview with Gary Thompson on April 23, 2002.

Page 256 "It doesn't matter how much money you have . . ." Interview with Dan Nita on April 20, 2000.

Page 256 "When we first received the call to accommodate them . . ." Interview with Brandi Jarva on August 22, 2000.

Page 256 "The most rooms I've ever seen connected together . . ." Interview with Cary Rehm on July 18, 2000.

Page 256 "They travel in a class of service . . ." Interview with Tom Jenkin on June 15, 2000.

Page 257 "During our first six months with high stakes tables . . ." Interview with Dave Hanlon on July 18, 2000.

Page 258 "The slot machines were subsidizing high rollers . . ." Christina Binkley, "In Las Vegas, Casinos Take a Big Gamble On the High Rollers," *Wall Street Journal*, September 7, 2001, p. A1.

Page 259 "When a casino has a customer from Bangkok or Taiwan . . ." Interview with Dave Hanlon on July 18, 2000.

Page 259 "How we work with each whale depends upon who the person is . . ." Interview with Tom Jenkin on July 18, 2000.

Page 260 "Last week a customer lost $200,000 . . ." Interview with Frank Quigley on September 19, 2000.

Page 260 "Austrailia's wealthiest man with an estimated net worth of $4.6 billion . . ." Dave Berns, "Magnate's Gambling Losses Big News," *Las Vegas Review-Journal,* September 16, 2000, p. 30.

Page 261 "I know Kerry Packer . . ." Interview with Dave Hanlon on July 18, 2000.

Page 261 "We were beaten for $3 million in three hours . . ." Interview with Jay Sevigny on January 22, 2001.

Page 261 "Kashiwagi regularly bet $200,000 on each hand of baccarat . . ." Interview with Gary Selesner on August 25, 2000.

Page 262 "He was a legitimate 'Sir,' . . ." Interview with Howard Klein on September 20, 2000.

Page 266 "Like the Diamond Lounges . . ." Interview with Brandi Jarva on June 17, 2000.

Page 266 "Our long-time employees will absolutely know our top 100 customers . . ." Interview with Michael Silberling on September 24, 2000.

Page 267 "The verdant mirage sits on 320 acres . . ." John L. Smith, *Running Scared,* New York: Barricade Books, 1995, p. 243.

Page 267 "Golfing is limited to a handful of players per day . . ." John L. Smith, *Running Scared,* New York: Barricade Books, 1995, p. 246.

Page 268 "Our customers are mainly from Phoenix and Tucson . . ." Interview with Janet Beronio on June 13, 2000.

Page 268 "We have the finest property in Chicagoland . . ." Interview with Joe Domenico on November 6, 2000.

Page 268 "For rated customers living nearby who prefer going home . . ." Interview with Michael St. Pierre on November 6, 2000.

Page 268 "Our people do go that extra mile for a rated player . . ." Interview with Michael Silberling on September 24, 2000.

Page 269 "If a high roller orders a veal chop dinner . . ." Interview with Marty Miles on June 15, 2000.

Page 269 "We like to keep these players in this area . . ." Interview with Tom Jenkin on June 15, 2000.

Page 270 "One of my good friends is a woman from California . . ." Interview with Brandi Jarva on August 22, 2000.

Page 270 "A gentleman wanted something done for his wife . . ." Interview with Jay Sevingny on January 22, 2001.

Page 270 "I'm not much of a celebrity gawker . . ." Interview with Geoff Andres on August 23, 2000.

Page 271 "Although the man was very formal . . ." Interview with Jerome Robinson on September 19, 2000.

Page 272 "I give naming rights for some of our suites . . ." Interview with Bill Keena on January 20, 2001.

Page 272 "The Kenai River is the most famous king salmon fishing in the world . . ." Interview with Russ McLennan on January 21, 2001.

Page 273 "We have some important customers in the Pacific Brim . . ." Interview with Phil Satre on February 14, 2001.

Page 274 "In a 2002 survey conducted by America's Research Group . . ." Interview with C. Britt Beemer on September 19, 2002.

Page 274 "Our management philosophy is truly a inverted pyramid . . ." Interview with Marilyn Winn on May 13, 2000.

Page 275 "We look for people who enjoy . . ." Interview with Marilyn Winn on August 28, 2000.

Page 275 "When our managers come across somebody . . ." Interview with Marilyn Winn on August 28, 2000.

Page 275 "Every customer is important to us . . ." Interview with Tom Jenkin on June 15, 2000.

Page 276 "Before we open for dinner . . ." Interview with Marty Miles on July 18, 2000.

Page 277 "A satisfied customer will tell six people . . ." Interview with Britt Beemer on March 22, 2001.

Page 282 "They actually thought God would give them good luck . . ." Interview with Mike Vitale on August 29, 2000.

Page 283 "A few years ago, a well-known NASCAR racer . . ." Interview with Bill Keena on January 20, 2001.

Page 283 "The driver handed the man . . ." Interview with Bill Keona on January 20, 2001.

Chapter 9

Page 286 "If the Harrah's management team were transposed . . ." Interview with Rich Mirman on August 28, 2000.

Page 286 "These are people that never had anything to do with the gaming industry . . ." Interview with Gary Loveman on September 28, 2000.

Page 287 "There are the antagonists . . ." National Gambling Impact Study Commission, April 1, 1999, p. 25.

Page 287 "That's something you can't do when you go on a vacation to Disney . . ." Interview with Charles Atwood on April 20, 2000.

Page 288 "In addition to the casino games . . ." Interview with Gary Loveman on September 28, 2000.

Page 290 "I believe that argument is sheer nonsense . . ." Interview with Gary Loveman on September 28, 2000.

Page 291 "There is probably a right way and a wrong way . . ." Interview with Dean Hestermann on February 13, 2001.

Page 292 "I look at it as being smart marketers . . ." Interview with Jan Jones on May 16, 2000.

Page 292 "There's an emotional attachment . . ." Interview with Gary Loveman on September 28, 2000.

Page 293 "A typical customer goes to Vegas once a year . . ." Interview with Tim Wilmott on October 6, 2000.

Page 294 "In a research study conducted in 2000 . . ." C. Britt Beemer and Robert L. Shook, *It Takes a Prophet to Make a Profit*, New York: Simon & Schuster, 2001, p. 222.

Page 294 "I was on a flight and sat beside a U.S. Congressman . . ." Interview with Gary Loveman on February 15, 2001.

Page 294 "Something is wrong with the system . . ." Gary Loveman, "Where Gambling Will Take Us in the 21st Century," speech at the 11th International Conference on Gambling and Risk-Taking, Las Vegas, Nevada, June 12, 2000.

Page 295 "For example, in Missouri, there's a $2 admission charge . . ." Interview with Michael St. Pierre on November 6, 2000.

Page 295 "There will be a lot of social engineering kinds . . ." Interview with Dean Hestermann on February 13, 2001.

Page 295 "I think the benefits to these states . . ." Interview with Dean Hestermann on February 13, 2001.

Page 296 "We will continue to look at acquisition opportunities . . ." Interview with Phil Satre on February 14, 2001.

Corporate Milestones

1937   Bill Harrah opens his first bingo parlor in Reno, Nevada.

1946   Bill Harrah opens Harrah's Club at its present location on North Virginia Street in downtown Reno.

1955   Harrah's purchases several clubs at Lake Tahoe in Stateline,

1956   Nevada, beginning what would become today's Harrah's Lake Tahoe.

1959   Harrah's begins expansion of the Lake Tahoe facility, including the world-famous South Shore Room.

1962   Construction of the 400-room hotel in Reno.

1966   Headliner Room opens at Harrah's Reno.

1971   The company begins public trading with issue of 450,000 over-the-counter shares.

1972   Harrah's is listed on the American Stock Exchange.

1973   Harrah's is listed on New York Stock Exchange—the first casino company to be listed.

The company opens a 250-room hotel tower at Lake Tahoe.

1976   A 290-room expansion opens at Harrah's Lake Tahoe.

1978   William F. Harrah, company founder, dies.

The board of directors of Holiday Inns of Memphis, Tennessee, approves proposal to build and operate a hotel/casino in the marina area of Atlantic City, New Jersey.

1980   At Harrah's Reno, construction begins on second tower with 240 rooms.

Holiday Inns acquires Harrah's hotel casino company. At the time, Holiday Inn had 1,600 hotels and interests in two casinos: a casino under construction in Atlantic City, and a 40 percent interest in River Boat Casino, a casino adjacent to the Holiday Inn Hotel on the Las Vegas strip.

1981   Michael D. Rose, president of Holiday Inns, elected chief executive officer.

1983   Holiday Inns acquires the remaining 60 percent interest in River Boat Casino. Harrah's assumes management of the casino and hotel.

Embassy Suites hotel division created as the new all-suite hotel brand of Holiday Inns.

1984   Holiday Inns, through its Embassy Suites hotel division, acquires Granada Royale Hometels, making Embassy Suites the leader of the all-suite hotel market.

The first Embassy Suites Hotel opens in Overpark, Kansas.

1985   Holiday Inns shareholders approve a new corporate name, Holiday Corporation. The new umbrella organization represents diversity of company products with brands like Harrah's Casinos, Holiday Inn hotels, Embassy Suites hotels, and Hampton Inn hotels.

1987   Holiday Inns completes recapitalization plan with the payment of a special one-time $65 per-share cash dividend to shareholders.

Bill's Casino opens in Lake Tahoe next door to Harrah's.

1988   Holiday Inns introduces new extended-stay hotel brand, Homewood Suites.

Holiday closes on sale of certain international assets and 13 domestic hotels to Bass PLC of Great Britain for approximately $475 million.

Harrah's property in Laughlin, Nevada, opens.

1989   Harrah's begins major renovation and modernization project in Reno.

Holiday Corporation's board approves acquisition of the Holiday Inns hotel business by Bass PLC.

The first Homewood Suites opens in Omaha, Nebraska.

1990   Holiday stockholders approve sale of Holiday Inn hotel business to Bass PLC. The remaining company, which now includes Harrah's, Embassy Suites, Hampton Inn, and Homewood Suites, is renamed the Promus Companies,

The Promus Companies Incorporated common stock begins trading on the New York Stock Exchange.

1991   Philip G. Satre was named president and chief operating officer for Promus.

Harrah's headquarters relocates from Reno to Memphis.

1992   Announcement of the company's first riverboat casino project in Joliet, Illinois, to open in early 1993.

Conversion of Holiday Casino in Las Vegas to Harrah's Las Vegas is completed.

Embassy Suites corporate headquarters relocates to Memphis from Dallas and establishes Memphis as the headquarters city for all Promus subsidiaries.

Promus acquires interest in Sodak Gaming Supplies, the exclusive distributor for International Game Technology (IGT) for gaming equipment on Indian reservations.

1993   Promus stock splits two for one.

Harrah's opens in Joliet.

Harrah's Vicksburg and Harrah's Tunica open.

1994   Harrah's Joliet expands with the opening of a second riverboat casino.

Harrah's Shreveport opens.

Philip Satre is named Promus chief executive officer. Michael Rose remains chairman.

Harrah's opens in North Kansas City.

Harrah's Ak-Chin casino opens near Phoenix. It is the first Indian gaming operation for Harrah's.

1995   The Promus Companies Incorporated spins off its hotel brands (Embassy Suites, Hampton Inn, and Homewood Suites) into a new corporation. The remaining company, which consists of the Harrah's brand, all Harrah's assets, and a majority of the Promus headquarters assets and its people, is then renamed Harrah's Entertainment. The move puts Harrah's name on the New York Stock Exchange for the first time since 1980. Its stock symbol is HET. Michael Rose remains chairman and Philip Satre remains president and CEO.

1996   Harrah's Tunica Mardi Gras opens—Harrah's second property in Tunica, Mississippi.

Harrah's opens an expansion of its North Kansas City casino, including a second casino boat and a hotel.

1997   Chairman Michael Rose retires. Philip Satre becomes chairman and keeps titles of president and chief executive officer.

Harrah's St. Louis-Riverport, a riverboat casino entertainment complex in Maryland Heights, Missouri, opens.

Harrah's consolidates its two Tunica casinos into a single, larger complex.

Harrah's Atlantic City completes expansion and renovation, including a new 416-room hotel tower, expanded casino space, and exciting restaurant concepts.

The company launches Total Gold, its integrated national players rewards and recognition program.

A $200 million expansion and renovation of Harrah's Las Vegas is completed. It is the largest-ever ground floor renovation in Las Vegas history.

Celebration of Harrah's sixtieth anniversary, highlighted by a highly successful Dazzling Diamonds tour. The six-month, 10-city national touring exhibition featured some of the world's most famous and costly diamond jewelry.

Harrah's Cherokee Smoky Mountains opens in the Great Smoky Mountains of North Carolina.

1998 Harrah's Prairie Band opens 15 miles north of Topeka, Kansas.

The company acquires Showboat, a gaming company with casinos in Atlantic City, East Chicago, Indiana, Las Vegas, and Sydney, Australia. The Sydney property operates under the name Star City.

U.S. Patient Office issues patent (#5,761,647) to Harrah's on its "National Customer Recognition System and Method," a patent to protect its Total Gold customer recognition and rewards program that tracks customer activity within and across properties.

Gary Loveman joins the company as chief operating officer; he is named to the three-person Office of the President later that year.

1999 Harrah's is named "Company of the Year" by *Casino Executive* and *Casino Journal* names Philip Satre "Gaming Executive of the Year."

Relocation of Harrah's corporate headquarters from Memphis to Las Vegas begins. The move is completed the following year.

The Showboat property in East Chicago is renamed Harrah's in a move to benefit from the company's strong national brand name.

Based on a readers' poll, Harrah's receives 81 awards from *Casino Player,* more than any other gaming company.

Harrah's Entertainment acquires Rio All-Suite Casino Resort, adding a true Las Vegas destination resort to complement its Harrah's Strip location.

Computerworld ranks Harrah's #2 in its Top 100 Best Places to Work in Information Technology.

Harrah's New Orleans opens, the only land-based casino in the famed city.

2000   For the second consecutive year, Harrah's is listed on *Forbes Magazine's* Forbes Platinum List of the 400 best-performing large U.S. companies, the only casino company to be named.

Harrah's signs a letter of intent with the Rincon San Luiseno Band of Mission Indians to develop a $100 million casino and hotel project just north of San Diego, marking the first agreement between a California Indian tribe and a major gaming company.

Total Gold becomes Total Rewards—the industry's first cross-brand, multitiered player loyalty program.

Harrah's acquires Players International, which operates a riverboat casino on the Ohio River in Metropolis, Illinois; two cruising casinos in Lake Charles, Louisiana; two dockside riverboat casinos in Maryland Heights, Missouri; and a race track in Paducah, Kentucky.

Harrah's sells the Star City Casino in Sydney, Australia, to TABCORP Holdings Ltd.

The company sells the Showboat Las Vegas Hotel, Casino and Bowling Center to VSS Enterprises, LLC.

2001   Harrah's relaunches its www.harrahs.com Web site, expanding customers' online options, offering E-Total Rewards features and garnering awards for its customer-friendly design.

The company acquires Harveys Casino Resorts. The purchase includes Harveys in Lake Tahoe; Harveys Casino and Bluffs Run casino in Council Bluffs, Iowa; and Harvey's Wagon Wheel in Central City, Colorado.

2002   The company celebrates its sixty-fifth year in business. As of June 30, 2002, the company has: 41,000 slot machines; 1,100 gaming tables; 1.5 million square feet of casino space; 14,200 rooms and suites; 13 showrooms and dinner theaters capable of seating 8,600 guests; 400,000 square feet of convention center space; 105 restaurants on its premises; and 42,000 employees.

The Harveys Council Bluffs is renamed Harrah's.

Harrah's ranks first in five major categories on *Fortune* magazine's list of top hotel, casino, and resort companies.

Harrah's Atlantic City opens a new 452-room hotel tower, part of a $200 million expansion to the property.

Harrah's Cherokee opens a 252-room hotel and casino expansion.

Harrah's Rincon opens near San Diego. The casino features 1,500 slots, 36 table games, and six restaurants.

Harrah's Entertainment buys the remaining stock of JCC Holding Co., the owner of Harrah's New Orleans. JCC is absorbed into Harrah's.

Harrah's announces a 544-room hotel addition to the Atlantic City Showboat, scheduled for completion in late 2003.

The company announces that Gary Loveman will take over as chief executive officer, effective January 1, 2003. Phil Satre will remain chairman with a two-year contract.

Index

ENTER TO WIN A TRIP FOR TWO TO HARRAH'S LAS VEGAS!

You can enter the sweepstakes by logging onto www.harrahs .com/jackpot. Two drawings will be held on or about March 4, 2003 for a prize valued at approximately $1,500. Prize includes:

- **Coach airfare for two**
- **Hotel accommodations at Harrah's Las Vegas for 3 days/2 nights**
- **$500 spending money**
- **Two show tickets**

Promotional period begins on December 6, 2002 at 12:00:00 A.M. and ends on March 31, 2003 at 12:00:00 A.M. pacific time.

General Rules:
- As used herein "Harrah's" means Harrah's Operating Company, Inc. and all of its parent, affiliated, and subsidiary companies.
- Customers can enter on line at http://www.harrahs.com/jackpot for their chance to win a trip for two to Harrah's Las Vegas for 3 days and 2 nights.
- No purchase necessary to participate.
- Void where prohibited or restricted by law.
- Must be at least 21 years of age to participate and participants must provide valid proof of age.
- This promotion is subject to all applicable federal, state, and local laws and regulations, including gaming, and all aspects of the promotion are subject to the approval of appropriate regulatory authorities.
- All entries are subject to review and verification.
- Odds of winning dependent upon number of entries received.
- Only one entry (either mail or online) per person throughout promotional period.
- Harrah's reserves the right to distribute additional entries via advertising, direct mail, or other promotional means.

- Winners must show valid picture identification (driver's license, state identification card, or military identification card) in order to collect prize. If winner is not a U.S. citizen, a current passport or alien registration card is required.
- Winners must sign an affidavit and release provided by Harrah's prior to receiving any prize.
- Winners agree to allow the use of their name and likeness for promotions/advertising and announcements without compensation where permitted.
- Winners are responsible for any and all taxes, licenses, registrations and other fees.
- Drawing times are approximate. Harrah's reserves the right to change drawing and event times due to unforeseen or extenuating circumstances.
- All decisions regarding the interpretation of rules, eligibility, etc. for this promotion lie solely with Harrah's whose decisions are final.
- Harrah's reserves the right to modify or cancel this promotion at any time, for any reason, subject to any applicable regulatory approval, provided that such modification shall not, as of the date of such modification, materially alter or change any participant's prize already awarded.
- Harrah's may disqualify any person for any prize based upon fraud, dishonesty, violation of promotional rules or other misconduct whether or not related to this promotion.
- Harrah's is not liable for injuries or losses arising or resulting from participation in the promotion and is not liable for any acts or omissions by employees, whether negligent or willful, in the conduct of the promotion and is not liable in the event of any equipment or software malfunction.
- Harrah's is not responsible for lost, late, mutilated, or illegible entries nor for electronic transmission errors or delays resulting in omission, interruption, deletion, defect, delay in operations or transmission, theft or destruction or unauthorized access to or alterations of entry materials, or for technical, hardware, software, or telephone failures of any kind, lost or unavailable connections, fraud, incomplete, garbled, or delayed computer transmissions, whether caused by Harrah's, users, or by any of the equipment or programming associated with or utilized in the promotion or by any technical or human error which may occur in the processing of submissions which may limit, restrict, or prevent a participant's ability to participate in the promotion.

- If for any reason the promotion is not capable of running as planned, including infection by computer virus, bugs, tampering, unauthorized intervention, fraud, technical failures, or any other causes within or beyond the control of Harrah's which corrupt or affect the administration, security, fairness, integrity, or proper conduct of this promotion, Harrah's reserves the right at its sole discretion to cancel, terminate, modify or suspend the promotion.
- Any attempt by any person to deliberately damage any program or to undermine the legitimate operation of this promotion may be a violation of criminal and civil laws and should such an attempt be made, Harrah's reserves the right to seek damages from any such person to the fullest extent of the law.
- Prizes and entries are non-transferable and not redeemable for cash.
- Entries will be retained for record keeping purposes in accordance with local legal requirements.
- Need not be present to win.
- Employees of Harrah's and its subsidiaries, affiliates, or parent companies and immediate family members are not eligible for this promotion. Immediate Family is defined as: mother, father, spouse, children, son-in-law, daughter-in-law, mother-in-law, father-in-law, step-parents, step-children, grandmother, grandfather, grandchildren and any relative or other person residing in the employee's place of residence.
- Individuals who are excluded from casino facilities, either through a government program or by their own request, are not eligible.
- By participating in this promotion, participants agree to the rules.
- A copy of these rules and any changes will be available at the Total Rewards Center throughout the duration of this promotion.
- This promotion is governed by Nevada law. By entering into this promotion, you are agreeing to submit to rules, statutes, regulations, and the jurisdictions of the courts of the State of Nevada.

Mail-in Entries:
- One free entry may be obtained by sending a request, along with a stamped, self-addressed, #10 envelope to: Harrah's Operating Company, Inc. "On-line Jackpot Sweepstakes" P.O. Box 98905 Las Vegas, NV 89193 (Vermont residents may omit return postage). The request must state that entry into the Jackpot promotion is being requested.
- Mail-in entry requests must be postmarked by March 31, 2003 and received by April 3, 2003 from a U.S. jurisdiction only.

- Limit one request per outer mailing envelope. Only one entry per person.
- Harrah's is not responsible for late, lost, damaged, incomplete, illegible, postage due, or misdirected mail.

Internet Entries:
- In the event of a dispute regarding the identity of the person submitting an entry, the entry will be deemed to be submitted by the Authorized Account Holder of the e-mail address of the entrant at the time the entry is received. Authorized Account Holder is defined as the natural person who is assigned the e-mail by an Internet access provider, on-line service.
- This promotion is intended for viewing in the United States only and shall only be construed and evaluated according to United States law. Do not proceed in this site if you are not a resident of the United States.
- All required fields must be completed to be eligible.
- One entry per person.

Drawings:
- Two Drawings will be held on or about March 4, 2003 at 12:00:00 P.M. pacific time in Las Vegas, NV.
- Winner will be selected by random drawing from all eligible entries.
- Entrants may win only once per drawing day.
- Winners will be contacted via mail, telephone, or any other available means and will have until 14 days after prize notification to claim their prize. Unclaimed prizes will be forfeited.
- Alternate winner will not be chosen if prize is not claimed within 14 days after winner has been notified.

- Two (2) Prizes valued at approximately $1,500.
  - Prize includes:
  - Coach airfare for two
  - Hotel accommodations at Harrah's Las Vegas for 3 days/2 nights
  - $500 spending money
  - Two Show tickets
- Certain restrictions and blackout dates may apply.
- Winner will receive roundtrip coach airfare for two to Las Vegas from the closest major continental US airport to winner's home.
- Travel is valid for 6 months from date of win and must be booked at least 30 days in advance.

- Travel arrangements must be made through Harrah's Passport Travel only.
- Winner will receive 2 nights' stay at Harrah's Las Vegas (room, tax & surcharge only).
- Hotel stay is valid 6 months from date of win.
- Both winner and guest must be 21 years or older to travel.